THE LUZON CAMPAIGN, 1945

THE LUZON CAMPAIGN, 1945

MacArthur Returns

NATHAN N. PREFER

CASEMATE

Pennsylvania & Yorkshire

Published in the United States of America and Great Britain in 2024 by
CASEMATE PUBLISHERS
1950 Lawrence Road, Havertown, PA 19083, USA
and
47 Church Street, Barnsley, S70 2AS, UK

Copyright 2024 © Nathan N. Prefer

Hardback Edition: ISBN 978-1-63624-424-2
Digital Edition: ISBN 978-1-63624-425-9

A CIP record for this book is available from the British Library

Printed and bound in the United Kingdom by CPI Group (UK) Ltd, Croydon, CR0 4YY

Typeset in India by Lapiz Digital Services, Chennai.

For a complete list of Casemate titles, please contact:

CASEMATE PUBLISHERS (US)
Telephone (610) 853-9131
Fax (610) 853-9146
Email: casemate@casematepublishers.com
www.casematepublishers.com

CASEMATE PUBLISHERS (UK)
Telephone (0)1226 734350
Email: casemate@casemateuk.com
www.casemateuk.com

Cover image: Soldiers of Company "K", 161st Infantry Regiment, 25th Infantry Division, cover a cave after tossing in a phosphorus grenade, near Balete Pass, April 19, 1945. (REAL WAR PHOTOS # A 2895)

Back cover image: Troopers of Company G, 187th Glider Infantry Regiment, 11th Airborne Division, advancing to Sulac, Luzon, April 9, 1945. (REAL WAR PHOTOS # A 2042)

A general is just as good or as bad as the troops under his command make him.
—General Douglas MacArthur, address to Congress, August 20, 1962

It is hard to imagine today, when the U.S. Military is entirely professional and widely regarded as the most skilled on the planet, that World War II was a time when the nation called its citizens to arms, blended them with a small professional force, and created a military that was the equal of any in the world. But it happened.
—John Prados, *Storm Over Leyte*, 2016

When things are going badly in battle the best tonic is to take one's mind off one's own troubles by considering what a rotten time one's opponent must be having.
—General Sir Archibald P. Wavell, *Other Men's Flowers*, 1944

Military History, accompanied by sound criticism, is indeed the true school of war.
—General Antoine Jomini, *Summary of the Art of War*, 1838

Highest honors must be accorded the officers and men of our combat units, who with incomparable skill, gallantry, determination and tenacity defeated the fanatical enemy in close and bitter combat on exceedingly difficult terrain. Theirs was the suffering, the intense physical hardship, and the mental strain inseparable from war—and theirs, as it should be, is the glory of the victory.
—Lieutenant General Walter Krueger, General Order Number 134, June 30, 1945

Contents

List of Maps

CHAPTER I

Introduction

It was the longest ground campaign in the Pacific War. It was also the largest in terms of manpower on both sides. It was commanded by one of the most revered—and reviled—American commanders of that war. The enemy commander was one of the most respected and proficient produced by Imperial Japan. After eight months of continuous struggle, the campaign was still ongoing, ended only by the surrender of Imperial Japan. Yet in the nearly 80 years since its conclusion, few studies of that battle have been produced. Instead, what has been produced are histories of incidents within that campaign, many of them excellent, but which do not do justice to the ordinary soldier who fought, and the many who died, in clearing the Philippine island of Luzon of Japanese occupation. This study hopes to fill that historical gap.

By January 1945, it was clear to the Allied Powers that they were well on the way to winning the world war that had begun more than four years ago. In Europe, American General George S. Patton's Third U.S. Army was attacking to clear the significant enemy penetration seized during what was now being called the Battle of the Bulge. Lieutenant General William H. Simpson's Ninth U.S. Army was about to reach the western side of the Kall River. To the south, Lieutenant General Jacob L. Devers's Sixth Army Group was defending itself against another major German offensive, Operation *Nordwind*, in which the Seventh U.S. Army of Lieutenant General Alexander M. Patch was heavily engaged. To the east, Russian Army forces were battling for the city of Budapest. In Italy, Lieutenant General Willis D. Crittenberger's IV Corps took over the Serchio River sector from the 8th Indian Infantry Division and prepared to assault the latest German winter line. On the other side of the world in Burma, the 124th U.S. Cavalry Regiment, a part of the newly established Mars Task Force, successors to Merrill's Marauders, crossed the Shweli River in a move to cut Japanese lines of communication. Not far away the British Fourteenth Army continued attacking the Japanese *Burma Area Army*, driving it deeper into the jungles. In China, Japanese forces renewed their attack along the Canton–Hankow Railroad to drive the Chinese forces away from their own communications. In Fleet Admiral

Chester W. Nimitz's Central Pacific Theater of Operations, the Seventh Army Air Force began the preliminary bombardment of the Bonin Islands, including Iwo Jima.

As these campaigns were progressing, a new one began. General Walter Krueger's Sixth U.S. Army began to land on the Philippine island of Luzon. Consisting of some 190,000 American soldiers, supported by thousands of sailors and Marines, the Sixth Army was to recover the former home of the commander of the Southwest Pacific Theater of Operations, General Douglas MacArthur.

The campaign to recapture the Philippine islands, and with it Luzon, was not predestined by the Japanese seizure of those islands in early 1942. When the American Chiefs of Staff met to discuss the offensive in the Pacific, they decided upon four options. Because of the vastness of the Pacific, and the great distances between each island group, the war in the Pacific was quite different from that in Europe. Japan is 3,400 miles from Pearl Harbor, then the main American base in the Pacific. It is also 3,600 miles from Australia, where American forces could be based within a friendly ally's territory. So, the problem was how best to cover that vast area and reach Japan itself. At the time it was believed by the Allies that only an invasion of Japan itself would force an end to the Pacific War.

Of the four avenues of attack discussed by the Americans, the route through the Indian Ocean, led by the British Royal Navy, was soon discarded. Clearly, the Royal Navy had its hands full in the Atlantic with the German submarine campaign already threatening to starve Great Britain into submission. The shortest route, through the Aleutian Islands, was also quickly ruled out due to the abominable weather in the area which would seriously hinder operations. A third route, from Australia, along the New Guinea coast and into the Philippines, was seriously considered and was consistently recommended by the senior American commander in Australia, General MacArthur. The problem seen here was that all American Army and Navy resources would have to be dedicated to this route, which was unsatisfactory to the Navy due to the narrowness of the waters, the surrounding enemy air bases, and leaving significant enemy forces on the flank of the advance. The last plan, favored by the U.S. Navy, called for an "island-hopping" advance through the Gilbert, Marshall, Caroline, and Mariana Islands before a major assault on Formosa, from which the ultimate assault on Japan could be launched.[1]

Discussions continued within the Joint Chiefs of Staff and some decisions made were subsequently altered as the war in the Pacific developed, but ultimately the choice was a combination of the latter two routes. The Navy and Marines, supported by the Army Air Corps, would attack across the Central Pacific while most of the Army troops would use the New Guinea–Philippines route, supported by the Navy, Marines, and Army Air Corps. Despite General MacArthur's continuing objections, by 1945 this dual offensive was well established and nearing completion.

Douglas MacArthur had graduated the U.S. Military Academy at West Point in the Class of 1903. The son of Civil War General Arthur MacArthur, who had earned

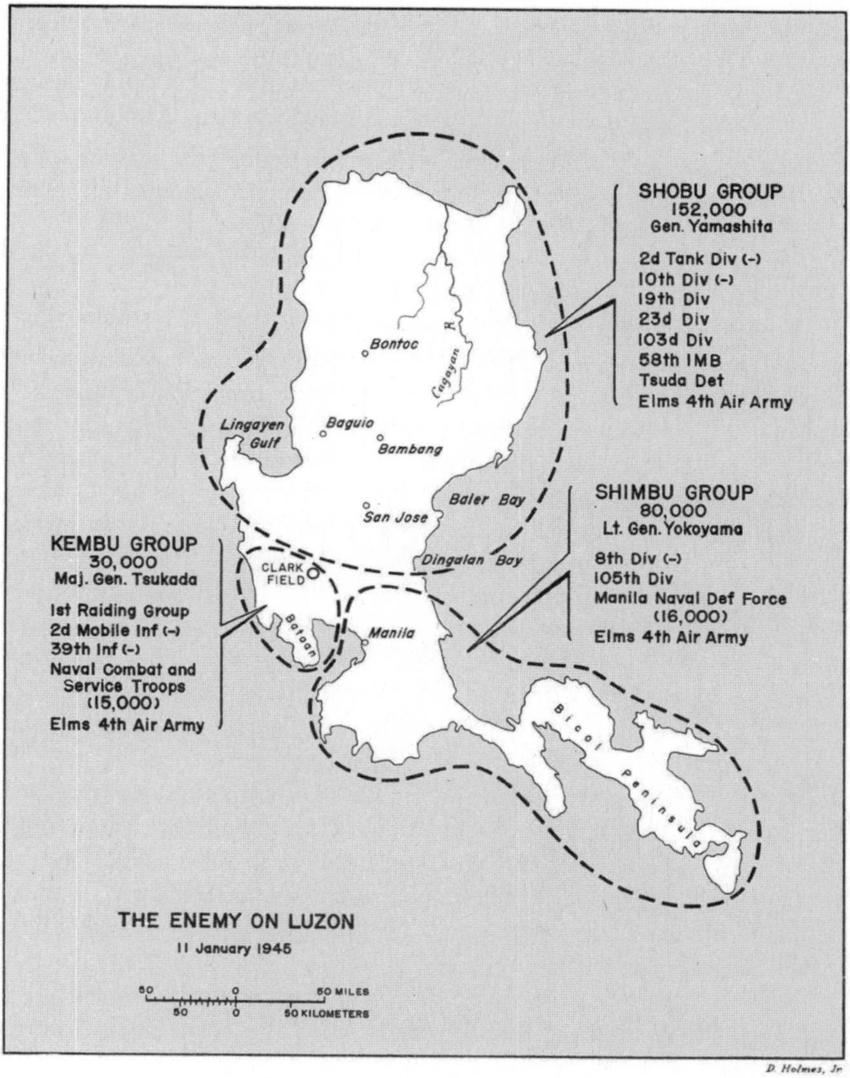
SHOBU GROUP
152,000
Gen. Yamashita
2d Tank Div (-)
10th Div (-)
19th Div
23d Div
103d Div
58th IMB
Tsuda Det
Elms 4th Air Army
SHIMBU GROUP
80,000
Lt. Gen. Yokoyama
8th Div (-)
105th Div
Manila Naval Def Force
(16,000)
Elms 4th Air Army
KEMBU GROUP
30,000
Maj. Gen. Tsukada
1st Raiding Group
2d Mobile Inf (-)
39th Inf (-)
Naval Combat and
Service Troops
(15,000)
Elms 4th Air Army
Bontoc
Cagayan R
Lingayen Gulf
Baguio
Bambang
Baler Bay
San Jose
Dingalan Bay
CLARK FIELD
Bataan
Manila
Bicol Peninsula
THE ENEMY ON LUZON
11 January 1945
50 0 50 MILES
50 0 50 KILOMETERS
D. Holmes, Jr

Japanese Forces on Luzon, January 11, 1945

Robert Ross Smith. *United States Army in World War II. The War in the Pacific. Triumph in the Philippines.* Washington, D.C.: Center of Military History, 1984. p. 95.

the Medal of Honor, Douglas's advance in the Army was rapid. He ended World War I as a brigadier general commanding the 42nd Division with a reputation for skillful leadership and personal courage. His subsequent career included many highlights, including serving as aide to President Theodore Roosevelt and Superintendent of

West Point. By November 1930, he was a general and chief of staff of the United States Army. Having peaked in his career, General MacArthur resigned from the U.S. Army to accept an offer to become a field marshal in the developing Philippine Army, then being organized in anticipation of declaring itself an independent nation as promised by the United States. He served in this capacity for six years, headquartered at a Manila hotel, until the Japanese attacked the United States at Pearl Harbor. Having been recalled to active duty in the U.S. Army in July 1941, he was the senior commander of American and Philippine forces during the dark years of the Japanese advance across the Pacific.

Having been defeated in the Philippines, he was ordered to Australia where he began the long, difficult, and bloody battles to return to the Philippines. Promoted to general of the Army in 1944, his Southwest Pacific Theater of Operations was assigned to conquer New Guinea and the Philippines preparatory to an invasion of Japan itself, should that be necessary. Using American, Australian, and New Zealand troops, the struggle took over two years before the first soil of the Philippines, the island of Leyte, would return to American control.[2] Throughout these long and difficult years, General MacArthur kept his promise to the Philippine people foremost in his thoughts, stating clearly when he first landed in Australia, "I came through, and I shall return."

General MacArthur's promise, which he deemed a personal point of honor, was not universally accepted by other American military leaders. Admiral Ernest J. King, the commander-in-chief of the United States Navy, passionately believed that a direct attack by his own Central Pacific Theater forces on the island of Formosa, off the Chinese coast, would be a better avenue to an eventual invasion of Japan. He believed that the Philippines should be bypassed, and a direct attack mounted on Formosa from the Mariana Islands, recently seized by Navy and Marine Corps forces under the command of Admiral Chester W. Nimitz. Admiral King did agree that some Philippine islands could be seized as support bases, mentioning Mindanao in particular.

At a conference in July 1944, at Pearl Harbor, General MacArthur made his case to President Franklin D. Roosevelt and Admiral Nimitz. President Roosevelt was aware of the views of Admiral King and wanted to hear those of General MacArthur. Those arguments included his claim that the United States was honor-bound to liberate the Philippines, where resistance to the Japanese had been encouraged by the Americans. He also argued that failure to redeem his pledge to return would reflect badly on American promises throughout Asia. Further, he noted that the establishment of American bases for the invasion of Japan on Luzon would be sheltered by a friendly population and at a distance from Japan that could not easily be directly attacked from Japan, unlike Formosa whose proximity to Japan exposed bases there to Japanese attack directly from Japan or coastal China, then in Japanese hands. He compared attacking Japan before liberating the Philippines to the Allies in Europe attacking Germany before liberating France. His arguments convinced both the President and Admiral Nimitz. Although Admiral King still opposed the plan, the Quebec Conference, in September 1944, made it clear that the Philippines, beginning with Leyte, would be liberated.[3]

Besides keeping General MacArthur's promise, the seizure of the Philippine islands would threaten Japan's overseas access to food and critical raw materials such as oil. Japanese war leaders fully expected an invasion of the Philippines as their defensive perimeters shrank under unceasing Allied attacks. To hold these critical islands against any such Allied threats, they sent 430,000 of their soldiers and sailors to defend the islands. They also sent, albeit at the last moment, their best field commander, General Tomoyuki Yamashita, who had earlier in the war defeated significant British, Australian, and Indian Army forces at Malaya and Singapore.

General Tomoyuki (Hobun) Yamashita was born in 1888 and commissioned as a second lieutenant of infantry in June 1906. He graduated from the Japanese War College in November 1916 and was attached to the Army General Staff. He then served as a military student abroad, visiting Switzerland and Germany before becoming a military attaché to Austria and Hungary. After commanding an infantry regiment at home, Colonel Yamashita served in several high-level staff appointments before assuming command of an infantry brigade. Promoted to lieutenant general in November 1937, he commanded a division in battle in China and rose to commander, *Kwantung Defense Army*. By November 1941, he commanded the *Twenty-Fifth Army*, which seized Malaya and Singapore from the British.

Soon after this significant success, however, he came into conflict with a powerful military clique and was "exiled" to Manchuria in command of a small army. The increasingly threatening Allied advance across the Pacific forced his return to active theaters, and he was, by October 1944, in command of the *Fourteenth Area Army*, assigned to defend the Philippines.[4] He arrived there barely weeks before the first American landings took place on Leyte, in the central Philippines. Here again he found himself at odds with the *Imperial General Headquarters* (*IGHQ*) in Tokyo. General Yamashita wanted to concentrate all his substantial forces on Luzon, the main Philippine island which contained the capital of Manila as well as the most significant air and naval bases, the American objectives. But *IGHQ* in Tokyo, misled by grossly inflated reports by the *Imperial Japanese Navy* of success at the Battle of Leyte Gulf, insisted that he defend Leyte. Believing that General MacArthur was trapped on the Leyte beachhead, they ordered an immediate reinforcement of the Leyte garrison, fully expecting to receive General MacArthur's surrender there. Forces were rushed to Leyte, against General Yamashita's wishes, from all over the Philippines and from as far away as Manchuria. In all, the *Fourteenth Area Army* lost more than 70,000 men during the unsuccessful Leyte campaign.[5]

General Yamashita took stock of his situation at the end of 1944. The Japanese air and naval forces were all but destroyed in earlier battles, particularly at the Battle of Leyte Gulf. He could expect little or no assistance from those quarters. The forces remaining to him, some 260,000 soldiers, sailors, and grounded airmen, had little artillery, transportation, armor, or other modern equipment to resist the inevitable invasion. Knowing his troops were unequal to the modern American Army in open warfare, General Yamashita decided that his best, indeed his only, option was to conduct a delaying defensive battle, keeping his army in the field as long as possible and keeping the American field forces tied down trying to eliminate him. Unlike General MacArthur, who in 1942 had decided that his critical defensive areas were Manila, the Central Luzon Plain, Manila Bay, and the Bataan Peninsula, General Yamashita understood that his most critical asset was his own army, which presented a "threat in being" for as long as it could maintain itself in the field. He intended to withdraw most of his forces into three widely separated mountain strongholds and defend these in a prolonged battle of attrition.

Fortunately for General Yamashita, the defeat on Leyte, following the prior defeats in Burma, India, and the Central Pacific, had now brought *IGHQ* to the same conclusion. Tokyo in January 1945 approved the "first joint operational plan of the war, indeed the first in Japan's modern history."[6] It consisted of Operation *Tengō* (Operation *Heaven*) in which the already notorious kamikaze tactic would be hugely expanded and employed against the Americans, and Operation *Ketsu-gō* (Operation *Decisive*), which was designed to improve defenses of the Japanese homeland. In this scenario the *Fourteenth Area Army* would continue fighting on Luzon to divert Allied strength while the Japanese Army and Navy hurried to strengthen the defenses of Iwo Jima and Okinawa. These two islands were regarded as critical outposts of homeland defense by the Japanese and preliminaries to the Battle of Japan itself. This planning accepted the idea that while the British and Chinese would continue to wear down Japanese strength on the continent, the Americans would continue to advance toward Japan, extending their lines of communication and supply. The Japanese military adopted a strategy of *shukketsu* (bleeding) the Americans to buy time to build up the defenses on Iwo Jima and Okinawa and hopefully make the Americans rethink any plans to invade the home islands.

Weeks before the Americans came to Luzon, General Yamashita had prepared his defenses. First, he divided his troops into three large groupings. Each was assigned a geographic region to defend. The largest group was known as the *Shobu Group*, under General Yamashita's personal command, which numbered about 152,000 troops and was concentrated in northern Luzon. A smaller force, known as the *Kembu Group*, with about 30,000 troops, defended the area around the prewar American airfield complex known as Clark Field, Bataan, and Corregidor. The remaining force, known as the *Shimbu Group*, included 80,000 soldiers and was assigned to the southern area of Luzon, including the long Bicol Peninsula and the mountains east of Manila. This group was sited to control the capital city's water supply.[7] Perhaps the only error on General Yamashita's part came when he expected the American invasion two weeks later than it occurred, thereby finding some of the Japanese units not yet in their assigned positions.

One problem that General Yamashita faced and which he could do little about was transportation. With food, ammunition, and communications equipment in short supply—the Japanese were by 1944 forced to import rice from Thailand and Indochina to feed both their own troops and the civilian population—General Yamashita knew that his troops would have to live off the land, another reason for withdrawing deep into the Luzon mountains where they could produce their own food. Transportation difficulties also included the near destruction of the Luzon road and railway system, preventing a swift movement of troops or supplies. Indeed, the Japanese logistical base at Manila, the central base for the entire Pacific, was chaotic and so uncoordinated that Lieutenant General Akira Muto, the chief of staff of the *Fourteenth Area Army*, described it as being filled with supplies "piled in an unsystematic ... helter-skelter way."[8] He also complained that there was a lack of supplies needed for the defense of the Philippines but an overabundance of unnecessary supplies.

General Yamashita did what he could to move these 70,000 metric tons of supplies from the Manila warehouses, but was told that with his available transportation, it would take six months to move it all. He ordered that the most vital supplies be moved first and only if time allowed would the rest be moved into the mountains. Time, and the Americans, did not allow. Only about 4,000 tons of these supplies were moved before the invasion.

General MacArthur had problems of his own. One of the objectives in seizing Leyte had been the need for airfields on which to base his land-based support aircraft. With most naval air support being used in the Central Pacific Theater of Operations, General MacArthur's forces relied heavily on U.S. Army Air Force units for ground support and to maintain air superiority over the battlefield. These he had grouped into a command known as the Far East Air Forces, commanded by Lieutenant General George Churchill Kenney. Born in Yarmouth, Nova Scotia, in 1889 and commissioned into the Air Service in 1917, General Kenney had graduated from the Command and General Staff School and Army War College. General Kenney had risen in the Army Air Force until he became General MacArthur's senior air officer. Under his command were the Fifth U.S. Army Air Force, commanded by Major General Ennis Clement Whitehead (University of Kansas, 1917), and the Thirteenth U.S. Army Air Force under the command of Major General St. Clair Streett.[9]

As noted, the seizure of Leyte had been designed in part to provide the necessary airfields for the supporting aircraft. But once on the ground it was found that the soil of Leyte was generally unsuitable for such airfields. Some could, and were, constructed and used, but there was not nearly enough suitable space on Leyte to support the numbers of aircraft that the Luzon campaign would require. More were going to be needed. To provide these additional airfields, the island of Mindoro was selected. This island was situated off the southeastern tip of Luzon, between Leyte and Luzon, making its location ideal for basing supporting aircraft. Research showed that the southwestern portion of Mindoro could be used to build these airfields, which in turn would provide the necessary support for the ground troops and provide cover for the convoys moving to Luzon before, during, and after the invasion.[10] About half the size of the state of New Jersey, it is roughly oval and very mountainous, except in the southwest. The island has coastal plains which could be used for airfield sites. But it rains nearly every day on Mindoro, the humidity is high, the climate enervating, and tropical diseases abound, especially malaria. At the time, the island was basically undeveloped and had few natural resources.

Allied intelligence accurately estimated the Japanese garrison on Mindoro as numbering about 1,000 soldiers. These were a mixed group of infantrymen from the *8th Infantry Division* and the *105th Infantry Division*, along with support troops. There were also some 200 others who had survived sinking ships and found themselves stranded on the island. Once again General MacArthur gave the job of taking a defended enemy bastion to General Krueger and his Sixth U.S. Army. To accomplish the task, General Krueger created a special headquarters he named the Western Visayan Task Force. Brigadier General William Caldwell Dunckel (University of Missouri, 1915) was placed in command of the 19th Regimental Combat Team of the 24th Infantry Division and the 503rd Parachute Regimental Combat Team. The latter, originally intended to parachute onto Mindoro, was instead carried there alongside the 19th Infantry when it was determined that there were not enough airfields on Leyte to accommodate the number of transports such a drop would require. The task force included support troops such as antiaircraft artillery, engineer boat and shore regiments, and a large group of airfield engineers intended to create the vital airfields.

The task force staged off the east coast of Leyte on December 12, 1944 and sailed for the objective. While transiting to Mindoro, the task force was sighted by the dreaded Japanese kamikazes and attacked. The light cruiser USS *Nashville* (CL-43) was hit and suffered severe damage. The 130 men that were killed included General Dunckel's chief of staff, Colonel Bruce C. Hill. General Dunckel was among the 190 men wounded and was severely injured and burned. Thankfully, the Japanese lost the convoy and searched for it in the wrong sectors. On the morning of December 15, 1944, the invasion force arrived off Mindoro and landed, protected by American aircraft. Despite the protection, two of the landing ships, tank (LSTs) were hit and eventually sunk. Other ships were damaged. But the landings were successful and even exceeded expectations. There was minimum opposition, and the Final Beachhead Line (FBL) had been established by late afternoon. One enemy airfield was captured intact and new fields were begun immediately, including one named Hill Field after Colonel Hill. The main opposition from that point on was the nearly constant Japanese air raids. The arrival of several fighter squadrons of the Far East Air Forces soon slowed and then stopped these raids.

Unknown to the busy infantrymen and engineers establishing a base on Mindoro, the Japanese *Southwestern Area Fleet* took exception to their invasion. They organized a naval raid against the new American beachhead which included two cruisers and six destroyers,[11] all that the skeleton *Imperial Japanese Navy* had available. Their mission was to bombard the American beachhead on Mindoro and sink any American shipping encountered before withdrawing. This force sailed from Camranh Bay, Indochina,[12] on December 24, 1944, but was quickly discovered by patrolling American submarines. Thanks to the early warning, the Japanese force was attacked by air beginning December 26, 1944, but managed to reach their objective where they conducted a 40-minute bombardment of the American beachhead, causing minimal damage. The Japanese then withdrew successfully, leaving many of the American pilots that had attacked them without a place to land, if they had launched from Mindoro. The Japanese lost one destroyer.[13]

Japanese air attacks continued through the middle of January, but for all practical purposes, the Mindoro operation was successfully completed. Infantry patrols searched the island for small groups of Japanese who more often avoided contact than initiated it. Philippine guerillas soon took over much of the duty of eliminating the Japanese. The 21st Infantry Regiment of the 24th Infantry Division came ashore to reinforce the beachhead, just in case the Japanese tried to land reinforcements. By the end of the month, the island was considered secured, with losses of 16 infantrymen killed, 71 wounded, and four missing in action. In an unusual turn of events, the supporting units, including naval and air forces, suffered 475 men killed and 385 wounded. Fewer than 200 Japanese were reported killed or captured by the end of January.

One of those killed while supporting the Mindoro and Luzon operations was Major Thomas Buchanan McGuire. The 24-year-old fighter pilot of the 475th Fighter Group, Fifth Army Air Force, was already an ace several times over, but insisted on flying to beat his closest rival, Major Richard Bong. The New Jersey native had already flown in the Aleutians before coming to the Southwest Pacific where he scored heavily, despite being shot down in October 1944. It was Christmas Day when his group was escorting B-24 bombers to hit Manila in preparation for the coming invasion. The group was attacked by more than a score of enemy fighters, and Major McGuire and his fellow fighter pilots turned to protect the bombers. He shot down one enemy fighter but his wingman, Lieutenant Floyd Fulkerson, was hit and shot down. More and more enemy planes arrived, and more of Major McGuire's fellow pilots were being shot out of the skies. As he shot down his fourth enemy plane his guns were emptied. Rather than leave the fight, Major McGuire remained and made "dummy" passes at the enemy fighters to keep them away from the vulnerable bombers. Two weeks later, he was attacking one enemy fighter over

Negros Island when another jumped him from behind. To outmaneuver the enemy, he pulled his P-38L fighter plane[14] into a vertical bank, but the heavily loaded plane stalled and crashed into the jungle below, killing Major McGuire. For his actions on Christmas Day, 1944, Major Thomas B. McGuire was awarded a posthumous Medal of Honor.[15]

Quite unlike Major McGuire was another pilot supporting the coming Luzon operation. Captain William Arthur Shomo was 26 years old and had been flying in the Pacific for 18 months, firing his guns only once. This was not unexpected, as his mission was reconnaissance, not combat. Flying with the 82nd Reconnaissance Squadron, Fifth Army Air Force, the mortuary college graduate from Jeanette, Pennsylvania, was flying the relatively new F-6D photo-reconnaissance version of the P-51D Mustang fighter plane.[16] While supporting the Mindoro landings on January 11, 1945, he was scouting near Manila in his aircraft "Snooks 5th" when he came upon an enemy dive-bomber and quickly shot it down. The next day, he and his wingman, Lieutenant Paul Lipscomb, spotted several enemy planes above them. Even though they could not see all the enemy planes, they decided to attack. They soon found themselves in contact with a dozen enemy fighters that were escorting a bomber. In moments Captain Shomo shot down three enemy fighters while his wingman scored as well. Sensing that the bomber was something important, given its large escort, Captain Shomo went into the attack. He quickly shot it down. Then another fighter fell to Captain Shomo's guns. Then another. One more came under Captain Shomo's deadly fire before the enemy counterattacked. Calling Lieutenant Lipscomb, who had himself downed three enemy planes, to join him, the two Americans left the scene. For his actions in taking on an overwhelming enemy force in a reconnaissance aircraft and shooting down seven enemy aircraft, Captain Shomo was promoted to major and awarded the Medal of Honor.[17]

The Mindoro operation was necessary for the creation of airfields, but it was also considered a diversionary operation, to convince the Japanese that the Americans were still building up their forces and were not yet prepared to conduct an invasion of Luzon. Other diversionary operations included naval demonstrations, dummy parachute drops, simulated landings, and radio and radar deceptions. Many of these took place along the south coast of Luzon to draw Japanese resources away from the planned landing site, Lingayen Gulf. General Yamashita, however, never veered from his conviction that the main landings would come at Lingayen Gulf, where the Japanese themselves had landed three years earlier.

Lingayen Gulf was the precise area where General MacArthur had decided to begin his long-awaited Luzon campaign. It was an area of sheltered beaches on the northwestern coast of Luzon. Luzon generally is a mountainous and heavily forested island of irregular shape. One of the few relatively flat areas on the island was the Central Plain, which opened onto Lingayen Gulf.[18] Putting his troops there would place them close to the best roads and railways on the island. These all ran over the

Central Plain and then on to Manila, General MacArthur's main objective. Manila Bay was one of the world's largest harbors guarded by fortified islands, the largest of which is Corregidor. Landing at Lingayen Gulf also provided maneuvering room for large forces, such as those the Americans were about to land. Possession of Manila Bay and the Central Plain would put the Americans in a central position to complete the conquest of the rest of the island. Certainly, the Japanese had thought so when they had used those very same beaches to begin their own invasion of the Philippines in 1941.

The force General MacArthur designated to seize Luzon was his oldest and most experienced army, the Sixth Army under General Walter Krueger. Its assault force would be the I Corps and XIV Corps, both experienced tactical headquarters, controlling the 6th, 37th, 40th, and 43rd Infantry Divisions, all veteran units. In reserve, General Krueger would have the 25th Infantry and 11th Airborne Divisions, along with the separate 158th Regimental Combat Team and 13th Armored Group.[19] The 6th Ranger Battalion, 13 artillery battalions, two chemical mortar battalions, two tank battalions, five engineer boat and shore regiments, four amphibian tractor battalions, and 16 engineer aviation battalions rounded out the troop list for Sixth Army's opening phase of the Luzon operation. In all, 191,000 men, including 131,000 combat troops, were heading for Luzon to face General Yamashita's 230,000 soldiers, sailors, and airmen.

CHAPTER 2

The Lingayen Beachhead

The first planning for the invasion of Luzon had envisioned a target date of December 20, 1944. But delays on Leyte, which required an additional amphibious landing at Ormoc Bay that tied up essential assault shipping, and the Mindoro operation, which further engaged critical assault shipping, deferred the attack. These shortages, combined with the slowing in establishing enough airfields for supporting aircraft, moved the assault date to January 9, 1945.

The Sixth Army had been created by a telegram from General MacArthur to General Walter Krueger on January 12, 1943. At that time, General Krueger was commanding the Third U.S. Army and on an inspection tour in Colorado. He received the telegram which read, "I have just recommended to the Chief of Staff that you and the Third Army Headquarters be transferred to this area. I am particularly anxious to have you with me at this critical time."[1] For General Krueger the message was a welcome surprise. At the age of 62, he understood few officers over the age of 50 were being sent overseas to command field units in the war. Most of them were relegated to training and administrative assignments within the United States. So, the order from Washington to leave his Third Army Headquarters behind and instead organize a new army headquarters at Fort Sam Houston, Texas, was not onerous, but merely another step toward his entering combat in this war. General Krueger took some key staff officers and was soon commanding the new Sixth U.S. Army in Australia.[2]

Lieutenant General Krueger took command of the Sixth Army on February 16, 1943, at Brisbane, Australia. With a small infantry force he began the long, bloody, and difficult fight up the north coast of New Guinea. Often it operated under the nom de guerre of "Alamo Force," since General MacArthur wanted to keep direct control of the Sixth Army and not have it inserted into the formal chain of command in the Southwest Pacific Theater where it would at least nominally be under Australian command.[3] For the next two years the Sixth Army fought its way toward the Philippines. It was the force that allowed General MacArthur to formally

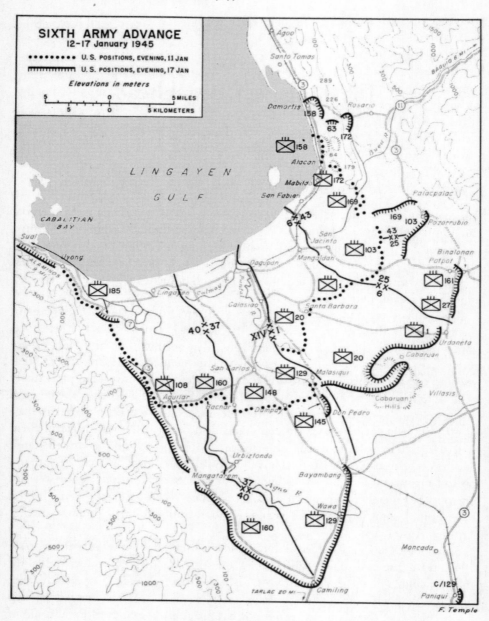

Sixth Army's Advance Toward Manila, January 1945

Robert Ross Smith. *United States Army in World War II. The War in the Pacific. Triumph in the Philippines.*
Washington, D.C.: Center of Military History, 1984. p. 116.

announce his return to the Philippines when it landed on Leyte. And it would be the force that brought him "home" to Manila.

Indeed, the recapture of Luzon was a major goal for General MacArthur. Even if his staff had not underestimated the Japanese forces on that island, he would have proceeded with the invasion. There were good and sufficient reasons for seizing Luzon. It held the best and most airfields in the Philippines, from which Allied air forces could interdict Japanese supply lines from southeast Asia and even parts of the China coast. Similarly, Manila Bay, Subic Bay, and lesser naval bases would provide the same advantage for Allied naval forces. But more than the valid military reasons for seizing Luzon, General MacArthur wanted to redeem his own military reputation which, in his own mind, had been soiled by his loss of the Philippines, particularly Luzon, in 1942.

By January 1945, the Sixth Army had come a long way from that small, ill-trained, and inadequately equipped army that had originated in Brisbane. It now had two corps headquarters, six combat infantry divisions, and scores of supporting troops, including tank battalions, engineers, antiaircraft units, quartermaster units, medical units, base units, and others. It was supported by two American fleets, the Seventh Fleet under Vice Admiral Thomas Cassin Kinkaid (USNA, 1908) providing close support, and the Third Fleet under Admiral William Frederick Halsey, Jr. (USNA, 1904), which provided long-range support by attacking Japanese bases within range of Luzon. The Far East Air Forces, which had long been companions of Sixth Army, accompanied it to the Luzon invasion.

Because Sixth Army was so spread out along the north coast of New Guinea, its units started for Luzon at different times. One of the most pressing concerns was the increasingly effective Japanese kamikaze threat, which had already destroyed or damaged numerous ships, including the Mindoro operation's flagship. To reduce this threat as much as possible, both Admiral Kinkaid's and Admiral Halsey's fleets began an intensive pre-assault bombardment of Luzon and neighboring airfields in early January. These operations included sweeping Lingayen Gulf for mines or other obstacles which might impede the landing force.

An often-ignored factor in any amphibious campaign is the journey to the battlefield. For Admiral Kinkaid's Seventh Fleet, the trip had many threats. Although the *Imperial Japanese Navy* had recently suffered significant defeats in the Mariana Islands and in Leyte Gulf, it still had impressive strength on paper.[4] But most of the surviving Japanese fleet was in hiding, repairing battle damage and conserving fuel. Only Japanese submarines were in the area, but these had repeatedly proven ineffective at striking a decisive blow against the American fleets. But during the Leyte campaign, another Japanese tactic had been implemented—the kamikaze, or suicide, attack. Japanese aircraft production had recently peaked at 2,000 aircraft per month, and many of these had been rushed to forward areas. The problem for the Japanese, however, was pilots. They had few experienced pilots left, and it took far too long to train new ones to a proficiency needed for aerial combat against the now-experienced Americans.[5] The kamikaze was their answer.

Vice Admiral Jesse Barrett Oldendorf (USNA, 1909) led the first echelon of the attack force. Followed by Admiral Kinkaid with the amphibious forces, they departed Leyte on January 2, 1945. At dawn the next morning, the first kamikaze struck the fleet oiler USS *Cowanesque* (AO-79). That began a day-long string of attacks by 120 enemy aircraft on the fleet. But other than some close calls, the Seventh Fleet had a successful day. January 4 was different. The escort carrier USS *Ommaney Bay* (CVE-79) was hit and eventually abandoned, losing 93 killed and 65 wounded. Next, an American plane reported two Japanese ships leaving Manila and heading for Formosa. Commander R. H. Holmes's destroyer, USS *Bennion* (DD-662) and two Australian frigates[6] were sent after them. One enemy destroyer was sunk; the other returned to Manila. Kamikazes struck again, and the heavy cruiser USS *"Lucky Lou" Louisville* (CA-28), which had thus far in the war escaped damage, was hit and set afire. Damage control efforts limited a potential disaster and the ship continued with the invasion forces. Even as the USS *Louisville* was fighting fires, another kamikaze hit the HMAS *Australia*, killing 25 and wounding 30. But the Australian cruiser also carried on. Then, in rapid succession, the light carrier USS *Savo Island* (CVE-78) was hit, then the light carrier USS *Manila Bay* (CVE-61). The latter ship was hit hard and lost 12 dead and 56 wounded. But 24 hours later she was able to resume air operations. Next, destroyer escort USS *Stafford* (DE-411) was hit and fell out of formation, eventually returning to Leyte for repairs. Destroyer USS *Helm* (DD-388) was clipped by a kamikaze, losing six wounded and losing her mast and searchlight.

On January 5, as the fleet was passing tiny Apo Island between Negros and Siquijor, the cruiser USS *Boise* (CL-47) was warned in time to avoid torpedoes aimed at her. Nearby, a Japanese midget submarine broached the surface and was immediately attacked and sunk by aircraft and the destroyer USS *Taylor* (DD-468). Another was believed to have escaped.

But the next day was the worst. On January 6, 1945, several minesweepers entered Lingayen Gulf with destroyer support to clear the gulf of mines. Commanding the destroyer USS *Walke* (DD-416) was Commander George Fleming Davis, a 33-year-old American naval officer born in the Philippines. While engaged in their mission, the ships came under attack by the dreaded kamikazes. Commander Davis immediately took a position on the exposed wing of his ship's bridge to command the defense. Under his expert direction, the first two enemy planes were shot down. Despite the third aircraft heading directly toward him, Commander Davis remained at his exposed command position directing his ship's antiaircraft fire. The third kamikaze, however, could not be stopped and crashed into the bridge of the USS *Walke* where Commander Davis stood. Despite serious wounds and burns from splashed gasoline, Commander Davis remained in command and directed the salvage of his ship while continuing to direct its defense, shooting down the last kamikaze. Only after ensuring the safety of his ship and crew did he consent to accepting medical treatment. He succumbed to his wounds several hours later. For his personal gallantry in saving the USS *Walke*, Commander George Fleming Davis received a posthumous Medal of Honor.[7]

The day continued to be bad for the U.S. Navy. The battleship USS *New Mexico* (BB-40) was hit on the bridge by a kamikaze. The blast killed British Lieutenant General Herbert Lumsden (Royal Military Academy, 1915), a personal representative of British Prime Minister Winston Churchill who was along as an observer. The ship's captain, Captain R. W. Fleming, and a *Time* magazine correspondent were also killed. Altogether 25 sailors were killed, and 87 men wounded. Another kamikaze crashed into the destroyer USS *Allen M. Sumner* (DD-692), killing 14 men. The minesweeper USS *Long* (DMS-12) tried to outrace an incoming kamikaze but lost, being crashed at the waterline. Communication difficulties caused the ship to be abandoned. When the captain, Lieutenant Stanley Caplan, USNR, and a salvage party returned to the ship, it was crashed again, this time capsizing the ship. Thankfully, casualties were light, with one killed and 35 wounded. Destroyer-transport USS *Brooks* (APD-10) was also hit, losing three killed and 11 wounded. The Pearl Harbor veteran battleship USS *California* (BB-44) was hit, losing 45 killed and 151 wounded. Light cruiser USS *Columbia* (CL-56) was hit, losing 13 killed and 44 wounded, and barely survived the significant damage suffered. HMAS *Australia* was hit a second time, adding 14 killed and 26 wounded to her losses the day before. USS *Louisville* was also hit again and set afire. Rear Admiral Theodore E. Chandler (USNA, 1915), commander of Cruiser Division 4, was flying his flag on *Louisville* and was severely burned in the crash. Despite his wounds he personally handled a fire hose and then waited his turn in the first aid line. But his wounds were too serious, and he died the next day, one of 31 killed and 56 wounded.[8] Only the arrival of a massive air umbrella from the Third Fleet drove off the attackers.

At dawn on January 9, 1945, Lingayen Gulf was filled with American and Australian ships of every description. Unlike the Japanese who had stormed these same beaches in the dark, the Americans chose to come ashore in daylight. To the soldiers about to land on the beaches the smoke and dust of the pre-invasion bombardment obscured much of the area except for the buildings of the towns of Lingayen and San Fabian. Indeed, the need for the bombardment had been questioned by Admiral Oldendorf. He was aware that the Japanese had adopted new tactics of leaving the beaches undefended, preferring a defense in depth. In fact, guerilla leader Lieutenant Colonel Russell W. Volckmann, who commanded guerilla forces in northern Luzon, had recovered some documents from a crashed Japanese aircraft that revealed General Yamashita's plans to concentrate his forces in the mountains of northern Luzon. He had signaled this information to General MacArthur's headquarters, stating, "There will be no, repeat no, opposition on the beaches."[9] But his message seems to have been overlooked.

The right flank of Sixth Army was the responsibility of the XIV Corps, which had first fought the Japanese at Guadalcanal. Commanded now by Lieutenant General Oscar Woolverton Griswold (USMA, 1910), it included the veteran 37th Infantry Division on its left and the experienced 40th Infantry Division on the right. Major General Robert Sprague Beightler's (Ohio State University, 1912)[10] 37th Infantry Division had originated with the National Guard of Ohio and first fought the Japanese at New Georgia in the Solomon Islands. Major General Rapp Brush (University of Illinois, 1911) and his 40th Infantry Division had relieved the Marines on New Britain and fought the remaining Japanese until relieved by Australian troops. Their assignment was to secure a Final Beachhead Line along the southwest shore of Lingayen Gulf and prepare to repel any Japanese counterattacks. Although tides delayed the landings by a few minutes the landings themselves were unopposed. By noon, the 185th Infantry Regiment of the 40th Infantry Division had advanced six miles and established a defense along the Agno River. The regiment had also secured the town of Lingayen, suffering no casualties.

It was much the same in the zone of the 37th Infantry Division. The 148th Infantry Regiment landed and found a bridge over the Calmay River destroyed but employed landing vehicles to cross without difficulty. On the left, the 129th Infantry encountered the only resistance, a small group of Japanese who defended a sand dune and house until they were evicted by the automatic weapons fire of the supporting landing vehicles, tracked (LVTs) and landing craft infantry (guns), or LCI(Gs). By afternoon the advance had contacted the adjoining I Corps units across the Pantal River near Dagupan. One of the landing craft crewmembers carrying the troops ashore remembered, "Dawn on the ninth found us off the beaches of Lingayen Gulf. Bow doors opened, the ramp went down, and we drove off into the water, fully loaded with 37th troops. As we emerged onto the beach I saw a dud sixteen-inch shell directly in our path. I quickly point it out to the driver and he narrowly avoided it. I quite likely saved us from disaster. I was apprehensive as were most all the way in but I think after so many months of training and waiting they were glad to start fighting. There was no return fire. The entire beachhead was virtually unopposed. Jubilant Filipinos greeted us, carrying American and Philippine flags."[11]

Major General Innis Palmer Swift's (USMA, 1904) I Corps had more difficulties conducting their landing. Their beaches were widely separated. Major General Edwin Davies Patrick's (University of Michigan, 1916) veteran 6th Infantry Division landed over Blue Beaches on a sandy coast near Dagupan. Here, too, tides delayed the landings slightly, but the initial landings were unopposed. By mid-afternoon contact had been established with the adjoining 43rd Infantry Division and the 37th Infantry Division of XIV Corps. Only one small group of Japanese opposed the advance inland of the 1st Infantry Regiment of the "Sightseeing Sixth" division. Otherwise only random air and distant artillery attacks marred the day.

It fell to Major General Leonard Fish Wing's 43rd Infantry Division to have the most difficulty.[12] Carried ashore in LVT-4As and LVT-4s of the 826th Amphibious Tractor Battalion, and supported by the 716th Tank Battalion and 98th Chemical Mortar Battalion, the landings were likewise initially unopposed.[13] The veteran New England National Guard division's sector was a series of low hills behind the White Beaches and then a series of ridge lines which provided good cover for the defending Japanese. To secure these potential defenses General Wing sent his 103rd Infantry Regiment to seize the hills immediately. The 169th Infantry was to seize another dominating point, Hill 470. Delayed by Japanese artillery and mortar fire, the 169th Infantry had reached but not secured Hill 470 by dusk. Patrols soon reported a strong Japanese presence on the hill.

As the 172nd Infantry came ashore it, too, suffered from Japanese artillery fire but moved rapidly inland and secured initial objectives. Japanese fire continued as the regiment advanced to Hill 385, which remained in Japanese hands at darkness. As a result, the battle became two separate fights, one by the 103rd Infantry Regiment and another by the 169th and 172nd Infantry Regiments.

The 103rd Infantry Regiment was directed on Hill 200, some 10 miles inland and an excellent observation point from which the Japanese could direct fire on most of the Sixth Army's assault beaches. Delayed slightly by small groups of Japanese, the regiment pushed forward almost four miles by darkness. On January 10, the regiment moved forward again, delayed slightly by a tractor-drawn Japanese 75mm artillery gun which continually moved, withdrawing slowly to Hill 200. By afternoon, the tractor had been knocked out by supporting artillery, but the determined Japanese manhandled the gun into the village of Manaoag. The regiment halted for the night just outside the town, out of contact with any other Sixth Army force. During the day, supporting artillery knocked out 13 enemy guns, including four captured U.S. 155mm artillery guns that had been taken during the fall of the Philippines in 1942.

January 11 saw the 103rd Infantry begin a direct attack on Hill 200. The Japanese defenders made it obvious early in the fight that they intended to hold their positions in the face of the American attack. With contact on the right with the 6th Infantry Division's 1st Infantry Regiment now established, the 103rd launched their attack. Meanwhile, the other regiments of the division had turned to secure the corps flank and found themselves facing a determined enemy in debilitating heat, steep-sided bare hills, and formidable defenses. The 169th Infantry seized Hill 470 but there were more hills just beyond it. Intense artillery, mortar, and machine-gun fire soon halted the attack. Naval air support and division artillery was insufficient to knock out the enemy defenses. The Japanese had tunneled into the hills and rock formations and had created the formidable cave and tunnel defenses for which they were already justly famous.

Typical of the combat faced by the 43rd Infantry Division at this point was the action of Company G, 169th Infantry, on January 12, 1945. The battalion was attacking near Hill 318. The enemy defenders, estimated to be a company of infantry liberally supplied with machine guns, grenades, and blocks of TNT, held a position that could only be reached across a narrow ridge 70 yards long. At the end of the ridge sat an enemy pillbox and several rifle positions on rising ground. The initial attack cost the life of the 3rd Battalion, 169th Infantry's commander. Halted by enemy fire, Company G sought a way to attack this menacing position. Staff Sergeant Robert E. Laws, a squad leader from Altoona, Pennsylvania, went forward alone under vicious enemy fire until he was close enough to toss grenades at the pillbox. Return enemy grenades wounded him, but he persisted in his one-man assault, using grenades passed forward to him by his squad mates. Finally, one of his grenades entered the pillbox and knocked it out. Determined to finish off the enemy defenders, Staff Sergeant Laws led the way forward again, knocking out successive enemy positions with grenades passed to him by his buddies. He was hit again, in the arms and legs, by enemy TNT blocks tossed in his path. Three Japanese charged at him with fixed bayonets, but he cut two down with his own automatic weapon and then engaged in hand-to-hand combat with the third. The two men fell to the ground and rolled some 60 feet down the steep ridge. When his men finally reached him, they found the enemy soldier dead and Staff Sergeant Laws climbing back up the hill to get back into the fight despite new wounds to his head. He was treated and evacuated, surviving to receive his Medal of Honor.[14]

By January 10, General Krueger understood that his beachhead was secure and that the main threat came from the far left facing the 43rd Infantry Division. It appeared that General Wing had uncovered the first enemy line of defense. Intelligence officers believed that the enemy was conducting a ruse, inviting the Sixth Army inland where it would be overwhelmed and destroyed. This perceived threat would strike from the left, where the Japanese were halting the American advance. General Krueger ordered the Sixth Army reserves to be landed behind his I Corps. Not only did I Corps face the only known Japanese threat, but its area was much larger than that of XIV Corps and its units were thinly spread over that extended ground, even after all corps reserves had been committed. First to arrive was the independent 158th Infantry Regimental ("Bushmasters") Combat Team, which quickly reinforced the 172nd Infantry Regiment.[15]

The estimated cost to Sixth Army in establishing their Lingayen Gulf beachhead was 55 killed, 185 wounded, with most of the losses occurring in the 43rd Infantry Division. For these losses, the Sixth Army had established a firm beachhead on Luzon, landed its first reserves, and identified the direction of the main enemy opposition. Operations to date had gone according to plan, unusual in military operations, and the Sixth Army was in its desired position to carry out the rest of its planned campaign. The only concern facing General Krueger by January 11, 1945, was, where were the Japanese and what were they planning?

As noted earlier, General Yamashita was not surprised by the location of the Lingayen Gulf landings, only by the timing of them. They occurred about two weeks earlier than expected. Knowing full well that he could not defend the entire island with the forces at his disposal, he elected to conduct a delaying action, defending only where he needed to retain the ground for his own purposes. There was no intent of trapping the Sixth Army, despite his superiority in numbers, for General Yamashita fully understood the might of the American supporting arms and his acute lack of the same. So, Lingayen Gulf was not defended, and the Central Plain and Manila Bay regions were also left largely undefended, for his own troops could not hope to match the overwhelming American superiority in an open field contest.

Because of General Yamashita's plans, the first Japanese encountered by the Sixth Army were members of the *Shobu Group*.[16] These were a detached battalion and reconnaissance troops of Lieutenant General Fukutaro Nishiyama's *23rd Infantry Division*.[17] The unexpected early landing of the Americans had caught General Yamashita in a last-minute restructuring of his forces, and these units had been dispatched to the area to delay the Americans until all the movements and realignments had been completed, which they were not at the time of the landing.[18] General Yamashita also faced resistance among his own staff as to his plans. Some of his staff, dismayed at the rapid advance of the Americans, urged him to launch a strong counterattack led by the *2nd Tank Division*.[19] This would, they argued, allow more time to move supplies from Manila to the mountains and might also allow the capture of American supplies to further enhance their prolonged defense. But General Yamashita declined, citing the strength of Sixth Army and its cautious movements which did not offer a good opportunity of catching it off guard. He added that the limited fuel supply of the *2nd Tank Division* and the many destroyed bridges and roads would only serve to impede the progress of an armored attack.

By the end of January 11, 1945, I Corps was facing the initial defenses of the *23rd Infantry Division*, the part of the *Shobu Group* closest to Lingayen Gulf. I Corps' objective was to seize control of the Damortis–Rosario road, a two-lane paved section of Route 3 that ran along the coast north into *Shobu Group* territory. Control of Route 3 would lead to Route 11, another two-lane paved road leading to the Philippine summer capital of Babuio, where General Yamashita had his temporary headquarters. The ground consisted of hills and ridges with many draws and ravines to provide cover and observation for the enemy. The ground was of soft rock and dirt, making the already proficient Japanese digging skills much easier to implement.

Blocking the attacking 43rd Infantry Division was the *58th Independent Mixed Brigade*, an independent force of the *Shobu Group* assisting the *23rd Infantry Division*. Major General Bunzo Sato's brigade contained five infantry battalions, each of about 900 soldiers, an artillery battalion with 15 75mm mountain guns, and the usual service troops. These 6,900 men were reinforced with additional artillery units containing guns as large as 300mm. Coincidentally, the first American unit to encounter General Sato's brigade was a similar independent unit, the 158th Regimental Combat Team under the command of Brigadier General Hanford MacNider (Harvard, 1911). The veteran "Bushmasters," an Arizona National Guard organization, had been fighting the Japanese since 1943 and were no novices to combat. Consisting of three infantry battalions and an artillery battalion,[20] the 4,500 men of the combat team moved past the 172nd Infantry Regiment and took the lead up the coast road, sending patrols into Damortis, which was found deserted. Determined to protect that flank of his army, General Krueger attached both the "Bushmasters" and the 63rd Infantry Regiment, 6th Infantry Division, to General Wing's 43rd Infantry Division. With his new resources, General Wing organized a three-regiment attack up the Damortis–Rosario road. If the attack by the 158th, 172nd, and 63rd Infantry Regiments succeeded then the observation points used by the Japanese to shell the beachhead would be eliminated. This would allow General Krueger to release the XIV Corps for further exploitation.

The attack began January 13 with the 172nd Infantry attacking Hill 580. Under intense fire from mortars, machine guns, and rifles, the Americans seized the hill at a cost of 15 killed and 25 wounded. Over the next few days, the regiment continued its attack, taking Hill 565 and others that provided observation for the Japanese. But the other regiments were not so successful. The 63rd Infantry Regiment captured Hill 363, but promised artillery support failed to materialize because of destroyed radios and communications wire. Enemy opposition and unrelenting heat slowed the advance. All water had to be hand-carried forward. General Wing, unhappy with the regiment's performance, relieved the commander and placed the regimental executive officer in command.

Meanwhile, the 158th Infantry was having problems of its own. Its attack went well for the first five minutes, until the leading troops entered a shallow defile half a mile east of Damortis. Japanese artillery and mortar fire struck with intense force, and enemy machine guns added to the din. The *58th Independent Mixed Brigade*, which had suffered under American air and naval bombardment for weeks, was taking its opportunity to strike back. From prepared positions in caves and tunnels, they fired unceasingly as the Americans sought cover from the deadly stream of fire. Taken by surprise in the ambush, the Americans withdrew, losing 20 men killed and 65 wounded.

The following day the Americans returned. The "Bushmasters" gained about a thousand yards, supported by their 147th Field Artillery Battalion and naval aircraft. In one instance the regiment's executive officer, Lieutenant Colonel George Colvin, spotted an enemy officer observing their attack. As he watched the enemy officer lower his binoculars and make notes on a clipboard, he called up the regimental 57mm guns and directed them against the enemy observation post. Colonel Colvin and his staff enjoyed the ensuing scene of the enemy officer running for cover, dropping his binoculars and map case to speed his getaway.

On the flank of the "Bushmasters," the 63rd Infantry had moved forward over a mile under constant Japanese artillery and mortar fire. They had a small advantage of their own, however. Captain William J. D. Vaughan, of the 6th Infantry Division's 1st Infantry Regiment, had been landed on Luzon by submarine back in November and been fully briefed on the area by Filipino guerillas before returning to report to his division, so the terrain was familiar. On January 14, the regiment advanced again, led by the 2nd Battalion, followed by the 1st Battalion. Hill 363 was secured against light resistance. That night, the Japanese counterattacked with infantry, mortars, and machine guns. In one section, all the Americans were killed or wounded, but Private First Class William Smith picked up a light machine gun and stood up in full view of the enemy, firing so effectively that he forced the enemy in his sector to withdraw.[21] Resistance increased the next day, and enemy artillery and mortars kept the men pinned to the ground. With wire communications destroyed, Staff Sergeant Manuel R. Kaufman kept his critical radio, receiving and sending messages from an exposed position until he was himself killed by an artillery blast.[22] Staff Sergeant Mike J. Mogab led his rifle squad against an enemy hilltop position only to be pinned down by intense fire. Moving forward alone, he knocked out one enemy machine gun, then returned for more grenades. He used these to knock out a second enemy gun. Shot in the chest, he rolled down the hill to his squad and refused medical treatment until he had pointed out the enemy positions to his men and directed their fire on it. His actions eliminated all enemy opposition on that hill.[23] Many others performed their duties despite the increasing risk of death or injury. By the time this area was cleared, the 6th Infantry Division had named it "Purple Heart Valley."

This continued strong resistance made General Wing realize that the enemy facing his 43rd Infantry Division must be stronger than expected. He ordered his 172nd Infantry to speed its advance toward Route 3 and seize Rosario to clean out much of the fire that had been striking the 158th and 63rd Infantry Regiments. Even as this order went out, a report came to General Wing that a Japanese motorized column was spotted moving south along Route 3 headed for Route 11. Once again, fears of a Japanese counterattack surfaced. Unless the 172nd Infantry gained control of the road junction of Route 3 and Route 11, such an attack could seriously affect the 43rd Infantry Division and by extension the entire flank of Sixth Army.

By the next day, the 172nd Infantry had established a battalion at the edge of Route 3 a mile and a half west of Rosario. Still anxious, General Wing ordered his 169th Infantry to send some troops up Route 3 to assist in knocking out Japanese artillery and capture the Route 3–Route 11 junction. The 172nd Infantry was to seize Rosario, while the 63rd Infantry was to clear the Damortis–Rosario road. The 158th Infantry were left to deal with the Japanese enclave that had stopped their advance earlier. But January 16 saw little progress in any of these missions. The

158th Infantry made little progress and lost 13 killed, 34 wounded, and 49 evacuated due to heat exhaustion. The other regiments suffered accordingly, and the 63rd and 172nd Infantry Regiments had the added problem of getting supplies through the rugged terrain, which also prevented tank support from reaching them. Until the engineers could build roads forward, all supplies of food, water, and ammunition had to be hand-carried forward by Filipinos or air-dropped. There were not yet on Luzon sufficient resources to do this on a scale that the two regiments required. A stalemate resulted.

Meanwhile, on his right flank General Wing had other problems. His 103rd Infantry Regiment, along with elements of his 169th Infantry Regiment, had run into elements of the *23rd Infantry Division* northeast of Hill 318. Lieutenant General Nishiyama had stationed his *64th Infantry Regiment* along the western approach to Route 3 with orders to delay the advancing Americans as long as possible. The understrength Japanese regiment was dug in on several hills overlooking Route 3. By January 15, the 169th Infantry had cleared Hill 318 and then Hill 355, at a cost of 15 killed and 30 wounded. Concerned at the cost of repeated frontal attacks, General Wing ordered the 169th Infantry to bypass the defended hills and move on Route 3 overland. Leaving one battalion behind to contain the *64th Infantry Regiment*, the rest of the 169th Infantry force marched throughout January 15 and finally reached its objective late on January 16.

The 103rd Infantry Regiment had been trying to reach Route 3 and clear it as well. Blocked by the *2nd Battalion, 64th Infantry Regiment*, at the Hill 200 complex, the regiment had been stymied for days. The 600 Japanese, supported by at least 15 artillery pieces and other support troops, had held the critical six square miles of essential terrain needed by the Americans for their continued advance. With close support from their artillery and the 716th Tank Battalion, the 103rd Infantrymen engaged in a deadly four-day battle which ended with the Japanese survivors pulling back into the hills above Pozorrubio. Two reinforced companies from the 3rd Battalion, 103rd Infantry Regiment, moved on to Potpot Barrio where they began to establish defensive positions for the night.

General Yamashita had refused his staff's entreaties to launch a major counterattack against Sixth Army. But he was not averse to local counterattacks to gain time to move more supplies into the hills and finish the interrupted reorganization of his defenses. In accordance with these intentions, he authorized such an attack by the *23rd Infantry Division* during the night of January 16–17, 1945. General Nishiyama passed on the order to General Sato, with instructions to have his *58th Independent Mixed Brigade* strike at the lines of supply of the 158th Infantry Regiment. Meanwhile, General Nishiyama would have his own *71st Infantry Regiment* send a small force to threaten the supply lines of the 169th and 172nd Infantry Regiments. Another small force, from the *72nd Infantry Regiment*, was to attack the rear of the 169th and 103rd Infantry Regiments at Pozorrubio. Still another small group, drawn from an attachment of the *2nd Tank Division*, was to send a tank-infantry force to strike the 103rd Infantry Regiment.

Whatever the attacks of the *58th Independent Mixed Brigade* were intended to accomplish, they failed miserably. The only attack of note in the American reports is an attack on the 147th Field Artillery Battalion, which was beaten off with little difficulty. All regiments of the 43rd Infantry Division reported "normal infiltration" during the night. A few Japanese did manage to set fire to a gasoline dump behind the 172nd Infantry Regiment but little else of concern developed. The *23rd Infantry Division* attack fared better. An enemy group seems to have accidently encountered a battalion of the 169th Infantry near Palacpalac Barrio and the ensuing fight lasted all night, resulted in 100 enemy dead at a cost of four Americans killed and 26 wounded.[24]

But the strongest attack of the night fell upon those two companies from the 103rd Infantry Regiment who had taken up positions at Potpot Barrio barely moments earlier. Just before midnight on January 16 these men were attacked by the *Shigemi Detachment*, the armored group attached to the *23rd Infantry Division*. Japanese tanks came racing out of the darkness, taking the Americans so by surprise that the antitank gunners failed to react as the first tanks raced through the barrio, spraying machine-gun fire in all directions. Two tanks disappeared down the road while others, supported by infantry, continued the attack. American gunners began to knock out enemy tanks, and after a two-hour confused brawl, the Japanese withdrew. But just as the Americans were thinking it was over, the two tanks that had earlier disappeared down the road returned at dawn. This time there was no surprise and American gunners finished off both enemy tanks. American losses were two killed and 10 wounded, plus a 37mm gun, a jeep, and an M8 Scout Car destroyed. The Japanese left behind 11 tanks destroyed and 50 dead. That morning the 43rd Infantry Division and its attachments were relieved by the newly arrived 25th Infantry Division. Having overcome the strongest resistance yet met on Luzon, the division withdrew for a well-earned rest behind the lines.

While the 43rd Infantry Division had been struggling to establish the Army Beachhead Line, its fellow I Corps division, the "Sightseeing Sixth," had been held back so as not to open a gap between the two divisions. General Swift, the corps commander, ordered the division to halt but allowed it to send forward reconnaissance patrols which identified two Japanese strongholds in front of the division, at Urdeneta and Villasis. Nevertheless, the division was held in support by the 43rd Infantry Division, and no immediate move was made against these Japanese. When the 25th Infantry Division relieved General Wing's command, General Patrick began his own forward movement.

Meanwhile, General Griswold's XIV Corps had moved deep inland. By January 11 they had established their portion of the Army Beachhead Line. In fact, so little resistance was there in the XIV Corps zone that some Allied naval forces landed at

Cabalitan Bay and established a seaplane base even before the advanced elements of the 40th Infantry Division arrived. Outside of a few skirmishes with elements of the *23rd Infantry Division*, little resistance was encountered by this division drawn from the California–Nevada–Utah National Guards. On the division's left the 37th Infantry Division soon joined Filipino guerillas and moved relatively easily south, reaching Route 13 by January 15. General Krueger ordered another forward advance, and General Griswold had his engineers build bridges over the Agno River to facilitate this movement. This was to be the start of a larger attempt to reach and secure the capital city, Manila. By January 17, advance elements of XIV Corps were at Moncada, on Route 3, 10 miles south of the Agno River. The cost had been 30 killed and 90 wounded compared with I Corps losses of 220 killed and 660 wounded. The Americans had returned to Luzon.

In Northwest Europe, the First and Third U.S. Armies were fighting to clear the ground seized by the enemy during the Battle of the Bulge. In the Seventh U.S. Army's zone, the 43rd Tank Battalion of the 12th Armored Division was wiped out at Herrlisheim. On the Eastern Front, the First White Russian Front overran Warsaw. In Italy, the Fifth U.S. Army relieved British units facing the Gothic Line. The American Mars Task Force had reached to within three miles of the Burma Road.

CHAPTER 3

The Central Plain

The Sixth Army's landings at Lingayen Gulf were soon known far and wide, announced personally by General MacArthur from the beachhead the day of the landings. One of the Army nurses who had been left behind in 1942 was now being held at Santo Tomas prison camp on the outskirts of Manila. Lieutenant Madeline Ullom recalled, "Internees who worked in a garden near the fence heard a radio broadcast from the outside which stated our forces landed at Lingayen. Navy bombers attacked sporadically during the day. Early in the morning residents of Shantytown found four-page leaflets with pictures of General MacArthur and 'MacArthur Has Returned. General MacArthur keeps his pledges.'"[1]

Landing against light opposition and moving inland swiftly were two different tasks on Luzon. Although the landings had gone off smoothly, the increasing resistance and the rugged terrain in which the Japanese had established their main defenses slowed the movement of critical supplies without which there would be no rapid conquest of the island. One of the main problems was bridge construction. Dozens of small streams and rivers crisscrossed the area over which Sixth Army was advancing and nearly all those bridges had been destroyed. Some had been demolished back in 1942 and never been repaired by either the Japanese or the Filipinos. The few found intact were too weak to carry the weight of the machines of a modern American army. Sixth Army needed bridges with a minimum 35-ton capacity, of which none had previously existed on Luzon. Improvisation was the order of the day. In the 37th Infantry Division, LVT and LCM (Landing Craft, Medium) ferries were put into operation to go forward. A slow but effective method, it was rivaled by the 43rd Infantry Division's use of a railroad right of way and railroad bridges to get its heavy equipment forward. On I Corps' left flank, bulldozers had to construct roads where none had existed before. This workforce included some 500 Filipinos each day hand-carrying tools and other supplies to assist in creating new roads. Although General Krueger had made provision for bringing heavy Bailey Bridges[2] along, these had been stored aboard several ships and came ashore piecemeal, making life difficult for the engineers. Yet as early as January 13, the Ohio Division's 117th Engineer

(Combat) Battalion had a Bailey Bridge across the Pantal River at Dagupan. The 6th Engineer (Combat) Battalion had put one in even earlier, on January 11, across the Binloc River. In the interim, the 5202nd Engineer Construction Brigade had been using pontoon bridges to get troops, equipment, and supplies forward. Other engineer units worked on repairing and restoring the rolling stock and roads of the Luzon railroad system. Still others worked on creating the vital airfields which would house the support aircraft upon which the Sixth Army depended. To make matters still more onerous, on January 10 a severe gale threw up eight-foot waves on Lingayen's beaches, making the landing of supplies temporarily impossible. All unloading had to be moved to the I Corps beaches, increasing congestion and making movement still more laborious.

By the middle of January 1945, both the Sixth Army and the *Fourteenth Area Army* were undergoing re-evaluations of their plans and deployments. General Krueger's growing concern about the enemy's strength—the *Shobu Group*—faced by the I Corps on his left flank along the Damortis–Rosario area, and the fears about a counterattack from that direction, made him believe that securing the road junction of Routes 3 and 11 was his priority. To accomplish this, he directed his newly landed reserve, the Regular Army 25th Infantry Division, to commit two-thirds of its strength to that area. The plan required the 103rd and 169th Infantry Regiments, 43rd Infantry Division, to attack north up Route 3. This, however, would leave a gap between the 43rd Infantry and 6th Infantry Divisions. The 25th Infantry Division was to fill that void. This would also allow the 6th Infantry Division, which had been held back to avoid such a break from opening, to resume its advance. Meanwhile, XIV Corps would mark time while I Corps reached the Army's Final Beachhead Line.

The 25th Infantry Division had been activated using Regular Army units at Schofield Barracks, Hawaii, just two months before the Pearl Harbor attack. After defending and training in Hawaii, it took part in the Guadalcanal and New Georgia campaigns before spending time in New Zealand rehabilitating. Its next landing was Luzon. Its commander since January 1944 was Major General Charles Love Mullins, Jr. (USMA, 1917). The division came ashore into a Sixth Army beachhead some 20 miles deep and 30 miles wide.

General Mullins's division was followed ashore by the 13th Armored Group, which assembled near the San Jacinto area on January 13. Sixth Army Field Order Number 42, January 16, 1945, ordered General Mullins to leave his 35th Infantry Regiment behind in Sixth Army Reserve while the rest of his division secured the line of Urdaneta–Binalonan. It was also on this day that the first U.S. Army Air Force squadrons landed at Lingayen and relieved the U.S. Navy carrier-based aircraft of close air support duties for Sixth Army.

Earlier, General Krueger had been called to a shipboard conference with General MacArthur, who was planning on landing a new force, the XI Corps, behind the

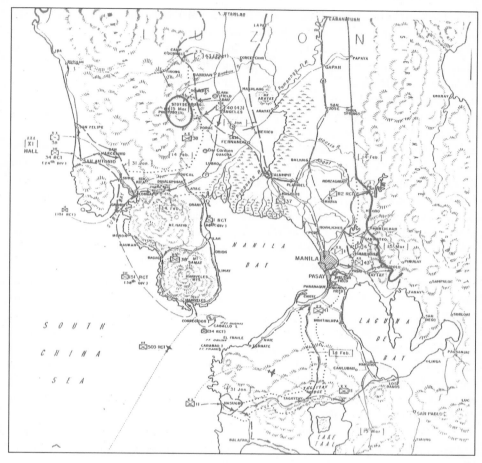

Manila Bay, Bataan, Corregidor, and Environs

Luzon. U.S. Army Campaigns of World War II. Commemorative Series. Washington, D.C. Center of Military History.

Japanese on the Zambales coast, north of Subic Bay. With this General Krueger concurred. But the other topic of the conference was more disturbing. Believing that his forces had suffered little thus far in the campaign, General MacArthur returned to his dearest subject, the liberation of Manila. He believed that an advance on Manila would encounter little enemy resistance and that the Japanese would evacuate Manila, as he had done in 1941. General Krueger stressed that his troops had encountered strong enemy forces to the northeast and that he had to commit some of his slender reserves to protect that flank. That left him with only the two divisions of XIV Corps to make any advance towards Manila, which was 120 miles away from his present positions. General Krueger attempted to explain that he was moving XIV Corps south toward Manila, but that his advance was necessarily slow to preserve the tactical integrity of Sixth Army. He believed that any rush toward Manila would expose Sixth Army to defeat in detail, one corps at a time. He also reiterated that his supply situation was not yet satisfactory and would only get worse if stretched another 120 miles. He proposed that once his follow-up reserve forces appeared—the 1st Cavalry Division and the 32nd Infantry Division, both veterans of previous campaigns—Sixth Army would launch an attack toward Manila. Although he clearly disapproved, General MacArthur reluctantly agreed to the delay. Indeed, General Krueger's operations officer, Lieutenant Colonel Clyde Eddleman, who was present later, said that it was "the only time I ever saw the two of them when they had cross words."[3] Nor did this settle the matter for General MacArthur, who badgered General Krueger with numerous messages throughout January about getting to Manila with speed, regardless of other factors, which he habitually discounted. In the end, General MacArthur remarked to an aide, "Walter's pretty stubborn. Maybe I'll have to try something else."[4]

"Something else" turned out to be a campaign to embarrass General Krueger into taking the risk he otherwise refused to take with his Sixth Army. First, General MacArthur moved his own headquarters ashore and placed it forward of General Krueger's own headquarters on Luzon. Then, he involved his other army, Lieutenant General Robert Lawrence Eichelberger's (USMA, 1909) Eighth Army, in the Luzon campaign by having it land at Nasugbu Bay, only 55 miles south of Manila, and giving General Eichelberger permission to advance on the capital city. Initially envisioned as a diversion to facilitate Sixth Army's advance on Manila, it soon developed into a "race" between the two armies. General MacArthur, knowing the two army commanders disliked each other, took full advantage of that situation.[5]

General Krueger was not fooled by these tactics and refused to take General MacArthur's bait. Having worked for him for two years under some of the most difficult conditions, he stuck to his decision to make the deliberate effort to seize Manila, even if his rival beat him to it, but maintaining the Sixth Army's integrity as he did so. He admitted later that "our advance toward the south was slower than desirable but its pace depended upon reconstruction of the many destroyed bridges, some very large ones, rehabilitation of the roads and the Manila–Dagupan Railroad. Shortage of vital bridge material, lack of locomotives and limited rolling stock complicated matters."[6] In this belief, he was supported by his own chief engineer, Major General Hugh J. Casey (USMA, 1918), who later wrote, "From the beginning, General Krueger had been confronted with the delicate problem of balancing on the one hand his urge to push the leading elements of the I and XIV Corps toward Manila as rapidly as possible and, on the other, the need to achieve fool-proof supply and support. He managed to attain that balance using brilliant tactics and by driving his engineers to the utmost."[7]

General Krueger was not the only one under pressure for speed, however. In addition to his personal interest in a quick liberation of the Philippine capital, General MacArthur had other concerns. The air bases at Lingayen Gulf were at best temporary, and would quickly flood, becoming unusable with the monsoon season which was fast approaching. Nor did they contain enough fields to accommodate the entire Allied air forces slated for the Luzon campaign. Only the all-weather fields at the Clark Field complex, on the way to Manila, could do that. These fields were also needed to provide the promised heavy bomber air support that General MacArthur had committed to the upcoming Central Pacific Theater of Operations' invasions of Iwo Jima and Okinawa. Further, the strategic concept upon which the Luzon campaign had been based, the cutting of Japanese supply lines to the East Indies, depended upon adequate base facilities to launch air and naval strikes against those supply lines. Resolving these issues centered on the conquest of the Clark Field air base complex and control of Manila Bay for naval forces.

It was at this juncture that Colonel Horton V. White, General Krueger's intelligence officer, revised his estimate of enemy forces and intentions. From various intelligence sources and enemy actions thus far in the campaign, Colonel White determined that the Japanese were not going to defend the Central Plain but defend northern Luzon instead. He felt that no significant enemy force lay between XIV Corps and Clark Field itself. He believed that only the *2nd Tank Division* remained in the Central Plain and that this force was moving north to join with General Yamashita's main forces. For once, Brigadier General Charles A. Willoughby (Gettysburg College, 1914), General MacArthur's intelligence chief, concurred with the Sixth Army's evaluation of Japanese intentions. With the upcoming XI Corps landing behind Clark Field, Japanese dispositions should be significantly disrupted to unhinge their defense of the airfields.

Although still reluctant because of Sixth Army's supply difficulties, General Krueger now agreed to push XIV Corps toward Clark Field. On January 18, he issued orders that directed a staged movement forward by XIV Corps to the critical airfields. To protect its own flank, XIV Corps was to echelon troops on its left and rear to protect it from any enemy encroachments from the north. Meanwhile, I Corps would continue efforts to secure the Routes 3 and 11 junctions at Damortis, thereby protecting XIV Corps' rear.

General Yamashita had problems of his own. Although I Corps had overrun the outpost line of defense at the Hill 355 area, these had always been intended as delaying defenses. His forces there, the *23rd Infantry Division* and *58th Independent Mixed Brigade*, still held excellent defensive terrain which would hold back any drive on Baguio, his temporary headquarters. Just to be sure, however, he strengthened that line with two battalions of his *19th Infantry Division*.[8] But his main concern was the protection of the approaches to his *Shobu Group's* enclave at San Jose. The I Corps advance in this area posed a direct threat to his forces sheltering in the

Cagayan Valley, from which he hoped to draw considerable food supplies. Another American thrust threatened the alternate route known as the Villa Verde Trail, which would halt his flow of supplies still being forwarded from Manila and also threaten the Cagayan Valley. Further, at this point elements of the *2nd Tank Division* had not yet cleared San Jose on their move north. Another force, elements of the *105th Infantry Division*, were even further from San Jose on their way north.[9]

To respond to these dangers, General Yamashita reverted to a previous plan that had then been discarded. The *2nd Tank Division* was to concentrate near San Nicolas and defend the Villa Verde Trail. To replace losses, it was to assume command over the *10th Infantry Division*'s *Reconnaissance Regiment* and other units. The rest of the *10th Infantry Division* would defend San Jose, holding that area until the *105th Infantry Division* passed on its way up Route 5. Then the *10th Infantry Division* would itself withdraw up Route 5. But confusion reigned within the Japanese command. Even as these orders were issued, General Yamashita learned that the *2nd Tank Division* could not maneuver its tanks along the rough terrain which composed the Villa Verde Trail. Then it was found that the *10th Infantry Division* was nowhere near where *Fourteenth Area Army* believed it to be. Lieutenant General Yasuyuki Okamoto, the division's commander, had decided on his own that his division was too weak to defend an open area against the American motorized forces. One regiment had remained with the *Kembu Group*, and another regiment was attached to the *103rd Infantry Division* in the north. With what was left of his division, General Okamoto had withdrawn his forces north of San Jose up Route 5 and disposed them along a line of defense meant to be manned later in the campaign.[10]

General Yamashita had little choice but to accept the *fait accompli*. He left General Okamoto's force in place and instead directed General Iwanaka's *2nd Tank Division* to defend the San Jose area, detaching a combat command built around the *6th Tank Regiment* to defend the town of Muñoz. Elements of the *105th Infantry Division* would drop off reinforcements as they passed through San Jose.

While both commanders struggled with their strategical, logistical, and tactical problems, the soldiers of both sides continued with the ground war. General Griswold, commanding XIV Corps, now had authorization to push forward his two divisions in stages. First, they would move up to a line from Tarlac to Victoria, a 10-mile stretch that would position them for a further advance south. Town after town fell with little or no opposition. On January 23, patrols of General Brush's 40th Infantry Division reached Camp O'Donnell, one of the original destinations of the "Bataan Death March" of 1942. This day it was deserted. Just the graves of those who had survived the "Death March" only to die of barbaric treatment and starvation remained to mark the location's brutal history.

The advance continued. In some instances, such as the town of Pura, advance elements of General Beightler's 37th Infantry Division found the town already in the hands of Philippine guerillas. In others, such as Tarlac itself, General Brush's

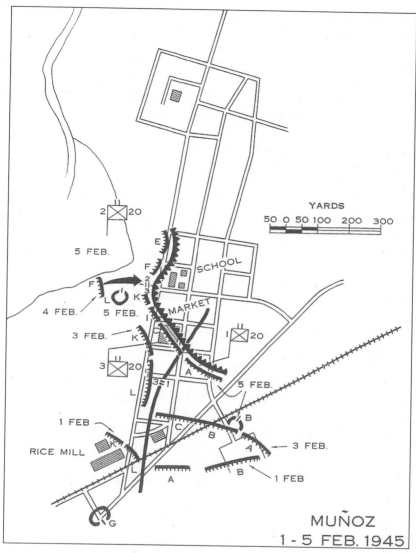

YARDS

50 0 50 100 200 300

MUÑOZ
1-5 FEB. 1945

The 6th Infantry Division's Battle for Muñoz

Division Public Relations Section. *The 6th Infantry Division in World War II*. Nashville, TN: Battery Press, 1983.

160th Infantry had to fight to clear the town of enemy troops. By January 21, the Tarlac–Victoria line had been established. The next day the XIV Corps advanced against no opposition. General Krueger now authorized General Griswold to seize Clark Field. Although the risk still existed, and supplies were falling short of needs, the opportunity was too good to pass up. General Griswold, with supply lines stretched to the limit and with a left flank exposed for 25 miles, began receiving reports of a Japanese force at Moncada, 20 miles to his rear. Battalions of the 37th Infantry Division's 129th and 145th Infantry soon removed this threat. But a Japanese attack at La Paz destroyed a vital bridge. With these difficulties, General Griswold reported to General Krueger that his advance needed to halt until more information about the enemy forces he faced was obtained. To do this, General Griswold, with General Swift's permission, sent patrols into the zone of the I Corps to ascertain the enemy situation there. General Krueger, still cautious about the advance of his XIV Corps, agreed. These patrols found evidence that a large enemy force had indeed been on XIV Corps' flank but had recently departed.[11]

With this information, XIV Corps' advance resumed. The 40th Infantry Division seized Bamban Airfield and cleared the town after a day-long fight. This indicated that XIV Corps had at last found the enemy force defending Clark Field. General Griswold took January 24 as a day of consolidation and rest, preparatory to making his attack to seize the airfield. He ordered General Brush to probe the enemy defenses while General Beightler's men remained poised to launch an attack. One of the Ohio's Division's regiments, the 129th Infantry, remained behind to protect the corps' exposed left flank.

The prewar American base at Clark Field was a vast complex of paved runways, taxiways, and dispersal areas. It ran along Route 3 for some 15 miles and offered the best possible airfields on Luzon. Located on flat open fields, rice paddies, and farmland, the terrain was open except to the west where the Zambales Mountains dominated the area. Assigned to defend the airfields, and then destroy them so that the Americans could not quickly restore them, were the 30,000 Army and Navy troops of General Tsukada's *Kembu Group*.[12] The *Kembu Group* was a mixed grouping of Army and Navy combat troops, service troops, and base troops, of which around half were trained combat troops. These were divided into nine separate detachments and assigned defensive sectors. These groups had little heavy artillery, mostly antitank guns and field artillery supported by a few heavy naval guns used as ground support weapons. They also had a variety of automatic weapons, some stripped from destroyed aircraft and ships.

General Tsukada planned three lines of defense. First, an outpost line of resistance northwest of the Bamban River, anchored at Fort Stotsenburg. Then a second intermediate line. But the main line of resistance (MLR) lay within the Zambales Mountains overlooking Clark Field. From here he could control use of the field from highly defensible terrain. A "last stand position," under Rear Admiral Ushie Sugimoto, was positioned deeper in the mountains.

First to attack was the 160th Infantry of the 40th Infantry Division. From the Manila Railroad, the regiment probed forward to the west toward objectives that turned out to be major defenses of the outpost line of resistance. Guerilla and civilian estimates of Japanese strength in the area varied greatly, but the division expected to meet some 3,000 enemy troops along a front 6,000 yards long. The 1st and 2nd Battalions began their assault on January 24. Naming the two objectives Stratta Hill and Stout Hill, after the battalion commanders, the 160th Infantry found the enemy deeply hidden in caves and tunnels seemingly impenetrable to air and artillery bombardment. Only close firing from tanks, self-propelled guns, flame-throwers, hand grenades, and demolitions could reduce such defenses. Using tanks and tank destroyers, the infantry blasted and burned each individual cave or tunnel entrance shut. Artillery and 6-inch naval guns blew away the natural vegetation that concealed these enemy defenses, and the attacking infantry finished the job. General Brush fed his 185th Infantry into the fight to reduce casualties and speed up the battle. The 108th Infantry moved west trying to gain the flank of the Japanese, but soon found itself under the same fire as the other regiments.

On January 26, the 640th Tank Destroyer Battalion's Reconnaissance Company, with a platoon of tanks attached, scouted the area around Clark Field. The Japanese responded by opening fire with their heavy guns, which in turn exposed these to American artillery fire. Several of these guns, along with pillboxes and machine-gun positions, were destroyed. The following day, the 160th Infantry reached the crest of Stratta Hill. The next day, Thrall Hill fell to the 108th Infantry Regiment. From one hill to the next, the 40th Infantry Division fought its way toward Clark Field. In doing so they destroyed the *2nd Battalion, 2nd Mobile Infantry, 2nd Tank Division* and penetrated General Tsukada's outpost line of resistance (OPLR). These defenses, which General Tsukada expected to hold a week, had fallen in three days. This victory had cost General Brush 35 killed and 115 wounded against Japanese losses of at least 1,000 killed in action.

The enemy resistance in front of the 40th Infantry Division had provided ample warning to General Beightler that his own 37th Infantry Division was now about to face the same enemy force. His first move was to seize the town of Angeles, a railroad stop on the Manila Railroad leading past Fort Stotsenburg. The 2nd Battalion, 145th Infantry, reinforced by the 37th Reconnaissance Troop and 637th Tank Destroyer Battalion, attacked against small-arms and machine-gun fire. During this fight, one enterprising soldier, Private First Class Hernandez, a machine gunner with Company E, thought he made a bargain when a local Filipino sold him a small pony for a pack of cigarettes. Now he would not have to carry his heavy pack and equipment on his own back. But the deal soon turned sour when the Military Police informed Private First Class Hernandez that he had purchased a stolen horse.[13]

The advance soon overran Clark Airfield runway number 1, which had last seen Americans 37 months earlier. The advance also found that Angeles had been abandoned by the Japanese and was held by Filipino guerillas. This advance placed the 37th Infantry Division beyond Clark Field and on what appeared to be an open road to Manila. The problem of what to do with the 37th Infantry Division now arose for Generals Krueger and Griswold. A strike for Manila would leave the right rear of the division open to a counterattack from the *Kembu Group*, which might not be held by the fully occupied 40th Infantry Division. Committing the division to seizing Clark Field would only further delay the advance on Manila, which was equally a prime objective of the campaign. The landing of XI Corps north of Bataan held out a promise, but not a certainty, that *Kembu Group* would be too distracted front and rear to launch a counterattack against XIV Corps. General Swift's I Corps was still bogged down, awaiting reinforcements before it could form a firm barrier against counterattack from the north. Although by this time, January 27, these reinforcements had arrived in Lingayen Gulf, they had not yet unloaded from their transports. After consideration, General Krueger decided to take the risk and ordered XIV Corps to continue with its advance on Manila.

General Griswold, however, was less sanguine about having his two divisions so far from each other. He preferred to retain both divisions to drive *Kembu Group* deeper into the mountains and away from Clark Field before detaching either for a push south. This would both protect his own supply lines and the engineers who were waiting to rehabilitate Clark Field. He directed General Beightler to join on the 40th Infantry Division's left flank and attack Clark Field and Fort Stotsenburg. To comply at least minimally with General Krueger's directive, he did allow General Beightler to send reconnaissance elements down Route 3 to San Fernando, 15 miles beyond Clark Field.

Leaving one battalion of his 129th Infantry to continue guarding the corps' left rear, General Beightler reshuffled his units for the attack. The rest of that regiment would strike for Fort Stotsenburg, reinforced with the 2nd Battalion, 145th Infantry. The remainder of the 145th Infantry would attack west from Angeles to clear the high ground south of Fort Stotsenburg. The 148th Infantry, reinforced with the 37th Reconnaissance Troop, would undertake the scouting mission. The attack began on January 28 and almost immediately ran into the *Kembu Group's* outpost line. Supported by the 754th Tank Battalion, the attack made progress until stopped by intense small-arms fire, machine guns, and a "friendly" air strike. The tanks were halted by a minefield. These mines were aerial bombs of between 15 and 150 kilograms, buried in the ground nose up, to blow up the heavy American tanks. The 117th Engineer (Combat) Battalion counted 1,349 such mines planted in the path of the 37th Infantry Division. They could only be removed after the aerial fuse was deactivated by hand and then the bomb itself pulled away by trucks equipped with A-frames.

The battle soon became one of each unit, be it a regiment, a battalion, or an infantry company, facing one of the nine Japanese detachments into which the *Kembu Group* had been divided. The Japanese conducted counterattacks, one of which forced a withdrawal by the 160th Infantry until its flanks could be stabilized. But the next day, January 29, this regiment of General Brush's division counterattacked and broke

THE CENTRAL PLAIN • 37

through the main line of resistance of their personal foe, the *Takaya Detachment*.[14] In addition to casualties of 10 killed and 70 wounded, another 50 Americans were evacuated due to heat exhaustion.

Meanwhile, the 129th Infantry beat off counterattacks by the Japanese before launching their own attack under artillery and air strikes. Within hours they had overrun the outpost line in their area and were entering the ruins of Fort Stotsenburg. As they did so, however, six enemy tanks attacked at Tacondo Barrio, striking the 3rd Battalion. The battalion's advance had been supported by tanks of the 754th Tank Battalion and tank destroyers of the 637th Tank Destroyer Battalion. But moments before the attack, the tanks had withdrawn to refuel and resupply. The Japanese knocked out a Cannon Company M-7 self-propelled 105mm howitzer[15] and struck Company I, 129th Infantry, with antitank fire and machine guns. The tank destroyers rushed into action, despite their vulnerability, and quickly knocked out four enemy tanks and crews. Two others retreated. Two of the tank destroyers were also disabled. So badly hurt was Company I that the battalion commander, Lieutenant Colonel Raymond C. Scheppach, had to have Company K send reinforcements to the front.[16]

These counterattacks had been intended to restore the Japanese outpost line of resistance. With the failure of the attacks, orders were issued to withdraw to the main line of resistance. It appears that these orders were issued even as General Beightler issued his own orders. General Krueger had been pressuring General Griswold to complete the seizure of Clark Field promptly. These instructions were passed to General Beightler, who in turn pushed forward the 129th Infantry. Due to the recent Japanese withdrawal, little resistance was encountered. Fort Stotsenburg was secured before dark on January 30. However, the 160th Infantry and 108th Infantry on the right continued to encounter fierce resistance from the *Takaya Detachment*, which had already been pushed back to its MLR.

Once again it was the 129th Infantry that made the most progress. While General Krueger personally raised an American flag over Fort Stotsenburg, where he had served early in his career, the 1st Battalion attacked on the morning of January 31 into the face of heavy enemy fire coming from 20mm, 25mm, and 40mm guns emplaced on the battalion's flanks. Yet within 20 minutes Company A had secured one of the key heights defending the position, known as "Top of the World," a large, bare-sloped hill mass commanding the plain containing Clark Field. Once "Top of the World" was taken, XIV Corps would have achieved all objectives at Clark Field. The 129th Infantry continued its attack throughout the day and by dark had managed to climb halfway up the heavily defended slopes. So close were the two sides that grenades were easily tossed back and forth. Despite heavy resistance, the Americans reached the crest of "Top of the World" before dark on February 1 and secured the area. The following day, February 2, Company I eliminated the last Japanese holdouts at the peak of "Top of the World." Clark Field was secured.

The exhaustion of the soldiers of the 37th Infantry Division is perhaps best typified by the tale of Private First Class Peter J. Cech. Ordered to run a communications line from an observation outpost to the company command post, he proceeded in complete darkness, tying the line onto any object he could find or feel in the darkness. He came upon a tree stump and began to tie the line onto it when it suddenly raced away at top speed. It was not until later that he realized that his "tree stump" was a carabao.[17]

With the seizure of "Top of the World" and the 40th Infantry Division isolating the remainder of the *Kembu Group* in the Zambales Mountains, the Central Plain had been secured. Over 2,500 casualties had been inflicted upon the Japanese, and the remainder of the armored force with *Kembu Group* wiped out. The determination of the defenders is highlighted by the fact that the Americans only captured 10 prisoners in this phase of the campaign. The Americans in turn had lost about 150 killed and 600 wounded, with the 129th and 160th Infantry Regiments suffering the most casualties. In addition, hundreds of men had to be evacuated due to injuries, sickness, heat exhaustion, and combat fatigue.

With Clark Field secured, the engineers could get to work to restore the field for the hundreds of American aircraft waiting to base there. Route 3 had been secured for the flow of American supplies, as had the Manila Railroad. Communications from Clark Field to Lingayen Gulf were now open and secure. True, the remainder of *Kembu Group* still lingered in the mountains, but one division could contain them while the other began the march to Manila. General Griswold directed General Brush to have his 40th Infantry Division continue attacking to the west, keeping the *Kembu Group* away from Clark Field and isolated. General Beightler's 37th Infantry Division was to begin its journey toward Manila, together with a new addition to XIV Corps, the recently arrived 1st Cavalry Division.

The 1st Cavalry Division (Special) was a unique organization within the U.S. Army during World War II. It was a prewar horse-mounted unit at Fort Bliss, Texas, when the war began. It was soon dismounted and organized as an infantry division, but with two brigades of two regiments each. One of its early commanders had been Major General Swift, who was now leading I Corps to the north. Its current commander was Major General Verne Donald Mudge (USMA, 1920) who had led it thus far in the war through the New Guinea, Bismarck Archipelago, and Leyte campaigns. The division's companies were called "troops" and battalions referred to as "squadrons," both holdovers from prewar days. Unlike infantry regiments, each cavalry regiment contained only two squadrons, for a total of eight rather than the usual nine infantry battalions within a division. It contained the usual supporting units, engineers, artillery, medical, signal, and reconnaissance, but with cavalry designations (except the artillery battalions). The division arrived on Luzon on January 26 and was sent to General Griswold's XIV Corps. What was soon to be termed "the Race for Manila" was about to begin.

In Northwest Europe, the Ninth U.S. Army's 102nd Infantry Division cleared the last remaining German enclave west of the Roer River. In the Third Army's zone, the 94th Infantry Division and 8th Armored Division cleared the enemy from Butzdorf in the Saar–Moselle triangle. On the Eastern Front, the Red Army reached the Gulf of Danzig. In the Central Pacific, Operation Plan CINCPOA 11-44—the invasion of Iwo Jima—became effective.

CHAPTER 4

Securing the Beachhead

While the XIV Corps was making the most dramatic advances of Sixth Army on Luzon, there remained the unglamorous but vital need to secure the Sixth Army's base of operations for the invasion to succeed. Uncomfortably aware that his Sixth Army was significantly outnumbered by General Yamashita's *Fourteenth Area Army* on Luzon, and as yet unsure of the Japanese plan for defending Luzon, General Krueger was anxious to secure his base of operations at Lingayen against the nearby enemy threat. This onerous task fell to General Swift's I Corps, holding the north side of the beachhead.[1]

General Wing's 43rd Infantry Division was still assigned to secure the junction of Routes 3 and 11. Even with its two attached regiments, the 158th and 63rd, this task had proved difficult. Alongside, General Patrick's 6th Infantry Division had been forced to slow its advance until that road junction was in I Corps hands. Blocking the way forward was General Nishiyama's reinforced *23rd Infantry Division*, with about 13,000 men holding ideal defensive terrain. Here, as usual, they had established well-prepared defenses in caves and tunnels, many interconnected. The well-known Japanese expertise in camouflage was fully in evidence. Artillery pieces were rail-mounted and pulled in and out of protecting caves as necessary. Some guns were camouflaged as nipa huts, hidden until the Americans stumbled over them.

As were all the American commanders at this stage of the campaign, General Wing felt pressure for speed but lacked firm intelligence on the enemy he faced. He decided on a two-pronged attack from two directions. Both of necessity would be frontal attacks. Three regiments, the 63rd, 158th, and 172nd Infantry Regiments, would attack from the west along the Damortis–Rosario road, while the 103rd and 169th Infantry Regiments drove north along Route 3 from Pozorrubio. He assigned four objectives. These were the Damortis–Rosario road and the terrain dominating it, the Hill 355–Mount Alava defense complex south of Rosario, the Hill 600–1500 ridge line east of Route 3, and of course the road junction and the heights dominating it.

The 169th Infantry, 43rd Infantry Division, left one battalion facing Hill 355 to occupy Japanese attention. The other two battalions spent January 17 and 18 seeking a way around the enemy defenses. They soon came upon a new section of Route 3 that rejoined the old road east of Sison. Despite perfect observation, the Japanese seemed content to leave the Americans to their search. But when the Americans secured Route 3 northeast of Sison, cutting their communications, they opened fire with machine guns, mortars, and artillery against the 169th Infantry. Eight tanks from the 716th Tank Battalion that had accompanied the advance were turned back, as they appeared to be the primary targets of the Japanese.

The next day Japanese troops from the *64th Infantry Regiment* encountered the 2nd Battalion, 169th Infantry, near the Bobonan Crossroads as the Japanese retreated from Mount Alva. This pressure from infantry and artillery forced the Americans, caught on open terrain, to withdraw to the Route 3 fork where the tanks had stopped the day before. Having lost a quarter of its strength, the 2nd Battalion continued the fight, killing 400–900 enemy troops. Six American Sherman M4 tanks were disabled. Among the 200 American casualties was the battalion commander, the second lost by the division since landing. Although forced to withdraw to the Bobonan Crossroads by heavy enemy artillery fire, the battle had eliminated the Japanese battalion. This left Mount Alva denuded of defenders, and the 169th Infantry was quick to take advantage of the situation. An attack on January 20 reached the crest. The following day was spent mopping up.

This left only Hill 355, which the regiment had already surrounded. With two battalions, a slow and costly attack took January 22 and 23 to clear the hilltop. The Japanese lost 500 men of the *1st Battalion, 64th Infantry Regiment*, and Hill 355. The 3rd Battalion, 103rd Infantry, came forward to "mop-up" the remaining enemy defenders. Another 150 enemy soldiers fell in this action, along with the capture of four 47mm antitank guns and seven 75mm artillery pieces. The first of General Wing's objectives had been taken.

The 103rd Infantry Regiment, after its sector had been reduced by the arrival of the 25th Infantry Division, had attacked Hill 600 in the face of automatic weapons, mortars, and artillery. Their supporting 181st Field Artillery Battalion was hit by an attack of about 200 Japanese soldiers led by a major. The attack was beaten off, and no guns were lost to enemy action. Other supporting artillery battalions were also attacked by infiltrators but continued to fire while repulsing these attacks. The American attack continued January 21, supported by tanks of the 716th Tank Battalion. Launched from three directions, this attack gained a foothold on the southern slopes of Hill 600 at the cost of 100 casualties. The open terrain gave the Japanese full view of the attacking Americans, and they took full advantage when a group of officers assembled at a command post on Hill 600's southern slope. Enemy artillery observers brought down a barrage of fire which killed four company commanders and seven enlisted men. Dozens of others were wounded. The 3rd Battalion, 103rd Infantry, had to withdraw to reorganize its shattered units.

General Wing directed the 103rd Infantry to concentrate on the northwestern slopes of Hill 600. Another objective, Hill 800, was also assigned, and the 169th Infantry was to cooperate in the assault. The attack began on January 25 with the attached 3rd Battalion, 63rd Infantry, seizing Benchmark Hill. Nearby, the 169th Infantry had taken most of Question Mark Hill[2] but left the eastern slope in enemy hands. The 103rd Infantry, less its 3rd Battalion, managed to reach the crest of Hill 600 until enemy fire from nearby heights drove them off. But patrols found that the Japanese had left undefended a saddle between Hills 700 and 800, and using this opening Company E, 103rd Infantry, captured Hill 700 that evening.

Late that afternoon, a vicious fight broke out on Hill 600, where Company F, 103rd Infantry, was holding the northwest slope. In a violent rainstorm, a strong Japanese counterattack caused serious damage to the battalion command post, shattered communications, and blew up an ammunition dump. After inflicting 19 casualties, the attack continued and hit Company E, causing another 15 casualties and driving the company off Hill 700. All night long enemy patrols struck throughout the 103rd Infantry's defenses between Hill 600 and Hill 800. Eventually, the Americans and Japanese came to an unwritten agreement to leave Hill 700 unoccupied if the other side didn't attempt to seize it. Although the Americans had not cleared the Hill 600 area, they had pushed the Japanese out of most of the area around Route 3 in their zone, eliminating observed enemy artillery, mortar, and machine-gun fire. The task of eliminating those guns was left to the artillery and Army and Marine Corps support aircraft. Patrols of the 43rd Infantry Division would seek out these guns and then call in air strikes to destroy them.

There remained the matter of the Damortis–Rosario road. Here the *58th Independent Mixed Brigade* had established strong defensive positions. These had already halted the advance of the 172nd, 158th, and 63rd Infantry Regiments. Between January 17 and 19, the 158th Infantry, heavily supported by air and artillery, cleared a crucial ridge line, but otherwise progress was limited. But constant patrolling and attacks finally destroyed Japanese resistance by January 21, when the 158th and 63rd Infantry made physical contact on Route 3 at a cost of 50 killed and 300 wounded. Nearly 650 enemy dead were counted in the area. It would take another five days for the 158th Infantry to reach the 172nd Infantry, despite strong artillery and tank support. The bulk of the Damortis–Rosario road was now open.

The advances of the 172nd Infantry Regiment had been slight, but constant patrolling had made some inroads into the Japanese defenses. On January 18, a Japanese 155mm howitzer battalion, supporting the *58th Independent Mixed Brigade*, had tried to withdraw to Rosario through a roadblock held by the 172nd Infantry. When the smoke cleared, five Japanese howitzers were destroyed and 100 crewmen lay dead, but not without cost. A shell from the enemy guns had hit the command post and aid station of the 2nd Battalion, 172nd Infantry, killing the battalion commander, the third lost by the 43rd Infantry Division since landing, and wounding two dozen others.

On this same day, elements of the 172nd Infantry managed to establish themselves on the southwestern slope of Hill 600. Using this as a base, other elements seized a hill 1,000 yards north of Rosario, which gave excellent observation over much of the Rosario area. From this location, the regiment sent patrols forward to Hill 606. Once there, patrols continued on into the town of Rosario which they found mined, booby-trapped, and defended by machine guns and riflemen hidden in shattered buildings. It took until January 28 to clear the town, but Route 3 was now open. The division's third task had been completed.

There remained only the seizing of that junction of Routes 3 and 11 just over a mile east of Rosario. General Wing sent two regiments, the 63rd and 172nd Infantry Regiments, to accomplish this task. Once again, the key to success were hills, this time Hill 900 and Hill 1500. The Japanese defenses were sited so that the hills were mutually supporting. An attacker could not attack one hill without the other firing on his flank or rear. To avoid this, each regiment made a simultaneous attack on January 25. The 172nd Infantry attacked Hill 900 successfully and quickly dug defensive positions just before two strong Japanese counterattacks struck. It would take four more days before the infantry could eliminate the last of the determined enemy resistance in the area.

It took the 63rd Infantry longer to get into position and attack, which they did on January 28. The attacking force took the southern crest of Hill 1500, but again it would take two more days before the entire area was cleared. Turning over the mopping up to the 172nd Infantry, the 63rd Infantry Regiment returned to its parent 6th Infantry Division at the end of January. It was at this time that the Americans took possession of the Route 3 and 11 road junction. In accomplishing the last of the 43rd Infantry Division's goals, the two regiments had lost 70 killed and 420 wounded.

In the center of General Swift's I Corps' zone the newly arrived 25th Infantry Division was assigned the job of securing a 10-mile stretch of Route 3 from Pozorrubio to Urdaneta. The terrain was flat and open, with dry rice paddies, pasture land, small woods, and streams. Little, if any, cover was available for an attacking army. Most of the streams were dry this time of year, and so were obstacles to maneuver. There were, however, some good all-weather roads in this sector. General Mullins's "Tropic Lightning" division was also shorthanded at this stage, with its organic 35th Infantry Regiment being held in Sixth Army Reserve.

Pozorrubio was held by what was left of the *Shigemi Detachment* of the *2nd Tank Division*. After counterattacking the 103rd Infantry during the night of January 16–17, the *Shigemi Detachment* had been ordered to withdraw and had started its journey when Major General Isao Shigemi learned that American forces were approaching Binalonan. General Shigemi halted his withdrawal and garrisoned that town. He had with him a company of the *2nd Mobile Infantry Regiment*, perhaps 10 tanks of the *7th Tank Regiment*, and several 75mm artillery pieces. He had also picked up some stragglers of the *2nd Battalion, 64th Infantry Regiment*, who had escaped Hill 200. His total force was estimated at about 350 officers and men. He quickly organized a rudimentary defense of trenches and dirt bunkers, with the tanks hidden and used as pillboxes. With insufficient forces to cover the whole town, he concentrated his defenses on the south and east, from which direction he expected the Americans to approach.

Those Americans were from the 161st Infantry Regiment of the 25th Infantry Division. Although the "Tropic Lightning" division was assigned to the Regular Army, the Washington State National Guard 161st Infantry had been assigned to it early in the war and had fought with it at Guadalcanal, New Georgia, Arundel, Kolombangara, and Vella Lavella. The regiment relieved elements of the 103rd Infantry Regiment on January 17 and sent patrols forward to Binalonan. On the right was the other division regiment, the 27th Infantry ("Wolfhounds"), which moved forward to secure Route 3 between Binalonan and Urdaneta.

Eight miles west of Binalonan, Company G of the 161st Infantry had been left as a flank guard for the attack at a village called Pao. On the afternoon of January 17, they were attacked and one of their outposts was overrun. The infantry formed a defense and fought until darkness when the Japanese withdrew, leaving 85 dead behind.

Colonel James L. Dalton II, the regimental commander, delayed his attack on Binalonan until he was satisfied that enemy attacks on the rear elements of his 161st Infantry were insignificant. He then pushed his 3rd Battalion into the north end of town and cleared it of minor opposition. But as the 1st Battalion approached the southern half of the town, it was stopped by rifle and machine-gun fire. Then a lone Japanese tank appeared and made a run across the front of Company B, spraying machine-gun and 47mm cannon fire until it was destroyed by bazookas and rifle grenades. Five more enemy tanks appeared and in a confused and disorganized attack raced about firing in every direction. It took a few moments before the tanks were destroyed by the infantrymen. The medium tanks of the 716th Tank Battalion were brought forward and the town cleared on January 18. Nine enemy tanks were counted destroyed; two artillery guns, five trucks, an artillery tractor, and a large quantity of ammunition were also destroyed. The cost to the 161st Infantry was 19 killed, 66 wounded, and three trucks destroyed.

During the fighting at Binalonan, Technician Fourth Grade Laverne Parrish, serving as a medical aid man with Company C, observed two wounded men lying under enemy fire. He immediately went to their rescue, crossing 25 yards of open ground. After pulling one man to cover he then administered first aid to the second man while still in the open fields under enemy fire. Both men managed to survive.

As often happens in combat, some Japanese soldiers failed "to get the word" that Binalonan had fallen. While the Americans were completing the mop-up of the town, three Japanese trucks loaded with ammunition and troops rolled up to the village at dawn on January 19, the drivers apparently unaware that it had changed hands the day before. They encountered a Company I roadblock, reinforced with the 2nd Platoon of the regiment's Antitank Company, and were soon made painfully aware of the change in the village's status.

General Swift now gave General Mullins another assignment. He was to advance to the Agno River, cross, and reconnoiter as far as 10 miles forward. This would give the 25th Infantry Division a front of some 30 miles, and with only two of its three infantry regiments available. General Mullins was, however, quite sanguine about the mission. He knew that there was no enemy facing the 27th Infantry Regiment and that the heavily damaged *Shigemi Detachment* was the only Japanese force on his side of the Agno River. That force was dug in at the town of San Manuel, protecting one of the Japanese routes to the main *Shobu Group* assembling to the north. Unknown to General Mullins, General Shigemi found himself cut off from other Japanese forces, and planned to fight to the death at San Manuel.[3]

At San Manuel, General Shigemi had about a thousand troops, most from the *2nd Mobile Infantry*, 40 medium and five light tanks of the *7th Tank Regiment*, 15 75mm and 105mm artillery guns of the *2nd Mobile Artillery Regiment*, several 47mm antitank guns, 25 machine guns, and 15 mortars. Knowing his tanks could not face the heavy American Sherman M4 tanks on an equal basis, he had dug in his tanks as pillboxes, although he kept about 15 as a mobile reserve. Several revetted strongpoints had been built, and troops could move from one to another via covered access.

Colonel Dalton's plan gave the 2nd Battalion the main effort, attacking from the north. The 1st Battalion would strike from the west. His 3rd Battalion was being held in corps reserve, guarding the Pozorrubio–Binalonan highway. Company A of the 716th Tank Battalion and Company D, 98th Chemical Mortar Battalion, with 4.2-inch mortars, would be in support.

After a 15-minute artillery preparation, the attack began early on January 24. Problems quickly surfaced. The tanks could not cross a tree-lined drainage ditch on the southwest side of town. Japanese 47mm antitank fire destroyed one of the 716th's tanks in the attempt. Four others were disabled, and a sixth fell into the drainage ditch itself. At a cost of eight killed and 63 wounded, the 1st Battalion's attack got nowhere. The 2nd Battalion's attack got off to a better start. Company F managed to get 50 yards inside the town but were stopped and pushed out of town by a tank-led Japanese counterattack. Another attack in mid-afternoon supported by self-propelled M7 cannons and 37mm guns from the Antitank Company left 2nd Battalion with a small foothold in northern San Manuel. Five enemy tanks had been destroyed and the volume of machine-gun fire noticeably reduced.

Reinforced with two rifle companies of his 3rd Battalion, Colonel Dalton renewed his attacks on January 25 through 27. Sending more tanks to reinforce the 2nd Battalion's foothold, the regiment began to inch its way through San Manuel. Company B moved around the enemy's eastern flank and blocked a bridge that might be used as an escape route. Midday on January 26, both assault battalions mounted a coordinated attack supported by two artillery battalions and pushed to the town's main road. That night the Japanese counterattacked with 13 tanks in successive waves. Supported by Japanese infantry, the tanks smashed into the 161st Infantry in the dark of night. The Americans soon knocked out 10 of the tanks and killed many of the attacking infantrymen. That was enough for General Shigemi, who took the remnants of his detachment out of San Manuel to the east, leaving a small rear guard behind. By midday the town was cleared of the enemy.

As he had earlier at Binalonan, Technician Fourth Class Parrish was on the front lines at San Manuel treating wounded. The North Dakota native was with his company when it was ordered to withdraw under heavy enemy fire. While treating the wounded who had returned, Tech 4 Parrish saw two wounded men still out in the field under enemy fire. He leapt from the cover of a drainage ditch, crawled forward under enemy fire, and brought both men to safety in two successive trips. Then he went out in the field and treated 12 additional casualties, crossing and re-crossing the field numerous times, each time under heavy Japanese gunfire. He then carried three more wounded men to safety. Finally, after having treated under fire 37 wounded men, and carrying five men to safety under fire, he was himself mortally wounded. For his actions at Binalonan and San Manuel, Technician Fourth Class Laverne Parrish received a posthumous Medal of Honor.[4]

Technician Fourth Class Parrish was among the 60 men killed and 200 wounded at San Manuel. The 716th Tank battalion also lost three tanks. Colonel Dalton later criticized the order for the attack, stating that since the Japanese did not hold the eastern end of the town American traffic could have passed unimpeded through the north side of the town and on to San Nicolas. This would have allowed the Americans to bypass the town. But that would have left a strong enemy force, including many tanks, astride the American lines of communication. With the fall of San Manuel, the 25th Infantry Division was free to advance to the Agno River without concern for the security of its flanks and rear.

Since the early days of the landing, General Patrick's 6th Infantry Division had been held back to ensure the integrity of the I Corps front line and to maintain contact with XIV Corps. On January 17, permission was granted to begin an advance toward the Cabaruan Hills where patrols had discovered a Japanese force. The object was to secure Urdaneta and the hill mass beyond it, which lay on the Army's Final Beachhead Line. The Cabaruan Hills were four square miles overlooking Route 3 and the Agno River. They were generally low hills, with few over 200 feet in height. Although patrols had uncovered a strong enemy force in the hills, they had not identified it. In fact, this was the southern anchor of the *23rd Infantry Division's* front line held by the *Omori Detachment*. Consisting mainly of the *2nd Battalion, 71st Infantry Regiment*, reinforced with artillery, a few tanks, and the *Gun Company, 71st Infantry*, these 1,500 Japanese soldiers had concentrated in the northwestern corner of the Cabaruan Hills.

General Patrick considered bypassing the *Omori Detachment*. He planned to launch a fierce attack by the 20th Infantry Regiment which would overcome the main Japanese resistance, after which he would leave a small detachment to contain the survivors and move his division forward. Using the 1st and 2nd Battalions, with his 3rd Battalion in reserve, General Patrick launched an attack on January 18 against a group of hills that had been determined to be the main Japanese position. While the 6th Cavalry Reconnaissance Troop covered the Agno River to the south, the 20th Infantry began the attack. Captain Robert E. Phelps led his rifle company across 1,000 yards of fire-swept ground until they were pinned down at the foot of a high ridge. Crawling forward alone, Captain Phelps threw a grenade into one pillbox, but the Japanese tossed it out again, wounding Captain Phelps. Seeing their captain lying wounded, the men of his command charged the pillbox, knocking it out. Technical Sergeant Efton A. Kitchens crawled forward under fire to find suitable locations for his machine-gun squad, then destroyed an enemy machine gun holding up his squad's advance, despite being mortally wounded.[5]

The initial advance went well, prompting General Patrick to believe that his plan was working. But on January 19 things began to go wrong. Overconfident, General Patrick ordered two of the 20th Infantry battalions to pull out, leaving only one battalion to finish the job. Reinforced with a company of 4.2-inch mortars and tanks of Company C, 44th Tank Battalion, this battalion advanced on January 22 after a disappointing air strike. For the first two hours, the assault proceeded as expected, but then strong Japanese resistance stopped the attack. All officers in Company G were killed or wounded, Company E was forced back, and Company F pinned down. Two supporting tanks were knocked out. Ten men were killed and 35 wounded. Artillery from the supporting 53rd Field Artillery Battalion was called down on the enemy.

Still the Japanese would not be moved. Private First Class (later Staff Sergeant) Harold E. Smith crawled forward alone and knocked out two enemy positions with hand grenades, then went on until he had destroyed four enemy machine guns single-handed. When his 60mm mortar squad came under direct enemy fire, Staff Sergeant Charles J. Baker sent his men to cover and alone took the enemy under fire with his mortar so effectively that the company he was supporting could renew its advance.[6] But this action convinced the regimental commander, Colonel Washington M. Ives, Jr., that more strength was needed, and he requested that of General Patrick.

Displeased with the delay, General Patrick ordered a battalion of the 1st Infantry Regiment to join Colonel Ives. The next day, January 24, the 1st Infantry's

2nd Battalion took over the attack and made limited gains. Once again, success seemed close at hand, and General Patrick pulled the 20th Infantry out of the Cabaruan Hills, leaving the single battalion of the 1st Infantry to finish the job. General Krueger, anxious to establish his Army FBL, urged General Swift to move quickly to clear the Cabaruan Hills, avoiding more delays in the advance of both the 6th Infantry Division and the adjoining XIV Corps. General Swift passed on this message to General Patrick, who in turn reported back to General Swift that the 1st Infantry would clear the hills in another day. He believed that there were no more than 100 Japanese soldiers remaining in the hills and that there was no need for more troops to be committed there.

As mentioned, the 1st Infantry's attack on January 24 gained only 500 yards, but not from lack of trying. Over the next four days the soldiers of the 1st Infantry repeatedly distinguished themselves trying to eliminate the enemy in the Cabaruan Hills. Private First Class Pelva J. Van Winkle crawled across open ground in full view of the enemy to toss grenades, destroying two enemy machine guns. Private First Class William S. Guest attacked an enemy strongpoint, killing 11 enemy soldiers and knocking out the position before being downed by the enemy. Then there was First Lieutenant Charles G. Canas, a howitzer platoon leader, who reconnoitered the forward area on foot, killing two snipers in the process, and then led his self-propelled guns forward in a move that encircled the enemy and knocked out a scout car and five pillboxes.[7]

Although the 2nd Battalion, 1st Infantry, would disagree with him, General Patrick declared the Cabaruan Hills free of organized resistance on January 25, exactly as he had promised General Swift. But there were at least 200 Japanese still active within the hills, and the 2nd Battalion, 1st Infantry, requested a dozen flamethrowers to eliminate the last resistance. January 26 proved the infantrymen correct, as a minimal 150 yards was gained at a cost of 12 men killed, 12 more wounded, and a tank destroyed. Convinced, General Patrick ordered another battalion of the 1st Infantry into the hills.

The 1st and 2nd Battalions, 1st Infantry, attacked together on January 28 and eliminated all remaining organized resistance within the Cabaruan Hills. Another 225 Japanese were counted killed against American losses of 20 killed and 50 wounded. A final estimate made later determined that more than 1,400 Japanese soldiers had been killed defending the Cabaruan Hills. This victory cost the 6th Infantry Division and its attached units 80 killed and 200 wounded. It also cost Colonel Ives his command, as General Patrick relieved him from command of the 20th Infantry.[8] But the *Omori Detachment* was no more.

While the battle for the Cabaruan Hills was ongoing, elements of the 1st Infantry Regiment had swept past into Urdaneta, finishing off a small remnant of the *Shigemi Detachment*. Relieved there by the 25th Infantry Division, the regiment then moved on to the Agno River against no resistance. Continuing on, the Americans found more and more small villages secured before their arrival by Filipino guerillas. Nearby, the 20th Infantry, after leaving the Cabaruan Hills, moved south to Cuyapo, taking the town on January 20 and establishing the 6th Infantry Division on the Army's Final Beachhead Line. The 6th Reconnaissance Troop had made contact with XIV Corps at Victoria on January 20, achieving the last goals of the I Corps.

The *23rd Infantry Division* and the *58th Independent Mixed Brigade* had done well in Japanese eyes. They had held the vital Route 3–11 road junction for two weeks against a strong enemy attack. They had in the process inflicted many casualties on the Sixth Army. Even with the loss of Route 3, the *Fourteenth Area Army's* headquarters at Baguio remained secure and could expect more time before being threatened by the American advance. General Yamashita's triangle defense sector had also not lost its southern anchor, which remained secure at San Jose, which the Americans had yet to reach.

On the other hand, Japanese losses had been severe. The *23rd Infantry Division* was down to about half its authorized strength, and two-thirds of the *58th Independent Mixed Brigade* was gone. The only replacements available to General Yamashita were ill-trained rear area soldiers or third-class provisional units. Most of the artillery of the two units was also lost or destroyed, along with much of their transport and ammunition. These losses convinced General Yamashita that there was no longer any point in trying to hold the Routes 3 and 11 junction, so on January 23 he ordered the *23rd Infantry Division* to begin a move further up Route 11. One result of these orders was the easing of the pressure on the 43rd Infantry Division.

Moreover, the destruction of the *Shigemi* and *Omori Detachments* had cost the *Shobu Group* more than an infantry battalion and a complete armored combat command. The modest delay imposed upon the American advance was not sufficient for their loss, nor was the loss of valuable equipment and some of the best trained troops within *Fourteenth Area Army*. About the only success these delaying actions had was to grant General Yamashita more time to deploy his forces in the defense of San Jose, a key anchor of his defensive area.

For General Krueger, his concerns over securing the Sixth Army base area at Lingayen were now largely alleviated. With I Corps now on the Final Beachhead Line and enemy forces pushed beyond observation and artillery distance, he could feel that the Sixth Army's left and rear areas were secure. For this, much credit goes to General Wing's 43rd Infantry Division and its attached 63rd and 158th Infantry Regimental Combat Teams (RCTs).

The end of January also saw on Luzon what one historian has called, "World War II's most dramatic mission."[9] Under direct orders from General MacArthur, General Krueger assigned Lieutenant Colonel Henry Mucci the mission of conducting a raid on the Cabanatuan prisoner-of-war camp with his 6th Ranger Battalion. This battalion had been formed by General Krueger, who had been following events in the European Theater of Operations and felt his own forces could use such a commando-type unit. Unlike the Ranger battalions in Europe and the Mediterranean, the 6th Ranger Battalion was not formed by calling for volunteers, but instead the 98th Field Artillery Battalion, which had fought in New Guinea, was selected for the special training. Only those within the battalion who volunteered joined the newly designated unit. Colonel Mucci, from Bridgeport, Connecticut, and a former provost marshal of Honolulu, was selected as the battalion commander.

Several companies of the battalion had landed prior to the Leyte invasion to secure critical offshore islands, protecting the main invasion force. But since Leyte, complained some of the Rangers, they had been acting more as a "palace guard" for General Krueger's Sixth Army Headquarters than a raiding command. Things changed on January 27, when Colonel Mucci was summoned to see General Krueger's operations officer. The mission assigned was to go behind enemy lines and rescue hundreds of prisoners of war held at Cabanatuan. The Allies had learned of a Japanese policy that when Allied forces approached Japanese-controlled prisoner-of-war camps, the prisoners of war in those camps were to be killed if they could not be safely moved away. This policy had already been implemented at several prisoner-of-war camps and neither General MacArthur nor General Krueger wanted to risk this happening on Luzon.

Company C, reinforced with part of Company F, was to infiltrate behind Japanese lines and rescue the prisoners at Cabanatuan. Working with the Alamo Scouts[10] and Filipino guerillas, the mission began on January 28 and on the night of January 30 the raid took place. The raid was a complete success, with 511 prisoners rescued at a cost of two Rangers killed.[11] With the danger of these prisoners being killed eliminated, General Krueger could now fully concentrate on the rest of his mission. There were, after all, still some 200,000-plus Japanese troops on Luzon facing his Sixth Army.

CHAPTER 5

The Kembu Group

At the end of January General Krueger's Sixth Army had established its Army Beachhead Line and was moving across the Central Plain toward Manila. Clark Field had been seized, and the initial contacts with the largest enemy group on the island had been successfully made. Under constant pressure from General MacArthur, General Krueger was now preparing to launch General Griswold's XIV Corps toward Manila. The 37th Infantry Division and the newly arrived 1st Cavalry Division would soon engage in a "race" for Manila.

But there remained the matter of the *Kembu Group*. This force of Japanese had defended Clark Field, and after XIV Corps pushed them into the Zambales Mountains, XIV Corps had moved on, leaving General Brush's 40th Infantry Division to deal with the remaining Japanese. General Brush had been directed to continue his attack to the west and drive the *Kembu Group* deep into the mountains where they could be isolated. To assist in this maneuver, General MacArthur had sent the XI Corps, of Eighth Army, to land on Luzon's west coast, seize Bataan, and hopefully "dislocate" the *Kembu Group*'s defenses.

There were several earlier plans to land the XI Corps on Luzon, but in the end, they were ordered to land in the San Antonio area of Zambales Province, 40 miles west of the Central Plain and 25 miles northwest of Bataan. Between there and the XIV Corps lay the Zambales Mountains. Commanded by Major General Charles Philip Hall (USMA, 1911), the XI Corps contained only the 38th Infantry Division, new to combat, and the 34th RCT, attached from the veteran 24th Infantry Division.

The 38th Infantry Division was drawn from the National Guards of Indiana, Kentucky, and West Virginia. One of its regiments, the 149th Infantry, had seen brief combat on Leyte when Japanese airborne raiders had landed in its staging area, but the division itself was new to battle.[1] Its commander was Major General Henry Lawrence Cullen Jones (University of Nevada, 1906), who had been commissioned into the cavalry in 1911 and had served with field artillery units in World War I. His mission was to land at San Antonio and the San Marcelino Airfield along Route 7 and the former U.S. naval base at Olongapo at the head of Subic Bay. Due to the fears of General MacArthur and his intelligence chief, General Willoughby, XI Corps was then to clear the Bataan Peninsula of enemy forces. It was believed by some that General Yamashita would copy General MacArthur's plan of defending Manila and Manila Bay by holding the Bataan Peninsula, which controlled access to both. However, as noted earlier, General Yamashita had no such plans and accepted that the defense of Manila and Manila Bay was beyond the capability of his forces. He viewed Bataan as a cul-de-sac which would allow the superior firepower of the American Army to cut his forces to pieces as they lay helplessly contained in the peninsula.

Intelligence estimated that there were about 13,000 Japanese troops in the Bataan–Zambales Province area, 5,000 on Bataan and the remainder in the interior. In fact, there were but 4,000 Japanese troops on Bataan, largely from the *39th Infantry Regiment, 10th Infantry Division*.[2] Originally intended to reinforce the Japanese garrison on Leyte, they had been diverted to Bataan when it became obvious that the Leyte campaign was concluded. They were reinforced by a platoon of tanks, a battery of artillery, and several Army and Navy base defense forces. Known as the *Nagayoshi Detachment*, after Colonel Sanenobu Nagayoshi, the regimental commander, they were technically under the command of General Tsukada of the *Kembu Group*. General Tsukada ordered Colonel Nagayoshi to block Route 7 to protect the rear of the *Kembu Group*, but once XIV Corps had secured Clark Field, the orders were for the *Nagayoshi Detachment* to join the *Kembu Group* in the mountains. But before Colonel Nagayoshi could implement his new orders, he was under attack by the XI Corps.

The planned pre-invasion naval bombardment for XI Corps was cancelled when Filipino guerillas rowed out to the U.S. Navy ships offshore and reported that there were no enemy troops in the vicinity. Accordingly, early on the morning of January 29 the XI Corps landed unopposed, with all four regiments landing abreast. Cheering Filipinos greeted them as they stepped ashore. Colonel Winfred G. Skelton's 149th Infantry rushed to seize San Marcelino Airfield only to find that it had already been taken by Filipino guerillas under Captain Ramon Magsaysay.[3] The 24th Reconnaissance Troop, part of the 34th RCT, drove up to Subic Bay without meeting any opposition. The sole casualty of the day was a member of Colonel Rolf C. Paddock's 151st Infantry Regiment, who was apparently gored by a local carabao.

The landing came as a surprise to the Japanese. In fact, Colonel Nagayoshi did not even learn of the landing until the next day, and even then, he assumed the landings had been made at Subic Bay. General Hall came ashore early on the morning of January 30, and with his arrival the XI Corps was transferred from the Eighth Army to Sixth Army. That day Lieutenant Colonel L. Robert Mottern's 2nd Battalion, 151st Infantry, seized Grande Island, in Subic Bay, without opposition. Colonel William W. Jenna's 34th Infantry moved on Olongapo, with Lieutenant Colonel Edward M. Postlethwait's 3rd Battalion in the lead.

By mid-morning the battalion had entered Subic Town without meeting any Japanese. Moving further along Route 7, led by the 24th Reconnaissance Troop, the battalion came up to a hairpin turn in the road about a mile west of Olongapo. Here Major Hironori Ogawa had placed Second Lieutenant Hiroshi Abe, an Antitank Company platoon leader of his *3rd Battalion, 39th Infantry*, with two 37mm antitank guns. Lieutenant Abe's orders were to oppose an expected American landing in Subic Bay. Reinforced with a machine-gun squad and an infantry squad, along with engineers prepared to blow up a nearby bridge, he was well dug in with interconnecting pillboxes, caves, and trenches prepared by the engineers.

The 24th Reconnaissance Troop came under artillery fire as they approached the curve. This later turned out to be "friendly fire" from the 63rd Field Artillery Battalion that was trying to lay down fire in front of the advancing infantry. No damage or casualties resulted, but the firing caused First Lieutenant Paul J. Cain to dismount his Company I, 34th Infantry, and advance on foot. One platoon was sent to cover the left flank just in case the firing came from the enemy. Meanwhile the 24th Reconnaissance Troop began to move through the hairpin curve when Lieutenant Abe's men opened fire. The Americans immediately responded with light and heavy machine guns and 37mm guns mounted on jeeps.

Several Japanese ran out to blow up the bridge along Route 7, but each in turn was cut down by the sharpshooting of an American sniper. Unsure of his opposition, Lieutenant Cain called for more firepower. Colonel Postlethwait sent up a platoon of the 603rd Tank Company and the regimental Cannon Company, whose 75mm and 105mm guns were mounted on M3 tank chassis. In pouring rain, the Americans attacked Lieutenant Abe's defenses, knocking them out one by one. One Japanese engineer managed to blow a hole in the road, temporarily blocking the further advance of the self-propelled guns. Engineers from Company C, 3rd Engineer (Combat) Battalion, quickly threw steel mats across the hole, allowing the American advance to continue. By late afternoon, the action was over. Three Americans had been killed and one wounded. Estimated Japanese casualties were 14 killed. In their retreat, the Japanese put the torch to Olongapo. The 34th Infantry nevertheless took possession that afternoon.

"At Subic Bay," wrote Lieutenant Ernest Chaplin, a forward observer from the 150th Field Artillery Battalion, 38th Infantry Division, "we drew artillery fire when we placed our guns and dug in. I saw one disaster when one of our L-4s was hit dead center over our position by a friendly artillery unit firing 155mm Long Toms from behind us. The L-4 belonged to our battalion and my close buddy, the pilot, was blown to pieces along with the observer. Flying these missions, you had only a .45 caliber pistol, carried field glasses and no parachute."[4]

To protect the rear of the *Kembu Group*, Colonel Nagayoshi had developed a series of defenses along both sides of Route 7 with the intent of holding off any American attempt to get to the group's rear. The main defenses were three miles north of Olongapo in a deeply jungled area known as ZigZag Pass. In addition to the thick jungle in this area, Route 7 twisted violently through the pass, following the line of least terrain resistance that must have been originally an animal trail. Stepping five feet off Route 7 blocked the trail from view. Every hill and knoll in the pass was covered with foxholes, tunnels, and trenches. Dirt and log pillboxes covered critical points along the trail. As usual, Japanese camouflage was excellent. Having been in the area since December, Colonel Nagayoshi had spent his time productively, creating a strong defensive position and stocking it with plenty of food, water, and ammunition.

Colonel Robert L. Stillwell's 152nd Infantry Regiment took the lead on January 31. Initial opposition was scattered rifle fire and some long-range machine-gun fire. The following day, however, things became serious. The twisting Route 7 and the thick jungle made it increasingly difficult for Colonel Stillwell to accurately report his position to headquarters. Inaccurate maps only compounded the difficulty, as did radios that failed to work in the heavy jungle. Such was the situation when the regiment came to a horseshoe curve on Route 7 approaching ZigZag Pass.

The Battle of Zigzag Pass is a confused and deadly struggle best described in detail elsewhere.[5] For the next two weeks the 38th Infantry Division, supported by the 34th RCT, fought a bloody and frustrating battle against Colonel Nagayoshi's *39th Infantry Regiment*. Every attempt by the Americans to either attack frontally or by a flank failed. Artillery and air support was limited due to the thick jungle and the impossibility of accurately reporting friendly positions on inaccurate maps. The frustration of the combat troops was also felt by their commanders, and resulted in the relief of one regimental commander and eventually the relief of General Jones, the division commander. At one point, General Hall took personal command of an infantry regiment, but nothing moved the *Nagayoshi Detachment*. To accomplish his mission, General Hall sent Colonel Skelton's 149th Infantry Regiment to bypass Zigzag Pass and make contact with XIV Corps, which they eventually did. But Zigzag Pass remained in Japanese hands.

The 34th and 152nd Infantry Regiments continued to pound away at the Japanese defenses.[6] General Hall decided a change in command was necessary and placed Brigadier General Roy Woodson Easley (Cumberland College, 1911), the assistant division commander, in temporary command. The next day Brigadier General William Curtis Chase (Brown University, 1916), who had commanded one of the 1st Cavalry Division's brigades, took command. As sometimes happens when commanders are changed, more troops suddenly became available. General Chase was given the 151st, 152nd, and 149th Infantry Regiments to renew his attack. With the 149th Infantry—returning from their mission to contact XIV Corps—now blocking their rear and retreat route, and with two full regiments attacking their front, the Japanese at Zigzag Pass began to crumble. General Chase also benefited from air support flying from San Marcelino Airfield, which began an intensive

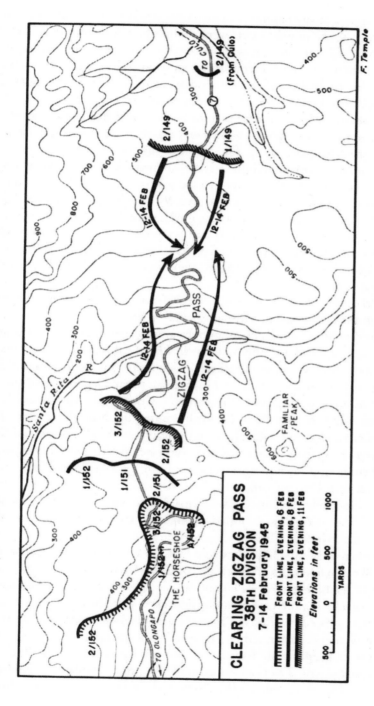

The 38th Infantry Division's Battle for ZigZag Pass

Robert Ross Smith. *United States Army in World War II. The War in the Pacific. Triumph in the Philippines.* Washington, D.C.: Center of Military History, 1984. p. 311.

bombing and strafing campaign against Zigzag Pass. Napalm was used for the first time in the battle. Still, the ground battle went on foot by foot, with the Japanese yielding ground only after intensive pressure. For nearly a week after General Jones's relief, small-scale battles continued, eliminating enemy posts one by one. Not until February 13 did the 149th Infantry and 152nd Infantry make physical contact, formally opening Zigzag Pass. Several more days were spent mopping up.

"If there is another war, I recommend that the military and the correspondents, and everyone else concerned, drop the phrase 'mopping up' from their vocabularies. It is not a good enough phrase to die for," wrote Lieutenant General Robert L. Eichelberger,[7] Eighth Army commander. This is perhaps best shown in the experience of Major Harry B. Manigold's 3rd Battalion, 152nd Infantry Regiment. Assigned to clear the north side of Route 7, the attack was preceded by a heavy artillery barrage and white phosphorus 81mm mortar fire to keep the Japanese troops sheltering while Companies L and K crossed a river and moved up the hill on which the Japanese were entrenched at an area known as the East Pass. The Americans faced the *5th Company, 39th Infantry Regiment*, protecting Colonel Nagayoshi's battle command post within the pass.

One of the Japanese caves received a direct hit from an American artillery round, killing all but one of the seven men sheltering in that cave. The shelling blasted off the jungle cover of the defenses of the *5th Company*, and by the time the American infantry approached, the company had been reduced to 41 survivors. Yet the Americans themselves were completely exhausted from the heat and the climb. They began to dig in for the night. As they did so two Japanese machine-gun squads opened fire and swept the American area with gunfire. The Americans began to dig with intensity. But the fire still threatened the men above ground. The company commander, himself only recently returned after being wounded earlier, and a sergeant grabbed automatic weapons and melted into the jungle, eventually eliminating both enemy squads. By February 13, signs of the Japanese disintegration were found everywhere. Battle flags, sabers, gas masks, uniforms, and food and ammunition were discovered abandoned. Yet the next evening, Japanese demolition squads destroyed three 57mm antitank guns and a truck right in the division headquarters sector.

Casualty reports listed some 2,400 Japanese killed at Zigzag Pass and 25 taken prisoner. The 300 survivors with Colonel Nagayoshi retreated deep into the Bataan Peninsula and remained there until the end of the war. The 38th Infantry Division and its attached 34th RCT suffered 1,400 total casualties, including 250 killed. But the bitterly frustrating Battle of Zigzag Pass was over. XI Corps now could secure Manila Bay's coastline and remain a threat to the *Kembu Group*'s rear areas.

The first step in clearing Manila Bay was to clear the Bataan Peninsula. Enemy guns along the coastline could threaten Allied shipping using Manila Bay. General Hall now planned to have one regimental combat team secure the east coast while another secured the west coast and seized Mariveles, at the southern tip of the peninsula. This latter operation would be an amphibious one, launched from Subic Bay. Delays caused by the ongoing battle at Zigzag Pass moved the operation back several days and required an additional infantry regiment be sent from I Corps. The 6th Infantry Division's 1st Infantry Regiment, then in reserve, was sent to XI Corps.

General Hall organized the 1st Infantry RCT as East Force and placed it under the command of Brigadier General William Spence (USMA, 1916), the artillery commander of the 38th Infantry Division. Its job was to clear the east coast, following much the same route as had the Japanese in 1942, drawing attention onto itself, to distract enemy attention from South Force. This latter group was built around the 151st Infantry RCT under General Chase's direct command. It was to land at Mariveles, clear southern Bataan, and then strike up the east and west coast roads until contact was made with the 1st Infantry Regiment. Intelligence reports indicated 6,000 Japanese on Bataan south of Zigzag Pass. In fact, Colonel Nagayoshi had fewer than 1,400 troops on Bataan, including survivors of Zigzag Pass.

The 151st Infantry loaded at Olongapo on February 14 and sailed the same day. The 1st Infantry moved out on February 12 but had a longer route to travel. The transport force, Rear Admiral Arthur Dewy Struble's (USNA, 1915) Task Group 77.3, faced serious obstacles in mine-sweeping and preliminary bombardment tasks. At least 140 mines were swept up near Mariveles Harbor, and two destroyers were damaged by them. Japanese guns from Corregidor added their voices to the operation. These guns scored a hit on the USS *Fletcher*, a destroyer. The shell hit the USS *Fletcher* in a most vulnerable spot, the number one gun magazine, and set fire to the powder stores. Watertender First Class Elmer Charles Bigelow, a naval reservist, had been standing on the deck when the shell hit. The sailor from Illinois immediately understood the danger and picked up two fire extinguishers and raced below to fight the fire. Refusing to waste time by donning protective rescue-breathing apparatus, he charged into the blinding smoke and fire through a hatch into the smoke-filled compartment. The acrid smoke burned his lungs with every breath, but Watertender Bigelow worked rapidly and with instinctive sureness to cool the cases of powder and the bulkheads of the magazine. His swift action with no regard for his personal safety saved the ship and put out the fires. Watertender Bigelow succumbed to his injuries the next day. His Medal of Honor was posthumously awarded.[8]

The U.S. Navy was already striking back, however. Off the coast Lieutenant Commander John K. ("Jake") Fyfe's submarine, USS *Batfish*, was in Luzon Strait on her sixth war patrol. The Americans suspected from radio intercepts that the Japanese were using submarines to bring in supplies and evacuate pilots and high-ranking personnel from Aparri, on the north coast of Luzon. Four Japanese submarines—*RO-46*, *RO-112*, *RO-113*, and *RO-115*—were believed engaged in this activity. While patrolling in Baboyan Channel on February 9, the USS *Batfish* picked up a radar contact at 11,000 yards. Commander Fyfe began tracking the contact, which was soon emitting radar signals of its own. Sailing on the surface, the USS *Batfish* fired four torpedoes on a target it had not seen visually. All four torpedoes missed. Commander Fyfe decided to try a new angle of approach, and this time moved to within visual range of his target. A Japanese submarine was sighted at 1,000 yards' range. Three more torpedoes were fired, one hit, and the explosion ended the career of the Japanese submarine *RO-115*.

A search for survivors proved futile. With dawn came friendly aircraft, and Commander Fyfe went deep to avoid "friendly fire." An attempt to return to the surface later resulted in more "friendly fire." As Commander Fyfe put it, "A tender moment and a very unfriendly act."[9] After spending the day underwater, the submarine surfaced at dusk and almost immediately picked up enemy radar signals. Shortly after 8 p.m. the contact was visually sighted by lookouts, but before Commander Fyfe could fire, the enemy submarine dived out of sight. USS *Batfish* remained on the surface, chagrined at missing another opportunity to sink an enemy submarine. As they were deciding on their next move, the sound operator reported hearing noises underwater that sounded like a submarine blowing its air tanks preparatory to surfacing. A moment later the radar discovered a contact 8,650 yards away. The enemy submarine had surfaced! Commander Fyfe rushed to reduce the range to about 6,000 yards, keeping his submarine low in the water to avoid detection, and fired four torpedoes. "The target literally blew apart and sank almost immediately," recalled Commander Fyfe.[10] The Japanese submarine *RO-112* was no more.

Two days later, February 12, the USS *Batfish* repeated its performance. An hour after midnight a radar contact was detected. Commander Fyfe approached and the contact disappeared underwater. Searching the presumed course of the enemy, Commander Fyfe had spent an hour cruising that course when once again radar picked up another contact, the same submarine that had dived away earlier that evening. Contact was regained at 6,800 yards, and once again Commander Fyfe lowered his submarine into the water until only the bridge was above the waves. Torpedoes were fired, an explosion was seen and heard, and the Japanese Navy lost submarine *RO-113*. Although other American submarines sank Japanese submarines, Commander Fyfe's USS *Batfish* ended the war with the record, sinking three enemy submarines in three days.[11]

Ashore on Bataan, the 151st Infantry landed at Mariveles Harbor against light machine-gun and rifle fire. A gun firing from Corregidor hit one of the landing craft and wounded 17 infantrymen aboard, while another carrying men of the 24th Reconnaissance Troop hit a mine and caught fire, causing additional casualties. By mid-afternoon General Chase was ashore and directing operations. No enemy troops were found in Mariveles itself. That evening about 100 enemy soldiers attacked Major Robert King's 3rd Battalion, 151st Infantry, but were chased off after losing about 60 casualties. South Force had lost three killed, 43 wounded, and 14 missing during the first day, mostly from mines and Corregidor's artillery.

The next few days were spent in patrolling the area and dispatching a group to contact East Force.

East Force had started down Bataan on February 14 and moved quickly, opposed by nothing more than the occasional sniper. The main obstacle was the many bridges that Filipino guerillas had demolished to prevent Japanese movement. These now hindered American progress, instead. During the night of February 15–16, about 300 Japanese attacked the perimeter of the 1st Infantry near Orion. The ensuing fight, which became hand-to-hand at one point, cost the Americans 11 killed and 15 wounded, but the Japanese lost 80 killed and were chased back into the jungles of Bataan. This was the last gasp of organized Japanese resistance on Bataan.

General MacArthur visited Bataan on February 16 to view his old battlefields. Motoring along in the East Force's zone, he drove five miles beyond the outposts, encountering no Japanese. But overhead American planes of the Fifth Army Air Force observed the movement ahead of the known American lines and believed they had a Japanese motor convoy in their sights. Fortunately, they requested permission before attacking, and General Chase, investigating the report, learned that this was General MacArthur's party. The request to attack was denied.

The next few days saw the 149th Infantry and other elements of the 38th Infantry Division drive across Bataan to eliminate any remaining Japanese. Only abandoned defenses and the occasional straggler were discovered. In securing Bataan, XI Corps had lost 50 men killed and 100 wounded. Colonel Nagayoshi's casualties were put at 200, leaving him with about 1,000 troops hidden in the deep jungle of the peninsula until the war's end. Many of them would die of starvation and disease, or roving guerilla patrols, before then.

Well off to the right of the main Sixth Army enclave on Luzon, the 40th Infantry Division was still dealing with the remnants of the *Kembu Group*. From the beginning the fight had been one of battling against a well-entrenched enemy holding rugged and dominating ground. Progress was often measured in yards, not miles. The 40th Cavalry Reconnaissance Troop, supported by the 620th Tank Destroyer Battalion, led the way. Nearby, the 37th Cavalry Reconnaissance Troop supported the attack. These three lightly armored forces soon realized that they were leading the attack on Clark Field. As Paul Gerrish of the 40th Infantry Division remembered, "It dawned on us that the three lightly armored reconnaissance units were the armor that would try to take Clark Field from the stubborn Japanese defenders."[12]

As mentioned, XIV Corps had overrun the *Kembu Group*'s outpost line of resistance by February 1, after which the 37th Infantry Division was redirected on Manila. This left the 40th Infantry Division to deal with the *Kembu Group*. The main defenses of the Japanese were divided into "Combat Sectors." These formed the main line of resistance and were numbered from 13 through 17. A combined Army–Navy force manned these sectors. There remained about 25,000 Japanese Army and Navy troops within General Tsukada's forces. Although prepared to defend to the death, the Japanese communications and supply problems precluded a prolonged defense. The only real advantage held by the Japanese was the highly defensible terrain which they held. Only a carefully thought-out plan, and heavy support from air and artillery forces, could breach that defense. But General Krueger wanted assurances that his base of operations and Clark Field were immune from enemy attack, and for this to occur *Kembu Group* would have to be annihilated or reduced to impotency.

General Brush was in no hurry. He spent the first week of February reorganizing his division and sending out patrols to find the enemy and learn as much as they could about the defense they would be facing. The 185th Infantry Regiment, which had earlier been held in reserve, rejoined the division. But while General Brush was in no hurry, General Krueger was. On February 6, General Brush received word from General Krueger to "proceed more expeditiously with the destruction"[13] of the *Kembu Group*. This order was the result in part of a mild anxiety for the security of Sixth Army's base area, and also because General Krueger knew that he was soon to lose the 40th Infantry Division to Eighth Army for other operations beyond Luzon.

General Brush drew up a plan for his 160th and 185th Infantry Regiments to make frontal attacks on the enemy center while the 108th Infantry moved against the Japanese right flank. The initial objective was some high ground seven miles west of Route 7. Once this area had been cleared the division was to overrun the entire Main Line of Resistance of *Kembu Group*. But even before the formal offensive began, the 160th Infantry became involved in mopping up Storm King Mountain. Here a strong Japanese force was defending from caves, bunkers, and foxholes. Armed with artillery, grenade dischargers, and more than two dozen machine guns, they held back the initial probes.

The 160th Infantry attacked on February 6 supported by tanks, tank destroyers, and Fifth Army Air Force aircraft. After two days of heavy fighting, the hill was cleared, but that night a banzai-type attack began which lasted until noon the next day. The following day, February 10, the regiment discovered that the remaining Japanese had withdrawn. They had left behind about 220 dead. An unintended consequence of this action was that the fight had eliminated a key position in the enemy's defense, making the attack of the 160th Infantry somewhat easier. This success also prompted General Tsukada to order a withdrawal from the MLR his troops were defending and take up "last-stand" positions.

The result of this order was to divide the left and right sectors of the *Kembu Group*, leaving each to be defeated in detail. But it would still take three days of bitter fighting for the 185th Infantry to seize Snake Hill North, a height from which the Japanese had poured fire on the 160th Infantry's flank. Meanwhile the 108th Infantry Regiment struck the Japanese right flank. Here strong defenses included 20mm cannon and 25mm machine guns along with cannons stripped from destroyed aircraft at Clark Field. The next four days were spent in clearing the approaches to

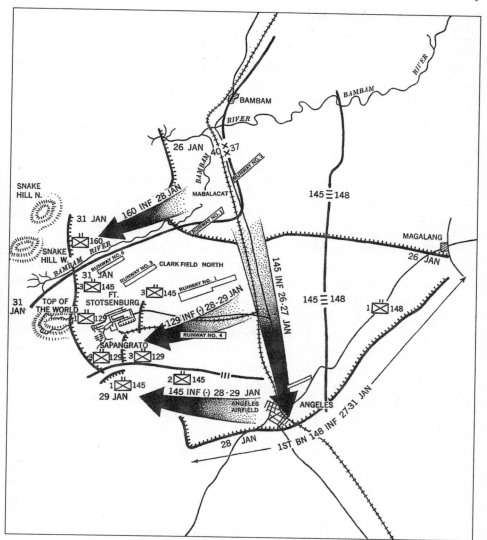

The 37th and 40th Infantry Divisions' Battle for Clark Field

US Army in World War II Atlas. The War in the Pacific. The National Historical Society. Harrisburg, PA. 1998, p. 72.

the main enemy defense in this area. Most territory gained was rendered untenable by Japanese shooting from heights just beyond the latest gains. Only after the divisional artillery began putting its rounds down dangerously close to the American front lines did the 108th Infantry begin to make noticeable progress. To further eliminate the opposition, the regiment's Cannon Company, the 640th Tank Destroyer Battalion, and the 754th Tank Battalion all moved up to lend the support of their guns to the advance, laying direct fire on enemy positions. By February 12 one wing of the defenses had been eliminated.

With the 108th Infantry Regiment turning the right flank of the *Kembu Group*, the next step was to attack the last stand areas, combat areas 13 through 17, into which the survivors of *Kembu Group* had withdrawn. The 185th and 160th Infantry immediately continued their attack into these areas. Battles raged around places with names like Snake Hill West, Scattered Trees Ridge, and Object Hill. A 90mm gun was towed up Storm King Mountain to bombard the Japanese, followed soon by some heavy 155mm artillery pieces. These guns began a direct fire mission against individual Japanese defenses, knocking them out swiftly and without infantry casualties. One battalion later recorded that the defenses they faced here were "the most complex and elaborate sector of the remarkable defense system encountered in the Bamban–Stotsenburg operation."[14]

During these days the 37th and 40th Cavalry Reconnaissance Squadrons and the 620th Tank Destroyer Battalion continued to push against the enemy defenses. Heavy enemy automatic weapons and artillery fire had deterred them repeatedly. Paul Gerrish recalled that after several failed attempts, "The next time we turned south we captured the Bamban airstrip after a brief skirmish. Japanese were still at the far end of the strip as a Piper Cub came in for a landing and under fire. The pilot jumped out, gave it a quick look and dashed over, saying, 'Look out for those Japanese. They are firing live ammunition.'"[15]

By February 15, the battle was down to the last few remaining combat sectors. There was no longer a Japanese MLR. Instead, each grouping defended a hill or series of hills until they were overwhelmed by American infantry, tanks, artillery, mortars, and tank destroyers. This type of fighting was costly, and battalions of the 160th Infantry were soon down to half strength. But the battles continued. Known to the men of the 40th Infantry Division as the Battle of the Seven Hills, it dragged on until February 20, when General Brush declared that the effectiveness of the *Kembu Group* as a threat to Sixth Army no longer existed. His men had overrun a huge enemy supply area, counting 210 vehicles, 167 machine guns, 63 20mm guns, 51 13mm guns, and two 75mm guns. Much in the way of radios, telephone equipment, transmitters, tires, generators, wire, tools, and food was also seized. Clearly the battle was all but over. Meanwhile, behind the infantry, the men of the 115th Engineer (Combat) Battalion had been busy clearing mines from Clark Field, mostly the same as the 100- to 500-pound aerial bombs discovered earlier. More than 550 mines were removed. Other engineers closely followed the infantry, sealing caves and tunnels with demolitions, later reporting more than 600 caves sealed. The division would remain on Luzon for the rest of the month, later taking part in the liberation of the Southern Philippines. Its task in mopping up the remainder of the *Kembu Group* was taken over by the XI Corps and the

43rd Infantry Division at the end of February. Only the *17th Combat Sector* still existed by that time.

The 43rd Infantry Division eliminated the *17th Combat Sector* in 10 days, and turned over responsibility for the *Kembu Group* to the 38th Infantry Division in early March. The 38th Infantry Division spent the next several weeks patrolling to find the Japanese, slowed more by supply problems in the untracked and unexplored wilderness than by the Japanese. Unknown to XI Corps, General Tsukada had already given up. On April 6, he ordered his forces to disperse and continue guerilla operations if they could. By May, the 38th Infantry Division had killed an additional 8,000 Japanese, most of whom were trying to escape Luzon or flee to the north to join General Yamashita. For the rest of the war, American divisions resting from the front lines were rotated through the area, patrolling to find any remaining organized Japanese resistance. They found none.

But these battles were not without their cost. On April 22, Company C of the 149th Infantry Regiment was attacking along a narrow, wooded ridge. The leading squad faced a strongly entrenched enemy in camouflaged emplacements on a hill beyond artillery support. The Japanese were hurling explosive charges on the attacking riflemen. Private First Class William H. Thomas, from Michigan, was with the leading squad serving as an automatic rifleman. One of these explosive charges blew off both of his legs below the knees. He nevertheless refused medical treatment and evacuation but insisted on remaining at his post, firing at the enemy until his weapon was disabled by an enemy bullet. Still refusing aid, he threw his last two grenades and destroyed three of the enemy. His platoon leader credited him with being the key factor that prevented the repulse of the platoon and assuring the capture of the enemy position. He died of his wounds later that day.[16]

The reduction of the *Kembu Group* had cost XI Corps 550 men killed and 2,200 wounded, not including hundreds of losses due to disease and heat exhaustion. It was estimated that in turn *Kembu Group* lost 12,500 killed and thousands of others lost to disease and starvation. At the end of the war, of the original 30,000 members of the *Kembu Group*, only 1,500 survived. About 500 others had already been taken prisoner. The *Kembu Group* was no more.

In the interim, contact had been made with the Philippine guerilla movement to the north. Things soon began to get difficult, as Lieutenant Jay Vanderpool, an artillery officer who had volunteered to go behind enemy lines to establish contact, would later recall. "I met with the guerillas. One leader was from the U.S. Naval Academy and another from the USMA. Other military schools were also represented. There were ten or twelve different [guerilla] outfits which would as soon fight one another as they would the Japs. We started getting revenue returns when we began swapping for pilots who had been shot down. They were real good trading material. The Navy and Marine Corps wanted their people back. We suggested that while picking pilots up they could bring in a load of this or that, so they packed a PBY or sub with a bunch of goodies. We salvaged and traded for twenty-two pilots in December 1944 alone."[17]

Lieutenant Vanderpool would soon lead a group of guerillas in supporting the 11th Airborne Division's drive on Manila. More and more smaller groups joined and were soon involved directly in tactical operations instead of hit-and-run guerilla tactics.

Meanwhile, in Northwest Europe the Third Army's 6th Armored Division overran the German West Wall (Siegfried Line) defenses in its area. In Seventh Army's zone, the 70th Infantry Division was still facing fierce opposition in its attack on Forbach. In northern Italy the 10th Mountain Division succeeded in capturing Mount Belvedere and moved on Mount Torraccia. On Iwo Jima the 4th Marine Division overran Airfield Number One.

CHAPTER 6

The Race to Manila

By the end of January, the Sixth Army had achieved most of its initial objectives. General Swift's I Corps controlled the Route 3 and 11 road junctions and was in position to attack San Jose. General Griswold's XIV Corps had pushed back the *Kembu Group* into the Zambales Mountains and secured vital Clark Field for American air power. General Krueger's Sixth Army base area was relatively secure, as were its communications. There remained only the securing of Manila and Manila Bay. It was to these objectives that General Krueger now turned his attention. He ordered General Griswold, on January 26, to send forces forward to the Pampanga River, about halfway between Clark Field and Manila.

General Griswold's first objective was the Manila Railroad and Route 3 intersection along the Pampanga River at Calumpit. This was a flat plain through which crossed the only highway and railroad connections providing a direct route to Manila. To the northeast was the militarily impassable Candaba Swamp. To the south and west were other swamps along Manila Bay blocking military movement. The only direct route to Manila from the Sixth Army beachhead was through the narrow gap at Calumpit, over which bridges, now destroyed by the Japanese, provided passage over the Pampanga River.[1] This area provided a natural defensive position for the Japanese in that it could not be flanked and would have to be broken by an overwhelming frontal attack. Intelligence had reported that there were no known Japanese defenses between XIV Corps and Calumpit.

General Griswold decided to try to beat the Japanese to Calumpit. He ordered the 148th Infantry Regiment, led by the 37th Reconnaissance Troop, both from the 37th Infantry Division, to strike for the bridges over the San Fernando River at San Fernando, 13 miles beyond Clark Field. General Beightler, commanding the 37th Infantry Division, had been visited on the battlefield by General MacArthur, and the latter had commented that he would love to see his old comrade from World War I lead the advance to Manila, but feared that the more motorized and heavily armored 1st Cavalry Division, which had now moved alongside the 37th Infantry Division, would get there first.[2] Each division was to take one route, the cavalry on Route 5 and the infantry on Route 3, to reach Manila.

Taking General MacArthur's hint,[3] General Beightler dispatched Lieutenant Colonel James Gall's 1st Battalion, 148th Infantry, toward Manila. Speed was stressed at every level of command. Racing down roads surrounded on both flanks by swamps, the troops moved quickly. General Griswold planned for the infantry to move forward as a blocking force for the faster moving cavalry units following. The major obstacle remained the Pampanga River. Once there, the engineers had to replace the destroyed bridges. Every piece of bridging equipment was used by the Sixth Army engineers, but there was a 60-foot gap between the end of the bridge and the far shore. General Beightler's own 117th Engineer (Combat) Battalion rushed forward heavy pontoon bridging material and finally closed the gap, but the delay cost the 37th Infantry Division the race to Manila.

Colonel Gall's battalion crossed the river on boats before the bridges were completed and raced toward the village of Plaridel, establishing contact with the enemy late on February 1. Company A eliminated the opposition and advanced to a point about 400 yards from the village, where they encountered the Japanese line of defense. Here about 200 Japanese held the forward line of defense, while other companies were echeloned in depth to defend the village. The Americans faced the usual line of tranches and well-prepared emplacements. The Battle of Plaridel continued for the next 24 hours. Japanese mortar fire tried to discourage the American attack, but, supported by the 140th Field Artillery Battalion, Captain Steve Losten, commanding Company A, led the attack through jungle, woods, and open ground to the eventual street fighting to clear the town. Private First Class Clifford R. Halyard saw a Japanese heavy machine gun in a destroyed building and, realizing the threat to his squad, raced with his Browning Automatic Rifle (BAR)[4] toward the gun, firing his weapon as he ran. When 15 yards from the enemy, Pfc Halyard was hit by three bullets and fell to the ground. Despite his serious wounds, he crawled forward into the enemy fire until he silenced the enemy gun with his own automatic rifle fire. By the time his buddies reached him, Pfc Halyard was dead. His Distinguished Service Cross was posthumously awarded.[5]

While Company A fought in the village, Company B sought out snipers disrupting communications and medical evacuations. By dawn on February 3 the Japanese had had enough and they withdrew, leaving about 350 dead and significant equipment behind. American losses in the Battle of Plaridel were 15 killed and 45 wounded. Leaving one company behind to garrison the town, Colonel Gall's battalion resumed the race for Manila. Under constant Japanese harassment, the 148th Infantry pushed past one Japanese delaying point after another. Each turn of the road and small village was a delaying point used by platoons or companies of Japanese infantry to delay the advance on Manila. In Malolos, for example, the Japanese fortified the strong Municipal Building and placed two companies of infantry in and around it to delay the advance. It took the heavy 155mm artillery of Lieutenant Colonel Wilbur H. Fricke's 136th Field Artillery Battalion, supported by the 140th Field

Artillery Battalion, to force the Japanese out and into the fire of the waiting American infantrymen.

There was no time for building bridges over the many streams and small rivers between the 37th Infantry Division and Manila. Even before the engineers came up, the infantry forded streams or worked their way across destroyed bridges. But bridges were necessary to bring forward the artillery and other supporting arms, so the engineers often worked under fire to build, or rebuild, these bridges. Amphibian tractors were used to keep the forward elements supplied with food and ammunition. Despite Sixth Army's best efforts, however, often the forward combat troops went hungry, thirsty, and with the bare minimum of available ammunition. Knowing his infantry was vulnerable without their artillery support, General Beightler restricted the advance of his forward infantry elements to the speed of that artillery. The division's artillery executive officer, Colonel Kenneth Cooper, ensured that the artillery took priority over all other units in the advance, leaving newsmen, photographers, and Army brass standing by the riverside. Division, Corps, and Army engineer units were all pressed into service to keep the forward movement flowing toward the Philippine capital.

For the men in the lead it was tough going. Inspired by tales of wine, women, and song in the capital city, they pushed ahead along the 160-mile march through heat, rain, and dust. Blisters made each step torture. Japanese resistance, although light, took its toll as well. And always there was more heat, more dust, more Japanese, and more blisters. Only the thought that there were Americans imprisoned in Manila needing their freedom kept many of these men on the march. No longer were they fighting for a "vital" air base or a "necessary" stepping stone to Japan; this time it was something concrete, something they could relate to, fellow Americans needing their help. Such thoughts kept many in the ranks who might otherwise have fallen out with exhaustion, heat stroke, or illness.[6] Every effort was expended to reach the city.

There were bright spots along the way. The leading infantry units uncovered cold beer at the Balintawak Brewery near the Tuliahan River on the outskirts of the city. While the riflemen were busy refreshing themselves, Captain Morgan Griffiths, commanding the regimental Antitank Company, discovered a large stock of lumber, including beams and planks, on the brewery grounds. Placing a guard over the lumber, he ordered up trucks to transport the find to the Tuliahan River. There his men, along with Company B and other units, worked in waist-deep water constructing a "weird-looking structure which combined the worst features of almost all types of bridges."[7] Oil drums were floated and combined with 2-by-12 beams, lashed, nailed, or pegged together while supporting beams were driven into the river bottom. By mid-afternoon the "bridge" was completed, and the first vehicle was slowly placed to cross. Captain Griffith and his men watched with trepidation as that vehicle began to cross. The bridge creaked, bent, and complained, but it held. So low did the "bridge" bend under the weight of some vehicles that jeeps

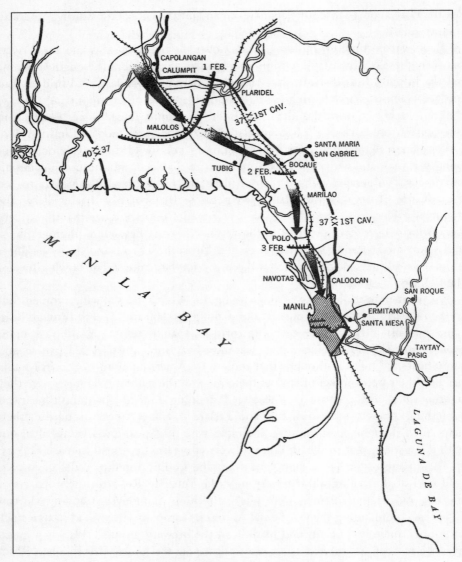

The 37th Infantry Division's Race for Manila

US Army in World War II Atlas. The War in the Pacific. The National Historical Society. Harrisburg, PA. 1998, p. 73.

crossing were hub deep in the water. But the "bridge" never collapsed, and vehicle after vehicle successfully, if dangerously, passed over to Rizal Avenue, leading into Manila. Captain Griffith's only complaint was that his own Antitank Company was given third priority in crossing his own bridge.

The "race" continued. At Banga, the leading elements encircled and destroyed a Japanese infantry company. At Mabolo the 3rd Battalion, 145th Infantry, which had now entered the "race," came up against an enemy battalion and was forced into a short withdrawal, while the 2nd Battalion, 145th Infantry, outflanked the enemy. Strong enemy counterattacks now began to develop, but the advance continued. Released from division reserve, the 1st Battalion, 145th Infantry, marched all day on February 4 under a broiling sun to the Pasig River. Reaching the river, the battalion cleared Grace Park, Obero, Tondo, and Nicolas sectors. Upon entering these districts, especially the Tondo sector, the first evidence of Japanese atrocities was uncovered when numerous civilians were found, hands tied, murdered by the Japanese.

The veteran 1st Cavalry Division had landed on Luzon at the Mabilao area of Lingayen Gulf on January 27. Understrength after the recently completed Leyte campaign, the division concentrated at Urdaneta and then moved to Guimba for its entrance into combat on Luzon. Even as the division moved forward, "behind the lines" it took casualties. As Troop A, 7th Cavalry, passed through the village of Labit in a truck convoy, enemy mortar and small-arms fire struck the Americans. Technical Sergeant John B. Duncan, of Los Angeles, quickly organized his platoon and eliminated the enemy opposition despite being mortally wounded in the attack.

The advance of the 1st Cavalry Division began on January 31 when a small force advanced from Cabanatuan. The advance was led by the 1st Cavalry Brigade.[8] Like General Beightler, the cavalry division commander, Major General Verne D. Mudge (USMA, 1920) had been visited by General MacArthur while at Guimba on January 30. General MacArthur told General Mudge, "Go to Manila. Go around the Nips, bounce off the Nips, but go to Manila. Free the internees at Santo Tomas. Take Malacanan Palace and the Legislative Building."[9] Inspired by these orders, General Mudge organized two reinforced motorized squadrons that soon became known as "Flying Columns." With no opportunity for reconnaissance and little knowledge of the terrain or routes they would encounter over the next 100 miles, the cavalrymen charged forward.

Lieutenant Colonel William E. Lobit, commanding the 2nd Squadron, 5th Cavalry, reinforced with antitank platoons, engineer and medical detachments, Battery A of the 82nd Field Artillery, and Company A, 44th Tank Battalion, led off. Alongside, Lieutenant Colonel Haskett L. Conner, Jr., commanding the 2nd Squadron, 8th Cavalry Regiment, reinforced with a reconnaissance platoon, antitank platoon, engineers, and medical detachments, Battery B, 61st Field Artillery Battalion, Company B, 44th Tank Battalion, and a section of heavy machine guns also moved to Manila. In reserve was a small group under Lieutenant Colonel Tom Ross, commander of the 44th Tank Battalion, with the remainder of his battalion and the 302nd Reconnaissance Troop.

With the focus on mobility, all unnecessary equipment was left behind to enable as many of the infantry to be mounted on trucks as possible. Barrack bags, kitchens, and anything else not needed in combat were left behind. Only the soldiers, their arms, ammunition, gasoline, four days' rations and communications equipment were carried. Even so, there was insufficient transportation for all the men of the "Flying Columns."

Departing at midnight, February 1, the three columns rolled over primitive roads in a complete blackout. Rivers and rice paddies were crossed, and by dawn the town of Cabanatuan, the first objective on the road to Manila, had been reached. Colonel Lobit's 5th Cavalry Squadron waded and swam the Pampanga River and captured the Valdefuente Bridge from the enemy side, driving off the Japanese demolition squads. General Mudge, leading from the front, saw that the Japanese had packed the bridge with 3,000 pounds of dynamite and were about to try to detonate it with mortar fire. Taking some nearby troopers with him, he led them onto the bridge through the mortar fire and threw the explosives into the river below. Meanwhile, Colonel Conner's 8th Cavalry Squadron had crossed to the southeast, and the move had placed a Japanese force in between the two cavalry squadrons. An American bazooka rocket exploded a Japanese truck filled with explosives, blowing a hole in the road ahead. Fierce fighting developed and lasted throughout the day and into the night. The 7th and 12th Cavalry Regiments arrived by truck and on foot and took over the battle, leaving the "Flying Columns" free to continue the "race" to Manila. Further to the south, Colonel Ross's tank column had crossed the river and run into more Japanese. The ensuing fight pushed the Japanese aside, but at the cost of the life of Colonel Ross.[10]

At dawn on February 2, the road had been repaired, the Japanese driven off, and the "Flying Columns" were once again racing forward. To streamline command arrangements, General Mudge placed Brigadier General William C. Chase (Brown University, 1916), normally the commander of the division's 1st Cavalry Brigade, in command of both "Flying Columns." The columns rolled down Route 5, while to the east strong Japanese forces on high ground constantly harassed their advance. Under orders not to be delayed by dealing with the enemy not actually stopping their advance, the columns rolled on. This became possible due to the superb air support provided to the columns by U.S. Marine Air Groups 24 and 32. Under the cover of this air cover, the "Flying Columns" could push down Route 5 to Manila. The speed of the advance varied with road conditions and enemy opposition. In places, the advance could proceed at 30 miles per hour, while at other places along the route progress slowed or halted altogether due to poor roads or enemy opposition. At other times, grateful Filipinos gathered by the roadside to cheer on the advancing Americans. Gifts of flowers, chickens, eggs, and bananas were common. The cavalrymen looked forward to seeing the Filipinos, as this meant that there were no Japanese about.

Destroyed bridges presented a constant problem to the advance. In many cases it was possible to bypass the destruction by fording the streams and crossing the vehicles through the shallow water. When the column reached Baliuag, Japanese opposition slowed the advance, but the enemy were pushed aside, and a security detachment was left in the town to protect the line of communication. But when the leading column reached the Angat River—a broad and deep river with a swift current—neither the cavalrymen nor their vehicles could be forced across this obstacle. The current denied them the opportunity of building a bypass. Contact was established with the 37th Infantry Division at Plaridel, and soon both leading cavalry battalions were crossing the river there. Bulldozers were used to fill holes in the riverbed and the physical strength of the cavalrymen were used to push, pull, and drag their vehicles across the river.

Once across the Angat River, the column divided. Colonel Lobit's troopers moved east toward the village of Angat, while Colonel Conner's men turned south on a secondary road toward Santa Maria. Here, both columns encountered the strongest enemy resistance of the day. Colonel Conner's 2nd Squadron, 8th Cavalry, found its way blocked by an enemy battalion entrenched on high ground commanding the road. Under the cover of close air support from Marine aircraft of Marine Air Group 32 (MAG 32), the battalion managed to maneuver itself into a good attack position and soon routed the enemy from their excellent defenses, Colonel Lobit's 2nd Squadron, 5th Cavalry, found itself slowed by several enemy roadblocks. Each had to be dealt with by dismounting troopers who swiftly eliminated one roadblock after the other. The column then came up to a bridge over a small stream. The bridge was too weak to carry the weight of the column's tanks, and the stream's banks were too steep for vehicles to ford the stream. As the Americans contemplated their next move, Japanese mortars, machine guns, and small arms opened fire on them. Battery A, 82nd Field Artillery, quickly dealt with the situation by shelling the Japanese, who soon retreated. Although sporadic enemy fire continued to harass the column, no serious opposition presented itself during the remainder of the afternoon. Behind the columns, General Mudge and his brigade commanders moved into Baliuag and set up division headquarters there. By that night, February 2, the leading columns were within 15 miles of the outskirts of Manila.

The following day the columns moved on. North of Novaliches they ran into heavy opposition from Japanese forces near the Ipo Dam, which the Japanese had decided to defend. The cavalrymen were forced to fight their way past the critical intersection and leave behind Troop E, 8th Cavalry, to keep the Japanese from closing the route behind them. Colonel Lobit's men had finally cleared Angat, forcing the Japanese to abandon some 75mm artillery guns in the village. General Chase sent his Marine Corps flyers to reconnoiter the way ahead. They reported the vital bridge at Novaliches apparently intact. This was good news, because the stream over which it crossed was narrow with steep banks, hindering the passage of vehicles. Colonel Conner hurried forward only to find that the Japanese had planted a large mine on the bridge, intending to destroy the structure. To prevent the Americans from saving the bridge, the Japanese had it covered with mortar and small-arms fire and the mine's fuse had already been ignited. A Navy bomb disposal officer who had long served with the cavalry division, Lieutenant (j.g.) James P. Sutton, from Tennessee, raced forward alone into the enemy fire and cut the burning fuse, saving the bridge for the cavalry. The column quickly crossed the bridge, drove off the Japanese defenders, and continued its march on Manila.[11]

As mentioned earlier, in June 1944 General MacArthur had been asked to submit his views on bypassing the Philippines in favor of a landing on Formosa. He argued forcefully for a landing in the Philippines, stating that the Formosa plan was "unsound" and the proposal to bypass the Philippines "utterly unsound." At the subsequent high-level strategy meeting in Hawaii in July, he reiterated this argument, giving his personal guarantee that "a Luzon Campaign could be completed in thirty days to six weeks" and that the losses in such a campaign would be "inconsequential."[12] Half of that projected time was now gone, and his forces had yet to reach Manila, the island's capital. His impatience grew with each moment the "race" dragged on. To preserve his image, he turned to the 11th Airborne Division, then in reserve with Eighth Army.

The 11th Airborne Division was activated on February 25, 1943 at Camp Mackall, North Carolina, with one parachute regiment and two glider infantry regiments, plus the usual artillery and supporting elements.[13] After completing training in the United States, the division was sent to New Guinea, where it trained in amphibious and jungle warfare operations. Its first combat was at Leyte where it participated—as infantry—in that jungle and mountain campaign from November 1944 to January 1945. It was one of the few American divisions in World War II to have only one commander throughout its combat existence.

Major General Joseph May Swing was born in Jersey City, New Jersey, and graduated from West Point in 1915 with a commission in the field artillery. He served in Mexico and in France during World War I. Between the wars he graduated from the Command and General Staff School and the Army War College. He served in a variety of inter-war appointments before taking command of the 82nd Infantry (later Airborne) Division's artillery. He was then assigned to activate, organize, and train the new 11th Airborne Division. He would remain the division's commander for the duration of the war.

Plans for the division during the Luzon campaign had changed often. Originally, they were to drop on the Central Luzon Plain in front of the Sixth Army to expedite its advance. These plans had been dropped when the Allied air forces reported that they had neither the aircraft nor the airfields to lift the entire division at one drop. General MacArthur's headquarters then decided to use them to stage diversionary operations along the southern and southwestern coast of Luzon. But the employment of these highly trained and specialized troops in such a manner seemed wasteful to many. In addition, the problem of supply, command, and administration so distant from support created insoluble problems. Other plans were also dropped when the Allied naval forces reported that they could not provide enough escort vessels nor fire support vessels to support other planned landings.

In the end, it was decided to land the entire division, less the parachute regiment, at Nasugbu on the southwest coast 45 miles from Manila. Due to the need to land XI Corps at Bataan, the airborne landings would have to wait until there was sufficient assault shipping available after XI Corps was safely established ashore. The planners hoped to pin down Japanese forces in southern Luzon and keep them away from the Sixth Army's drive on Manila. There was also the hope that the troopers could use a good existing road that led the 45 miles directly to Manila from Nasugbu. Finally, there was the intent to land the reserve 41st Infantry Division behind the paratroopers to reinforce Sixth Army. By January 20, General Eichelberger, commanding Eighth U.S. Army, recommended to General MacArthur that the division be landed amphibiously at Nasugbu, using the two glider infantry regiments, and after enough progress had been made by them, the parachute infantry regiment would be dropped on Tagaytay Ridge to expedite the advance forward to Manila.

Despite his anxiety to reach Manila quickly, General MacArthur hesitated. He ordered that one regiment land first to ascertain enemy strength, estimated by intelligence as about 7,000 soldiers of the *17th* and *31st Infantry Regiments* of the *8th Infantry Division*. The airborne division was not as strong as a standard infantry division, numbering at full strength 8,200 officers and men. The two glider infantry regiments had only half the strength of a standard American infantry regiment, while the parachute regiment had only about two-thirds that strength.

In fact, the *Shimbu Group* had placed the *Fuji Force* to defend the area around Nasugbu Bay. Under the command of Colonel Masatoshi Fujishige, commander of the *17th Infantry Regiment*, *Fuji Force* consisted of some 8,500 men, including a battalion of the *31st Infantry Regiment*, a battalion of combat engineers, artillery, and service units. Nearby and available to Colonel Fujishige was the *2nd Surface Raiding Base Force*, a Japanese Army unit of suicide boat squadrons with their own support units. Most of these squadrons had already lost their suicide boats to Allied air and naval strikes. Because he had such a large area to cover, Colonel Fujishige had spread his forces widely, with few holding any decisive point.

The 11th Airborne Division staged for the assault on Leyte and, carried by Rear Admiral William M. Fechteler's (USNA, 1916) Task Group 78.2, sailed for Luzon on January 27. General Swing, however, had been concerned about the lack of information on his proposed landing beaches. On January 14, he ordered First Lieutenant Robert L. Dickerson, of the 188th Glider Infantry Regiment, to report to him. General Swing told Lieutenant Dickerson to get a non-commissioned officer to volunteer for a dangerous mission and report back. With Staff Sergeant Vernon W. Clark in tow, he returned to General Swing who ordered them to Mindoro. There they found out that they were to reconnoiter the proposed landing area with the help of Philippine guerillas. Proceeding by PT boat, they landed, joined the guerillas, and completed their mission, finding no enemy forces in the immediate beach area and providing accurate maps for the division.

With 22 officers and 934 enlisted men newly received to replace losses on Leyte, the division began its journey to Luzon, along the way dropping off the 511th Parachute Infantry Regiment on Mindoro from where it would later fly to Tagaytay Ridge. General Eichelberger accompanied the division and tried to talk General Swing into a "fast drive to Manila," promising to "back him if he gets his pants shot off."[14]

At first it seemed that the idea of a run for Manila might work. The initial landing by the 188th Glider Infantry was lightly opposed, and soon the town of Nasugbu was in their hands. The troopers then started down the road, Route 17, toward Tagaytay Ridge and Manila. Only light rifle, machine-gun, and mortar fire occasionally opposed the advance. Satisfied that the landings were a success, General Eichelberger released the rest of the division for a landing. By the end of the day all the combat troops of the division, except the 511th Parachute Infantry, were ashore. The 188th Glider Infantry seized intact a critical bridge over the Palico River, avoiding a time-consuming detour. With this success, General Eichelberger again ordered the division to use all possible speed to continue to surprise the Japanese, who seemed unaware of the Americans' presence. By late afternoon the 188th Glider Infantry and elements of the 187th Glider Infantry were five miles from Nasugbu and across the Palico River on the road to Manila. So excited was General Eichelberger with the division's progress, that he contacted the Fifth U.S. Army Air Force and ordered the 511th Parachute Infantry be dropped on Tagaytay Ridge on February 2 instead of the planned February 3. He also ordered the 19th Infantry Regiment of the 24th Infantry Division, assigned as the operations reserve force, to be rushed to Nasugbu from Mindoro.

February 1 was an equally good day for the airborne troopers. The leading elements headed for Tagaytay Ridge but came up against Japanese troops holding a defile with machine guns and rifles, supported by artillery. The Japanese were well positioned on high ground overlooking the path that the Americans needed to advance. Despite little natural cover, Captain Raymond Lee and his Company A of the 188th Glider Infantry Regiment used what they could to advance on the key Japanese position atop Mt. Cariliao. A Japanese counterattack was beaten off after Captain Lee sheltered his men in Japanese caves. The rest of the battalion followed and soon had the Japanese pushed off the heights. But this delay, however brief, affected the arrival of the 511th Parachute Infantry Regiment. Under orders from General MacArthur to ensure that the drop would be made only when he was sure that contact with the paratroopers could be made within 24 hours of their arrival, General Eichelberger was forced to return to the original drop schedule of February 3.

It was just as well that he did, since despite strong air and artillery support, the 188th Glider Infantry made slow progress on the morning of February 2. But when they overran the Japanese command post at Aga village, progress soon picked up. Here large stores of ammunition, engineer supplies, and general supplies of all types were captured intact. "The assault was so vigorous and fast that the enemy was driven back in complete rout. This was verified by the capture of an enemy regimental command post (later found to be the headquarters of the Japanese *31st Infantry Regiment*—Colonel Fujishige's CP) at Aga at 1300 hours, which showed the haste in which their personnel had departed. Large stores of ammunition, food, clothing, engineer equipment and cigarettes were captured. Several cases of liquor, many documents, weapons, and a Japanese sabre was also found by the writer."[15]

Now Lieutenant Colonel Harry Wilson's 1st Battalion, 187th Glider Infantry, took the lead and moved to a position two miles short of Tagaytay Ridge before stopping for the night. The night passed quietly, and with dawn the Americans renewed their advance. A strong enemy position atop a bare ridge at a sharp bend in Route 17 on the western edge of Tagaytay Ridge halted the advance. The 188th Glider Infantry left a battalion to deal with this resistance and continued forward. The advance soon encountered men of the 511th Parachute Infantry Regiment who had landed on the ridge earlier that morning.

The 1,750 men of the 511th Parachute Infantry had begun landing atop Tagaytay Ridge right on schedule, but other than that things went badly. The drop was widely scattered, and only the absence of enemy opposition prevented a disaster. Only about one-third of the troopers landed in their designated drop zones. Some landed as far as five or six miles from their zones. A great deal of confusion marred the operation, with jumpmasters and aircraft captains disagreeing about the correct drop zone, and with some following the drop of supplies instead of waiting for the actual drop zone. But with no enemy present and with the 188th and 187th Glider Infantry Regiments already in the area, a disaster was averted. The 50 jump casualties were serious enough, with one man killed and one seriously injured.[16] By mid-afternoon, Colonel Orin D. Haugen, commanding the 511th Parachute Infantry, had his regiment organized and was sending out reconnaissance patrols.

Generals Eichelberger and Swing now decided to leave the 188th Glider Infantry to deal with the Japanese strongpoint while continuing to secure Tagaytay Ridge. The 511th Parachute Infantry would lead the advance to Manila. To expedite their advance, General Swing "motorized" the regiment, using much of his division's limited motor transport to speed the troopers' advance. General Eichelberger wanted to "bluff" the Japanese into thinking his force was much larger than it was and told General Swing to raise as much dust as he could while advancing.

Leaving the guerillas to deal with the small scattered groups of Japanese that occasionally resisted the American advance, the airborne division moved to Manila. Resistance still took a toll, however. In one instance, the Americans were confounded by the amazing first-shot accuracy of the Japanese artillery. It wasn't until later they learned that the Japanese had pre-recorded the range of certain trees along the road, marking each with a large white cross. When the Americans reached these trees, the Japanese already had the range to fire immediately, without the necessity for "ranging fire." On February 3, one such barrage caught General Eichelberger, General Swing, Brigadier General Albert E. Pierson (Cornell University, 1918), the assistant division commander, Brigadier General Frank Farrell (USMA, 1920), the division artillery commander, and several battalion commanders grouped together. Several were killed, and Lieutenant Colonel Harry Wilson, commanding 1st Battalion, 187th Glider Infantry, and others wounded.

CHAPTER 7

The Tragedy of Manila

It was called the "Pearl of the Orient." This was Manila, the capital of the Philippines. Multi-culturalism was a fact, not a theory, in Manila in 1940, with indigenous Tagalog Filipino culture sharing space with 300 years of Spanish rule overlaid by 40 years of American occupation and assimilating heavy Chinese and Japanese populations. There were also strong Scottish and German influences to be seen in what many considered a beautiful city. There were problems, of course. The city was prone to earthquakes and floods. But most citizens, Manileños, as they called themselves, took such incidents in stride. In 1940 the city ranged from nipa-thatched huts to modern air-conditioned apartment buildings. The city, older than any in the United States, owed its station to the fine Manila Bay and the port with which it hosted shipping from around the world. With a population of about 800,000, swelled to over one million by war refugees, it was one of the larger cities in the Orient. Divided by the Pasig River, which ran through the city center, Manila was divided into a more modern area north of the river, with retail stores, movie houses, and restaurants. Along the bay front were much of the native population, laborers, fishermen, and others. To the east were the more affluent residential districts and most of the European residents. North of the river lay the Filipino White House and Malacañan Palace, the seat of the American government officials. On the south lay the famous old Walled City known as Intramuros, built by the Spanish and bordered on three sides by a moat that had been filled and converted to a public park. Many of the port facilities, including piers, warehouses, fuel storage, and machine shops, were located here.

When the Japanese invaded the Philippines in late 1941 General MacArthur had at first tried to defend the entire archipelago but soon realized his forces were woefully inadequate even to defend all of Luzon. As a result, he belatedly activated a prewar plan, War Plan Orange-3, and withdrew his forces into the Bataan Peninsula and Corregidor, a fortified island guarding Manila Bay. In 1941, he had declared Manila an "open city," which by international agreement meant that it would not be used for military purposes and therefore should be spared attacks. The Japanese, however, chose to ignore the proclamation and bombed Manila on several occasions. Damage was relatively slight, and although some damage still existed from the earlier battles, Manila was largely intact in February 1945. The Japanese had made some repairs, but much remained to be done, and with their war going badly, many work projects, including road and building repair, were ignored.

As mentioned earlier, General Yamashita did not intend to repeat General MacArthur's mistakes of the 1942 campaign. He had no intention of retreating to Bataan, nor did he intend to defend Manila. Given his plan to abandon the Central Plain and Manila Bay, it was only logical that Manila, which lay at Manila Bay, was to be left undefended as well. With insufficient resources to feed and protect the one million residents of the city, he knew the city was in large part highly inflammable, and lying as it did on a flat plain, it offered no good defensive positions. He determined to abandon Manila once all his supplies, troops, and equipment could be moved out of the city. He would leave only a small number of Army troops to maintain order, protect his supplies, and eventually to blow up the city's bridges to delay the American occupation and their ability to advance against the *Shimbu Group*, east of the city.

That was the plan, but as sometimes happened between the *Imperial Japanese Army* and the *Imperial Japanese Navy*, communications failed. Despite issuing plans to his subordinate units, as the *Imperial Japanese Army* moved out of Manila, the *Imperial Japanese Navy* moved in to the city. Vice Admiral Denshichi Okochi,[1] the commander of the *Southwestern Area Fleet* and the highest-ranking Japanese naval officer in the Philippines, decided on his own to defend Manila with his own naval forces. These forces were significant, since Manila had been a major port for the Japanese during their conquests and occupation of Southeast Asia. Designating a new force, which he labeled the *Manila Naval Defense Force*,[2] he ordered 4,000 navy men into the city for its defense. He placed Rear Admiral Sanji Iwabuchi,[3] commander of the *31st Naval Special Base Force*, which already had troops in Manila, in command. Admiral Okochi ordered all *Imperial Japanese Navy* troops then on Luzon to the defense of Manila, further disrupting General Yamashita's plans. Transportation difficulties would prevent most of those troops assigned to the *Kembu Group* from reaching the city before the Americans arrived. Even without these troops, Admiral Iwabuchi had 16,000–17,000 men under his command, including the 4,000 soldiers General Yamashita had left as a rear guard. He immediately set about preparing defenses in and around Manila. Although few defenders were combat troops, it didn't matter much, as defending within an urban setting made each sailor a competent opponent.

As he left Manila for the mountains with the *Fourteenth Area Army Headquarters*, Admiral Okochi placed Admiral Iwabuchi's forces under the command of Lieutenant General Shizuo Yokoyama and his *Shimbu Group*, but there was little or no communication or command authority between the two forces. At a series of meetings between January 8 and 13, Admiral Iwabuchi quickly made it clear to General

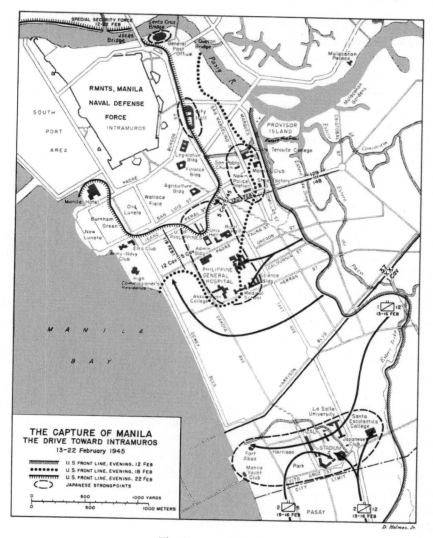

The Capture of Manila

Robert Ross Smith. *United States Army in World War II. The War in the Pacific. Triumph in the Philippines.* Washington, D.C.: Center of Military History, 1984. p. 276.

Yokoyama that his mission to defend Manila to the death took priority over any assignments he might receive from the *Imperial Japanese Army*. With little alternative, General Yokoyama placed the 4,000 army troops left in Manila to conduct final destruction under Admiral Iwabuchi's command and left the navy to its desired fate. General Yokoyama did, however, get Admiral Iwabuchi to agree to defend with his naval troops Fort McKinley, southeast of Manila, and the San Juan del Monte area, which connected the city with the *Shimbu Group*'s main defenses to the east.

Admiral Iwabuchi had to use his forces to cover an area of about 250 square miles. To cover this vast area, he had 12,500 navy and 4,500 army personnel, while another 3,500 naval troops defended the islands in Manila Bay or had been sent to maintain communications with the *Shimbu Group* in the mountains east of Manila. In Manila itself, he retained 14,000 troops, divided into five different commands. Each command was assigned a sector to defend, under a commander responsible directly to Admiral Iwabuchi. The main group, consisting of about 5,000 naval troops and known as the *Central Force*, was under the admiral's personal command.

Admiral Iwabuchi had no detailed plan to defend Manila. He proposed only a suicidal fight to the death in place, keeping Manila and Manila Bay from Allied hands for as long as possible. He got off on the wrong foot, however, when he decided that the main attack would come from the south, and ignored the XIV Corps' advance until they were in sight of the city, allowing the Americans to approach with little interference. While awaiting the attack he planned a destruction of all "military installations" within the city. His definition of "military installations" was, however, somewhat suspect, since it included the entire port area, all bridges, all transportation facilities, the water supply system, and the electric power supply. However, he made no effort to control his troops' demolitions, and they soon got far out of hand. Nor were his defenses laid out along purely military lines. While some defense lines were mutually supporting, others were not. No provision was made for withdrawal from one line to the next, the idea being that when a defense was overrun there would be no survivors. The most effort at constructing defenses was made at Intramuros, using the well-constructed government buildings of the Walled City as a core of the defense.

Buildings were made into fortresses. Sandbags blocked the entrances, barricades blocked corridors and stairways within the buildings, while firing slits were carved through the walls. Tunnels connected the basements of many of the buildings while machine guns were mounted with only the muzzles showing. Bunkers and pillboxes, constructed throughout the city, added power to the defense. Mines were liberally placed around the defenses. Barbed wire, oil drums filled with dirt, vehicles of every description, and even heavy factory machinery blocked the streets. The defenders armed themselves with a high proportion of automatic weapons, many stripped from sunken naval vessels and destroyed aircraft. Thousands of grenades were distributed. Available artillery ranged from dual-purpose 120mm guns to 47mm antitank guns, widely distributed throughout the defense. There was even a good supply of 200mm rockets from *Imperial Japanese Navy* supply bases.

The Americans did not anticipate a strong defense of Manila. Everyone from General MacArthur down the chain of command expected some form of desultory fighting for the city before it was occupied quickly. General MacArthur's headquarters had even issued plans for a great victory parade led by the theater commander in person. Only General Krueger believed that the Japanese would defend the city, and he was in the distinct minority until intelligence sources, coming late in January, appeared to support his opinion. But the strength and depth of the defenses came as an uncomfortable surprise to the Americans, revealed only when they were fired upon from those defenses. Plans for the big victory parade were then quietly laid aside.

General MacArthur loved the city, which had been his home for many prewar years. As a result of his concern for the city, he issued orders that severely limited artillery and air support to the ground forces attacking within the city. Only observed supporting fires against clearly identified targets, such as Japanese gun emplacements, were permitted. General Krueger, meanwhile, set as priorities the seizure of the city's water supply and its power supply. The Novaliches Dam, the Balara Water Filters, the San Juan Reservoir, and the pipelines connecting these installations to Manila were XIV Corps' first objectives.

The battle for Manila can be said to have begun February 3, 1945, when the 2nd Squadron, 8th Cavalry Regiment, crossed into the city that evening. Their initial mission was to free the civilian internees held at Santo Tomas University. General MacArthur had also assigned General Mudge the seizure of the presidential palace, Malacañan Palace, and the Legislative Building. This latter objective was beyond the division's zone of operations, but was no doubt targeted because by taking possession of the seat of government, General MacArthur could rightfully claim that he had seized Manila, regardless of whether much of it remained in enemy hands.

Led by tanks of the 44th Tank Battalion and two Filipino guerillas,[4] the 8th Cavalry reached the gates of Santo Tomas University and broke down the gate. Japanese guards, mostly Formosans, gave little resistance, and moments later some 3,500 civilian internees from various countries were freed. But another group of internees, perhaps 275 mostly women and children, were being held by a Japanese force under Lieutenant Colonel Toshio Hayashi, the camp commander, in another building about 60 yards from the main university buildings. Colonel Hayashi demanded a guarantee of safety for his men if he released the hostages and left the area. With little alternative, General Chase, of the 1st Cavalry Division, agreed to the proposal, and the last of the internees were freed.[5]

As the Americans arrived, the internees were at first pleased to hear that one of them, a Briton from Worcestershire named Ernest Stanley, was called out of the crowd by the American commanding officer. Mr. Stanley was universally loathed by the rest of the internees as a collaborator. Arriving at Manila only weeks before the war began, he had been interned with the rest, but soon developed a position as an intermediary between the internees and the Japanese camp commander. That he spoke fluent Japanese was another reason for suspicion. His close relationship with a Japanese civilian connected with the camp, one Tobo, only reinforced suspicions. Yet when the tanks of the 44th Tank Battalion, "Battlin' Basic," "Georgia Peach," and others came roaring into the camp, Mr. Stanley was called out and handed a helmet and rifle by the Americans. Stunned, the internees would not learn until later that Mr. Stanley was in fact a spy, operating an intelligence network through Mr. Tobo—who was in reality a Nisei-American pretending to be a hairdresser—which led directly to guerilla forces.[6]

Meanwhile Troop G of the cavalry regiment had moved on to the third objective, the Legislative Building. But as they rode down Quezon Boulevard they came to a great stone building, known as Old Bilibid Prison. There the Japanese had dug in strongly and opened fire with rifles, machine guns, and antitank guns. Drivers tried to turn their vehicles in the narrow streets, resulting in confusion and casualties. Aided again by local guerillas, the cavalry managed a withdrawal back to Santo Tomas University, where they reunited with the rest of the squadron and the newly arrived 2nd Squadron, 5th Cavalry. There they learned that Captain Emery M. Hickman's Troop F, 8th Cavalry, had secured the Malacañan Palace against slight resistance.

It was on February 5 that General Chase learned that the Novaliches Bridge, his only supply and communications route to the rear, had been blown up by the enemy. With all supplies and reinforcements cut off until a new route could be established, General Chase had serious problems. His force—two small cavalry squadrons, some tanks, and engineers—was too small to do more than patrol their own area. He had no information about the Japanese defenses he was facing, nor did he know much about the position of the neighboring 37th Infantry Division. For the next 24 hours General Chase and his "Flying Columns" were at risk of a Japanese counterattack that, if strong enough, could wipe them out. His choices were to make a stand at Santo Tomas University or to abandon the internees and conduct a fighting withdrawal. However, General Chase's immediate opponent, Colonel Katsuzo Noguchi and his *Northern Force*, were surprised by the sudden appearance of the Americans, and poorly disposed to launch such a counterattack.

Under orders from General Mudge, General Chase sent the 2nd Squadron, 5th Cavalry, to seize another bridge, the Quezon Bridge, about a mile south near the Far Eastern University. The attempt failed when strong Japanese opposition halted the advance at a roadblock on Quezon Boulevard. The roadblock, consisting of a minefield, trucks wired together covered by four machine guns, halted all forward movement. Even as the cavalrymen withdrew, the Japanese blew up the Quezon Bridge. But as the cavalrymen returned to Santo Tomas University, they were cheered by the arrival of troops from the 37th Infantry Division.

Perhaps the measure of the confusion by the Japanese is best judged by an incident that occurred while the 5th Cavalry Regiment was moving into the city. A convoy of trucks carrying elements of the 5th Cavalry Regiment moved forward, racing through the streets at 40 miles per hour, when they encountered four trucks moving toward them. As the Japanese trucks passed them by, the entire American convoy raked each truck with rifle and automatic weapons fire, destroying the trucks and killing several Japanese. The American convoy continued, little realizing that at the tail of their convoy four more Japanese trucks, mistaking the Americans for their own, had tagged onto the rear of the convoy. Darkness prevented early detection, but eventually the troopers in the rear truck realized that they were being followed and opened fire with machine guns mounted on their vehicles. A moving firefight broke out, and the Japanese trucks and crews were eliminated at a cost to the 5th Cavalry of two killed and several others wounded.

General Beightler's 37th Infantry Division had marched into Manila through the Tondo and Santa Cruz Districts west of Santo Tomas University. The leading 2nd Battalion, 148th Infantry, had reached Old Bilibid Prison without knowing that the cavalry were nearby, fighting their own battle. The cavalry had been heavily engaged in their battles, and had largely ignored the prison, but the infantrymen had broken into the prison and discovered 828 Allied and American prisoners of war and 447 civilian internees being held there. Because of the heavy fighting, the prisoners, now in American hands, remained within the relatively safe prison walls until the area was cleared of the enemy.[7]

Not that the rescue was so easily done. When Captain Sidney Goodkin's Company F, 148th Infantry, approached the prison they did so with great caution, having been alerted that the Japanese planned to blow it up using the store of ammunition kept within the prison walls. Captain Goodkin's men were slowed by crowds of cheering Manilaños who showered them with gifts of food and drink, but upon reaching the prison, enemy machine guns and snipers halted the advance. Captain Goodkin sent a patrol to investigate other avenues of approach, but when that patrol failed to return after an hour, he sent a second platoon under Sergeant Rayford Anderson. Sergeant Anderson managed to get close to a rear entrance, where he observed two sentries. After dispatching the sentries, the patrol shot off a lock to a rear entrance and entered a storage area. Peering into the courtyard area, he saw several Caucasians he believed to be prisoners. But his whispered calls to them were ignored. The internees feared a Japanese trick. His new-style helmet and other modern equipment added to their suspicions. Even singing a few bars of "God Bless America" elicited no response. Only when he tossed in some cigarette packages that were obviously American did the internees respond and open their internal gates. Soon the entire battalion occupied the prison.[8]

The advance of the 37th Infantry Division into Manila had begun to reveal what would soon become one of the great tragedies of the war in the Pacific. As the Americans advanced, they came upon groups of Filipinos, men, women and children, who had been gathered together by the Japanese, bound, tortured, raped, shot, stabbed, burned, and eviscerated. The bodies were left to decay in the streets, parking lots, or buildings of the city. As the Americans advanced deeper into the city, more and more such atrocities were uncovered. Mass rapes, executions of innocent civilians, and mass murder were everywhere in the city. The Japanese, knowing they were about to die, had no qualms about killing as many Filipinos as they could before their own inevitable end. By the time the battle was over, it was estimated that between 60,000 and 100,000 Filipino civilians were killed during the battle, the clear majority by deliberate action by individual or small groups of Japanese soldiers and sailors.

General Beightler divided his zone into two, with the 145th Infantry attacking west of Highway 3 and the 148th Infantry attacking on the east. Whole sections of Manila were already on fire, and as the Americans advanced the enemy exploded dynamite-filled buildings in their path. Japanese machine-gun fire and 20mm gunfire from pillboxes at every corner slowed the advance and increased casualties. Fire began to threaten Bilibid Prison, and the internees there were hurriedly evacuated on all available transportation under enemy fire from nearby buildings. While this was occurring, General MacArthur visited the division, intending to move on to the cavalry division sector. But his route was blocked by the enemy; disappointed, he returned to his headquarters without officially setting foot in Manila.

The advance continued. Captain Gus Hauser's Company I, 148th Infantry, advanced to a point 200 yards from the Pasig River at about noon on February 6, but intense heat from burning buildings forced a withdrawal. That night was spent picking off snipers who were silhouetted against the fires of Manila. Company K had been ordered to seize and hold the Jones Bridge across the Pasig River. Under increasing Japanese rocket, mortar, rifle, and machine-gun fire, the company advanced slowly. As they approached the bridge leading to their objective, they discovered a minefield and a 500-pound bomb attached to the bridge for demolition. Despite these obstacles, the company managed to cross single file. They continued through streets covered with enemy fire. Discouraged by the continued advance of the Americans, the Japanese then set fire to the buildings directly in front of Company K. These had already been mined and prepared for demolition. The ensuing flames engulfed several blocks and threatened the Americans with a fiery death. Captain Labin W. Knipp, the company commander, ordered a withdrawal.

Leading the advance during the day was Second Lieutenant Robert M. Viale, of Bayside, California. During the morning's advance, he had led his third platoon forward personally. He had taken on two enemy pillboxes, destroying them after screening his advance with smoke grenades. During this action, he was painfully wounded in his right arm but refused evacuation and remained with his command. Pushing ahead through mortar fire and flames, he had led his platoon in the forefront of the company's advance. Now ordered to withdraw, he discovered that his withdrawal route was well covered by Japanese machine guns. Entering a building, he managed to acquire a position overlooking the enemy post but encountered civilians inside the building. His platoon followed him inside. Still trying to eliminate the enemy gun, he placed a ladder against a high window, armed a grenade, and climbed up, prepared to destroy the gun with the grenade. He was left-handed and could throw the grenade despite his wounded right arm. But in climbing the ladder his right arm gave way, and while steadying himself on the ladder the grenade dropped to the floor amid the civilians and his own men. Jumping down from the ladder, he sought a way to safely dispose of the weapon, but the room was full of civilians and his own soldiers. He raced to a corner of the room, covered the grenade with his body, and absorbed the full blast of the grenade to save his men and the innocent civilians. His Medal of Honor was posthumously awarded.[9]

Captain Knipp led his men along burning streets so hot that the pavement melted under their feet. Exploding buildings shattered around them. Undeterred, Captain Knipp organized his men for a breakout, picked up a Browning Automatic Rifle, and stepped out into the middle of the street, attacking an enemy machine gun. His rapid fire caused the enemy to duck. Taking advantage of the pause in enemy fire, he tossed smoke grenades between his men and the enemy guns. The Japanese, now unable to clearly see the Americans, were unaware that Captain Knipp was moving his company directly across their line of fire. Eventually, the entire company managed to escape. Captain Thomas Downey, the battalion surgeon, organized litter teams to bring in the wounded and worked on them by the light of an oil lamp in a dark, shattered building. As the withdrawal continued, Captain Knipp encountered two more enemy machine guns blocking the way. He repeated his earlier heroism but this time was seriously wounded in the stomach before the smoke obscured him. Refusing to seek cover, he remained out in the open tossing grenades until his company had reached safety, then commanded the rear guard.[10]

The enemy forces facing the Americans were Colonel Noguchi's *Northern Force*, which was holding the area only until they completed their mission of destroying military installations, military stores, and delaying the enemy's advance. By February 6, Lieutenant Colonel George T. Coleman and his battalion of the 145th Infantry had cleared all but a small pocket of the enemy, but at the cost of Colonel Coleman's life. Clearing the Japanese required close cooperation between the infantry and the division artillery, tanks, and Cannon Company's M7 mounted guns. Destruction—between the deliberate Japanese destruction and the American firepower used against the enemy—would soon reduce Manila to rubble, making it the second most heavily destroyed city of World War II. Only Warsaw, Poland, suffered more damage and destruction after being fought over twice during the war in Europe.

On February 6, the boundaries were again altered. The 37th Infantry Division took over the eastern portion of the city itself, while the 1st Cavalry Division moved to clear the suburbs east to the San Juan River. There was little opposition in the suburbs, and that task was completed the next day. To the north, the 7th Cavalry Regiment managed to capture the Novaliches Dam, finding no prepared demolitions. They did intercept three Japanese soldiers who were carrying demolitions to the dam, however. The nearby Balara Water Filters were also captured intact. Patrolling along the main water pipelines, the cavalrymen next captured the San Juan Reservoir. But even as the cavalry was securing the area, an artillery shell hit the reservoir's main outlet valve, forcing the valve to be worked by hand. For the remainder of the battle, the 7th Cavalry Regiment, the only unit of the 1st Cavalry Division not to fight within Manila, protected the city's water supply.

The 8th Cavalry Regiment was less fortunate. They were passing into the New Manila Subdivision across the San Juan River when they came up against the *1st Independent Naval Battalion*, supported by a heavy weapons detachment. These streets were heavily mined and covered by 20mm cannon, machine guns, and small arms. Many of the homes had been turned into machine-gun positions. Supported by tanks from the 44th Tank Battalion and artillery from the 61st and 947th Field Artillery Battalions, the cavalrymen were forced to make short rushes from house to house, avoiding mined streets and the still surviving machine guns. But at the end of the day, February 8, the area had been substantially cleared at a cost of 41 men wounded. The tank battalion, which had suffered from the mines, lost 11 killed and 12 wounded along with three tanks destroyed. Captures included 22 20mm cannons, three 6-inch naval guns, five 13.2mm machine guns, a 105mm howitzer, and smaller arms. About 500 enemy dead were left behind. The 8th Cavalry went on to capture El Deposito, an underground reservoir a mile southwest of the San Juan Reservoir.

By February 10, the XIV Corps had cleared all of Manila and its suburbs north of the Pasig River. Colonel Noguchi's *Northern Force* had been seriously depleted and pushed south across the river. Colonel Noguchi, who had accomplished all his assignments, had withdrawn over the Pasig, destroying the bridges behind him. His *1st Independent Naval Battalion* had lost approximately 1,500 men, but most of these were ill-armed service troops or stragglers. The Americans, in turn, had gained valuable knowledge of urban street fighting and seized intact most of the city's water supply. General Krueger now issued orders for the seizure of the city's power supply. This involved seizure of Provisor Island, in the Pasig River, where the key generating plant lay. General Griswold gave this assignment to the 37th Infantry Division. The 1st Cavalry Division would join them after it cleared the northern suburbs.

General Beightler selected the 148th Infantry to make the assault, followed by the 129th Infantry and the 1st Battalion, 145th Infantry. The remaining two battalions of the latter regiment were occupied in guarding the division's line of communications. To guard the northern portion of the city, General Beightler created a provisional task force he called Special Security Force, consisting of the 637th Tank Destroyer Battalion, the 37th Cavalry Reconnaissance Troop, and Company A, 754th Tank Battalion.

Intelligence reports put the main Japanese resistance well east of Malacañan Palace botanical garden grounds. General Beightler ordered his 148th Infantry to land at the gardens to avoid any immediate enemy resistance. The attack would clear the Paco and Pandacan Districts before turning south to Intramuros and Manila Bay.

The 129th Infantry's assignment was to cross and then swing west along the river to seize Provisor Island and the power plant. The 672nd Amphibian Tractor Battalion would use its LVTs to carry the troops across the river. Facing them was Admiral Iwabuchi's *Central Force's 1st Naval Battalion*, about 800 riflemen supported by machine gunners and heavy weapons units. This force was concentrated around the Paco District south of Provisor Island, half a mile west of the Malacañan gardens. The center of this defense was at the Paco Railroad Station on the Manila Railroad line.

The 672nd Amphibian Tractor Battalion assembled its LVTs in the protection of a small bend of the river near the palace. The division's organic engineers, the 117th Engineer (Combat) Battalion, assembled every engineer assault boat they could lay their hands on and gathered them at the same location. The two groups would cooperate in shuttling the assault troops of the 37th Infantry Division across the river. The assault began in the mid-afternoon of February 7 with a barrage of 105mm guns covering the assault of the 3rd Battalion, 148th Infantry. The first wave crossed against no opposition, but as the second wave moved out into the river they were struck with intense machine-gun, mortar, and artillery fire. Targets included both the river and the landing site at the Malacañan Palace. But once ashore the leading waves found only a few scattered Japanese in the area, and a bridgehead was quickly established. By early evening two battalions had successfully crossed and were holding a bridgehead of some 300 yards along Cristobal Street and then inland about 1,000 yards to a bridge over the Estero de Concordia. The cost had been 15 men killed and 100 wounded, nearly all as the result of machine-gun and artillery fire.

General Beightler set up an advanced headquarters across the river by the end of the day, thankful that he had ignored General MacArthur's advice that the area seemed so quiet that he (Beightler) could cross the river and clear all southern Manila with a platoon.[11] The 148th Infantry, supported by the 136th and 140th Field Artillery Battalions, spent the next three days clearing the Pandacan District. Behind them the 129th Infantry moved forward. The troops, "tired and hot, with dried tongues and parched lips after marching all day,"[12] moved along hoping for a break at the Balintawak Brewery along their route. As they marched along they began to pass the men they were relieving, carrying containers of every description filled with the "cool, tempting, amber-colored brew," which the relieved troops shared with the incoming 129th Infantrymen.[13] That evening, despite a close call when the regiment appeared to be marching past the brewery, orders at the last moment permitted the men to bivouac within a few hundred yards of the precious drinking establishment and acquire beer for each squad.

The 145th Infantry had been assigned the task of securing what was termed the Pasig River Line. This entailed ensuring that no Japanese troops crossed the river back into the rear areas of XIV Corps. The regiment was spread out along the river, preventing Japanese infiltration. Here they discovered Japanese forces in the Tondo District, bypassed earlier. Other small groups of Japanese, also bypassed in the earlier advance, began to make a nuisance of themselves by attacking the division's line of communications. Both these problems fell to the 145th Infantry to deal with while protecting the Pasig River Line. Company G, reinforced with elements of the regimental Cannon Company and a heavy machine-gun platoon, dealt with the enemy in the Tondo District. As the regiment was dealing with these problems, the Japanese struck back. An amphibious attack occurred on February 7 aimed at the 2nd Battalion, 145th Infantry, in the North Dock Area of Manila Bay. These Japanese were apparently attempting to reinforce those in the Tondo District but were mostly destroyed by the American mortar, cannon, and antitank fire which sank all the Japanese barges before they could land. The approximately 20 Japanese who managed to reach the shore were eliminated by rifle and machine-gun fire. To expedite the clearing of the Tondo District, Company F was sent forward to assist Company G. During the move, Private First Class Pahr of Headquarters Company, 2nd Battalion, 145th Infantry, noticed a ragged Filipino civilian was walking toward his post carrying a rifle. Pfc Pahr thought little of the man, as by now surviving Manileños armed themselves with discarded weapons simply to survive Japanese atrocities. Turning back to his duties, Pfc Pahr was shocked to hear a bullet whizz past his head, and then a second. Turning, he saw that the ragged Filipino was lying dead in the street, having been shot by one of Pfc Pahr's buddies who was suspicious of the man. A closer examination revealed that the ragged "Filipino" was in fact a disguised Japanese soldier.

The 129th Infantry had been assigned the capture of Provisor Island. After crossing behind the 148th Infantry, the regiment turned west toward the island. A company was sent ahead to seize a bridgehead over the Estero de Tonque east of the island, but enemy rifle, machine-gun and mortar fire repelled this attempt. The island, about 400 yards east to west and 125 yards north to south, contained five large buildings and several smaller shelters which covered nearly all the island's surface. Three large buildings were of concrete; the others were frame structures sided with sheet metal. The Japanese garrison, members of the *1st Naval Battalion*, could be reinforced via a bridge over the Estero Provisor on the west side of the island. Once again, the Japanese had improvised defenses among the buildings and built sandbagged bunkers at entrances to the buildings. From across the river, other Japanese forces could support the garrison by fire.

After a scheduled artillery bombardment, Company G, 129th Infantry, moved to the mouth of the Estero de Tonque on February 9, where they planned to use two engineer assault boats to shuttle themselves to Provisor Island. The initial target was a boiler plant at the northeast point of the island. The first boat, carrying eight men, made the crossing safely. A second was hit, causing two casualties. The survivors swam to the island. In the first half hour only 15 men made it to the island. They entered the boiler plant, only to be thrown back by a Japanese counterattack. The men took position behind a coal pile lying outside the boiler plant. There they remained, pinned down by enemy fire from the boiler plant and the main powerhouse just to the south. The rest of the assault force could not reach them as enemy fire was targeting the route of approach. An attempt at withdrawal cost two more casualties. Company G called in their battalion mortars to protect the survivors until nightfall, when they could be withdrawn. After dark, Company G's commanding officer, Captain George West, swam to the island, dragging behind him an engineer assault boat. Despite being wounded himself, he shuttled his men back across the water. A final count revealed that six men had been killed, five wounded, and six were missing of the 17 Americans, including Captain West, who landed on Provisor Island.[14]

With Company G hors de combat, the task now fell to Company E. A prolonged artillery barrage hit the island late afternoon and well into the night. This time Company E had six engineer assault boats to use, and the first two boats made it safely across before the moon came up and revealed the operation. The next three boats were sunk by Japanese machine guns and mortars. A fuel dump on the island then erupted in flames, exposing the men already ashore. Once again, the Americans hugged the coal pile until the fire burned itself out and the moon disappeared. Taking this opportunity, the men dashed into the boiler plant and began a deadly game of hide and seek among the huge machinery. By dawn the Americans had taken possession of the eastern half of the building, while the Japanese retained the western half.

The following day Company E cleaned out the rest of the boiler plant. But any attempt to move beyond the plant received a hail of enemy fire. While Company E waited, division mortars and artillery blasted the remaining buildings on the island, supported by shore-based tanks and tank destroyers. Such close fire resulted in some "friendly fire" casualties, and Japanese fire killed seven more Company E men. That night another squad came across to the island to reinforce the men already there. As Company E prepared to renew their assault on February 11, resistance on the island collapsed. A cautious search of the island found only stragglers. By midafternoon, the island was secured. It had cost the 2nd Battalion, 129th Infantry, 25 men killed and 75 men wounded. But the Japanese had succeeded in destroying the power plant before they left, and what they had missed, American firepower had destroyed. It would be some time before this power plant provided electricity to Manila again.

The issue of artillery and air power had become one of controversy. General MacArthur had forbidden the use of American artillery or air power in close support of the infantry in a desire to preserve the historical and cultural significance of Manila. But as the battle progressed and as casualties mounted due to the fanatical Japanese defense, more and more of the ground force commanders argued for a revision of the restrictions. By the time of the Provisor Island battle these restrictions had been all but lifted. The consequences, necessary as they were, would again present themselves in the battle for the Paco Railroad Station.

The 148th Infantry had crossed the Pasig River and was now assigned to clear the Pandacan District. After that the objective was to clear the Paco District. In the face of the heaviest Japanese weapons—200mm and 447mm rockets so huge that they could be seen while in flight—these weapons relied more on concussion for damage than explosive power. Finally, American forward observers located the source of these monsters and silenced them. With these out of the way, the Pandacan District was soon cleared. Attention turned to the Paco District. Here even greater trouble was encountered at the Japanese stronghold around the Paco Railroad Station, Concordia College, and Paco School.

About a battalion of Japanese held these strongpoints. American artillery, now fully unleashed, pounded the area, but by the end of February 9 the Japanese were still strongly holding out. The attacking Americans, from the 1st and 3rd Battalions, 148th Infantry, came up against the core of Japanese resistance in Manila. Here the Japanese held an unbroken succession of heavily fortified buildings, mutually supporting pillboxes, thickly strewn minefields, and mined structures. They were fully supplied with weapons and ammunition, and food seemed plentiful. For the next three weeks, the 37th Infantry Division would be faced with these strong defenses.

First to encounter these was Captain Buster Ferris's Company B, 148th Infantry. Ordered to seize the Paco Railroad Station, they found an elaborate system of machine-gun positions surrounding the station, covered by riflemen in foxholes. Inside the station itself, sandbagged fortifications contained 20mm guns and a pillbox with a 37mm antitank gun. About 300 enemy troops defended the station. They had excellent observation over the entire area and directed artillery and mortars on every American advance.

Despite the strength of the enemy stronghold, Captain Ferris ordered his 2nd Platoon to make a frontal attack against the railroad station, while the rest of the company provided supporting fire. The men raced across a debris-strewn field until they were stopped a hundred yards from the building by enemy fire. Private First Class Elbert E. Jones, a bazooka man, managed to snake his way an additional 50 yards forward, dragging his weapon with him. Hiding behind the only cover, a dirt mound no higher than six inches tall, he fired 20 rounds of antitank ammunition directly into the station before return machine-gun fire killed him. His fire drove the Japanese from the left wing of the station and kept the Japanese occupied, while behind Pfc Jones medical aid men carried off the wounded.

Meanwhile, two other Pfcs of Company B, John R. Reese and Cleto Rodriguez, carried their BARs forward to within 60 yards of the station. Both men carried as much ammunition as they could and spent the next two and a half hours firing into the Paco Railroad Station, expending over 1,600 rounds. They knocked out the 20mm enemy gun, killed an estimated 82 enemy soldiers, and disabled a Japanese heavy machine gun. Their aggressiveness unnerved the defenders and started a retreat which turned into a rout. As they were withdrawing, taking turns covering each other, a final burst of fire killed Pfc Reese.[15]

The rest of the 1st Battalion, 148th Infantry, bypassed the Paco Railroad Station and headed for the Manila Gas Works. Here the situation was the same, and numerous casualties resulted. Indeed, so many were wounded that the medical detachment couldn't handle the casualties, and 30 men from front-line companies were assigned temporary duty evacuating those wounded men. One such individual was Private First Class Joseph J. Cicchetti, a platoon messenger of Company A, 148th Infantry. He immediately organized a litter team and led it through tangled wreckage and enemy fire to seek out and evacuate casualties across a 400-yard open space covered by Japanese fire. In four hours, constantly under enemy fire and harassed by close explosions from mortars and artillery, Pfc Cicchetti led his team in evacuating 14 wounded soldiers. In one instance, an enemy machine gun blocked his team. Standing straight up to draw the enemy fire, he located the gun and killed the crew with his rifle while the rest of his team successfully evacuated the casualty. He then came upon a group of wounded men trapped under an enemy bombardment. As he approached he was himself seriously wounded by a shrapnel wound to the head. Despite his own severe wounds, he carried one injured man to safety across 50 yards of fire-swept ground. He laid the man gently on the ground at the aid station, then collapsed himself and died moments later.[16]

The fanatical Japanese defense cost the Americans higher casualties than expected, but the defense itself was hopeless. Surrounded by either the enemy or physical obstacles, such as Manila Bay, there was no way out for any organized band of Japanese, although stragglers would be able to slip through American lines. Even as they cost General Beightler's division heavy losses, the Japanese themselves were further compressed when the 1st Cavalry Division crossed the Pasig River near the Philippine Racing Club. The leading 8th Cavalry elements crossed on the evening of February 9, and the rest of the regiment was safely across by dawn the next day. There was no opposition in the landing area but mines slowed the advance. Patrols established contact with the 37th Infantry Division near the Paco Railroad Station. The two bridgeheads of the XIV Corps were now one. The 5th Cavalry secured the Makati Electrical Power substation against no opposition, although they were harassed by fire coming from across the river at Fort McKinley. That same day, XIV Corps was assigned the 11th Airborne Division to add to its troop strength. With this addition, XIV Corps now had the enemy within Manila cut off from retreat or reinforcement.

CHAPTER 8

Intramuros, the Walled City

Admiral Iwabuchi was particularly concerned when the XIV Corps crossed the Pasig River on February 9. He decided that his positions within Manila had succumbed far more rapidly than expected. His losses had been severe. Perhaps it was time to order his men out of Manila. While contemplating this move, he moved his headquarters to Fort McKinley, probably hoping to direct his troops' withdrawal from that point.

Just as Admiral Iwabuchi was moving his headquarters, his *Imperial Japanese Army* counterpart, General Yokoyama at *Shimbu Group* headquarters, became aware of the situation within Manila. Determined to support the defenders of Manila, General Yokoyama prepared to counterattack. However, the general had little information on the true situation within Manila, and what he had was often outdated. He believed, for example, that the American force within Manila was at the strength of one regiment, when in fact the bulk of two American divisions were engaged in and around the city. He hoped to isolate the American force while at the same time pulling the remnants of the *Manila Naval Defense Force* out of the city to reinforce his own *Shimbu Group* to the east. The counterattack was scheduled for the night of February 16–17. General Yokoyama ordered Admiral Iwabuchi to have his *Manila Naval Base Defense Force* hold its positions within the city until the counterattack could open a line of retreat for them. There was no plan to reinforce the Manila garrison, which General Yokoyama wanted to free to add to his own command. He also hoped that the counterattack would open a route for additional supplies to be moved out of Manila and added to his *Shimbu Group*'s reserves.

Communications between Admiral Iwabuchi and General Yokoyama continued to deteriorate significantly in the interim. Admiral Iwabuchi had changed his mind about the retreat and had returned to his headquarters in Manila on February 11 before he received word of General Yokoyama's planned counterattack. It took two more days, until February 13, before General Yokoyama learned enough about the situation within Manila to decide that his counterattack idea was impractical. He then ordered Admiral Iwabuchi to withdraw his forces without depending upon a counterattack by *Shimbu Group*. All of this had been monitored 125 miles to the north, at *Fourteenth Area Army Headquarters* at Baguio. General Yamashita voiced his displeasure to General Yokoyama on February 15, demanding to know why Admiral Iwabuchi had returned to Manila and ordering General Yokoyama to get all Japanese forces out of the city immediately. Again, two days elapsed before Admiral Iwabuchi received a copy of General Yamashita's orders and General Yokoyama's instructions to abandon Manila. By that time, it was too late, for XIV Corps had the city surrounded and all routes of retreat were blocked. Admiral Iwabuchi made no attempt to break out of Manila, and General Yokoyama's planned counterattack failed.

That counterattack was organized in two columns. To the north, two battalions of the *31st Infantry Regiment, 8th Division*, reinforced with two provisional infantry battalions of the *105th Division* were to cross the Marikina River[1] out of the *Shimbu Group*'s defensive area and seize the Novaliches Dam and Route 3 north of Manila. To the south, three provisional infantry battalions of *Kobayashi Force*—formerly titled the *Manila Defense Force*—were to also cross the Marikina River and seize the Balara Water Filters and unite with the northern force at Grace Park in Manila. The attack began on February 15 and lasted until the 18th.

While the Japanese planned, General Krueger had continued to push forward troops to support the main action within Manila. One such unit was the 112th Cavalry RCT, an independent non-divisional unit. This former Texas National Guard outfit—now despite its designation as "cavalry" operating as an infantry unit—had earlier fought in New Guinea and Leyte. After relieving the 12th Cavalry Regiment of the 1st Cavalry Division along the XIV Corps line of communications at Novaliches, the Texas cavalrymen fought off the *Shimbu Group*'s attack for three days, before the Japanese conceded defeat and withdrew. The Japanese left behind 300 dead, while the cavalrymen lost two killed and 32 wounded. The disparity in losses stems from the series of uncoordinated attacks launched by the inexperienced Japanese against the veteran Americans. The Japanese withdrew in disorder.

The southern attack wing launched by the *Kobayashi Force* was turned back in a day. American artillery caught this group crossing the Marikina River and decimated it. Although piecemeal attacks continued for another two days against the 7th and 8th Cavalry Regiments, the main power of the Japanese counterattack had been lost. Another 650 enemy dead were counted, while the 2nd Cavalry Brigade lost 15 killed and 50 wounded. General Yokoyama did not appear to be particularly disappointed by the failure of his counterattack. He had little hope for success since communications from Admiral Iwabuchi had made it clear that he had no intention of abandoning Manila. The admiral informed General Yokoyama on February 17, the second day of the attack, that he believed that withdrawal of his forces was no longer possible. In any case, he went on, he still firmly believed that the defense of Manila was of utmost importance to Japan. He refused to move his headquarters out of the city nor allow any portion of his force to withdraw, believing that such a withdrawal would lead to a rapid annihilation of his force.

Despite repeated orders from General Yokoyama, on February 19 and 21, Admiral Iwabuchi prohibited retreat from Manila. General Yokoyama's suggestions that a retirement by small groups over a period of nights would reduce losses, based upon past successful Japanese experience, was ignored. By February 23 all communications between Admiral Iwabuchi and the *Shimbu Group* ceased. The battle for Manila would continue.

While the Japanese argued, the Americans continued fighting. In the zone of the 1st Cavalry Division the 2nd Brigade Reconnaissance Platoon was guarding an important road junction when a communications jeep drove up only to be caught by enemy fire in an exposed position. Three men were trapped with the vehicle. Private First Class Melvin H. Amundson, of Wisconsin, took in the situation and crawled forward using what little cover was available. He instructed the men on how to withdraw to safety and was about to follow them when he realized that the communications equipment in the jeep would aid the enemy if captured intact. On his own initiative, he returned to the jeep, jumped in, and turned it around. Racing to safety under enemy fire, he successfully rescued the jeep and its vital equipment, earning himself a Silver Star.[2]

Technical Sergeant Andrew J. Bridgewater, of Arkansas, was leading a patrol of the division's 302nd Reconnaissance Troop deep behind enemy lines on February 12 when they observed a U.S. Marine aircraft crash several hundred yards away. They also spotted an enemy patrol hurrying to the crash site. Sergeant Bridgewater saw the two Marine Corps pilots extricate themselves from the crash, but also noted that they were disoriented and unfamiliar with their surroundings. Making a split-second decision, he stepped out of his concealed hideout and shouted to the Marines to come to him. They did so immediately, but the Japanese saw him as well. Before they could arrive, Sergeant Bridgewater and his observation post team changed locations and went into hiding. By the next day there were enemy troops all over the area searching for him and his team as well as the Marine pilots. When his hiding place was compromised, Sergeant Bridgewater led his team and the pilots back to safety within American lines.[3]

During the counterattacks of the *Shimbu Group* on February 16, a group of engineers was trapped behind enemy lines. A patrol from the 640th Tank Destroyer Battalion was dispatched to their rescue. The group was led by First Lieutenant Rupert K. Allsup in an armored car. Accompanying the armored car was a machine-gun jeep manned by Private First Class Hugo Ruede of South Dakota and Private First Class Earl C. Wrights of Pennsylvania. As they approached the ambush site, enemy guns opened fire, killing Lieutenant Allsup. Privat First Class Ruede immediately assumed command, moving his jeep forward and taking the enemy under fire. Under cover of Pfc Ruede's machine gun, the armored car withdrew. Despite his own wounds, Pfc Wrights assisted in manning the jeep's machine gun, firing over 2,000 rounds at the enemy. The jeep was covered with bullet holes from front to back. So hot did the jeep machine gun become that it fired automatically, without control. When it became clear that there was nothing more they could do, Pfc Ruede ordered Pfc Wrights to safety. He remained behind to reload the machine gun, directed it against the enemy, and then fired it, then left it firing automatically while he made his own withdrawal. The diversion created by the courageous battle of Pfc Ruede and Pfc Wrights allowed the engineers to safely escape.[4]

Meanwhile, Admiral Iwabuchi's retreat possibilities had been dashed by the arrival of General Swing's 11th Airborne Division at the northwest sector of Laguna de Bay. They had to fight most of the way. After securing Tagaytay Ridge, the division had moved north, encountering Japanese opposition along the way. In one instance, Captain Steve Cavanaugh's Company D, 511th Parachute Infantry Regiment, were following the leading scouts down Route 17 when they were halted by one of the scouts near the town of Imus. The scout informed Captain Cavanaugh that the bridge across the Imus River had been destroyed but that they had located a second bridge west of the road. However, that bridge was protected by a group of Japanese sheltering in an old Spanish barracks of stone construction surrounded by a stone wall.

Captain Cavanaugh was ordered to secure the bridge by Lieutenant Colonel Frank ("Hacksaw") Holcomb, the division's operations officer, who was accompanying the leading troops. As Company D moved into position, Colonel Holcomb assigned Battery A, 674th Glider Field Artillery Battalion, and two M8 self-propelled cannons[5] to support the attack. Assisted by their own mortars and the attached artillery, Company D attacked and breached the stone wall but could not get into the Japanese-held building. The artillery and cannons were fired extensively but seemed to have no effect on the building's occupants.

Observing all this, Technical Sergeant Robert C. Steele of Company D saw that no amount of artillery pounding with the small M8s and 75mm guns would penetrate the thick stone walls. Taking matters into his own hands, he ordered his platoon to provide cover fire while he climbed up to the building's roof under enemy fire. Once on top, he punched a hole in the roof with an ax he had brought along and then poured gasoline down into the building. Next he tossed in a white phosphorous grenade to start a blazing inferno. Japanese troops began to rush out of the burning building, only to be cut down by Captain Cavanaugh's troopers. Learning that two of the enemy were still in the building and resisting, Technical Sergeant Steele entered that inferno and eliminated the last of the opposition. For his actions, Sergeant Steele was awarded a Distinguished Service Cross.[6]

General Eichelberger and General Swing were anxious to reach Manila. To accomplish this with the best possible speed, the 11th Airborne Division became momentarily motorized, in a manner of speaking. Every vehicle the division quartermaster, Lieutenant Colonel John Conable, could lay his hands on was added to the Airborne's motor column. The 408th Quartermaster Company carried the division forward, adding vehicles as they went. "We had a supply line 69 miles long and 50 to 200 yards wide," recalled Colonel Conable.[7] He went on to explain, "In addition to our own truck drivers, we had most of the division band as drivers."[8] The division's chemical warfare officer, First Lieutenant Kenneth Murphy, became the wagon master, leading each convoy in a jeep to discover ambushes before they caught the convoys under fire. At the end of each run, Lieutenant Murphy would check each driver, to see if they were alert enough for another run. Those that appeared exhausted could sleep in a designated area at each end of the convoy route. Most drivers averaged a 19-hour day. The 11th Airborne Division was determined to get to Manila.

Not all the troopers rode forward. Colonel Edward H. Lahti's 511th Parachute Infantry walked much of the way. Lieutenant Colonel Henry Burgess and his 1st Battalion marched the entire way from Tagaytay to Paranaque, some 36 miles. He recalled, "As we made the last few miles, we received many greetings, fresh fruit, and young men offering to help carry our packs and ammunition, which was a godsend. One older woman ran out to a trooper in front of me, threw her arms around him and said, 'Thank god you are here.' His reply was, 'Lady, I would have been here a year ago if it hadn't been for that damn basic training.'"[9]

The advance of the 11th Airborne Division to Manila had cut off the *Southern Force's Abe Battalion* near Mabato Point on the northwest shore of Laguna de Bay. In the four days between February 14 and 18, a battalion of guerillas led by Major John D. Vanderpool, a special agent of Southwest Pacific General Headquarters, contained the Japanese until the 11th Airborne Division sent three infantry battalions, supported by artillery and tank destroyers with Marine Corps air support, to finally eliminate the enemy battalion, which lost 750 men. The cost to the 11th Airborne Division was 10 killed and 50 wounded. Once again, this disparity was due to a skillful use of artillery, air support, and firepower.

While the *Abe Battalion* stood and died at its post, the *4th Naval Battalion* was less dogmatic. Cut off at Fort McKinley when the 5th and 12th Cavalry Regiments united at Manila Bay, the Japanese withdrew as the 1st Cavalry Division and the 11th Airborne Division cleared that area. Whether this was with the permission of Admiral Iwabuchi is unknown. Joined by elements of the *3rd Naval Battalion*, which had defended Nichols Field, the combined group would withdraw to the *Shimbu Group* during the night of February 17–18, bringing some 1,400 additional troops to General Yokoyama.

The 11th Airborne Division had reached the Parañaque River by February 4, barely three miles from the Manila city limits. They were faced by the *3rd Naval Battalion* reinforced with elements of the *1st Naval Battalion*, along with a random grouping of artillery, holding what the Americans labeled the Genko Line. This defense included long-established concrete pillboxes which had been covered with vegetation and dirt, making them difficult to see from any distance. Machine guns were carefully concealed in trees. Northeast of Parañaque lay Nichols Field, a former

U.S. Army Air Force base recently utilized by the *Japanese Naval Air Service*. Here dozens of antiaircraft guns of various calibers, equally well camouflaged, defended the abandoned base. All approaches were over flat, fully exposed terrain. Northeast of Nichols Field lay Neilson Field, itself lightly defended but covered by elements of the *4th Naval Battalion* holding Fort McKinley.

As the troopers approached Manila, they encountered a flood of refugees. Lieutenant Colonel Henry Burgess, whose 1st Battalion, 511th Parachute Infantry, was in division reserve, remembered the scenes all too well. "Many nursing women had been bayonetted in their breasts, some had the tendons in the back of their necks severed by sabers and could no longer hold their heads up. Small children and babies had been bayonetted ... We had been admonished to keep our medical supplies for ourselves, and not to help others. Of course, we couldn't, and didn't refuse them assistance."[10]

While the 511th Parachute Infantry moved into Manila, Colonel Robert H. Soule's 188th Glider Infantry Regiment, reinforced with Lieutenant Colonel Norman Tipton's 2nd Battalion, 187th Glider Infantry Regiment, were directed against Nichols Field. Beginning February 7, the attack gained little ground. Heavy field artillery, mortars, and machine guns slowed the attack to a crawl. That evening the Japanese counterattacked, during which "the Japs tried to enter our positions by boat drifting down the Parañaque River past the bridge which marked the front line. Filipinos who had carried the wounded awoke the personnel along the dike and in the command post. Fire was withheld to almost point-blank range."[11] The counterattack failed.

The 11th Airborne Division was transferred on February 10 from the Eighth Army to Sixth Army's XIV Corps, placing the units fighting for Manila under one tactical command. General Griswold welcomed his new troops and directed them to continue to seize Nichols Field and Fort McKinley. General Swing, having cleared his assigned portion of the Manila suburbs, turned his last regiment, the 511th Parachute Infantry, east to join the attack on Nichols Field. But little changed. The fighting remained as difficult as ever. When First Lieutenant Henry G. Hynds led his platoon of Company A, 188th Glider Infantry, forward on February 10, they managed to seize a minor elevation, giving the Americans a slight height advantage. The Japanese immediately contested this small advance with machine guns on the ridge's reverse slope. One man was killed and three others, including Lieutenant Hynds, were wounded. Despite his own wounds, Lieutenant Hynds pulled the other wounded men to safety. Then, despite being under direct flat trajectory antiaircraft fire, he went out into the open again to rescue additional wounded men. Over the next two days, Lieutenant Hynds led his platoon defending against two banzai charges. During one attack, enemy fire killed one man and wounded three others, opening a gap in his lines. Despite his wounds, which left him physically weak, Lieutenant Hynds personally filled the gap and prevented an enemy breakthrough. For his actions, he would receive a Distinguished Service Cross.[12]

The vicious battles for Nichols Field and Fort McKinley continued. Major Charles P. Loeper took command of the 1st Battalion, 188th Glider Infantry. So intense were the battles that he soon found himself leading the forward elements of his battalion and was killed in action within days of assuming command. Suicidal banzai attacks repeatedly hit the 2nd Battalion, 511th Parachute Infantry, breaking their lines and overrunning the battalion command post. One survivor was forced to lie beneath the body of a fellow soldier throughout the night, until the Japanese had been driven off. So intense was the battle that the division historian would write, "The Japanese defended Nichols Field as if the Emperor's Palace itself were sitting on the center runway."[13] One company commander, awed by the powerful weapons used by the Japanese to defend the Genko Line, sent a message to the division's command post which read, "Tell Halsey to stop looking for the Jap Fleet. It's dug in on Nichols Field."[14]

General Griswold assigned the massive guns of the XIV Corps' artillery to support the paratroopers, and a new attack on February 12 made some excellent progress. By dark, most of the field had been overrun by the paratroopers and the next day was spent mopping up. But Nichols Field was far from ready to support Allied air forces. Its runways were still mined and heavily pitted and there was the occasional artillery fire from nearby Fort McKinley. With their last objective during the battle for Manila taken, General Swing could take stock of his losses. Since landing at Nasugbu, his division had suffered more than 900 casualties, the majority at Nichols Field. Of these, about 170 men had been killed and 750 wounded. The division now turned to mopping up, counting over 3,000 enemy dead before clearing Fort McKinley and Cavite.

The battles on the outskirts of Manila changed the situation within the city but little. By February 12, Admiral Iwabuchi had lost most of the *1st Naval Battalion* at Provisor Island, and the *2nd Provisional Infantry Battalion* had been decimated by the 1st Cavalry and 37th Infantry Divisions along the Pasig River. The *2nd Naval Battalion* had lost heavily to the 1st Cavalry and 11th Airborne Divisions south of the city. All other Japanese units within Manila had suffered casualties from American air, artillery, and mortar fire. The best intelligence estimates placed about 6,000 Japanese troops still within Manila under Admiral Iwabuchi's command by February 12. Most of his artillery had been destroyed, and his few remaining mortars were being destroyed one by one by American artillery. The defense was reduced to fighting with rifles, machine guns, and hand grenades. Yet there seemed no lack of fierce opposition as the Americans moved deeper into the city.

The battle degenerated into one of attrition. Advances were made street-by-street, sometimes room-by-room or yard-by-yard. Some days there was no progress at all. All pretense at "civilized warfare" vanished. The Japanese, now certain that their only fate was death at the hands of the enemy, unleashed all their basest instincts. Atrocities against civilians increased, and random destruction to no purpose abounded. Soon it was clear that Japanese command had disintegrated, and that control had been totally lost.

The Americans placed heavy reliance on their artillery, tanks, tank destroyers, mortars, and bazookas to knock out enemy opposition, but these could accomplish only so much. In the end, it came down to the individual rifleman to dig the enemy out of his holes, pillboxes, bunkers, and fortified buildings personally. Soon a system developed. Small groups of Americans worked their way from one building to the next, usually securing the roof first, and then working their way down the buildings one floor at a time. Using the stairways as their line of advance, line of supply, and route of evacuation, the American soldiers fought their way down one floor after the other. To avoid Japanese defenses along stairwells, they blew holes in walls and floors to gain access to the rear of the Japanese. Hand grenades, flamethrowers, and demolitions were used to finish the job. Although difficult and painful, these methods rarely resulted in high casualties. The 129th Infantry, for example, gained 150 yards on February 12 at a cost of five killed and 28 wounded. Not a particularly high loss for one day, but continued day after day, the drain on the front-line infantrymen was becoming severe.

It quickly became clear that the final Japanese stand within Manila would be within the famous Walled City of Intramuros. But getting there was no easy task. The 5th and 12th Cavalry Regiments turned north after reaching Manila Bay. The first obstacle was Harrison Park and the Rizal Memorial Stadium near the bay just inside the city limits. It took the cavalrymen two days of bitter fighting to clear these strongpoints. These battles destroyed the remnants of the *2nd Naval Battalion*, which lost 750 killed. The cavalrymen counted 40 killed and 315 wounded of their own.

By February 19, the 12th Cavalry was attacking the Army-Navy Club and Elks Club, site of Admiral Iwabuchi's former headquarters. Closely supported by artillery and tanks, the attack overran both strongpoints. Admiral Iwabuchi had abandoned his former headquarters and moved into Intramuros. The Manila Hotel was next. It took all day to clear out the many Japanese defenses built into the building's strong earthquake-proof structure. When it was over, the penthouse, General MacArthur's former residence, was found gutted. Its only occupant was a Japanese officer who had committed ritual suicide.

The 37th Infantry Division faced the identical problem, just with different names. For the 129th Infantry, after having secured Provisor Island, they were faced with a group of strongly built buildings known overall as the New Police Station. This area, at the corner of San Marcelino and Isaac Peral Streets, included a concrete shoe factory, the Manila Club, Santa Teresita College, and San Pablo Church. All approaches to these defenses lay across open ground covered by machine guns hidden within the buildings. The veteran 129th Infantry, who had fought on New Georgia,

Bougainville, and against the *Kembu Group*, would record these defenses as the most formidable encountered during the war. But it had to be taken, or else the entire drive to Intramuros would be stymied by a strong enemy enclave amid the 37th Infantry Division's lines. The initial attacks on February 13 were unsuccessful, despite heavy artillery fire. Artillery, as large as 155mm shells, had no effect on the concrete buildings of the New Post Office and the Manila Club. Point-blank fire from a tank destroyer's 76mm gun fared no better. High-explosive 105mm shells fired from the regiment's Cannon Company merely scratched the concrete exterior.

It wasn't until the next day, February 14, that progress was made. Supported closely by M4 Sherman tanks of the 754th Tank Battalion, Company B, 129th Infantry managed to gain access to the Manila Club. Nearby, Company A also entered the New Police Station through its broken windows, while a platoon of Company C entered the basement. Attacking before dawn, the Americans had surprised the Japanese, who had not yet manned their defensive posts. For the next several hours, however, the Japanese fought hard in the corridors and rooms of both buildings. In one case alone, the 129th Infantry was obliged to knock out three sandbagged machine guns before clearing that one room. Japanese began to drop hand grenades from the upper floors on the attacking Americans. Interior stairways were destroyed or well defended, forcing the infantrymen to eventually withdraw from the building. Company B, however, could retain its hold on the Manila Club.

The next three days were spent in smothering the Japanese with artillery, tank, tank destroyer, and cannon fire. Even in these days when no ground assault was launched, the 129th Infantry reported 16 men killed and 58 wounded. One man who fortunately did not make the casualty list was Private First Class Robert Hoyt of the 129th Infantry Intelligence Section. He was crawling through a hole in a fence to establish an observation post when his entrenching shovel fell between his legs and tripped him in an open field under enemy observation. Under enemy rifle and machine-gun fire, his first impulse was to get up and run, but before he could do that, he realized that he had lost his glasses. With poor eyesight without those glasses, he couldn't even see which way to run. Private First Class Hoyt then spent moments under fire on his hands and knees seeking his glasses. After four excruciating minutes, the glasses were found, and Pfc Hoyt dashed to safety. He had barely realized that he was safe before a battalion commander, who had observed the entire proceedings, came up to him and asked, "What in hell were you doing out there, looking for a cigarette butt?"[15]

The 129th Infantry was relieved by the 145th Infantry on February 18. They attacked and found themselves facing the same fierce resistance. Although the shoe factory and Santa Teresita College were seized, the attack on the New Police Station failed. The following day, heavily supported by artillery, tanks, tank destroyers, and self-propelled 105mm cannon, the attack resumed. San Pablo Church, whose fire supported the defenses of the New Police Station, was seized. This allowed

Company B, 145th Infantry, to gain access to the east wing of the New Police Station, but after a day-long fight the Americans were once again forced to withdraw. It wasn't until February 20, after the constant American support fires had all but demolished the building, that Company C, 145th Infantry, seized the New Post Office for good. It had taken eight days and cost the 37th Infantry Division 25 killed, 80 wounded, and three tanks destroyed.

The tale of the New Police Station can be repeated for every American regiment then fighting in Manila. There was the City Hall and General Post Office, the Philippine General Hospital and the University of the Philippines, Assumption College, Rizal Hall, the Manila Hotel, and many others, each of which slowed the American advance and inflicted casualties on the attacking battalions. But in the end the *Central Force* was destroyed, and the *5th Naval Battalion* was reduced to stragglers trying to get to Intramuros.

The Walled City of Intramuros was the last stand for the Japanese defenders of Manila. The battle would be one between American artillery, tanks, and tank destroyers against the medieval Spanish walls and buildings. It was known that the Japanese defenses were the strongest on the southern and eastern sides of the Walled City. This was because the Japanese expected the coming attack to be aimed at these defenses, a logical conclusion given the power of the American forces in those directions. Japanese defenders in the Legislative, Finance, and Agriculture buildings southeast of Intramuros could oppose any attack from those directions. American planners believed that a better approach would be from the west, where enemy defenses were weaker. But this approach had its own problems. The attack would first have to clear the South Port Area and would be attacking toward their own supporting artillery. The supporting artillery would have to be moved largely to the north and northeast to prevent "friendly fire" casualties.

To the northeast the ancient wall ended at the Government Mint, allowing direct access to the city. Only a low sea wall on the Pasig River obstructed direct access in this area, and Japanese defenses were believed to be weak here as well. Staff planners of the 37th Infantry Division decided that an amphibious assault here stood a good chance of success. Once again, close support by artillery, tanks, and tank destroyers was planned to ensure success. But General Beightler was aware that the Japanese had dug tunnels throughout the Walled City to communicate and move reserves from one threatened spot to another. Hoping to keep the Japanese off balance, the planners decided to make more than one assault. Accordingly, a second assault was planned for the area near the northwestern entrance to the Walled City, at Quezon Gate. But this area was known to be heavily defended with pillboxes inside the walls. The only way to deal with this opposition was to smother it with heavy artillery, blasting a way for the infantry to enter by blowing a hole in the thick Spanish walls just south of Quezon Gate. Enfilading fire from the three government buildings to the south would also threaten such an assault. These, too, would have to be neutralized by a heavy protective fire. As a final precaution, the 1st Cavalry Brigade was to position itself west and southwest of Intramuros to prevent the Japanese from escaping in that direction.

The planners considered a night attack. The wall along the north side of Intramuros had crumbled under American fire in many places, and it was believed that assault troops in LVTs would be able to crawl across the rubble and land their troops inside the Walled City. But the need to coordinate supporting fires—difficult if not impossible in darkness—and fear of having to conduct a night withdrawal, forced a decision for a daylight assault. After submitting his plans to General Griswold at XIV Corps, General Beightler ordered the assault to begin at 0830 hours on February 23.

Having concluded his planning, General Beightler began to think of reducing his casualties to a minimum. He considered calling in air support to raze the Walled City. Later he would deny that he thought of destroying the entire city, only that he wanted to destroy the northeast corner to allow the easiest access for his assault troops. Meanwhile, XIV Corps made several attempts to induce the Japanese defending Intramuros to surrender. XIV Corps also asked for the thousands of Filipino civilians known to being imprisoned within Intramuros by the Japanese to be released. Neither appeal was answered.

General Beightler's request for heavy air support was passed up to General Griswold, who in turn passed it on to General Krueger at Sixth Army headquarters. General MacArthur, who had severely restricted American air strikes within the city of Manila,[16] was queried. He peremptorily refused to sanction any air strikes on "a city occupied by a friendly and allied population."[17] Denied their air support, Generals Griswold and Beightler organized a massive artillery support program. This included a pre-assault bombardment lasting from February 17 to February 23 and would include indirect, direct, and point-blank fire by an assortment of artillery. Every corps and division artillery battalion would participate, from 240mm to 75mm and 105mm guns. Assisting were the 60mm, 81mm, and 4.2-inch chemical mortars. From the highest buildings on the American side of the river, machine guns would blanket Intramuros with fire. Whether or not it was intended, Intramuros was about to be razed.

The 8-inch howitzers of the 465th Field Artillery Battalion opened the bombardment by creating a breach in the wall along the east side. A 155mm howitzer of the 756th Field Artillery Battalion followed by blasting apart the Quezon Gate. Then the 8-inch howitzers pounded the rubble of the gate into an easy ramp into the city. Meanwhile, on the north, the 240mm guns of the 544th Field Artillery Battalion pounded the north wall and tried to knock out Japanese defenses near the Government Mint. The 76mm guns of the 637th Tank Destroyer Battalion blasted footholds on the South Quay and along the rubble at the riverbank to facilitate the infantry's passage. Firing into the city continued throughout the days of preparation.[18] In all, 7,487 high-explosive, 300 armor-piercing, and 116 smoke and white phosphorus shells were fired into the Walled City before the first American soldier set foot inside its walls.

The assault force at the Government Mint landing site was the 3rd Battalion, 129th Infantry, carried once again by the assault boats of the 117th Engineer (Combat) Battalion. The landing was unopposed, and the troops raced into Intramuros. The battalion directed its advance toward Fort Santiago and soon had established contact with the 2nd Battalion, 145th Infantry Regiment, which had charged across the open space from the Post Office to the north gate of the east wall, at Letran University. The Japanese seemed shocked by the powerful bombardment and resistance was slow in developing, but as the infantrymen moved deeper into the city, scattered resistance from single machine guns and riflemen began to appear. By noon, the 129th Infantrymen had reached the west wall of the city without suffering any casualties. Only 10 Japanese had been killed during the morning.

Both assault regiments found enemy resistance weak, and only at the Market Place did Company G, 145th Infantry, have a serious battle to overcome enemy resistance. Observing the assault, Brigadier General Clyde D. Eddleman, the Sixth Army operations officer, commented that this attack, "was one of the most beautifully conceived and perfectly executed plans I have ever known."[19] Even as the Americans advanced, their lungs were filled with the dust and smoke still saturating the air from the bombardment. Nevertheless, the 129th Infantry had reached and entered Fort Santiago, fighting hand-to-hand with the defenders until darkness. Here the Japanese sheltered in tunnels and recesses, tossing hand grenades at the attacking Americans. Staff Sergeant Maynard E. Mahan, of Company D, 129th Infantry, was taking a brief break behind a large concrete block and about to enjoy his last cigarette when a mortar shell landed nearby. A piece of flying metal clipped the cigarette from the sergeant's mouth without so much as scratching him. Instead of relief, Staff Sergeant Mahan immediately complained to a nearby buddy, "Damn it, that was my last butt."[20]

The 145th Infantry was briefly delayed when about 200 refugees came running out of the Del Monico Church on Gral Luna. These refugees had been held by the Japanese and consisted of women and children, nuns, and several priests. The males of the group had been separated and placed within Fort Santiago, where they were later found, murdered. Lieutenant Ross Linton and Sergeant Harold Riggs of the 37th Quartermaster Company were assigned to bring some trucks forward to remove the civilians. But access to Intramuros, with the battle still raging, was difficult. By the time Lieutenant Ross and Sergeant Riggs arrived, there were at least a thousand civilians at the pickup point. With the fighting close to the site, the trucks intended to pick up 200 civilians were filled with more than 1,000 and then quickly evacuated the battlefield. During the battle, an additional 1,000 civilians were evacuated, many by wounded 37th Infantry Division soldiers who were themselves being evacuated for medical treatment. By the end of the first day, much of the eastern half of Intramuros was in American hands, at a cost of five killed and 62 wounded.

The next day began with the Japanese, now clearly losing the fight, trying some deceptions. Several appeared wearing American uniforms and carrying American weapons, trying to move to new positions under American observation. Others put a white flag in the belfry of the Del Monico Church and then opened fire with rifles. But neither of these had any impact on the American advance. By the end of February 24, the city was largely cleared of the enemy, although many holdouts remained within the ruins. The 12th Cavalry Regiment moved swiftly through the port district, seized the Customs House, port area, and Engineer Island. The 3rd Battalion, 129th Infantry, spent the day using demolitions to eliminate the remaining enemy stragglers hidden in the rubble.

It was during the battle for the Customs House that Private First Class William J. Grabiarz distinguished himself. The soldier from Buffalo, New York, was acting as a scout with Troop E, 5th Cavalry, and leading his troop and some tanks down a Manila street when enemy machine-gun and rifle fire from concealed positions within the Customs House opened on the troop. The troop commander was struck down and the rest of the cavalrymen forced to shelter. Seeing his troop commander lying helpless in the open exposed to point-blank enemy fire, Pfc Grabiarz voluntarily ran out from behind a tank to carry him to safety. While doing so, however, he was himself severely wounded in the shoulder. Despite the intense pain of his wound and ignoring his buddies' cries to seek shelter for himself, Pfc Grabiarz continued to drag his wounded commander out of the enemy's range. When this proved impossible due to his wounds, Pfc Grabiarz covered the wounded officer with his own body to shield him from the enemy fire. As he did so, he called for a tank to move into position between him and the enemy. Before the tank could intervene, however, enemy fire struck Pfc Grabiarz again and again. After the tank finally reached position, it was found that although Pfc Grabiarz was mortally wounded, his selfless act had saved the life of his troop leader. His Medal of Honor was posthumously awarded.[21]

Although officially "mopping up," there remained one significant Japanese pocket within Manila. These were the Legislative, Finance, and Agricultural buildings which had been bypassed to clear the rest of Manila and Intramuros. These buildings were detached from all others and were in an open park area. Each was four stories and built strongly with concrete to make them earthquake proof. The only approach was across the open grounds of the surrounding park. Admiral Iwabuchi himself was headquartered in the Agricultural Building. He had perhaps 700 men left under his command. Defenses included several 37mm and 75mm guns along with the usual rifles, mortars, and machine guns.

To deal with these last holdouts, General Griswold organized an assault force consisting of the 1st Cavalry Brigade, the 637th Tank Destroyer Battalion, 716th Tank Battalion, 754th Tank Battalion, 82nd Chemical Mortar Battalion, and elements of the 37th Infantry Division. At first Generals Griswold and Beightler considered simply starving the Japanese out, but it was realized that this could take too much time when troops were needed elsewhere in the campaign. Instead, another two-day bombardment was organized using XIV Corps artillery, 37th Infantry Division artillery, and tank destroyers. Battery B, 136th Field Artillery Battalion, rolled their huge 155mm guns forward until they were placing direct fire on the buildings and were themselves under enemy fire from those same buildings. The 1st Cavalry Brigade began the ground attack against the Agriculture Building, while the 148th Infantry took on the other two strongholds.

The 5th Cavalry attacked three times on February 26, only to be repulsed each time. Once again, Battery B, 136th Field Artillery, came forward, and after an hour of bombardment, the 5th Cavalry attacked at midday and secured the building by nightfall. Nearby the 148th Infantry, supported by two platoons of Company B, 754th Tank Battalion, a platoon of the 117th Engineers, and Company A, 82nd Chemical Mortar Battalion, assaulted the other two buildings. Under cover of a smoke screen, the engineers cleared the mines leading to the two buildings. After two hours, the tanks rolled forward to attack earthen emplacements and other obstructions in front of the buildings.

The 1st Battalion, 148th Infantry, took up positions on February 25 preparatory to assaulting the enemy-held buildings. Complaints soon arrived from the 1st Cavalry Division that 155mm shells fired against the buildings were landing in the cavalry division's area. It was found that these heavy shells, fired at short range, were passing through the buildings and exploding within the cavalry division's sector. All fire was ceased until corrections could be made. That same evening a surrender appeal made by a Nisei interpreter assigned to the 37th Infantry Division was issued, but no reply was recorded.

The following day, the 148th Infantry crashed the gate at the Legislative Building, led by Company B. Initial opposition was slight and few Japanese encountered. Within an hour the company had secured the first floor except for a pillbox in the southwest corner. Under fire from Japanese firing up from the basement, Company B cleared the second and third floors. Flamethrowers eliminated the pillbox. Gasoline cans with thermite grenades attached eliminated other strongpoints. But Captain Ferris's men could not clear the building. They withdrew and called for more artillery. Another bombardment reduced a good part of the building to dust. In mid-afternoon Company B returned and began digging their way through the enemy defenses.

Once again, a leadership role was assumed by Sergeant Cleto Rodriguez, whom we have seen in action earlier at the Paco Railroad Station. Still carrying his BAR and now known by his buddies as a "one-man army," Sergeant Rodriguez went around to the rear of the building, instead of taking the obvious approach to the front. He found himself behind an enemy machine gun, which he knocked out. With the rest of his platoon behind him, the first floor was cleared. He then led the way up the stairs to the second floor, killing a Japanese who tossed a grenade which wounded him in the face. For this and subsequent actions during the Legislative Building battles, Sergeant Rodriguez added a Silver Star to his decorations. By the day's end, the building was cleared except for the tunnels and dugouts in the basement. Six Americans had been killed and 28 wounded.

The 3rd Battalion, 148th Infantry, took the Finance Building. Attacking on March 2, the battalion pounded the building as the others had been and the standard surrender appeal sent. Unusually, however, this time the surrender appeal resulted in the actual surrender of 22 Japanese, who emerged under a white flag. Another white flag flew from the roof, indicating that others wanted to surrender, but heavy fire from within the building prevented any acceptance of surrender. As the fight continued other white flags appeared, and some additional Japanese, including an officer, surrendered successfully while others were shot down by their more determined comrades. Repeated attempts by the replacement 1st Battalion, 148th Infantry, to clear the building met strong resistance, and this in turn was answered by more artillery, until by mid-afternoon the Americans had secured the first floor. By evening the building was secured, although enemy ammunition was still exploding from the many fires still blazing within it. On March 3, the last remaining Japanese were killed atop the elevator in the elevator shaft. The battle for Manila was over.

The *Manila Base Defense Force* was destroyed. About 16,000 Japanese died in and around Manila during the battle. Of these about 12,500 were Admiral Iwabuchi's men, while another 3,500 were members of the *Shimbu Group* defending the suburbs and participating in the abortive counterattack of late February. The city itself was a wreck, much of it destroyed and beyond repair. Public transportation no longer existed, and the water supply and sewage systems needed significant repair. There was no electricity. Most streets needed to be rebuilt and one-third of the city's bridges had been destroyed. Most public, and many private, buildings were destroyed. Manila would have to be rebuilt from scratch.

The battle for Manila in February and March 1945 cost the U.S. Army 1,010 killed in action and 5,565 wounded in action.[22] Tens of thousands of civilians had also been victims before, during, and after the battle. Yet the battle for Manila was just one aspect of a campaign that would continue to inflict casualties on both sides for months to come.

CHAPTER 9

The Shimbu Group

The conquest of Manila did not provide the Americans with unfettered control of the essential Manila Bay. That body of water held several fortified islands with which the Americans were quite familiar from their time governing the Philippines in the first half of the 19th century. These islands included Corregidor, Caballo, Carabao, and El Fraile. Of these the only significant threat to unobstructed Allied use of Manila Bay was the fortified island of Corregidor, which had been defended by the American and Filipino forces for several months before the surrender of the Philippines in May 1942.

The situation in 1945 was quite different than that of 1942. The Japanese, just as they had decided not to stand in Bataan, had no significant plan for these islands. Although the *Shimbu Group* had staffed these islands, they were not a part of any integrated defense, nor were they intended to do more than defend to the death, thus delaying American use of Manila Bay. In effect, these island garrisons were isolated outposts with no chance of relief or escape. The intent was merely to harass and delay the American development of the Philippines as a base from which to attack Japan.

Once again General MacArthur's intelligence service failed him. They estimated the Corregidor garrison at one-sixth of its actual strength and based all plans on that faulty estimate. Guessing that a mere 850 Japanese troops garrisoned the island, they would find that in fact there were over 5,000 there, nearly all naval troops. Then, anxious to make "proper" use of its available airborne troops, the plan involved both an airborne drop on the island combined with an amphibious assault. Little account was taken of the enemy defenses, nor the terrain on which the troopers would be dropped. In addition, experience had shown that coordinating an airborne and amphibious operation against the same target was fraught with difficulties. Yet an airborne attack did promise to include the element of surprise, as the island was an unlikely airborne target. It was hoped that an airborne attack would divert some of the enemy fire from the more exposed amphibious assault troops.[1] In addition, the use of paratroopers may have been intended for "dramatic effect," to redeem the defeat suffered there by the Allies in 1942.

Selected for the airborne phase of the operation was the separate 503rd Parachute Infantry RCT. The 503rd Parachute Infantry Regiment had been organized at Fort Benning, Georgia, in February 1942. The regiment trained at Fort Bragg before sailing, less its 2nd Battalion, for the Pacific in October 1942.[2] There it found itself the only airborne unit in the entire Southwest Pacific Theater of Operations. In September, the regiment took part in the unopposed occupation of Nadzab in New Guinea, dropping into the jungles despite the unfavorable terrain. After returning to Australia, the regiment next dropped on the offshore New Guinea island of Noemfoor. Here again, the landing ground was unsuitable, a hard-surfaced runway littered with vehicles and other obstacles. The regiment suffered severe jump casualties but participated in the conquest of the island for the next several weeks. The regiment next landed on Leyte in mid-November as a reserve force. Then came the amphibious seizures of Mindoro and Palauan Islands in the Philippines. It had less than a month to prepare for the Corregidor operation, during which it was reorganized into a regimental combat team (RCT), adding Company C, 161st Airborne Engineer Battalion, and the 462nd Parachute Field Artillery Battalion to the command.

Corregidor is an island shaped like a tadpole, with a large "head" and a tail slowly tapering into the sea. It is three and a half miles long and half a mile wide at its widest point. Near the larger end Malinta Hill rises to 350 feet while the ground drops away precipitously. Indeed, the island was full of potential obstructions to paratroops. The amphibious troops, infantrymen of the 34th Infantry Regiment, 24th Infantry Division, would land near the tail while the troopers were landing above them. Colonel George M. Jones,[3] the commander of the 503rd RCT, made a personal aerial reconnaissance and urged a drop onto a prewar landing strip known as Kindley Field, at the central part of the tail. General Krueger overruled the suggestion, feeling that a drop onto the island's tail would not separate the Japanese defenders sufficiently. Instead, he ordered Colonel Jones to drop on a parade ground and golf course near the top of Malinta Hill, thereby trapping the Japanese garrison between a "high" and "low" attack. The date of the attack was set for February 16.

The paratroopers boarded the C-47 transport aircraft of Colonel John Lackey's 317th Troop Carrier Group which formed two columns of planes, one passing over each drop zone. Even though the aircraft were flying southwest to northeast to allow the most time over the island, allowing more paratroopers to jump at the same time, the paratroopers could still only land fewer than 10 at a time from each plane. After repeated runs over the island to drop all its paratroopers, the aircraft would have to return to Mindanao, load the second lift, and return. It would take over an hour just to land 1,000 troopers, violating the principle of mass. But there was no other choice. The aircraft could not drop the second lift until five hours after the first. Given the situation, planners estimated jump casualties at 20 percent. Colonel Jones thought they could run as high as 50 percent. Casualty estimates for the 34th Infantry Regiment ran nearly as high.

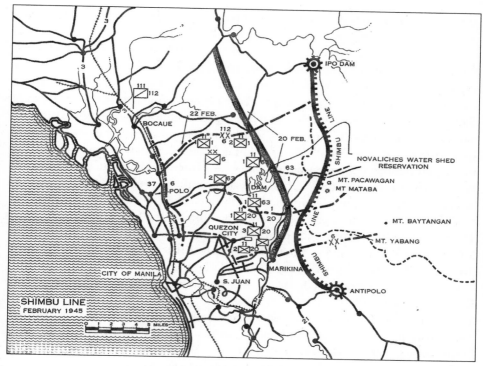

The *Shimbu Group* Line North of Manila

Robert Ross Smith. *U.S. Army in World War II. The War in The Pacific. Triumph in the Philippines.* Washington, D.C. Center of Military History. 1984. Map section.

The Japanese knew that the Americans were coming. Clearly, they would not be permitted to remain undisturbed on their islands in Manila Bay and allowed to harass Allied shipping using the port of Manila. These defenders were known as the *Manila Bay Entrance Force* under the command of Captain Akira Itagaki, *Imperial Japanese Navy*. Captain Itagaki's immediate superior was Admiral Iwabuchi, then fighting in Manila. At his headquarters on Corregidor, Captain Itagaki expected an American attack any day. What he did not expect, however, was an airborne assault. Much of his defenses were sited to defend against an amphibious attack somewhere on the island's "tail," where the Japanese had themselves landed in 1942. A reserve force was sheltered at Malinta Hill to counterattack any such landing.

Allied air forces had been bombing Corregidor since January 22, when General MacArthur designated it as a target. Both the Fifth and Thirteenth U.S. Army Air Forces had dropped bombs totaling 3,125 tons of explosives on the island. On the morning of February 16, B-24 and B-25 bombers concentrated on the known and suspected Japanese gun positions on the island, while A-10 light bombers bombed and strafed anything which caught their attention. Even tiny Caballo Island, a mile to the south of Corregidor, was hit by the air bombardment.[4]

The Allied naval forces had been shelling the island since February 13 and sweeping for mines as a prelude to the seizure of Mariveles, previously discussed. Rear Admiral Russell S. Berkey's (USNA, 1918) Task Group 77.3 concentrated its attention on the north coast of Corregidor, where the Japanese seemed to have concentrated their defenses. The light cruisers USS *Phoenix* (CL-46), USS *Montpelier* (CL-57), and USS *Denver* (CL-58), supported by several destroyers, pounded Corregidor and the fortified islands in Manila Bay, including El Fraile, Carabao, and Caballo. But this action frustrated Admiral Berkey, since he wanted the Japanese to respond and reveal their heavier weapons, so he could destroy them. "Juicy targets were placed under the Nip's nose, but he declined to take a crack at them."[5]

But the Japanese did not take this beating quietly. The following day, February 14, return fire from Corregidor damaged two destroyers and so severely damaged a minesweeper that it had to be sunk. Concerned that the Japanese still had such powerful weapons at their disposal, Admiral Kinkaid, commanding Seventh U.S. Fleet, added three heavy cruisers and five more destroyers to the bombardment force on February 15.

The naval forces shifted their attention to the south side of the island on February 16, preparing the way for the amphibious assault by the 3rd Battalion, 34th Infantry. Patrol Torpedo (PT) boats were stationed along the flight path of the paratroopers to rescue those who missed the island and fell into the bay. Even as the first C-47 aircraft came into sight, the A-20 aircraft intensified their bombing and strafing of Corregidor and Caballo.[6]

The initial assault force was organized under the title "Rock Force" and consisted of the 503rd Parachute RCT plus the 3rd Battalion, 34th Infantry Regiment. Colonel Jones commanded Rock Force and once on the ground would report to General Hall's XI Corps, Sixth Army. After a breakfast of dehydrated eggs and coffee, Lieutenant Colonel John R. Erickson's 3rd Battalion, 503rd Parachute Infantry's drop began at 0833 hours on February 16 against no immediate ground opposition. Joined by Battery A, 462nd Field Artillery Battalion, and Company C, 161st Parachute Engineer Battalion, the drop was observed by Colonel Jones flying overhead. Battery D, 462nd Parachute Field Artillery Battalion, also dropped a platoon armed with heavy machine guns. Once again, as he had at Noemfoor, Colonel Jones sustained serious jump injuries upon landing, but remained in command.

Captain Itagaki, who had rushed to the beach to observe the amphibious assault coming from Bataan, was caught in the open by paratroopers who wiped out his command group, leaving the *Manila Bay Entrance Force* leaderless. For the Japanese troops on Corregidor, the repeated passes by the American planes dropping paratroopers in white, red, yellow, and camouflaged parachutes inflated their estimate of the assault force, deceiving them into believing that some 8,000 paratroopers had landed, when in fact no more than 1,000 were on the island. This caused them to hesitate in organizing a counterattack, and further confusion resulted from the total disruption of their communications.

As expected, not all the paratroopers landed on the island. One PT boat, *PT 376* under the command of Lieutenant (j.g.) John A. Mapp, rescued seven who had been blown past the island and landed in the bay. Those that did land correctly immediately set about their first task—to secure and hold the drop zones for the second lift. They were to clear all enemy from the area, known as "Topside," and provide fire support for the incoming amphibious assault of Lieutenant Colonel Postlethwait's 3rd Battalion, 34th Infantry.[7] The drop zones were cleared, secured, and heavy machine guns sited to cover the landing of the infantry within the first hour.

Colonel Postlethwait's battalion had come to Mariveles with the 151st Infantry Regiment during the Bataan clearing operations. Climbing aboard 25 LCMs manned by soldiers of the 592nd Engineer Boat and Shore Regiment, the battalion circled around to the west end of Corregidor and landed on the beach at 1028 hours, two minutes ahead of schedule. Despite earlier concerns, there was no opposition at the beach. But as the follow-up waves landed, Japanese machine-gun fire began to impact the area. Supporting vehicles detonated several mines as they came ashore, and a tank of the 603rd Tank Company, a self-propelled cannon of the regimental Cannon Company, and an antitank gun of the regimental Antitank Company were destroyed. But despite the increasing opposition, Companies K and L, 34th Infantry, surged forward and reached the top of Malinta Hill within the hour. Casualties to the infantry were two men killed and six wounded. The paratroopers suffered more, with 25 percent (280) jump casualties or mis-dropped troopers. This was attributed to a higher jump altitude than originally planned and a faster wind than normally accepted during parachute operations.

The Japanese were caught completely off guard. The heavy pre-invasion bombardment, the continuing air attacks until the arrival of the paratroopers, and the airborne assault completely threw off the Japanese defenses. Combined with the early loss of their commander, the remaining Japanese were left to their own devices. By the time junior officers tried to organize a defense, the Americans were in control of all their initial objectives and were prepared to clear the island.[8]

The second lift arrived shortly after noon and dropped Major Lawton B. Caskey's 2nd Battalion, 503rd Parachute Infantry, and Battery B, 462nd Parachute Field Artillery Battalion, along with the regiment's service and headquarters companies. This time the correct altitude was maintained throughout the jump and most troopers landed on the correct drop zones. Japanese automatic weapons fire opposed the jump but resulted in few casualties. Another 2,050 Americans were on "the Rock."

But as was their norm, the Japanese did not admit defeat. Heavy fire began to come against the drop zones from prewar coast defense batteries Cheney, Crockett, and Wheeler. To address this, Captain Henry W. Gibson of Battery B, 462nd

Parachute Field Artillery Battalion, disassembled a howitzer, carried it to the second floor of a ruined officer's quarters building, and then had his crew reassemble it. A parachute caught in debris blocked the gun's field of fire, so Private First Class John P. Prettyman attempted to remove it, but he was killed by enemy fire.[9] Despite this, the gun was able to fire and knock out several enemy automatic weapons from its vantage point. Major Arlis E. Kline, commanding officer of the 462nd Parachute Field Artillery, was another jump casualty, suffering a jaw separation in the landing, but like Colonel Jones, remained in command until medically evacuated and replaced by Major Melvin Knudson.

By the end of February 16, the 503rd Parachute Infantry could assess their condition and status. Two men had refused to jump, resulting in their being court martialed and dismissed from the paratroops. Three parachutes had failed to open. Eleven other men had died due to jump injuries. Fifty others had been wounded while they had been in the air. Another 210 troopers were injured, usually suffering from fractures or concussions. Casualties for February 16 were 21 killed, 267 wounded, and an unknown number missing. Many of these missing men were on Corregidor, hiding from the enemy. Wounded or injured paratroopers hid by themselves or were protecting injured buddies behind Japanese lines until they could escape or be rescued by an American advance. Many did not last long enough to be rescued, and as the American advance continued, their bodies were found.

As always in combat, the medical aid men were in the thick of the battle. One unusual instance on Corregidor involved Captain Emmet R. Spicer, a surgeon attached to the 462nd Parachute Field Artillery. He set up his aid station and then went to the RCT headquarters to report his position and status. In returning to his post, Captain Spicer came upon a trooper who had lost an eye. After treating the man's injuries, he sent him to the aid station. This scenario was repeated several times on Captain Spicer's journey back to his aid station until a Japanese sniper mortally wounded him. Incredibly, Captain Spicer sat down, although dying, and proceeded to write out his own medical tag, which was attached to all the wounded. After entering his name, rank, and serial number, he supplied the diagnosis, "gunshot wound, perforation left chest, severe, Corregidor, 16 February 1945."[10] A patrol later found his body, tag attached. He received a posthumous Silver Star for his life-saving efforts at the cost of his own.

Colonel Jones, evaluating the enemy resistance as slight and seeing no need for further jump casualties, cancelled the last drop and ordered his 1st Battalion, 503rd Parachute Infantry, to be brought to the island by sea. Major Robert A. Wood's battalion boarded transports and flew to San Marcelino Airfield near Subic Bay, dropping their pre-packaged supply and equipment bundles on Corregidor as they passed overhead. They then proceeded to Corregidor by boat from Luzon. During the equipment drop, 16 of the 42 transports were damaged by Japanese antiaircraft fire from Corregidor, proving the wisdom of Colonel Jones's decision to cancel the final drop.

With no place to go, and no intent of surrendering, the Japanese fought on within Corregidor. One typical action was repeated numerous times while the island was cleared. Private First Class Lloyd G. McCarter, from Washington State, had landed on February 16 and immediately raced across 30 yards of exposed ground to knock out an enemy machine gun with hand grenades. Two days later, he killed six enemy snipers while leading his platoon's advance. That night a strong Japanese counterattack hit his company's position. He volunteered to move to an advance exposed position to get a better view of the attackers. Repeated attacks came against his position, only to be repelled. Finally, only Pfc McCarter remained on his feet, unwounded. And still the Japanese attacked. Shouting encouragement to his wounded comrades around him and yelling defiance at the enemy, he continued to beat off attacks singlehanded. He repeatedly crawled back to American lines for more ammunition between assaults. He burned out one automatic rifle and acquired another, burned this one out as well, and grabbed an M-1 rifle. As dawn broke, the Japanese made one last desperate effort to overrun the Americans. Private First Class McCarter stood erect blazing away at the enemy. He was soon seriously wounded but refused to leave his position until he had directed others on the best avenue for the American counterattack.[11] He received his Medal of Honor from President Harry S. Truman at the White House the following year.

The Japanese continued to try to counterattack American positions and to infiltrate behind their lines, especially during darkness. This often required the Americans to clear the same defenses a second or third time—a dirty, trying business. Frustrated, the Japanese began to blow up their own positions and supply dumps. On February 19, they blew up an ammunition dump near Breakwater Point, killing 15 paratroopers who had unwittingly taken possession of a building directly over the hidden dump. After their last major counterattack had been halted by Pfc McCarter and his buddies, the Japanese made small banzai counterattacks between February 19 and 23.

The 3rd Battalion, 34th Infantry, had occupied Malinta Hill since the day of landing. Several small Japanese counterattacks had been beaten off over the next several days. In the interim, the infantrymen secured the roads and other access points to facilitate the evacuation of wounded and the transport of supplies. Numerous small caves were cleared out or sealed with explosives. On the night of February 21–22, a sudden deafening explosion rocked Malinta Hill. Flames shot out of tunnel entrances, rocks and debris flew through the air, fissures opened in the ground. Six men of Company A, 34th Infantry, were buried alive in the rubble. Subsequent investigation revealed that perhaps 2,000 Japanese had taken shelter under Malinta Hill. They planned a controlled explosion to prepare the way for a major counterattack, but that blast had gotten completely out of control, killing many of the hidden Japanese. Several hundred others managed to escape, while dozens of others were cut down by the 34th Infantrymen. Other Japanese, hidden around the island, thought the blast was some sort of signal, and many other explosions rocked the next few nights. The last such blast occurred at Monkey Point on February 26, killing 50 Americans and blowing an American tank 50 yards, killing all but one of the crew. The battle for Corregidor was over. The cost to the Americans had been 1,000 killed, wounded, injured, and missing.[12] The Japanese casualties were calculated at 4,500 killed, 20 captured, and 200 escaped.

Caballo Island was no real threat to the Americans, and so it was left idle until mid-March, when the 38th Infantry Division asked permission to reconnoiter the island. General Chase sent a platoon of the 2nd Battalion, 151st Infantry, then garrisoning Corregidor, in an LCM to investigate. They landed unopposed on the east end of the island and found a Japanese strongpoint at the center of the small island. General Chase scheduled an assault for March 27. After the usual bombing and naval bombardment, the 592nd Engineer Boat and Shore Regiment landed the 2nd Battalion against no opposition. The Japanese garrison, about 400 soldiers, was shell-shocked and hiding near the center of the island. A brief but fierce two-day battle cleared the island of all enemy opposition. One last group took shelter in prewar pits and tunnels from which they could fire on the Americans but the Americans could not reach them. Tanks could not depress their guns enough to be of help. Finally, engineers poured diesel oil into the tunnels and set it afire. The effort failed as there was not enough oil to cover the steep slopes within the tunnels. The 113th Engineer (Combat) Battalion then set up a pipeline to pump the oil uphill using assistance from the U.S. Navy. After 2,500 gallons of diesel fuel were pumped in and set alight, a huge flash fire erupted, followed by several explosions. Two more days of such treatment secured Caballo Island.

El Fraile Island was five miles south of Caballo. Originally a reef, the U.S. Army had turned it into what was termed a "concrete battleship" named Fort Drum. With walls up to 36 feet thick and covered by a concrete roof 20 feet thick, it was a formidable obstacle. It boasted four 14-inch guns and four 6-inch guns, which could present a serious threat to shipping. Japanese machine guns prevented access to the only entrance to Fort Drum. That the Japanese defended it was discovered in late February when a PT boat crew, believing the fortress abandoned, landed and tried to enter the fort. The 70-man Japanese garrison allowed the first Americans to enter before opening fire and killing one naval officer and wounding a second.

Fort Drum waited until April before the Americans got around to it. Once again, General Chase's 38th Infantry Division, still garrisoning the area, got the assignment. Taking the successful example of Caballo Island as their lead, the 113th Engineer (Combat) Battalion again prepared to feed oil down the ventilator shafts and set it afire. Company F, 151st Infantry, landed on the island and moved to cover all entrances and exits of Fort Drum. The engineers followed and set up their equipment, once again relying on the U.S. Navy for pumps and other support. Adding TNT charges to increase the damage, the engineers set a 30-minute fuse and departed. But as they did, rough seas broke the oil lines. Major Paul R. Lemasters, commanding 2nd Battalion, 151st Infantry, raced back to the island and cut the demolitions fuse. The engineers repaired the broken lines and resumed pumping.

Other than the occasional rifle shot, the Japanese within Fort Drum remained quiet. No apparent resistance to 3,000 gallons of fuel oil being pumped into their shelter appeared. The explosion, when it came, was disappointingly small and without many fireworks. The Army and Navy commanders on the scene were disappointed and discussing next steps when the fire reached the fort's ammunition magazine. A sudden deafening roar was followed by great clouds of smoke and fire reaching well into the sky. Steel plates and chunks of concrete flew hundreds of feet out into the bay. Smoke and flames poured from every vent and sally port at Fort Drum. It would be five days before the area cooled down enough for American infantry to enter the blasted fort, where they found the bodies of 69 Japanese. The cost to the Americans was one man wounded.

The last objective was the small island of Carabao, about a mile off the Ternate shore. Two days of bombardment were followed by an amphibious attack by the 1st Battalion, 151st Infantry. Other than a shell-shocked pig, there was no living thing on the island. Apparently, the garrison had managed to escape sometime before the assault. General Hall at XI Corps could now report that the entrance to Manila Bay was secured.

While Manila Bay was being cleared, General Krueger turned his attention to the two remaining enemy groups on Luzon. With the Central Plain, Clark and Nichols Fields, and Manila, along with Manila Bay, now secured, his initial objectives had all been taken. Yet none of these could be considered secured when tens of thousands of enemy troops were still in organized groups within striking distance from these objectives. The necessity of securing his initial objectives had delayed any efforts against the two groups, the *Shobu Group* in the north, and the *Shimbu Group* to the east. But in February, Sixth Army began to organize for the drives against the two largest groups of enemy troops on Luzon. General Swift's I Corps was still positioned along the northern edge of the Central Plain and was poised to attack north against General Yamashita's *Shobu Group*. There was some anxiety among Sixth Army planners that if they delayed the attack for too long against General Yamashita, his forces would build formidable defenses that would cost Sixth Army dearly in casualties and time. On the other hand, the essential security of the Manila area could not be ensured until General Griswold's XIV Corps could at least pin down General Yokoyama's *Shimbu Group* in the mountains northeast of Manila and then destroy it. This latter concern was made more ominous since that area controlled much of Manila's water supply.

General Krueger had known during the planning stages for the Luzon campaign that his Sixth Army would not have sufficient resources to undertake two offensives at the same time. Now, he could not launch I Corps to the north without strengthening it with divisions pulled from XIV and XI Corps, which in turn weakened those units to the point that they could not drive out their enemy opponents. His plan called for as many as six divisions for I Corps when it attacked north, but there were not six divisions yet available. He counted on reinforcement units to add the necessary power to his attacks, plus the fact that he expected to retain all the combat divisions then on Luzon as well as those scheduled to reinforce his Sixth Army in the coming weeks.

But that was not to be. General MacArthur, relying on inaccurate intelligence estimates, soon decided that Sixth Army could clear the important strategic objectives with less strength than originally planned. He further decided that once driven into the mountains, the *Shobu* and *Shimbu Groups* would have assumed a secondary importance. In a letter to General Krueger on February 5, 1945, he wrote, "It is possible that the destruction of enemy forces in the mountains of north and east Luzon will be time consuming because the nature of the terrain will probably channelize operations and limit development of full power. Initially, hostile forces should be driven into the mountains, contained and weakened, and our principal effort devoted to areas where greater power may be applied." General MacArthur preferred to secure the Allied shipping lanes through the Philippines by clearing the Southern Philippines using General Eichelberger's Eighth Army. But that army needed troops, and some of them would come from General Krueger's Sixth Army on Luzon.[13] The Japanese forces who he believed had numerous suicide boat squadrons and some coast artillery on the Southern Philippine islands were more of a threat, believed General MacArthur, than were the 150,000-plus Japanese troops on Luzon.[14]

While reducing General Krueger's forces, General MacArthur added to his list of important objectives. In addition to clearing southern Luzon for American use, he ordered the clearing of Batangas Bay, on the south-central coast of Luzon, for Allied shipping. This was to be one of the staging areas for the invasion of Japan. Further, General MacArthur ordered that additional port facilities along the northwestern coast of Luzon be seized and developed for the same purpose.

With a limited freedom of action and fewer resources than expected, General Krueger set out to accomplish his new and former assignments. Contrary to his earlier planning, his forces shrank considerably. On February 7, he was informed that the 41st Infantry Division, already loaded on transports for Sixth Army, was instead assigned to the Eighth Army for employment in the Southern Philippines. Next, the 34th Infantry RCT, which had been fighting with General Hall's XI Corps on Bataan and Corregidor, was being withdrawn for the same purpose. They would be accompanied by other combat units of the 24th Infantry Division which had been fighting with the 11th Airborne Division south of Manila.[15] The 40th Infantry Division and the 503rd Parachute RCT soon followed. These were accompanied by numerous supply and service units previously assigned to the Sixth Army. Finally, General MacArthur designated General Beightler's 37th Infantry Division, then still fighting within Manila, to be the city's garrison force for a period of the next two months. Rather than the 11 combat divisions and four separate regimental combat teams he had originally planned for to complete the Luzon campaign, General Krueger was left with only nine, one of which was tied down for two months as garrison troops in Manila, and only two separate regimental combat teams.[16]

Because of this unexpected change, General Krueger was forced to shuffle his units and to change plans. First, he had to find a replacement for the 40th Infantry Division, then in I Corps fighting the *Shobu Group*. Fortunately, the 33rd Infantry Division was about to arrive as a reinforcement from New Guinea. But since he had permission to retain the 40th Infantry Division until March, General Krueger used the newly arrived troops to relieve the 43rd Infantry Division and the 158th RCT, allowing them some rest before they pushed north. The 43rd Infantry Division, after two weeks' rest, would return to the line, replacing the 40th Infantry Division, which would then depart Luzon. He ordered the 11th Airborne Division to seize Batangas and Balayan Bays in southern Luzon, reinforced with the 158th RCT. For the time being, he would concentrate his main efforts on the *Shimbu Group*, to finally secure the entire Manila Bay area.

Assembling forces to attack the *Shimbu Group* was difficult. Only the 2nd Cavalry Brigade, 1st Cavalry Division, was available, having just cleared the northeastern Manila suburbs. The separate 112th Cavalry RCT, protecting the long XIV Corps line of communications, could also be made available. But these two small units were clearly insufficient to attack a force estimated at 20,000 soldiers in the hills east and northeast of Manila. General Krueger reluctantly assigned the 6th Infantry Division, less its 1st Infantry Regiment then on Bataan, to the task, moving it from I Corps to XIV Corps. This made it even less likely that I Corps would be able to make any immediate progress against the *Shobu Group*, but General Krueger had little choice. General Hall's XI Corps was ordered to release the 1st Infantry Regiment and return it to the 6th Infantry Division.

General Griswold's XIV Corps already held some of the key water supply sources for Manila. But the Japanese held the Ipo Dam, 25 miles northeast of Manila, which provided a third of the water for the city. An aqueduct from the Ipo Dam to the Novaliches Reservoir was also in Japanese hands. A smaller dam, the Wawa Dam, along the Marikina River 15 miles northeast of Manila, was also an integral part of the water system. General Krueger ordered the seizure first of the Wawa Dam, then the Ipo Dam and the other portions of the water supply system. General Griswold assigned the 6th Infantry Division, the 2nd Cavalry Brigade, and the 112th Cavalry RCT to these objectives. The attack was to begin February 20.

Once again, the American intelligence underestimated the opposition. General Yokoyama's *Shimbu Group* numbered 50,000 troops, largely from the *8th* and *105th Divisions*, reinforced with members of the suicide boat squadrons and base battalions of the *1st Surface Raiding Base Force*. Some 30,000 of these were firmly entrenched in the area in which XIV Corps was about to attack. The terrain was excellent for defense, and the Japanese positions had been well prepared. Artillery was available for support. Strong forces were held in reserve in the Bosoboso Valley just behind the Japanese front lines.

The 7th Cavalry led the attack, crossing the Marikina River[17] without opposition. The next day, February 21, the regiment moved up Route 21 to Taytay, with negligible opposition. The cavalry began to probe within the Sierra Madre Mountains followed by the 8th Cavalry Regiment. As the cavalrymen moved deeper and higher into the mountains, they uncovered the initial Japanese defenses. There were largely improved caves, one of which was later found to have 32 separate entrances. Machine guns blocked all avenues of approach. Artillery hid in caves, coming out briefly to fire and then withdrawing back into the cave. Beginning February 23, the cavalry measured progress in feet per day. Despite support from the 75mm howitzers of the 99th Field Artillery Battalion, the cavalrymen were pounded by enemy artillery and 120mm and 150mm rockets, along with mortar fire, from hidden caves. The Cavalry History records, "It was not the haphazard, inaccurate fire that had been encountered on Leyte, but the carefully coordinated and prepared massed fires of the artillery elements of two enemy combat divisions."[18]

Undeterred, the troopers resumed their proven small-unit tactics for eliminating machine guns and mortars in caves. Supported by engineers, artillery, and air power, the brigade pushed forward. "The enemy had ideal positions from which to observe the advance of the troopers and to adjust barrages of accurately placed shells. It was an uphill battle for the cavalrymen. When one ridge had been captured, there always seemed to be another one ahead, higher and more dominating."[19] Observing the attack of his men, General Mudge was watching a cave being demolished when he was struck by a grenade and seriously wounded. General Hugh F. T. Hoffman assumed command of the division, while Colonel William J. Bradley, formerly of the 8th Cavalry Regiment, took command of the 2nd Cavalry Brigade.[20] The attack continued.

On March 4, the Japanese launched a counterattack that knocked out two tanks but made no progress. Two days later, the 1st Cavalry Brigade, relieved from duty in Manila, moved up on the 2nd Brigade's north, joining with the 6th Infantry Division, and attacked as well. The Japanese continued to defend, waiting until the Americans began the use of flamethrowers on their caves, then embarking upon suicidal banzai attacks only to be cut down. On March 10, the 8th Cavalry counted 402 enemy dead from such operations.

Meanwhile, the 6th Infantry Division attacked as well. Major General Edwin D. Patrick's 20th Infantry Regiment had found little initial resistance, but as the days passed that resistance increased much as it did in the cavalry's sector. When the 3rd Battalion, 63rd Infantry, attacked Hill 400, they found themselves under fire from 47mm and 70mm guns, which they knocked out while securing the hill. They, too, received heavy artillery and rocket fire, including 8-inch rockets whose siren screamed and caused every infantryman within hearing to dive for cover. Division artillery fired counter-battery missions, reducing the threat considerably. Army and Marine Corps aircraft were also directed on known and suspected enemy gun positions.

The 1st Battalion, 63rd Infantry, sent patrols up the steep slopes of Mount Pacawagan, but enemy fire forced their withdrawal. The attacks were renewed during which First Lieutenant J. H. Childs's mortar platoon came under attack while a mortar barrage cut the communications lines to his mortars. Knowing that his support was vital to the forward troops, Lieutenant Childs left his foxhole under intense small-arms and mortar fire and repaired the lines, despite serious wounds. He survived to wear his Silver Star. Even though he was already bleeding from numerous wounds, Technician Fifth Grade Gust Rosin, an aid man in the 63rd Infantry, ran from man to man, treating the wounded under an intense mortar barrage. Then he organized litter squads to remove the wounded until he finally lost consciousness from his own loss of blood. He, too, received a Silver Star. When the infantry company his battalion was supporting withdrew under a hail of enemy artillery, Second Lieutenant Charles F. Hudson, of the 53rd Field Artillery Battalion, remained at his observation post and accurately and continuously directed fire, which allowed the infantry to reorganize and seize their objective, earning his own Silver Star. The struggle continued, with many American soldiers distinguishing themselves. Indeed, it would take another three days before Mount Pacawagan was secured.

The constant slow struggle to advance convinced General Patrick that he needed to change tactics. With the arrival of his 1st Infantry Regiment, he changed his main effort to the zone of the 20th Infantry, where the terrain was better and the possibility of cracking the "*Shimbu Line*" at its center existed. If that happened, XIV Corps could roll up the flanks and reach its objectives.

Unable to penetrate Mount Mataba, the 20th Infantry managed on March 4 to move along the Ampid River and advance almost two miles into the Japanese defenses. General Griswold was also concerned that his XIV Corps was beating itself against a formidable defense. He decided also to concentrate his main force against a perceived weak spot. The attack was designed to break through the "*Shimbu Line*" and enter the Bosoboso Valley, getting into the rear of the Japanese and among their reserves and supplies. The area selected was between the Ampid River and the Nanca River, at the 1,000-foot-high Mount Baytangan. The attack was scheduled for March 8.

The cavalry attacked toward the village of Antipolo, making slow and painful progress. Reinforced by the 103rd Infantry Regiment, 43rd Infantry Division, which General Krueger had assigned to relieve the 1st Cavalry Division, the attack moved slowly. The 6th Infantry Division's attack had more success. General Patrick's idea to strengthen his attack by concentrating his 1st and 20th Infantry Regiments attack on a two-mile front at the Nanca River made good initial progress. Using the 112th Cavalry RCT to guard his now exposed flanks, General Patrick's two infantry regiments secured the western end of Mount Baytangan. The 1st Infantry seized Benchmark 8, another hill portion of the defender's line. This opened a path to Wawa Dam, and General Patrick directed the 20th Infantry to drive north for the dam.

These advances greatly concerned General Yokoyama. He decided that one of his main forces defending against the Americans was outflanked and needed to withdraw to a second line of defense. To halt future American penetrations of his defense, he also decided upon a counterattack. This was to be conducted by seven infantry battalions who would attack from Mount Mataba and strike the 6th Infantry Division enclave. It would be supported by artillery. Other battalions from other operational groups would support the attack by striking at Benchmark 8 Hill and against the 6th Infantry Division forces at the Marikina River.[21]

As he had earlier during the Battle of Manila, General Yokoyama expected too much of his forces. Few had worked together before, many had never trained as complete units, and communications were abominable. He was sending a weaker force against XIV Corps than he had done in February. Further, unknown to General Yokoyama, he had planned his attack to begin on the same day as General Patrick had scheduled his new attack, March 12.

The air and artillery strikes supporting the planned March 12 attack of the 6th Infantry Division knocked out much of the artillery expected to support General Yokoyama's counterattack. They also blasted many of the paths that the Japanese were using to advance to the attack. Command posts and communications were knocked out or destroyed. The Japanese counterattack of March 12 largely evaporated in the pre-attack preparations of General Patrick. The survivors dispersed into the hills, commanders lost control of their units, and contact with and between those units ceased. Suffice to say that the 6th Infantry Division's records indicate that it was entirely unaware that it was under attack. General Yokoyama called off his offensive on March 15.

Even as the Japanese attacked the 6th Infantry Division, the 43rd Infantry Division renewed the attack begun by the cavalrymen. The 103rd Infantry Regiment seized Antipolo and then Benchmark 7 Hill. Expecting a strong defense of the latter hill, they were pleasantly surprised when they found it undefended. It seemed that a flank of the "*Shimbu Line*" was exposed and vulnerable to the Americans. General Wing next set his sights on Mount Yabang and Mount Caymayuman, which would put the division through the enemy defenses. Unaware that this section of the enemy line was withdrawing under orders, the 103rd and 172nd Infantry Regiments attacked on March 14 against light opposition. In the first day, they advanced a mile and a half, more than the cavalrymen had managed in the previous 10 days. Confidence grew that a breakthrough had been achieved.

A similar situation existed within the 6th Infantry Division. Between March 12 and March 14, the 20th Infantry Regiment had cleared its sector and reached the foot of Mount Mataba. The 1st Infantry had more opposition, but advanced nevertheless. As they did so, on March 14 a sudden burst of machine-gun fire struck among a group of senior officers who had incautiously bunched up in the open at the regimental command post. General Patrick was mortally wounded, and Colonel James E. Rees, commanding the regiment, was killed. The assistant division commander, Brigadier General Charles E. Hurdis, assumed command, and Lieutenant Colonel Francis J. Corbin, commander of the 1st Battalion, took over the regiment.

By the end of March 14, the XIV Corps had made substantial progress against the *Shimbu Group*. That progress had been slow and costly in terms of casualties, but it had been steady. A deep wedge had been driven in to the Japanese lines, nearly separating two of its main sub-units. One of those units had been forced to withdraw to a second line of defense. The XIV Corps attack had prompted a major Japanese counterattack that had been decimated, further reducing the *Shimbu Group*'s ability to resist. These successes had been made against a force more powerful than expected, fighting from prepared defenses in terrain which favored that defense. It had also been heavily supported by a strong artillery force that had made the defense that much more formidable.

On the other hand, no direct assault had yet been launched against the Ipo Dam, and ground had been lost near the Wawa Dam.[22] Although good ground for a renewed assault on both dams had been achieved, the dams themselves remained in enemy hands. Losses had been totaled at 295 killed and 1,040 wounded. To this total battle casualty list must be added another 2,000 troops disabled by sickness or battle fatigue.

March 14 also saw a change in command. Effective on that date, General Hall's XI Corps relieved General Griswold's XIV Corps in command of the attack to the dams. With the 6th and 43rd Infantry Divisions under command, the problem of the *Shimbu Group* now became General Hall's responsibility.

CHAPTER 10

Seizing the Dams

General Hall's XI Corps made few changes in the plans to seize the dams. With the 6th Infantry and 43rd Infantry Divisions under command, the battle continued. General Hall would strike at the *Shimbu Group*'s left flank as had the XIV Corps. The only change made by General Hall was to concentrate his forces even further, striking against the *Noguchi Force* instead of both that force and the *Kobayashi Force* alongside. Again, faulty intelligence had reported that these two forces were out of contact with each other and that the latter force had been badly hurt by recent attacks, reducing its ability to defend around Mounts Pacawagan and Mataba.

In fact, however, the 6th Infantry Division attack struck the *Kobayashi Force*'s left flank, while General Wing's 43rd Infantry Division continued the attack against the *Noguchi Force*. This attack on March 15 caught the *Noguchi Force* still trying to occupy its second line of defense. Although they had successfully occupied Sugarloaf Hill, blocking the Nanca River, they had yet to occupy Benchmark Hill 23. Instead, a reinforced battalion of the *105th Division* had taken up positions at Mount Tanauan in incomplete defenses. The American attack caught them still trying to organize those defenses. General Yokoyama committed some of his reserves to this sector to prevent a breakthrough. He intended to contain the attack of the 6th Infantry Division rather than allow a breakthrough.

The Japanese made repeated and strong efforts to stop the American advances. The soldiers of the 6th Infantry Division spent their nights huddled in foxholes trying to escape heavy artillery and rocket concentrations or burning out machine-gun barrels fending off repeated banzai attacks by the Japanese. On March 16, for example, Private First Class Edwin N. Johnson was manning one such machine-gun post when his squad was attacked by an estimated 40 enemy soldiers. Within moments two of his crew had been killed and two others wounded. Operating the gun alone, Pfc Johnson fought off the enemy attack all the while under rifle, grenade, and mortar fire. Soon his machine gun overheated and ceased to function. Undeterred, Pfc Johnson continued his battle with his pistol and grenades. After four hours of furious fighting, the Japanese conceded defeat and withdrew, leaving 36 dead behind.[1]

The 103rd Infantry Regiment, supported by Company C, 44th Tank Battalion, attacked Benchmark 7 Hill and the Route 60–A road, which was needed for an American supply route. After three days of bitter fighting, some 250 Japanese were counted killed and the two objectives were in American hands. The attack continued to Mount Tanauan where more heavy fighting occurred before three more days of fighting uphill against machine guns, rifles, mortars, artillery, caves, and bunkers secured that objective. Some 300 enemy dead were counted on the hill. Other units of the regiment patrolled north and entered the Japanese rear areas in the Bosoboso Valley. One of these patrols reached Mount Balidbiran on the east bank of the Bosoboso, outflanking the *Noguchi Force*'s left flank.

The division's 172nd Infantry Regiment meanwhile had struck out for Sugarloaf Hill. Here the Japanese had time to prepare their defenses, and the initial American attack was stopped cold by intense enemy resistance from the usual caves and bunkers. With no progress on March 19, the regiment pulled one battalion out of the fight, and moving north and east launched new attacks against Mounts Yabang and Caymayuman. Seizure of the latter height would place them in the left rear of the enemy strongpoint at Sugarloaf Hill. The 1st Battalion, 172nd Infantry, and elements of the 754th Tank Battalion passed through the village of Teresa and attacked along the western side of the Morong River Valley. Benchmark 20 Hill was seized and small enemy detachments were bypassed to facilitate the advance. Roadblock after roadblock was overcome, and a battery of Japanese 155mm guns was overrun. By dark on March 22 the battalion was within three-quarters of a mile of Mount Caymayuman.

Here the infantry encountered steep hillsides that required them to crawl on hands and knees to advance up the hill. After a heavy artillery and mortar barrage, the 172nd Infantrymen attacked and reached the crest of the hill, encountering lightly held enemy defenses. At Sugarloaf Hill, however, the rest of the 172nd Infantry made slow progress and were under constant counterattack by small groups of Japanese. Artillery fire caused many casualties, and the regiment—along with the rest of the 43rd Infantry Division, in combat since landing on January 9—was showing signs of fatigue. Several rifle companies were down to 50 officers and men, some had fewer. Little progress could be expected with such weakened forces.

During the night of March 20–21, Japanese forces counterattacked the American hold on Mount Caymayuman in strength. Awakened to the threat to Sugarloaf Hill, a battalion of Japanese were determined to push the 1st Battalion off Mount Caymayuman. Their attack was halted by 800 rounds of artillery fire from the 103rd Field Artillery Battalion and supporting mortars of the 82nd Chemical Mortar Battalion. Apparently, this attack weakened the defenses of Sugarloaf Hill, as almost immediately the 172nd Infantry elements attacking there felt resistance slackening. The attack pushed ahead, overrunning artillery caves and machine-gun bunkers. The same day, March 21, the 103rd Infantry and 754th Tank Battalion assaulted Mount Tanauan under a smoke screen and, after counting 167 dead enemy soldiers, secured the height. Their losses amounted to one man killed and 20 wounded. Captures included 12 heavy machine guns, numerous artillery pieces, and 100 tons of ammunition.

Brigadier General Hurdis's 6th Infantry Division delayed its attack until March 17 when the 1st Infantry Regiment attacked toward Mount Baytangan and Benchmark 8 Hill. Initially the attack went well, and by late afternoon the battalions were digging in on a ridge just a mile from Mount Baytangan's crest. Barely an hour after the advance halted, a barrage of 150mm artillery fire struck the leading companies. Mortars soon joined in the barrage. Japanese infantry began to attack the battalion's exposed flanks. Outflanked and under severe fire, the battalions withdrew to their line of departure. Twelve men had been killed and 35 wounded. Lost in the withdrawal were an artillery radio, a jeep, two 37mm antitank guns, two 60mm mortars, and considerable ammunition.

During the fighting on March 19, Staff Sergeant Charles H. Lanham of Company K, 63rd Infantry, found his squad cut off from friendly forces by a strong enemy counterattack. Situated atop a steep brush-covered hill accessible only by a steep trail that had been mined earlier in the day, they fought off the enemy while awaiting reinforcements. When a column of friendly troops arrived at the bottom of the trail, Staff Sergeant Lanham led them over the mined and booby-trapped trail in complete darkness, feeling for the mines and trip wires blindly with his hands. In order to hurry up the relief, he then stood up on the trail and used a flashlight, which revealed his position to the enemy. After deactivating seven mines and deliberately exploding two others, he searched for the last one known to be on the trail. Unable to locate it, and rather than delay any further his platoon's relief, he boldly walked down the path in the area he knew the mine had been placed. He hit the trip wire with his foot, exploding a phosphorus grenade, but somehow escaped personal injury. He then led the relief column to his platoon and helped in repulsing the enemy attack.[2]

General Hurdis changed tactics. Patrols went out to reconnoiter the area ahead of the regiment while others mopped up bypassed enemy holdouts. The Japanese in the area put up a spirited resistance, with regular nightly counterattacks and constant artillery and mortar harassment. After five days, the 1st Infantry was no closer to Mount Baytangan than they had been on March 17. The situation was similar in the 20th Infantry's zone. Although the defense was not particularly well organized, it was constant and difficult to destroy. By March 22, the regiment was within a mile and a half of Mount Baytangan with one rifle company on a ridge leading to the crest of that vital hill.

General Hall decided that the only promising advance lay with the 103rd Infantry Regiment. But his troops were exhausted and casualties had significantly reduced effectiveness. The 20th Infantry Regiment, for example, was at one-third its authorized strength, as was the 1st Infantry Regiment. They were losing infantrymen

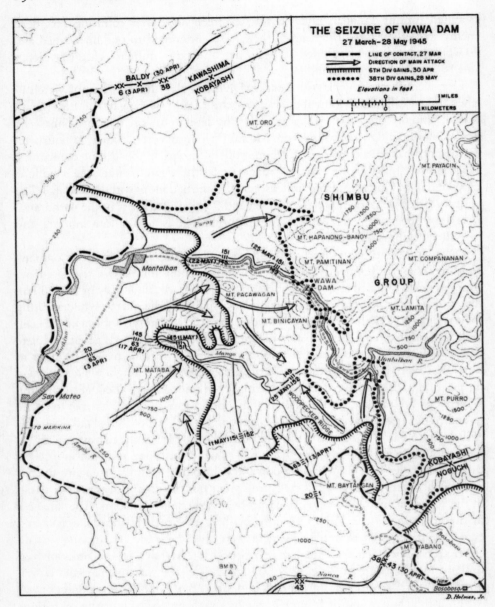

The Seizure of Wawa Dam, March–May 1945

Robert Ross Smith. *United States Army in World War II. The War in the Pacific. Triumph in the Philippines.* Washington, D.C.: Center of Military History, 1984. p. 393.

at the rate of 55–60 per day in killed, wounded, or sick. If this kept up much longer, these regiments would cease to exist. With no choice, General Hall called a temporary halt to operations to bring his assault regiments up to strength.

But before this halt could be implemented, General Yokoyama took a hand in events. Convinced that the situation on the left of his line had become hopeless, and to preserve his forces, he again ordered a withdrawal to the east of the Bosoboso River. These orders were issued on March 20, but so bad were the Japanese communications that it took several days, until March 23, for them to reach all the units of the *Shimbu Force*. Just as General Hall was about to issue orders for a halt in his offensive, the Japanese began their withdrawal on March 22. When the XI Corps assault regiments attacked the next morning, they encountered only scattered, disorganized opposition. This would remain the situation for the next three days, until March 26. The 20th Infantry cleared Mount Baytangan and reached the Bosoboso River. The 1st Infantry occupied Mount Baytangan and moved on to make physical contact with the 172nd Infantry, 43rd Infantry Division, northwest of Mount Yabang. Sugarloaf Hill fell to the 172nd Infantry on March 27.

The 103rd Infantry Regiment advanced along both sides of the Bosoboso River against minimal opposition. As they did they captured great quantities of Japanese supplies stored in the area. Signs of a hasty Japanese withdrawal were everywhere. The only signs of an organized Japanese force were foot and motor movements spotted along a trail leading to the northeast deep into the Sierra Madre Mountains.

With the *Shimbu Group* withdrawing from the immediate area, XI Corps could now turn its attention to its primary assignment, capture of the dams. First, the Americans took stock of their own losses. Against a total of 7,000 enemy killed,[3] XIV and XI Corps operations against the *Shimbu Group* had cost the U.S. Army 435 killed and 1,425 wounded, a total of 1,860 casualties. Once again, however, this does not consider the hundreds of American soldiers felled by disease or combat fatigue. Nevertheless, using only a portion of its strength, the American assault force had succeeded in pushing the main *Shimbu Group* into the hills.[4]

General Hall now redirected his XI Corps efforts to the north against the Wawa Dam. As they went, his troops were to secure the area west of the Bosoboso River, attacking toward the final objective line, from Mount Oro to the Wawa Dam and then to the Bosoboso River. Most of this sector was assigned to the 6th Infantry Division. General Hurdis's men were to attack from Mount Baytangan to Mount Oro, cross the Bosoboso River and clear Mount Purro, reduce any remaining strongpoints of the *Shimbu Group*, and then seize the Wawa Dam.

The 103rd Infantry was assigned to protect the rear of the 6th Infantry Division. They set up a roadblock and patrol base at Hill 1200 along the road that the *Shimbu Group* had used to withdraw. This trail, little more than a horse trail, ended in the mountains northeast of New Bosoboso, a village along the river. The rest of the 43rd Infantry Division would patrol the area east of the river until May, making sure that those elements of the *Shimbu Group* that had withdrawn did not return. These operations cost that division 30 killed and 120 wounded against 830 known enemy killed. Later, these duties would be taken over by the 112th Cavalry RCT.

Once again, General Hurdis chose the 1st and 20th Infantry Regiments as his assault units. They were to attack in wooded terrain covered by ridges, hills, and mountains. Facing the 1st Infantry was what came to be called "Woodpecker Ridge," after the constant chatter of Japanese machine guns coming from the ridge. The 20th Infantry faced Mount Mataba, a 1,000-foot-high bare ridge on which they already had one rifle company a mile and a half short of the hill's peak. The new attack would begin March 28. The 63rd Infantry would conduct diversionary operations on the slopes of Mount Mataba to divert enemy resistance. General Hurdis hoped that his initial attacks, especially those by the 63rd Infantry, would force the Japanese to expose the locations of their artillery, mortars, and machine guns which could then be destroyed by American artillery.

The 6th Infantry Division was facing the *Kobayashi Force*, a unit of the *Shimbu Group* that had been left behind to defend the dams. This force had quickly reoriented itself to defend the approaches to the dam, facing generally to the west. It contained two infantry regiments, some of which had yet to engage in combat. Reinforcements from the *Shimbu Group* reserve had recently arrived, further strengthening the force. The American attack moved slowly. With only 2,085 men left in the ranks, the 20th Infantry Regiment was too weak to push more aggressively. The 1st Infantry Regiment had only a few more. Companies were down to the size of platoons, and combat efficiency was rated only as "fair."[5]

To compensate for the lack of infantrymen, Generals Hall and Hurdis made some adjustments. The front of the 6th Infantry Division was reduced. Next, a provisional brigade was formed, including the 112th Cavalry RCT and the 169th RCT of the 43rd Infantry Division. This brigade took over a section of the line north of Mount Oro. It was under the command of Brigadier General Julian W. Cunningham, commander of the 112th Cavalry RCT. Known as "Baldy Force," from General Cunningham's lack of hair, the provisional brigade would allow the 63rd Infantry Regiment to be freed up for more active operations.

With 2,425 men in its ranks, the 63rd Infantry relieved the depleted 20th Infantry. While the 1st Infantry marked time in front of Woodpecker Ridge, the 63rd Infantry Regiment attacked on April 6. After three fruitless days, the attack was redirected against Mount Mataba, where the 1st Infantry had been stymied earlier. This time the defense was found to be weak and the southwestern slope was seized. But Japanese reinforcements were quickly dispatched and the advance halted again. It took another week before the Americans secured the crest.

Once again, it was the individual riflemen who carried the day. Led up the slopes by Captains William C. Beachler, Milburn W. Beitel, and William J. Moran, the infantrymen faced significant resistance. Private First Class Frank E. Phillips crawled to the crest of a ridge, then proceeded to drop grenades on several enemy machine guns below him, knocking them out one by one. Captain Moran, after two wounds, continued leading his men in attacking enemy caves holding machine guns, eventually knocking out six of them. Technical Sergeant Kenneth C. Johnson and Sergeant Henry A. Timmerman crawled over terrain exposed to enemy fire and then dropped demolition charges into enemy positions, eliminating them. Staff Sergeant Bummand M. Epps stormed an enemy pillbox, knocking out the two machine guns and seven enemy riflemen using his rifle and grenades. Actions like these soon overcame enemy resistance.

Another attempt by the 1st Infantry to seize Woodpecker Ridge failed on April 17. General Hurdis now had to address the problem that had been put off earlier. His 1st Infantry rifle companies averaged barely 105 men, about half strength. The 20th Infantry had an average of 125 while the 63rd Infantry's average was 120, all far below authorized strength. In addition, his men had been fighting continuously since January with little or no rest. There was a clear need for fresh troops if the battle for the dams was to succeed. To provide these, an exchange was worked out between General Hurdis and General Beightler whereby the 145th Infantry of the 37th Infantry Division would replace the 20th Infantry, who would move into Manila and garrison the city. The 145th Infantry had enjoyed a month of rest while performing garrison duties in Manila, and was better prepared for combat than the depleted 20th Infantry Regiment.

The new arrivals drew the assignment of Mount Pacawagan while supported by the 63rd Infantry. The 1st Infantry remained in defensive positions pending the results of the coming attack. To ensure the success of the 145th Infantry's attack, General Hurdis provided an overwhelming artillery support force, including three 105mm battalions, two 155mm battalions, a 155mm gun battery, a 240mm howitzer battery, an 8-inch howitzer battery, and two 90mm antiaircraft batteries. In addition, the 63rd Infantry provided fire from five 105mm self-propelled cannons, eight 81mm mortars, eight 4.2-inch mortars, two 57mm antitank guns, 11 heavy machine guns, and a dozen light machine guns. As expected, Japanese defenses were pulverized by this onslaught, but the determined defenders kept the 145th Infantry off the hill for another week and, even then, maintained defenses on a spur of the hill on the northeastern peak. The 145th Infantry lost 55 killed and 220 wounded in nine days of battle, more than any regiment of the 6th Infantry Division during April.

The end of April also brought relief to the depleted regiments of the 6th Infantry Division. The 1st and 63rd Infantry Regiments were relieved by the 151st and 152nd Infantry Regiments of the 38th Infantry Division. At the same time, General Chase's division relieved General Hurdis's men of the responsibility for seizing the dams. Against American losses of 790 killed and wounded, the estimated Japanese casualties were in excess of 3,000. The 6th Infantry Division had been hard hit during the series of battles in March and April, losing more than 4,000 men from all causes. The constant problem suffered by General Krueger's Sixth Army—a lack of replacements which in turn prohibited a rotation of front-line units—had only made these losses greater by keeping combat units in action long after they should have been relieved and absorbed replacements.

It was now General Chase's 38th Infantry Division's turn to attack for the dams. After clearing Bataan and Manila Bay, the division had been mopping up until called upon to relieve the 6th Infantry Division in XI Corps. General Chase was informed by General Hall that he believed from intelligence reports that the *Kobayashi Force* was withdrawing after suffering significant casualties. He believed that only small delaying forces lay between General Chase and the Wawa Dam.

Once again American intelligence failed. General Yokoyama was not only still holding on to the dams, but he was also preparing a counteroffensive in the form of a series of small counterattacks designed to delay and harass the Americans. He believed that the *Kobayashi Force* was still strong enough to launch these attacks while protecting the dams. He had provided reinforcements from the *Shimbu Group* reserve as well as attaching units from the withdrawn *Noguchi Force*. This gave him at least 6,500 soldiers available on May 3, to protect the dams. To further oppose the Americans, General Yokoyama had another 3,000 troops of the *Shimbu Group* reserve prepared to move forward from Mount Purro. General Yokoyama, whose record of counterattacks was less than successful, nevertheless decided upon a new attack because he believed that the American attack in April had shown that they were weakened, whether due to transfers to other fronts or to other Philippine islands, he did not know. The lull at the end of April had strengthened his view. He had no idea that the lull was caused by the need to rotate front-line units. The lull and his belief that the American forces had been weakened by transfers elsewhere threatened to invalidate his mission, which was to tie down as many American ground combat forces as possible for the longest possible time. The best way to do that, he believed, was to counterattack, thereby drawing upon the *Shimbu Group*, more American combat units.

General Yokoyama had no illusions. He knew that he could not regain the ground lost thus far. Instead he wished to launch a series of strong infiltration attacks where his troops would attack at night, hide by day, and severely harass the American rear areas, causing chaos and confusion, thus delaying the American offensive and prolonging the battle for the dams. These attacks began on May 10, with two battalions harassing the left rear of the 38th Infantry Division at Montalban, followed two days later with the main attack from the *31st Infantry* of the group reserve. Four more battalions, each numbering fewer than 300 men, would attack the town of Marikina, supported by raids from the remnants of the *Noguchi Force* on XI Corps' southern flank.

Unfortunately for General Yokoyama, his skills at launching a counterattack had not improved. He was completely unaware of the status of XI Corps, its intentions, or its strength. He did not know the 43rd Infantry Division had moved toward the Ipo Dam, nor that the relatively fresh 38th Infantry Division had taken over the attack on the Wawa Dam. Instead, as we have seen, he believed that the XI Corps was transferring troops to other fronts. Basically, he lacked even the most rudimentary tactical knowledge of his enemy.

In any case, General Hall didn't sit and wait for General Yokoyama to act. During the first week of May, XI Corps directed probing attacks during which the 145th Infantry, now attached to the 38th Infantry Division, secured all the important points of Mount Pacawagan, forcing the *Kobayashi Force* to pull back. During this same period, Colonel Washington M. Ives, Jr.'s 152nd Infantry gained a half a mile along Woodpecker Ridge. These movements placed the 145th Infantry in position to go directly for Wawa Dam, supported by the 152nd Infantry. Colonel Ralf C. Paddock's 151st Infantry guarded the division's flanks and secured Mount Mataba. Additional advances over the next few days continued to place XI Corps in a better position to achieve control of the dams.

These attacks made General Yokoyama realize that his original estimate had been wrong. The XI Corps was not withdrawing. Instead, they were attacking on a large scale directly into the center of his line. Worried that he had waited too long, he changed his orders and started his counteroffensive on May 4, rather than waiting until May 10 as originally planned. As the Japanese hurriedly made their dispositions for the attack, the 145th Infantry attacked and seized the pinnacle of Mount Binicayan, which lay on the south bank of the Marikina River at Wawa Dam. The American success had cost the *Kobayashi Force* another 400 men and placed the XI Corps in striking distance of one of their main objectives. In addition, the need to defend Mount Binicayan and Woodpecker Ridge had depleted any forces that the *Kobayashi Force* could contribute to General Yokoyama's planned counteroffensive. In fact, the 145th Infantry never realized it had been counterattacked. To further impede General Yokoyama's plans, the 152nd Infantry began to make wide envelopments of established Japanese defenses. In one such envelopment, they ran directly into the troops of the *Shimbu Group*'s reserve who were moving up to take part in the counteroffensive. Although slowed by the encounter, the 152nd Infantry continued advancing, overrunning the Japanese assembly areas for launching the attack. The 152nd Infantry began fighting off infiltration attempts on May 14 and continued doing so for the next week without realizing they were fighting off a major Japanese counterattack. In front of the Ipo Dam, the 43rd Infantry Division attacked directly into the assembling enemy counterattack force and forced it on to the defensive before the attack had even begun.

With his plans thwarted by the unexpectedly rapid American attacks, General Yokoyama called off his counteroffensive on May 15. These orders included instructions to withdraw, an order that took a week to reach the Japanese holding Woodpecker Ridge. This delayed the 38th Infantry Division for several days, but between May 4 and May 18 the Americans had, at a cost of 85 killed and 305 wounded, eliminated more than 1,300 enemy troops of the *Kobayashi Force*.

General Chase had some difficult problems to resolve before striking directly for the Wawa Dam. Japanese positions on high ground north of the dam could support the dam's defense by fire. His only supply line along the south bank of the Marikina River was controlled by Japanese artillery, mortar, and machine-gun fire from those same heights. A wide gap between his 145th and 152nd Infantry Regiments allowed significant enemy infiltration between his lines along the east bank of the Bosoboso River. Worse, lack of sufficient artillery and 81mm mortar ammunition had forced him to retain Colonel Winifred G. Skelton's 149th Infantry Regiment in reserve, since it could only be resupplied at the expense of his other two assault regiments.

General Chase decided that the 152nd Infantry would continue its attack to clear Woodpecker Ridge while the 151st Infantry would attack the heights north of the Marikina River at Mount Pamitinan and Mount Hapanong-Banoy. The 149th Infantry Regiment would relieve the 145th Infantry in place, and after some success in the attacks of the other two assault regiments, it would attack for the dam with secure flanks and a safe supply route. To accomplish this, the 113th Engineer (Combat) Battalion bulldozed roads to the front under enemy fire. Medium tanks soon appeared, along with flame-throwing tanks and armored half-tracks with multiple heavy machine-gun mounts. With this support the 152nd Infantry resumed frontal attacks against Woodpecker Ridge on May 21 and Japanese resistance soon began to crumble. By May 25 the attack had cleared the ridge and the Japanese were in retreat. The 38th Infantry Division now controlled the junction of the Bosoboso River and Marikina Rivers. Patrols probed as far as Mount Purro.

Similarly, the 151st Infantry had moved north of the Marikina River on May 21 and within days was pushing the Japanese defenders of Mount Pamitinan and Hapanong-Banoy off their perches. The following day, May 27, the 149th Infantry attacked toward Wawa Dam, finding that the Japanese had withdrawn. By mid-morning on May 28, Wawa Dam was in American hands. It had cost the 38th Infantry Division, including the attached 145th Infantry Regiment, about 750 casualties, including 160 killed. For all practical purposes, the *Kobayashi Force* no longer existed.

Meanwhile, General Wing's 43rd Infantry Division had been moved toward the Ipo Dam, the other major objective of XI Corps. Originally, both General Krueger and General Hall had planned on a series of attacks from south to north to eliminate the *Shimbu Group* and to capture the dams. But by early May General Krueger had decided that a more direct approach to the Ipo Dam was necessary. Manila's water supply problems were becoming critical, and a water shortage existed which could only be resolved by an early capture of both dams. In the interim, water to citizens south of the Pasig River was being provided by Army tank trucks and wells, most of which were contaminated. Sanitary conditions were deteriorating rapidly with insufficient water to carry off the refuse. General MacArthur looked to General Krueger for an early resolution of these dangerous conditions. Fear of an epidemic was a growing concern.

General MacArthur's concerns, voiced in late April, had caused Sixth Army to rethink their plans. In short order, General Krueger passed on these concerns to General Hall, who in turn redeployed General Wing's 43rd Infantry Division to rejoin its own 169th Infantry Regiment already facing the Ipo Dam and prepare to attack. To cover the ground left behind by the 43rd Infantry Division, General Hall disbanded "Baldy Force" and ordered General Cunningham to have his 112th Cavalry RCT cover those positions. With the rainy season fast approaching, speed was now paramount.

Speed in the rough and jungle-covered terrain was relative. It was not until May 7 that General Hall could schedule an attack on the dam. The best approach was on Route 52, a two-lane graveled road that ran from Manila, through Novaliches, and then to the dam. Six miles from the dam another route, Route 64, joined Route 52 at a junction soon to earn the nickname of "Hot Corner." Here Japanese artillery of the *Kawashima Force* had already harassed the 1st Cavalry Division as it passed on its way to Manila earlier in the campaign. "Baldy Force," which had held this area prior to its relief, had scouted the area thoroughly and determined that Route 52 was deeply fortified by the *Kawashima Force*. Rather than directly attack a known enemy defensive line, General Wing had his soldiers seek an alternate route. The terrain did not help, with thick jungle covering and rock formations appearing seemingly at random. Overlooked on three sides by high ground defended by the Japanese, limited options were available to seek an undefended approach to the dam.

General Wing was determined to avoid a frontal assault, if possible. South of the dam there was open ground along Route 52 that was rough, trackless, and uninhabited. The only way to launch an attack from here was if the division's engineers, the 118th Engineer (Combat) Battalion, bulldozed trails for supply and evacuation over rocky outcroppings where the enemy could observe every movement. But with scout reports indicating that the southern route was the least defended by the Japanese, General Wing, hoping for tactical surprise and weak defenses, made his decision. He would make his main effort along Route 52. Once again, the 103rd Infantry Regiment would make the main attack.

The 103rd Infantry was to launch its attack from two miles east of "Hot Corner" and drive four miles to Mount Katitinga, at the end of a broken, rocky ridge line running four miles to the Angat Gorge at the Ipo Dam. The regiment intended to use that ridge line as its avenue of approach to the dam. Meanwhile, the 172nd Infantry Regiment, acting in support, was to strike for the dam on a two-mile front to the left of the 103rd Infantry Regiment. The division's last regiment, the 169th Infantry, on the left of the 172nd Infantry, would execute diversionary attacks along Route 52 to pin down Japanese forces in that area.

The attack was strongly reinforced. Units included Colonel Marcus V. Augustin's Marking's Fil-American Yay Regiment, also known as the Marking Guerillas,[6] half the 754th Tank Battalion, Company A, 82nd Chemical Mortar Battalion, Battery D, 198th Antiaircraft Artillery Automatic Weapons Battalion, the 161st Antiaircraft Gun Battalion, and two batteries of the 227th Antiaircraft Artillery Searchlight Battalion. In addition, corps artillery support included a battalion of 155mm guns, another of 155mm howitzers, and a battery of 8-inch howitzers.

General Wing tasked the guerillas with another diversion. They were to cross the Angat River and drive east of the river toward Mount Kabuyao, three miles north of the Ipo Dam. There they were to await an American success and be prepared to exploit such a success. Brigadier General Alexander N. Stark,[7] the assistant division commander of the 43rd Infantry Division, would be commanding this phase of the assault.

General Wing decided to enhance his chances of surprise by sending forward his combat units in small increments. Over the three days, between May 2 and May 5, the division assembled behind the screen of the 169th Infantry, limiting reconnaissance to avoid discovery and deploying for the attack under cover of darkness. General Wing scheduled his attack for the hours of darkness on the night of May 6–7. Night attacks were inherently risky, especially without sufficient reconnaissance, but General Wing was determined to achieve surprise, allowing his vulnerable infantrymen an advantage in the opening phases of the attack. To enhance the attack's direction, artillery would fire white phosphorus shells to mark initial objectives. Under pressure for an early capture of the Ipo Dam, General Wing massed his forces in the hope that overwhelming force would carry the day.

Major General Osamu Kawashima's *Kawashima Force* had no information that a complete American infantry division, heavily supported by corps artillery, was in their front. The 7,000 remaining members of the Japanese force—American intelligence estimated they numbered 5,250—had been in the area for several weeks, constructing strong defenses. The unit itself, however, had weaknesses. Only one of the several battalions within the force was a trained combat unit, the *358th Independent Infantry Battalion, 105th Division*. Other battalions included in the force were provisional units hastily organized into infantry battalions and regiments to defend the area of the dam. Defending against the coming attack of the 103rd Infantry Regiment was the *Tomono Detachment*. They defended the ridge along which the Americans hoped to approach the Ipo Dam.

The American attack got off to a good start. Surprise was in fact achieved, and both the 103rd and 172nd Infantry Regiments made good initial progress on May 6. The 103rd Infantry moved against scattered opposition and reached Hill 1000, less than three miles from the dam. The 172nd Infantry also moved fast, and the Marking Guerillas were opposed only at Hill 535, where a battalion of Japanese had repulsed a company of the regiment. Nevertheless, the guerillas moved seven miles to the east and camped that evening only a mile and a half from Mount Kabuyao, its first objective.

So weak had been the initial Japanese defenses that General Wing ordered his division to continue attacking during the night of May 7–8. Indeed, the advance continued so well that it went on until May 11 with little serious opposition. But on that date the rough terrain and an early monsoon rainy season, along with increasing resistance, slowed the advance. By this time the 103rd Infantry was within two miles of the Ipo Dam and the 172nd Infantry was keeping pace alongside. Colonel Augustin's guerillas were equally successful. They had overrun a Japanese outpost on Mount Kabuyao and reached strong Japanese defenses less than two miles from the dam. Known as Four Corners Hill, three attacks by the guerillas had been repulsed.

By May 11 General Wing understood that all his units were in firm contact with the main Japanese defenses at Ipo Dam. The Japanese, at first caught by surprise, had reacted well and manned their defenses against the American attack from the south. Hoping to halt the flow of troops to the south in front of his assault regiments General Wing ordered the 169th Infantry Regiment to attack along Osboy Ridge, to distract and pin in place any additional reinforcements General Kawashima intended to move. He also redirected the Marking Guerilla Regiment. Originally designed as a feint, the guerilla advance had been unexpectedly successful. He ordered that the guerillas coordinate with the 103rd Infantry to execute a double envelopment to seize the dam. In effect, the attack became a race between the 103rd Infantry and the guerillas to see who could reach the dam first.

That race began with the guerillas, for the first time supported by the 43rd Division artillery, seizing Four Corners Hill. Losing 90 men while eliminating about 80 Japanese, the guerillas chased the surviving garrison to Hill 803, only half a mile from the dam. General Kawashima still had sufficient forces available to make the seizure of the dam costly for the Americans. But suddenly he received orders from General Yokoyama that ruined his plans. With the Japanese front against the 38th Infantry Division collapsing, and unaware that a full American division was attacking the *Kawashima Force*, General Yokoyama ordered General Kawashima to counterattack the left and left rear of the 38th Infantry Division. With his own defenses about to crumble, General Kawashima protested to General Yokoyama against the attack. But the order stood, and a battalion of the *Kawashima Force* was dispatched to launch the attack as ordered.

The result was exactly what General Kawashima had feared. Forced to spread his defense thin to cover the area formerly protected by the departed battalion, the 103rd Infantry pierced General Kawashima's lines at Hill 805 and Hill 860, reaching to within three-quarters of a mile of the dam. The Marking Guerillas also captured Hill 803. General Kawashima, fed up with orders that made no sense, recalled his battalion without consulting General Yokoyama. This battalion, commanded by a particularly competent officer, Major Tetsuyuki Kasama, had observed the American attack and started to return before receiving General Kawashima's orders. Finding its former positions in American hands, the battalion counterattacked but failed to recover the lost ground. By dawn on May 14, that battalion had but 250 effective soldiers left within its ranks.

Meanwhile, the Marking Guerillas had not been idle. With the Japanese occupied by the attack from the south, a guerilla patrol moved down Hill 803 and made its way along the Angat River to the dam. They found it intact and the powerhouse undamaged. Too weak to hold their positions, the patrol returned to report. General Wing now decided to fully commit his last regiment, the 169th Infantry Regiment. They were to attack and clear the road to the dam. The rains had made supply and evacuation difficult, and a good road was now vital for continued operations. Air supply had filled in some gaps, but it was not enough for a prolonged offensive. Weather now began to halt aerial resupply, further emphasizing the need for a ground supply line. Knowing that significant groups of the Japanese defenders had shifted to meet the attacks of the 103rd and Marking Guerilla Regiments, General Wing thought that the frontal attack he had previously avoided might now face reduced strength. The 169th Infantry was ordered to attack along Route 52. This would be part of a coordinated attack with the 103rd Infantry and 172nd Infantry Regiments, attacking within their zones.

Poor weather conditions delayed the attacks for two more days. In the interim a heavy concentration of artillery and air power was leveled against the Japanese.[8] More than 50,000 gallons of napalm were dropped on the Japanese holding the Bigti–Osboy Ridge alone. Route 52 was not neglected, either, with another 62,500 gallons of napalm being dropped along that road. Yet conditions remained poor. "Dawn broke on a gray sky on 13 May. By seven o'clock sheets of rain were drowning the landscape. The critical engineer roads which had been pushed behind the 103rd Infantry and the 172nd Infantry as far as Hill 805 became impassible mud holes. Vehicles loaded with ammunition, rations, and medical supplies sprawled hub deep along the road. The walking casualties started to the rear, knowing the ambulances would not come; the non-walking casualties waited patiently where they lay knowing some provision would be made to evacuate them."[9]

Despite these difficult conditions, the attack was renewed on May 17 and resulted in a dispute between the 103rd Infantry and the guerillas. It seems both units sent patrols down to the dam from different approaches, neither aware of the other's presence. While the 103rd Infantry patrol returned to report, the guerilla patrol raised an American flag over the powerhouse. Spotting this, the Americans sent a large combat patrol down to the dam to contact the guerillas. By the time the Americans arrived, over 200 guerillas were at the dam. Colonel Joseph P. Cleland, commanding the 103rd Infantry, refused to concede to the guerillas. He later messaged General Wing, "We're not conceding anything to guerillas. We had patrols at [the] dam this morning and saw no guerillas. When we returned this evening, they were there."[10]

Regardless of which unit claims credit, the fact remained that the Wawa and Ipo Dams, providing essential water to Manila, had both been captured largely intact. Japanese demolitions had been placed on the dam and powerhouse, but neither had been detonated. Although the dams had been secured, the fighting went on. General Wing still had to eliminate the *Kawashima Force* as a threat to the dams. He also had to secure Route 52 to supply his troops.

Eliminating the *Kawashima Force* proved easier than expected. The Japanese lines had been pierced and disorganized. Artillery and air strikes had further disrupted their organization. By May 17 General Kawashima decided that his troops were through and that any further attempts to hold or recover the dams were useless. He withdrew his forces to Mount Maranat, three miles east of the dam. Mopping up around the dams continued until May 31, as isolated Japanese groups attempted to infiltrate east to join the remnants of the *Kawashima Force*. Route 52 was cleared by the 169th Infantry. Meanwhile, the *Kawashima Force* reorganized itself for a withdrawal deep into the Sierra Madre Mountains. The Manila dams were safe.

CHAPTER 11

Southern Luzon

With the Manila dams secured, attention now turned to the final elimination of the *Shimbu Group*. General Hall's XI Corps had by the end of May destroyed the four strongest sub-groups of General Yokoyama's forces, but another large group, the *Kogure Detachment*, remained. It had originally been deployed to protect the rear of the *Shimbu Group* in the Bicol Peninsula and along the shore of Laguna de Bay. While there it had lost about half of its force by transfers to other groups, particularly the *Noguchi Force*. Philippine guerillas, patrols from the 43rd Infantry Division, air attacks, and sickness had further reduced the force from a high of 2,250 to perhaps 800 effectives. But they had been reinforced by some 2,000 Japanese troops retreating from the XIV Corps clearance operations south of Laguna de Bay, and more were expected. Concerned that these survivors and the *Kogure Detachment*, possibly totaling as many as 10,000 troops, would attempt to break out and rejoin the remnants of the *Shimbu Group* in the mountains east of Manila, General Krueger made plans to stop these Japanese troops before they reached General Yokoyama.

No Japanese soldier's experience within the *Imperial Japanese Army* of the Pacific War may be labeled as "typical," but all went through the process of becoming an *Imperial Army* soldier. One such soldier was a 35-year-old literary critic named Shōhei Ōoka of Tokyo. A graduate of Kyoto Imperial University and working with a small group of young intellectuals studying the literature of Europe, he was busy translating several such works into Japanese when his summons to report for duty arrived in January 1944. Within days he was no longer a college graduate translating foreign literature into Japanese; he was now Second Class Private Shōhei Ōoka.[1] As a *Nitōhei* (Second Class Private), he was immediately indoctrinated to a brutal world, far from college or literary life. Discipline in the Japanese Army was physical, with non-commissioned officers permitted, even encouraged, to use physical punishment for any real or perceived errors.

Japanese military indoctrination began as early as age eight, when in the third year of primary school all boys were given semi-military training by their teachers. As these children progressed in school, the training was soon taken over by Regular

Army officers. This training occupied two or more hours of each school day with up to six days of annual maneuvers. There were numerous post-graduate schools which included advanced military training, depending upon the graduate's vocation. Every Japanese male between the ages of 17 and 40 was subject to conscription. Although there were five classifications a Japanese conscript could fall under, by 1944 these standards had fallen much lower than at the war's opening. No exemptions were allowed under the law except for criminals and the permanently disabled. Even Japanese living abroad were subject to conscription, but these could request an extension for up to one year.

As a conscript, *Nitōhei* Ōoka was subject to a minimum of two years of service in the *Imperial Japanese Army*. As were most conscripts, he was assigned to the *Arms and Services Branch*, in his case the infantry. His recruit training included general instruction, squad training, bayonet training, and target practice. Soon he was marching with his unit and bivouacking overnight, sometimes for five days in a row. This was followed by more target practice, building field works, platoon and company training, more bayonet training, and more marching, as far as 20 miles a day. Later came company and battalion training, field work, combat firing, swimming, more bayonet practice, and marches up to 25 miles per day. The training ended with a final cycle of battalion and regimental training, combat firing, and maneuvers. *Nitōhei* Ōoka was now ready for combat.[2]

As soon as he completed his training, *Nitōhei* Ōoka was assigned to the newly formed *359th Independent Infantry Battalion*. As did many Japanese units of the period, this unit had more than one unit designation. It was also known as *Philippine Expeditionary Force Unit 10672*. This type of battalion usually consisted of a headquarters and train, commanded by a major, with four rifle companies, a machine-gun company, a battalion gun company, and a battalion antitank company. Armaments included four 70mm guns, eight 20mm antitank guns, four heavy (7.7mm) machine guns, 49 grenade launchers, 37 light machine guns, and 730 rifles. At this stage of the war, many such units were understrength and underequipped.

Nitōhei Ōoka was assigned to the *Number One Company*, also referred to as the *Nishiya Company*, after the commanding officer, First Lieutenant Nishiya Masao. The battalion traveled by rail to the port of embarkation where they boarded a civilian transport pressed into service. Nine ships, including four protecting destroyers, made up the convoy, which sailed for the Philippines on July 2, 1944. It was off Okinawa when word came of the American landings in the Mariana Islands. As the convoy cruised off the coast of Taiwan, one of the transports suddenly slowed, then the escorts began dropping depth charges. The transport soon sank, stern first. An American submarine, the USS *Piranha* (SS-389), had scored with torpedoes.[3] Rumors ran rampant as to the cause of the ship's demise, as no explosion had been heard aboard the other transports. Only one of every six men aboard the sunken transport was rescued.

That evening, July 12, 1944, the convoy reached Aparri on the north coast of Luzon. After waiting for the rescue ship carrying the survivors of the sinking ship to arrive, the convoy sailed on to Manila. Upon arrival, most of the battalion was assigned to the *105th Division*, protecting southern Luzon. But because it was under the division's responsibility, *Number One Company* was sent on to Mindoro, charged with "policing" that island. There they encountered a hostile population but otherwise spent a quiet and peaceful holiday period of 1944. To cover their large area of responsibility, the company was divided into platoon sectors, widely dispersed. Each man carried a Model 38 infantry rifle with 180 rounds of ammunition, plus normal field equipment.[4] Tents were set up at each platoon's base camp. In November, many of the enlisted men were promoted one grade, and *Nitōhei* Ōoka became *Ittōhei* (First Class Private) Ōoka.

Although what happened to the *Nishiya Company* occurred on Mindoro, it was a microcosm of what happened to similar companies on Luzon and other Philippine islands. Subjected to random guerilla attacks which caused a constant flow of casualties, but which kept the Japanese on alert constantly, they were also bombed regularly. This constant state of alert made many men susceptible to disease, which soon arrived in the form of malaria, dengue fever, and other maladies. When the Americans landed on Mindoro on December 15, several of the Japanese were already ill with one or more of these diseases, and one had already died. The officers immediately ordered a retreat into the thick jungles. There the company found a refuge in the mountains where they set up a base camp. Each night they watched for guerillas, and in the daytime for the Americans. Although for a while they remained in radio contact with their headquarters on Luzon, no help or assistance was forthcoming. More and more men fell ill. Repeated probes by the Americans and the guerillas forced several moves to new base camps. Each time a few men were left behind, too weak to move with the rest. Soon they were supplementing their food rations with bananas and potatoes from the native fields. Hunting parties went out in search of wild game for food.

The Japanese of the *Nishiya Company* remained soldiers and sent out patrols to obtain information which could be radioed back to headquarters, and to strike against the enemy when possible. But more and more of the patrols that were sent out failed to return. More and more of the men fell ill. Every few days they were forced to relocate their camps. Attrition from enemy attacks, raiding parties, and disease steadily eroded their ranks. *Ittōhei* Ōoka's time came after several weeks of struggling with malaria and dysentery. When it came time once again to move the base camp, he simply could not go on. He tried but fell behind and passed out. When he awoke, he found himself in the custody of two American soldiers. His war was over. "With this day, the activities of *Nishiya Company* as a unit came to a close. In the thirty-five days between February 9 and March 16, Second Lieutenant [*Shō-i*] Tanaka and eighteen other men from the unit, as well as one shipping engineer, were captured by guerillas, either alone or in small groups, as they straggled northward from the mountains behind Bongabong toward Calapan, surviving only on nuts, roots, tadpoles, and the like."[5] Of the 180 men in the *Nishiya Company*, that left one officer, four non-commissioned officers, and 16 privates, a total of 21 Japanese soldiers, less than 12 per cent, who would reunite in American prisoner-of-war camps on Leyte by the end of the campaign. It was a story repeated many thousands of times on Luzon.

* * *

General Krueger had tasked General Hall's XI Corps to clear up the eastern and northern shores of Laguna de Bay and block the Santa Maria Valley, closing Route 21 by physically joining with XIV Corps. General Hall gave the assignment to General Wing's 43rd Infantry Division. General Wing, fully engaged in other assignments, in turn gave the assignment to the 103rd RCT. Keeping its movements under as much concealment as possible, the regiment turned east on March 30. The following day the regiment moved into the Santa Maria Valley, catching the Japanese by surprise. Three days of sharp skirmishing brought the 103rd Infantry to physical contact with XIV Corps near Pagsanjam, on Laguna de Bay's southeastern shore. The movement had cost the Americans 10 killed and 20 wounded, while 240 enemy dead had been counted during the advance.

The Americans were surprised that the Japanese had failed to seriously defend the Santa Maria Valley, as it would have provided considerable food for the Japanese. They found that instead the *Kogure Detachment* had moved back to defensive positions at Kapatalin Sawmill, along Route 455, blocking the road to Lamon Bay. It now fell to XIV Corps to eliminate this defense.

But General Griswold had his hands full of other business, and it was not until nearly three weeks later that one regiment, the understrength 7th Cavalry, could be spared. The cavalrymen began a drive along Route 455 and found the Japanese dug in on hilly, densely jungled terrain at a horseshoe bend on Route 455. In many ways, it resembled the defenses of ZigZag Pass on Bataan earlier. Patrols and captured documents gave the cavalry a good intelligence picture of the enemy defenses, while artillery, bombs and napalm rained down to reduce them. The attack by the 7th Cavalry overran the enemy positions, killing 350 against American losses of four killed and 17 wounded. Six more casualties were sustained by the supporting Filipino guerillas. Marching without vehicles, the cavalrymen reached Lamon Bay on May 13, where boats of the 592nd Engineer Boat and Shore Regiment brought them supplies and vehicles. They also brought a battalion of guerillas under Lieutenant Colonel Bernard L. Anderson, an American officer.

The combined task force attacked Infanta only to find that the Japanese garrison had fled into the Sierra Madre Mountains. The 7th Cavalry cleaned up the remaining Japanese stragglers in the area while the 8th Cavalry did the same in the Santa Maria Valley. The 112th Cavalry RCT came up and relieved the 43rd Infantry Division. American intelligence officers calculated that this brief campaign had cost the Japanese 1,250 killed by ground attacks and another 500 men due to air and artillery strikes.

General Yokoyama agreed with the American intelligence estimates. Acknowledging by May 27 that his *Shimbu Group* was no longer an effective fighting force, he directed a withdrawal of all his units, some 26,000 men, less than half of which were still in organized units. The remaining 13,000 men were stragglers, with about 5,000 under medical treatment of one kind or another. Supplies were mostly gone, despite the vast stockpiles they had moved out of Manila. These had been abandoned along the way when American offensives had forced a rapid withdrawal. Only ammunition for small arms and machine guns remained plentiful. Lack of food remained the most difficult problem, causing an increased number of illnesses and straggling when individual or small groups of soldiers left the ranks in search of food. The sudden ejection from the Santa Maria Valley and Infanta region had deprived the group of any hope of gathering additional food. These Japanese were now issued only two ounces of rice per day per man, and that supply would be consumed within the month. Troops were already reduced to eating roots, bark, grass, and food stolen from local Filipinos. Not a local pig, carabao, or dog was left alive in the regions where the Japanese had passed.

General Yokoyama tried to move his remaining troops to an area where they could raise their own food. This he hoped to do by scattering them in the Sierra Madre Mountains. But General Hall at XI Corps decided otherwise and directed the 38th Infantry Division to mount limited attacks east from the Wawa Dam area. To assist in these attacks, General Chase was given the 2nd Provisional Regiment, East Central Luzon Guerilla Area. Organized and equipped by XI Corps, these guerillas were commanded by Major Edwin P. Ramsey, an American officer who had remained in the Philippines after the surrender and joined guerilla forces. Other forces, including General Wing's 43rd Infantry Division, General Cunningham's 112th Cavalry RCT, the 2nd Cavalry Brigade, and the Anderson guerillas would continue to patrol and clear out other sections of those mountains.

The fighting here continued for several more weeks. The Americans were striving to reach Santa Inez, the end of the *Shimbu Group*'s supply line into the Sierra Madre Mountains. Using native trails and river valleys, the 112th Cavalry RCT reached Santa Inez against light opposition by June 9. But the 151st Infantry, 38th Infantry Division, found the going much more difficult. Following the main road to Bosoboso, it took the 151st Infantry nine more days to contact the cavalry at Santa Inez. Alongside, the rest of the 38th Infantry Division and the 169th Infantry of General Wing's division also pushed forward into the mountains from the Wawa Dam. The

38th Infantry Division innovated the use of antiaircraft searchlights to illuminate its front lines at night, preventing infiltration or counterattacks. Both the 112th Cavalry RCT and the 38th Infantry Division employed the newest technology, helicopters, to evacuate seriously wounded soldiers from otherwise inaccessible mountains. The 38th and 43rd Infantry Divisions also combat tested the use of the new 57mm and 75mm recoilless rifles and 4.2-inch recoilless mortars. The latter was found to be unsatisfactory, but the two rifles were later widely distributed. This type of fighting did not end with a bang, but more of a whimper. The *Shimbu Group* was slowly ground down in many small, but usually fierce, small-unit actions. By the end of June, the *Shimbu Group* was in terrible shape, with most of the formerly organized units now broken up into small groups concerned only with the acquisition of food and survival. At this point the Japanese were losing three men from starvation or disease for every man killed in action. Within a month this ratio would rise to 10 for one. Although American intelligence estimated that General Yokoyama had about 6,500 men still under his command at the end of June, in fact he still had almost 15,000 men under his nominal command.

It fell to General Chase and his 38th Infantry Division to finish off the *Shimbu Group*. The 149th and 151st Infantry Regiments, with some 10,000 guerillas attached, continued to operate in the *Shimbu Group* area until the Japanese surrender in September. Each regiment rotated battalions to the front lines in the mountains, but these operated mainly in support of the guerillas, who carried the main burden of eliminating the Japanese. By August, another 5,000 enemy dead had been counted and others captured. At the end of the war, when word of the Japanese surrender penetrated the mountains of southern Luzon, only 6,300 Japanese troops remained to surrender. An additional 2,000 prisoners of war had been captured during the campaign. Some 5,500 remained unaccounted for.[6] That was all that remained of the original 50,000 members of General Yokoyama's *Shimbu Group*.

There remained only what is known as the Visayan Passages in southern Luzon. General Krueger had planned for logistical bases to be established on the shores of Batangas and Balayan Bays. He expected the XIV Corps to clear these areas during the first week in March, by which time the *Shimbu Group* would have been pushed far enough north to not be a factor in the defense of that area. The operation would entail securing the northern shores of the Bicol Peninsula and clearing the Batangas–Balayan Bay area. Then an amphibious operation would be launched against the southeast sector of the Bicol Peninsula to complete the securing of the Visayan Passages. The forces on the peninsula would attack north to meet XIV Corps forces attacking south toward them, thereby clearing the area of the enemy.

This region contains some mountainous areas, but the bulk of it was flat agricultural land with gently rolling terrain well suited for General Krueger's logistical bases. To execute this plan, General Griswold had only General Swing's 11th Airborne Division and the independent 158th RCT available. The final plan had the 511th Parachute

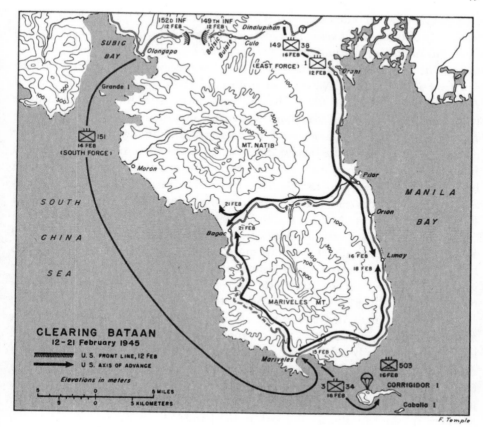

Clearing Bataan

Robert Ross Smith. *United States Army in World War II. The War in the Pacific. Triumph in the Philippines.* Washington, D.C.: Center of Military History, 1984. p. 333.

Infantry and 187th Glider Infantry Regiments attacking toward Lipa from the north and northwest, while the 158th Infantry RCT assembled near Nasugbu and then attacked southeast on Route 17 toward Balayan and Batangas Bays. Securing these objectives would give XIV Corps control over the Lipa Corridor. Then the 158th Infantry RCT would strike north to contact the 11th Airborne Division.

American intelligence estimated that there were between 10,000 and 17,000 Japanese troops in the area. The American units selected for this operation were outnumbered by the enemy they were to attack. Even if the 188th Glider Infantry Regiment, which had to be left to guard the force's line of communications, had been included in the assault force, they would have still been outnumbered by the Japanese.

General Yokoyama's defensive forces in the area consisted of the *Fuji Force*, all that was left of the original *Kogure Detachment*. This group included the *17th Infantry* (less *3rd Battalion*), the *3rd Battalion, 31st Infantry Regiment*, and an assortment of support and provisional units with a battalion and a half of artillery, all from the *8th Division*. Colonel Masatoshi Fujishige, regimental commander of the *17th Infantry*, commanded this force. He also had under his command several suicide boat squadrons, without boats, and base battalions of the *2nd Surface Raiding Base Force*, along with naval troops that had garrisoned the Manila Bay islands but escaped to Luzon. The *86th Airfield Battalion*, part of the *4th Air Army* stationed at Lipa, was also within *Fuji Force*. All told, there were about 13,000 Japanese troops in *Fuji Force*, of which perhaps 3,000 were trained infantry. Several of these widely separated units had already encountered Americans, specifically the 11th Airborne Division on its dash to Manila, and had suffered accordingly.

Colonel Fujishige's mission was not to hold the Visayan Passages. General Yokoyama had specifically ordered that his main objective was to protect the eastern flank of the *Shimbu Group* as it fought north of Manila. Otherwise, Colonel Fujishige was left to his own resources, a factor that was enhanced when communications between him and General Yokoyama broke down completely after March 1.

Colonel Fujishige's defenses were based on positions extending from Mount Macolod, on the southeast of Lake Taal, running across to Route 417, a good road leading to Batangas Bay. He placed small detachments at various road junctions in the Tayabas Bay plain. His best unit, the *17th Infantry Battalion*, was split among the various detachments, hoping that their training and expertise in infantry tactics would be extended to the rest of his troops by their presence.

Those troops had already suffered at the hands of the Americans. The 11th Airborne Division had destroyed his *West Sector Unit* in February, during their march to Manila. The paratroopers had also trapped 1,350 of his men at Ternate, cutting them off from Colonel Fujishige's other troops. All the suicide boats of the *2nd Surface Raiding Base Force* had been destroyed by Allied air and naval forces, with PT boats striking right into the heart of his base. Then, Philippine guerillas had appeared in force, creating what had been described as a "hornet's nest" of raids, ambushes, and sniping against his force. Finally, almost under the eyes of Colonel Fujishige, American forces had rescued over 2,000 American and Allied civilian internees from the Los Baños prison camp.

The raiders were a task force drawn from the 11th Airborne Division. The selection of units to participate in the raid was based upon those who had suffered the least casualties thus far in the Luzon campaign. These included Major Henry A. Burgess's 1st Battalion, 188th Glider Infantry Regiment; Lieutenant Colonel Michael Massad's 675th Glider Field Artillery Battalion; the 472nd Parachute Field Artillery Battalion; Captain Louis Burris's Battery D of the 457th Glider Field Artillery Battalion; Company B of the 637th Tank Destroyer Battalion; a platoon

General of the Army Douglas MacArthur, Commander, Southwest Pacific Theater of Operations. (NARA)

Lieutenant General Walter Krueger, Commander, Sixth U.S. Army, speaking with his troops. (NARA 208-PU-111-BB-005)

Lieutenant General Tomoyuki (Hobun) Yamashita, Commander, *Fourteenth Area Army*, defending the Philippines, 1944–45. (NARA 242-GAP-32W-14)

Vice Admiral Thomas C. Kinkaid, Commander, Seventh U.S. Fleet ("MacArthur's Navy"), 1944–45. (NARA 80-G-320652)

Major General Innis Palmer Swift, who commanded the I Corps during the Luzon campaign. He had earlier commanded the 1st Cavalry Division in New Guinea. (NARA 111-SC-264134)

Major General Oscar W. Griswold commanded the XIV Corps during the Luzon campaign, 1944–45. (NARA 208-PU-83K)

Soldiers of Company I, 103rd Infantry Regiment, 43rd Infantry Division, in action in the Philippines, 1945. (NARA 111-SC-310814)

Soldiers of the 2nd Battalion, 128th Infantry Regiment, 32nd Infantry Division, firing a 37mm antitank gun against Japanese positions on Luzon. (NARA 111-SC-270995)

The crew of the escort aircraft carrier USS *Manila Bay* (CVE-61) fights fires after being hit by a Japanese kamikaze off the coast of Luzon, January 5, 1945. (REAL WAR PHOTOS # N956A)

Soldiers of the 1st Infantry Regiment, 6th Infantry Division, advance with tank support in the Cabaruan Hills, Luzon, under a smoke screen. (REAL WAR PHOTOS # A 2658)

Soldiers of Company K, 161st Infantry Regiment, 25th Infantry Division, cover a cave after tossing in a phosphorus grenade, near Balete Pass, April 19, 1945. (REAL WAR PHOTOS # A 2895)

Company I, 20th Infantry Regiment, 6th Infantry Division, attack up a steep hill on the Kobayashi Line near Manila, April 4, 1945. (REAL WAR PHOTOS # A 2649)

Under enemy artillery fire, tanks of the 775th Tank Battalion support the attack of the 37th Infantry Division on Lantap, Luzon, June 12, 1945. (REAL WAR PHOTOS # A 3224)

North of Bubabag in the Cagayan Valley, Company A, 63rd Infantry Regiment, 6th Infantry Division, are climbing up to relieve an advanced outpost. (REAL WAR PHOTOS # A 2651)

Ignoring enemy dead, soldiers of the 37 Infantry Division blast enemy positions alor a highway on Luzon, June 12, 1945. (REA WAR PHOTOS # A 3228)

Infantrymen of the 129th Infantry Regiment, 37 Infantry Division, fighting in a Luzon cemeter April 24, 1945. (REAL WAR PHOTOS # A 3231)

Troopers of Company G, 187th Glider Infantry Regiment, 11th Airborne Division, advancing to Sulac, Batangas Province, Luzon, April 9, 1945. (REAL WAR PHOTOS # A 2042)

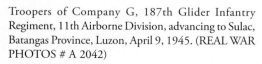

Soldiers of Company B, 82nd Chemical Mortar Battalion, supporting the 63rd Infantry Regiment, 6th Infantry Division, take up positions in front of the Shimbu Line, in the Sierra Madre Range east of Manila, April 26, 1945. (REAL WAR PHOTOS # A 2670)

Men of the 117th Engineer (Combat) Battalion, 37th Infantry Division, use a bulldozer to retrieve a Sherman tank of Company B, 775th Tank battalion, near Baguio Luzon, April 2, 1945. (REAL WAR PHOTOS # A 3247)

ldiers of Company A, 149th Infantry Regiment, 37th fantry Division, cover an advance patrol along the arkina River on the approach to Wawa Dam, May 28, '45. (REAL WAR PHOTOS # A 3285)

Soldiers of Company L, 128th Infantry Regiment, 32nd Infantry Division, fighting on Hill 604 along the Villa Verde Trail, April 1, 1945. (REAL WAR PHOTOS # A 3076)

Original 1941 National Guard members of the 123rd Field Artillery Battalion, 33rd Infantry Division, pose for a group photo with their 155mm guns on Luzon, May 26, 1945. (REAL WAR PHOTOS # A 3094)

Japanese troops fording a river somewhere in the Philippines. Undated, captured Japanese photo. (NARA 111-SC-334313)

Posed photo of a Japanese Navy machine-gun team in action. This photo, captured from the Japanese, shows the heavy machine gun model 92 deployed for action. Similar guns were often used in the Luzon campaign against the Americans, who called it the "woodpecker" from its stuttering noise when fired. (NARA 208-AA-247-XX-1)

Staff Sergeant Raymond H. Cooley, Company B, 27th Infantry Regiment, 25th Infantry Division, who earned his Medal of Honor near Lumboy, Luzon, on February 24, 1945. (NARA 111-SC-313644)

Private First Class Thomas E. Atkins, Company A, 127th Infantry Regiment, 32nd Infantry Division, who earned his Medal of Honor on the Villa Verde Trail on March 10, 1945. (NARA 111-SC-263485-B)

Private First Class (later Technical Sergeant) Cleto Rodriguez, of Company B, 148th Infantry Regiment, 37th Infantry Division, who earned his Medal of Honor at the Paco Railroad Station, near Manila, on February 8, 1945. (NARA 111-SC-313757)

Staff Sergeant Howard E. Woodford, of Company I, 130th Infantry Regiment, 33rd Infantry Division, who earned his posthumous Medal of Honor near Tabio, Luzon, on June 6, 1945. (NARA 111-SC-313797)

Differing reactions: Japanese prisoners of war bow their heads as they listen to Japan's Emperor Hirohito announce Japan's surrender, August 1945. (NARA 80-G-490320)

Differing reactions: Men of the 151st Infantry Regiment, 38th Infantry Division, react to the news of Japan's surrender, August 1945. (REAL WAR PHOTOS # A 3281)

from Company C, 127th Airborne Engineer Battalion; the 672nd Amphibious Tractor Battalion; elements of the 511th Parachute Infantry Regiment, and attached Philippine guerillas. When informed of his mission on February 19, Major Burgess's reaction was, "Why us?" He later recalled, "I. was shocked to learn that only our battalion of about 412 men and officers (a very small battalion even by parachute infantry standards) was expected to make the raid."[7] Major Burgess was informed that his battalion was in fact the strongest infantry battalion left within the 11th Airborne Division.

Intelligence sources had provided Lieutenant Colonel Henry ("Butch") Muller, the division intelligence (G-2) officer, with precise details of the camp and its defenses. Colonel Douglass P. Quandt, the division operations (G-3) officer, evolved an operations plan. Basically, First Lieutenant George E. Skau's 31-member Division Reconnaissance Platoon would move two days before the main force, contact the guerillas, and coordinate their actions with the task force. At the designated moment, First Lieutenant John Ringler's B Company, 511th Parachute Infantry Regiment, would parachute into a drop zone selected by Colonel Quandt and verified by Lieutenant Skau. Lieutenant Ringler met with General Swing, who "informed me that my mission was to take my company and drop on Los Baños prison camp, release all internees, and organize the people so we could start to march them to the point where they were to be evacuated."[8] The pick-up was to be conducted by the task force's commander, Colonel Robert H. ("Shorty") Soule, hence the name "Soule Task Force." Colonel Soule, commanding the 188th Glider Infantry Regiment, would then sail aboard vehicles of the 672nd Amphibious Tractor Battalion over Laguna de Bay and land nearby. There, protected by the field artillery which kept the estimated 10,000 Japanese nearby occupied, he would load the internees and troopers, and withdraw.

That is how it went. Jumping from 400 feet, Company B landed at the prison camp which had been attacked by the guerillas and Lieutenant Skau's reconnaissance men the moment Lieutenant Ringler's parachute opened. The combined force attacked the prison guards, cut the wire surrounding the camp, and began rounding up the civilians. Meanwhile, Lieutenant Colonel Henry ("Hank") Burgess's other two companies of the 1st Battalion, 511th Parachute Infantry, arrived at beaches secured by the guerillas near the prison camp exactly on schedule. Captain Thomas Meserau's C Company marched out to Mayondon Point, where they wiped out a small Japanese force that threatened the evacuation route. Company A likewise moved in the opposite direction to establish a block, protecting that route. Captain Louis Burris and D Battery, 457th Parachute Field Artillery, remained on the beach to provide support if needed. It soon was, and Battery D knocked out four enemy machine guns protecting Mayondon Point. Colonel Burgess's column came under some small-arms fire on the way to the camp but ignored it and pressed on. The amphibious tractors reached the camp and began to load the civilian evacuees. Colonel

Burgess ordered Lieutenant Ringler, who had not lost a man, to torch the prison camp. The paratroopers carried or otherwise assisted some 130 internees who could not walk to the tractors. Despite great confusion due to the celebrations among the internees, the paratroopers nevertheless managed to load the vehicles, each carrying 35 internees and a few paratroopers as guards, and began the return journey. With Company B and the Reconnaissance Platoon providing a rear guard, the column returned to the beach. A total of 2,122 civilian internees had been rescued at a cost of two guerillas killed, two wounded, and two troopers of the Reconnaissance Platoon wounded.

Meanwhile, Colonel Soule and the rest of his task force had the 188th Glider Infantry Regiment make a strong diversionary attack on the enemy front lines before Los Baños. Reinforced with the 637th Tank Destroyer Battalion, they kept the front-line Japanese occupied while the paratroopers cleared the prison camp. By late morning, the task force was advancing so fast the colonel could see the amphibious tractors returning across Laguna de Bay back to the starting point, Mamatid. The Soule Task Force had accomplished its mission, blocking any Japanese attempt at sending reinforcements to the prison camp. With a bridgehead across the San Juan River, Colonel Soule called a halt to operations for the day.[9] General MacArthur, impressed with the raid's success, sent a message which read, "Nothing could be more satisfying to a soldier's heart than this recue. I am deeply grateful. God was certainly with us today."[10]

Whatever embarrassment Colonel Fujishige might have felt at the successful raid by the Soule Task Force, it quickly was replaced by anxiety to maintain his own defenses. His concerns grew when the 187th Glider Infantry came down off Tagaytay Ridge and cleared the Japanese to the northern shore of Lake Taal. It continued until the Americans met *Fuji Force* defenders two miles west of Tanauan. These were overcome with support from air and artillery. The glider infantrymen then halted to await the results of an attack by the 511th Parachute Infantry through the Lipa Corridor toward Santo Tomas.

The 511th Parachute Infantry was to clear a path through the *Fuji Force* defenders along Route 1 from Manila to Tanauan and then along Route 21 to Laguna de Bay. The major block was at Mt. Bijang, which controlled both routes. Several unsuccessful attacks over three days were followed by a heavy barrage of air and artillery support, finally clearing the hill with guerilla support. But by that time the paratroopers had bypassed the block and moved to within a mile of Santo Tomas. Here strong Japanese positions faced both regiments, which even together were outnumbered by the defenders. Rather than risk heavy losses from frontal attacks, the two regiments mopped up their rear areas while directing air and artillery against the Japanese.

Meanwhile the 158th Infantry RCT had left Nasugbu on March 4, moving quickly to Balayan on the northwestern end of Balayan Bay. Resistance was described as "negligible." The "Bushmasters," as they called themselves, soon cleared the shores of Balayan and Batangas Bays and by March 11 were in the town of Batangas. This advance bypassed strong elements of the *2nd Surface Raiding Force* on the Calumpan Peninsula, separating Balayan and Batangas Bays. Before either could be secured, Calumpan Peninsula would have to be cleared of Japanese. Brigadier General Hanford ("Jack") McNider sent one of his battalions to clear the peninsula, where most of the Japanese garrison was busy trying to escape to the islands in the Verde Island Passage or to the Lubang Islands. Other battalions of the "Bushmasters" fought Japanese blocking Route 417, the Batangas–Lipa road at Mount Macolod. Here some 1,250 Japanese, supported by a 300mm howitzer, 81mm mortars, and many machine guns stripped from Japanese aircraft at nearby Lipa airstrip, held positions. Supported by two 105mm and two 155mm artillery battalions, the 158th Infantry overran the defenses of Mount Macolod in a four-day battle and cleared most, but not all, of the area. There were still some Japanese defenders in place when the combat team was withdrawn to clear the Bicol Peninsula.

But before the "Bushmasters" left the area, Lieutenant Colonel Boysie Day drove into a local village and stopped by an old, white-haired Filipino. The man said the Japanese had gone and that the village was deserted. Entering the village, Colonel Day saw "scores of bodies lay sprawled in the yellow dirt." Moving closer, he saw that "clouds of bluebottle flies hovered around the bodies." Entering the church, he noted, "the stained-glass window had been blown out and the holes let enough sunlight through for him [Day] to see what the Japanese had done before a few survivors confirmed his guess: the entire town had been herded into the church. The ruse to get them there was a familiar one, he [Day] learned later,[11] 'the commanding officer had something to tell them.'" The Japanese had then locked the doors and tossed in torches and dynamite. Hundreds of Philippine civilians lay dead in and around the church.

The 11th Airborne Division and the 158th RCT had by March 23 cleared the shores of Balayan and Batangas Bays, securing the northern side of the Verde Island Passage. Lake Taal was relatively secure as well, with *Fuji Force* units there now isolated. But General Krueger was eager to implement his plans for clearing the northern side of the Visayan Passage. To do this the Bicol Peninsula needed to be cleared of Japanese. This was why the "Bushmasters" had been withdrawn from Mt. Macolod. Concerned that the 11th Airborne Division's remaining strength was now so low that the entire division would be required to secure southern Luzon as well as acting as the Army reserve, General Krueger assigned only the "Bushmasters" to the Bicol Peninsula operation. Advised that the Allied air and naval forces for the Bicol Peninsula operation were not yet ready, he moved the attack back to April 1. He used the interim to move the 1st Cavalry Division to southern Luzon to replace the infantrymen, which is why the 43rd Infantry Division replaced the cavalry in the fight for the dams. The Japanese holdouts in the Mt. Macolod sector then became the responsibility of the 11th Airborne Division. Both the paratroopers and the cavalry would spend the next several weeks mopping up bypassed pockets of Japanese, fighting and in some cases dying in little recorded battles to liberate Philippine territory.

* * *

Once everything had been coordinated between Sixth Army, the Allied air forces and the Allied naval forces, the Bicol Peninsula attack was set for April Fool's Day. In the week prior, air and naval bombardment struck known and suspected Japanese defenses on the peninsula. Staging from Balayan Bay, the 158th Infantry RCT would go ashore at Legaspi two companies at a time, due to a shortage of appropriate landing craft. After securing a beachhead, they were to attack north and south until contacting the XIV Corps. Sixth Army intelligence placed about 1,500 Japanese troops on the peninsula, most from the *35th Naval Guard Unit* and a reinforced company of the *26th Independent Mixed Regiment*. There were also various ground service units of the *4th Air Army* in the area. Once again, the only purpose of the Japanese defending the peninsula was to protect the rear of the *Shimbu Group*.

As the 1st Battalion, 158th Infantry, came ashore at Legaspi Port there were a few rounds of Japanese artillery from a gun which was quickly eliminated by naval gunfire. The town, port, and nearby Japanese airfield were quickly secured by the "Bushmasters." Troops soon began moving deeper into the peninsula until the leading company was halted by enemy machine-gun fire. The company stopped for the night and found themselves surrounded later that evening. An attack by the rest of the battalion freed the trapped company the next morning. The "Bushmasters" had found the Japanese first line of defense. General MacNider now faced a dilemma. He could attack frontally or try an amphibious end run to secure one of his main objectives, the Sorsogon Peninsula. But a shortage of landing craft took the decision out of his hands. Based upon reports from U.S. Navy ships patrolling the area and knowing the Eighth Army had cleared the southern shores of the Visayan Strait, he decided that his RCT, numbering barely 2,000 soldiers, would attack overland. For the next eight days, April 2 to April 10, the "Bushmasters" fought over rough jungled terrain to overcome Japanese resistance. At a cost of 45 men killed and 200 wounded, they pushed the Japanese back and counted more than 500 enemy dead. Still anxious to meet his timetable, on April 6 General MacNider loaded his regiment's antitank company aboard five LCMs of the 592nd Engineer Boat and Shore Regiment and landed it on the Sorsogon Peninsula. There they found no opposition, secured the Philippine end of the transpacific cable, and moved over the rest of the peninsula against no resistance. Later the 2nd Battalion, 158th Infantry, supported by the 147th Field Artillery Battalion, cleared the entire peninsula, killing 150 Japanese against a loss of six men wounded.

The remainder of the regiment spent the next several days clearing the Bicol Peninsula of stragglers. The enemy made stands in the Cituinan Hills and around Daraga but were overcome by determined attacks. At a cost of 40 men killed and 235 wounded, the peninsula was cleared of Japanese troops. Almost 700 enemy dead were counted. Except for a prolonged mopping up of the entire area of southern Luzon, mainly by Philippine guerillas supported by American units, the campaign for southern Luzon was over.

* * *

In Northwest Europe, the Canadian I Corps was driving on Arnhem from the Nijmegen Bridgehead. In Ninth U.S. Army's zone, the 17th Airborne Division had captured Münster, while the 5th Armored Division moved to the Weser River. In First U.S. Army zone the 8th Infantry Division was fighting for the German towns of Siegen and Netphen. In Seventh U.S. Army's area, the 45th Infantry Division continued the vicious fight for Aschaffenburg. In Italy, the British Eighth Army continued its attacks at Lake Comacchio. Near the Ryukyu Islands, the convoy carrying the 77th Infantry Division to Okinawa was struck by kamikazes and suffered damage and casualties. On Luzon the battle turned to the north.

North to Baguio

While the other two corps of Sixth Army drew the assignments of seizing Manila, Corregidor, and the dams, Major General Innis P. Swift's I Corps had the unglamorous and unheralded yet critical job of not only protecting the rear of the entire Sixth Army, but also facing the major Japanese troop concentration on Luzon.

The initial movements went well. Ordered to move up to a line running from Licab to Lupao, General Swift had sent his 6th Infantry Division toward that line on January 28. The "Sightseeing Sixth" moved into Victoria and Guimba against limited resistance and the following day relieved elements of the 37th Infantry Division at Licab, east of Victoria. Finding no Japanese present, the division pushed on to Talavera, 12 miles east of Licab and, after a brief skirmish, secured the road junction at the barrio of Baloc, on Route 5. Almost without difficulty, the line of communications, Route 5, between the *Shobu* and *Shimbu Groups* had been nearly severed.

The 6th Reconnaissance Troop pushed down Route 5 to Muñoz, which marked the northern end of the Licab–Lupao line. Here they found no Japanese, but when the leading elements of the 20th Infantry Regiment approached the town the following day, January 28, the town was found occupied by the enemy. An initial attempt to take the town was repulsed. The days of advancing easily were obviously over. Continuing patrols by the 6th Reconnaissance Troop established that the Japanese had set up a counter-reconnaissance screen west of Muñoz and San Jose with a strong force located at Cabanatuan, seven miles south of Talavera.

While the "Sightseeing Sixth" had successfully occupied the Licab–Lupao line, the neighboring 25th Infantry Division had not. Major General Mullins's division had come out of Army reserve status on January 28 and marched unopposed along Route 8 until they had reached Gonzales, 10 miles west of Lupao. Other than a brief skirmish with a Japanese outpost at Pemienta, no enemy hindered that advance. But unknown at the time to the Americans was that a small armor-infantry force of the *2nd Tank Division* had been bypassed between Gonzales and Pemienta. During the evening of January 29–30, this force tried to break through the perimeter of the 27th Infantry Regiment. They left behind 125 dead, eight tanks, and eight 105mm howitzers destroyed, and numerous vehicles abandoned.[1] Additional battles were fought until the division came up against the same counter-reconnaissance screen that faced the 6th Infantry Division alongside.

These late January battles had provided Sixth Army with enough information to conclude that I Corps faced the *2nd Tank Division* around San Jose, Muñoz, and Lupao. There was also information to support the presence of the *10th Division* in the same general area. This information—that there were no Japanese west of Route 5—also relieved some of General Krueger's anxieties over the rear of XIV Corps, indicating that the Japanese were not as threatening as had earlier been feared. Nevertheless, the presence of perhaps two Japanese divisions in the area still indicated the possibility that they were preparing for an attack on the Sixth Army's communications and supply sources. To reduce this threat even further, General Krueger ordered General Swift on January 30 to have his I Corps drive east to seize San Jose and build a defensive line from there to Cabanatuan and Rizal, 20 miles to the south and southeast, respectively.

General Yamashita was also interested in the San Jose area, but for entirely different reasons than General Krueger. While the latter was interested in establishing a line facing the *Shobu Group* for future offensive operations while at the same time protecting his army's rear, General Yamashita was concerned with safeguarding the passage of the rest of his supplies, which had been temporarily stockpiled in and around San Jose, to his jungle fortress in the mountains to the north along Route 5. He also needed to hold the San Jose area until the *105th Division*, transferred from the *Shimbu Group* to the *Shobu Group*, passed through San Jose. General Yamashita estimated that the transfer of supplies, mostly ammunition, would take until the end of the first week of February. He hoped that the *105th Division* would also be clear of the area by then. The result of these opposing moves was the Battle of San Jose.

General Yamashita viewed the defense of San Jose as a limited duration operation, to last only long enough to secure his supplies and gain the bulk of the *105th Division*. Although they were unaware of it, if the Americans of I Corps could rapidly secure San Jose, both of General Yamashita's objectives would be lost, with serious consequences for the Japanese defensive battle for northern Luzon.

General Yamashita had deployed his defenses of San Jose in a defense in depth, with various detachments scattered throughout the area. Although General Yamashita ordered the *2nd Tank Division* to defend Lupao and Muñoz, Lieutenant General Yoshiharu Iwanaka ordered his troops, reinforced with battalions of both the *10th* and *105th Divisions*, into eight separate localities. These defending units were, as had become common practice in the Japanese Army, thrown together without any previous experience of working together. Lupao, for example, was held by a tank company each from the *7th* and *10th Tank Regiments*, two companies of the *2nd Mobile Infantry Regiment*, three 75mm guns, and engineers from the *2nd Tank*

Division. Having learned from earlier Pacific battles that the standard Japanese tank was no match for the standard American M4 Sherman tank, the Japanese buried their tanks as pillboxes. Only San Jose itself, long a target of Allied air power, was left undefended.[2]

The Japanese planning left much to be desired. There was no plan to defend the open ground along Routes 5 and 8 which led to San Jose from the American lines. The third-class Route 99, connecting Lupao to Muñoz, was left completely undefended. The Japanese flanks were left hanging in the open. All defenses were fixed and immobile. There were no plans for a withdrawal after the purpose for defending San Jose had passed. In postwar interviews, surviving officers of the *2nd Tank Division* claimed that fuel shortages, Allied air superiority, terrain difficulties, and the inferior quality of the Japanese armor was the cause of the defense arrangements at San Jose. It also appears that General Yamashita was willing to sacrifice most or all the *2nd Tank Division*, which would be difficult to utilize in the jungle-covered mountains of northern Luzon, to secure his supplies and additional reinforcements.

General Swift decided upon a simple plan for seizing San Jose. It would be a pincer movement, with the 6th Infantry Division making the main attack along Route 5 through Muñoz. The 25th Infantry Division would support the advance with an attack up Route 8 through Umingan and Lupao. Both divisions were reinforced with heavy artillery guns and tanks. The recently arrived 32nd Infantry Division would protect the attack's rear.

The attack began February 1, with the 20th Infantry Regiment, 6th Infantry Division, attacking Muñoz and the 27th Infantry Regiment, 25th Infantry Division, attacking Umingan. Situated among the rice paddies, which makes the area known as the "rice bowl of Luzon," Muñoz contained several hundred nipa huts spread over a wide area. Although the attacking Americans could "see a line of pillboxes and other emplacements paralleling the road at the west end of town," there was no sign of the enemy.[3] After a bombardment by the 51st Field Artillery Battalion, the attack began.

Company K, 20th Infantry, attacked from the northeast and crossed the railroad, then moved forward 200 yards without opposition. Suddenly and without warning, "a stream of automatic weapons fire from emplacements hitherto invisible pinned down the assault platoons."[4] Unable to find cover in the flat open terrain, the infantrymen began to dig into the ground to set up their own machine guns. They remained pinned down for the rest of the day. As evening approached, the rest of the 3rd Battalion, 20th Infantry, managed to join with Company K, digging in alongside. By that time enemy artillery and 47mm antitank fire had joined the automatic weapons firing at the Americans.

American artillery and tanks were called upon to even the odds. These knocked out two dug-in tanks and several other positions, but the enemy fire seemed not to slacken. Private First Class Gerald L. Halverson stood erect despite withering machine-gun fire and fired two rounds from his rocket launcher, destroying a dug-in

Japanese tank. He then worked his way forward to within 15 yards of an enemy machine gun, knocking it out with another rocket. As he fired at an enemy 47mm gun firing at his buddies, he was fatally wounded by a shell from that gun.[5] Captain Charles A. Figley, Jr., used a rifle to eliminate several enemy riflemen firing on his men, then used rifle grenades to destroy a Japanese tank and kill its crew. Technical Sergeant Harold W. Bieraugel knocked out another tank and crew with grenades and a bayonet, earning a Silver Star and Purple Heart when one of the enemy took a bite out of his hand. Sergeant Paul Blodgett and Corporal Emil C. Barta, of the 6th Engineer (Combat) Battalion, covered others who were ambushed while building a road into the enemy position, allowing several wounded men to be safely evacuated until they were themselves killed by enemy fire.

A coordinated attack by the 20th Infantry on February 2 fared no better. Heavy fire from tanks, artillery, machine guns, mortars, and riflemen crisscrossed the open approaches to Muñoz, blocking any advance. Three enemy tanks left the protection of their dugouts and charged the 3rd Battalion, but were soon disposed of by bazookas, rifle grenades, and the 51st Field Artillery Battalion. Two of the supporting Japanese 47mm antitank guns were also knocked out in this attack. That night several tank-stalking parties successfully knocked out more tank and some machine-gun positions. February 3 saw another attack, with 3rd Battalion attacking directly while 2nd Battalion, 20th Infantry, hit the Japanese left flank. A heavy artillery and mortar bombardment preceded this attack, which breached the outer defenses of Muñoz. Staff Sergeant Chester G. Johnson crawled forward toward a dug-in enemy tank until spotted by an enemy artillery observer. Artillery was directed at Sergeant Johnson, who sprinted forward and destroyed the enemy tank with his rocket launcher. Nearby, Sergeant Robert E. Millious of the attached 98th Chemical Mortar Battalion knocked out two tanks with his accurate observations from a post well in advance of the infantry units he was supporting.[6] First Lieutenant James L. Giangrosso led his platoon in the attack, then directed the repulse of an enemy counterattack. While withdrawing to better night positions, he noticed that two of his men were missing. Leaving his platoon in charge of his platoon sergeant, Lieutenant Giangrosso returned alone to the battlefield where he found the two men, both seriously wounded. He carried one man back under enemy fire, and then returned for the second. This man was too seriously wounded to be moved without a litter, and Lieutenant Giangrosso was advised that a litter team was unavailable until morning. Undeterred, Lieutenant Giangrosso remained in no-man's land with the wounded man all night, hiding from several enemy patrols scouring the area. Both were successfully rescued at dawn.[7]

* * *

Meanwhile the 1st and 63rd Infantry Regiments were attacking San Jose itself. Again, tanks and strongly held emplacements blocked any advance. Here the Japanese were also particularly motivated to hold the area, since any American advance beyond San Jose would expose their route of retreat to the north, blocking the way to Balete Pass and northern Luzon. But the 2nd Battalion, 1st Infantry, managed to establish itself along the Rizal Highway near Bicos, and the 3rd Battalion seized the Talavera River Bridge intact, destroying three enemy tanks and capturing an ammunition and fuel supply dump. The 63rd Infantry, with only two battalions available,[8] moved past Muñoz and seized the Agricultural School between Muñoz and San Jose. Leaving Company L to mop up the school, the rest of the 63rd Infantry advanced on San Jose but were halted by enemy fire. But while the Japanese were occupied with the 63rd Infantry, the 1st Infantry moved into San Jose and secured it on February 4.

Despite the success, General Patrick had lost patience with the commander of the 20th Infantry Regiment, Colonel Washington M. Ives, Jr. He relieved him of command and replaced him with Lieutenant Colonel Harold G. Maison.[9] Nevertheless, the battle for Muñoz remained a house-by-house and street-by-street fight for several more days.

Meanwhile, the 25th Infantry Division was faring no better. Attacking on February 1, they had run into the same defenses that faced the "Sightseeing Sixth." Troops of the 27th Infantry Regiment, under a heavy artillery and mortar concentration, managed to get to within 250 yards of the outskirts of Umingan before they were stopped by machine-gun and rifle fire. Antitank fire was used against American tanks and drove them off. Irrigation ditches in the area acted as antitank ditches, preventing the American tanks from maneuvering, but providing cover for the attacking infantry. General Mullins, the division commander, brought up the 35th Infantry Regiment to help. They were to bypass Umingan on the south and seize San Roque barrio on Route 8 four miles southeast of Umingan and a mile north of Lupao.

The attack of the 35th Infantry met surprisingly little resistance, for the Japanese had withdrawn into the foothills of the Caraballo Mountains. By midday on February 2, the 35th Infantry had cleared Umingan, leaving two pockets of resistance to be dealt with by the 27th Infantry. The mopping-up operation counted 150 enemy dead, eight destroyed 47mm antitank guns, and large quantities of ammunition for both antitank guns and artillery. Unwilling to allow the main Japanese force to escape into the mountains, General Mullins pushed the 35th Infantry toward Lupao immediately. Estimating the Japanese force in Lupao as a company of Japanese infantry supported by 20 tanks, the 35th Infantry dispatched its 1st Battalion to Lupao.

The advance on Lupao met no resistance until within 750 yards of the town, when Japanese machine-gun, mortar, and artillery fire halted the advance in its tracks. Attempts to outflank the enemy defenses over the open ground failed. With darkness approaching, the battalion withdrew 500 yards to allow the artillery and mortars to weaken the enemy defenses. But a renewed attack the next morning would again make no significant progress. Like General Patrick on his flank, General Mullins now worked to bypass Lupao. Leaving the 27th Infantry clearing Umingan and the 35th Infantry to deal with Lupao, General Mullins sent his third regiment, the Washington State National Guard-originated 161st Infantry Regiment, to move across country to Route 99 and then push forward to Route 8 between San Isidro and San Jose. Once there, they were to patrol and be prepared to assist the 6th Infantry Division in seizing San Jose, if necessary.

The 35th Infantry placed its 3rd Battalion on Route 8 southeast of Lupao on February 3. This battalion managed to get into the town the following day against heavy opposition, but the other two battalions could make no headway against the strong Japanese defenses. Meanwhile, the 161st Infantry had set up roadblocks along Route 8 southeast of San Isidro and awaited orders to assist the 35th Infantry. But that would prove unnecessary.

The seizure of the Talavera River Bridge allowed the 1st Infantry, 6th Infantry Division, to cross that river and move along the north bank. They gained a position within 1,000 yards of San Jose by February 3. On the east, the 63rd Infantry Regiment had cleared the Agricultural School and was poised to move on San Jose as well. With his two regiments in position, General Patrick ordered a concentric attack. The attack itself was anti-climactic. Two companies of the 1st Infantry walked into San Jose without opposition on the morning of February 4. The 63rd Infantry, slowed by the need to dispose of a Japanese tank-infantry force at Abar Number 2, never attacked San Jose. The main source of casualties for the 1st Infantry in San Jose came from "friendly fire" by B-25s of the Fifth Air Force that made an unscheduled strafing run across San Jose after it had been seized by that regiment.

* * *

The capture of San Jose had relieved General Krueger of any remaining concerns he may have felt for his Sixth Army's line of communications. The Japanese commitment of their only armored force to a prolonged defense of the Muñoz and San Jose area, rather than husbanding them for an offensive against Sixth Army, convinced General Krueger that no attack was coming from the *Shobu Group*. He removed all previous restrictions on the XIV Corps' advance on Manila. For General Yamashita, the battle had also been successful. The bulk of the *105th Division* had moved through San Jose and joined his *Shobu Group* before that town had been seized by the Americans. The last of the critical supplies needed by the *Shobu Group* for a protracted stand in the mountains of northern Luzon had also cleared San Jose during the night of February 3–4. With all his objectives at San Jose accomplished, General Yamashita ordered the withdrawal of the *2nd Tank Division* and its attachments up Route 5 on February 4.

The cost to the Japanese was high, however. General Swift's I Corps had cut off most of the *2nd Tank Division* at San Jose and cut the last line of communication between the *Shimbu* and *Shobu Groups*. Such was the confusion within the Japanese command that it took two days for the withdrawal order to retreat to reach Lieutenant

General Iwanaka. As a result, the battles of Lupao and Muñoz continued for those two days, even while the rest of the Japanese force was withdrawing. For those days the 20th Infantry besieged Muñoz, making small gains each day. By the end of February 6, the regiment reported knocking out 35 enemy tanks and several antitank guns, but that the enemy still had at least another 25 tanks in the half of the town they still held.

During these days, Technical Sergeant Donald E. Rudolph, of Company E, 20th Infantry, 6th Infantry Division, distinguished himself. The soldier from Minneapolis, Minnesota, was acting as a platoon leader at Muñoz on February 5 when he stopped to aid a wounded man. As he did so he observed enemy fire coming from a nearby culvert. Crawling forward, he eliminated the position with his rifle and grenades. Then he crawled across open terrain to a line of enemy pillboxes which had halted Company E's advance. At the first pillbox, he hurled grenades and then charged the enemy post. With his bare hands, he tore away the wood and tin covering the position and then dropped a grenade inside, killing the enemy gun crew and destroying their weapon. After ordering several of his men to provide covering fire, Technical Sergeant Rudolph seized a pick mattock and made his way to a second pillbox. Using the mattock to pierce the pillbox's covering, he dropped a grenade into the hole and then covered it with earth, to increase the power of the grenade explosion. He then repeated this process six more times, all the while under enemy fire and fully exposed to the enemy weapons. Returning to his platoon, he led them forward only to find them under attack by an enemy tank. Leaving his men under cover, Technical Sergeant Rudolph climbed atop the tank and dropped a white phosphorus grenade down the turret opening, destroying the crew and tank. For his courage and leadership on February 5, 1945, Technical Sergeant Donald E. Rudolph received a Medal of Honor and a promotion to second lieutenant.[10]

Having suffered casualties of 40 killed and 175 wounded in the 20th Infantry alone by this time, General Patrick decided upon other methods. Much of February 7 was spent pounding Muñoz with air, artillery, and mortars. Bombs and napalm were freely used. Corps and division artillery followed. Then, following a rolling barrage, the infantry would attack in the afternoon. Elements of the 63rd Infantry would join with the 20th Infantry in this attack.

The Japanese did not wait for the Americans to get set. The *Ida Detachment*, garrisoning Muñoz, decided to pull out. First, they launched a minor diversionary attack against the 20th Infantry. Under cover of this attack, the main body began an escape up Route 5 before dawn on February 7. With the current state of Japanese communications, it is not surprising that the *Ida Detachment* had no knowledge that San Jose was already in American hands. As a result, they ran into a series of roadblocks manned by the 63rd Infantry, 53rd and 80th Field Artillery Battalions, and the 2nd Battalion, 161st Infantry Regiment. The *Ida Detachment* was destroyed. At daylight on February 7, the 20th Infantry Regiment entered Muñoz unopposed.

The Japanese left 52 tanks, 41 trucks, 16 47mm antitank guns, and four 105mm artillery guns behind. Some 1,500 men of the *2nd Tank Division* died at Muñoz. The cost to the 6th Infantry Division was 90 killed and 250 wounded, not counting the casualties of the 1st Infantry at San Jose.[11]

Events at Lupao followed a similar pattern. The 35th Infantry Regiment continued to attack throughout February 4–7. Slowly, the garrison was compressed into a smaller and smaller area. The night after the *Ida Detachment* attempted its escape, 11 tanks left Lupao and five managed to get through the 35th Infantry Regiment's lines and disappear into the foothills east of the town. They were later found abandoned there. The dismounted garrison seemingly melted away, infiltrating through American lines to reach safety to the north.

Earlier, on February 7, Master Sergeant Charles L. McGaha, of Company G, 35th Infantry, 25th Infantry Division, was acting as a platoon leader when his and another platoon were pinned down by the enemy. Fire from five Japanese tanks and 10 enemy machine guns, supported by a platoon of riflemen, held the Americans on the ground. When one of his men fell wounded in the open, Master Sergeant McGaha crossed the road under heavy enemy fire and moved the wounded man 75 yards to a place of safety. During the move, he suffered a deep arm wound but returned to his platoon. He again assumed command and rallied the men. Then he again exposed himself to heavy Japanese fire to protect a litter party carrying a wounded man. When a shell exploded in their midst, Master Sergeant McGaha was again seriously wounded in the shoulder. Two of the litter party were killed. Master Sergeant McGaha picked up the wounded man and carried him to a protected spot, and then deliberately exposed himself to draw off enemy fire while the rest of his men withdrew to safety. Only then did he withdraw, where he collapsed from loss of blood and exhaustion.[12]

By noon, February 8, the 35th Infantry had secured Lupao. Here the Japanese left behind 33 tanks, 26 trucks, and three 75mm artillery guns, along with 900 dead. The cost to the 35th Infantry was 95 killed and 270 wounded. At San Isidro, the Japanese withdrew before the 161st Infantry could mount an attack.[13]

* * *

General Krueger now ordered I Corps to complete its remaining tasks. These involved moving to the Cabanatuan–Rizal line and reconnaissance of Baler and Dingalan Bays on Luzon's east coast. General Swift passed on both tasks to General Patrick's "Sightseeing Sixth." By February 7, the 63rd Infantry had captured Rizal against scattered opposition, and the next day the 20th Infantry secured Bongabon, six miles south of Rizal, finding only stragglers opposing their advance. A mixed force from the 20th Infantry and 6th Reconnaissance Troop reconnoitered Dingalan Bay, while a similar combined force from the 63rd Infantry did the same at Baler Bay. Only abandoned defenses were found. Leaving Filipino guerillas in charge, both forces returned to base. The 25th Infantry Division performed mopping-up and patrol duties along Route 5 until February 10, when General Swift began realigning his troops for the next advance. The next objective of I Corps was the *Shobu Group* in northern Luzon.

Overshadowed by the awesome presence of General MacArthur, General Walter Krueger is often overlooked as an American Army commander in World War II. Yet he repeatedly fought successful battles with the odds usually against him, and on Luzon this was evident. In February, his Sixth Army had three corps headquarters under command. One (XIV Corps) was busily engaged in and around Manila, The XI Corps was clearing southern Luzon and the Visayan Passages. The third (I Corps) was miles away from both, protecting the rear and preparing to attack a Japanese force that, on paper at least, outnumbered it. Not unlike General Patton's Third Army in France, General Krueger's Sixth Army was attacking in multiple directions, but not against a defeated enemy, rather one that was implementing its own plans as it had intended. Further, General MacArthur's sudden and unplanned removal of important follow-up forces originally intended for Sixth Army's clearing of Luzon to clear the entire rest of the Philippine archipelago forced General Krueger to delay and restructure his own plans for that operation "on the fly," as it were. The result was a lesson in generalship under pressure.

One of the delays forced upon General Krueger was the launching of I Corps against the *Shobu Group* in northern Luzon.[14] This force, under the direct leadership of one of Japan's most capable generals of the Pacific War, was also the largest, best equipped, and best supplied. Without the reserves which had been diverted by General MacArthur, General Krueger had to delay any major offensive to the north until other combat units already within Sixth Army could be made available. Despite acknowledging that any delay worked to the advantage of General Yamashita, General Krueger had no options. This was confirmed by intelligence reports that indicated that the *Shobu Group* was realigning its forces for a prolonged stand in the rugged mountains of north Luzon.

General Yamashita had problems of his own. He had to reorganize his forces, particularly those that had engaged Sixth Army and had suffered accordingly. He planned a triangular defensive position protecting his supplies and the Cagayan Valley from which he hoped to produce additional food. Even if the food and supplies could be protected, distribution of them over the heavily jungled and mountainous terrain would remain a problem.

Shobu Group's defenses were based around that Cagayan Valley, which ran from the seaside town of Aparri on the north some 200 miles south to Bambang at the Magat River. It was bordered on the east by the largely unexplored Sierra Madre Mountains, which separated the valley from the Pacific Ocean. On the west lay the equally forbidding Cordillera Central, or Malaya, Mountain Range which shielded the valley from the South China Sea. A lesser but equally difficult Caraballo Mountain Range blocked the valley from the south. The only "easy" access was from Aparri, which would require a large amphibious assault force, something that Sixth Army did not have at its disposal, with much of that capability assigned to Eighth Army, then clearing the rest of the Philippines. Otherwise, access was over poorly paved, winding, and tortuous paths through mountain passes easily defended by a military force.

The best way into the Cagayan Valley from the south was Route 5 through Balete Pass. A secondary route, Route 11 northeast of Baguio, was less attractive. These routes led to one of the three tips of General Yamashita's triangle defense, the Philippine summer capital of Baguio, where General Yamashita had established his headquarters. The other tips, Bontoc and Bambang, held the other main concentrations of Japanese defenders. To protect his rear, the *103rd Division* headquarters, with two regiments and artillery, protected Aparri. Other *103rd Division* elements garrisoned possible landing sites along Luzon's north coast. This division was also tasked with protecting *Shobu Group*'s rear against an airborne attack. For this they were reinforced with a provisional regiment formed from *4th Air Army*, antiaircraft units, and some Japanese paratroopers. Although originally posted to protect the coast and blocking Routes 9 and 11, the *19th Division* had been forced by increasing Filipino guerilla activity to move to Bontoc when General Yamashita began fearing an amphibious landing at Libtong and a subsequent drive on Bontoc. The *58th Independent Mixed Brigade* was moved to protect Routes 9 and 11. This was strengthened by the *23rd Division*, which established a line of defense between Rosario and Baguio. The remnants of the *105th Division*, perhaps 7,000 men that had escaped to northern Luzon, defended Bagabag and Bambang, reinforced with a regiment of the *10th Division*. Elements of the latter division were employed fighting Filipino guerillas within General Yamashita's triangle. The *10th Division* also held the critical area along Route 5 in front of Bambang. Another route, known as the Villa Verde Trail, outflanked Route 5 and was also guarded by the *10th Division*. Dozens of other trails and rudimentary routes forced a dispersion of Japanese strength to guard as many as they could. The *10th Division*, for example, guarded a stretch of over 25 miles of jungle and mountains, concentrating on any likely avenues of approach. Finally, the shattered *2nd Tank Division*, what was left of it, deployed a 250-man group on the Villa Verde Trail while the remainder assembled at Dupax, off Route 5 near Aritao. There they began reorganizing as an infantry division, accepting all kinds of replacements into its ranks, few if any of whom had infantry training.

Once again Japanese communications forced General Yamashita to divide the command arrangements of his forces. Major General Haruo Konuma, a former chief of staff of the *Fourteenth Area Army*, now commanded the *Bambang Branch*, *Fourteenth Area Army*, which controlled the *10th* and *105th Divisions*, the *2nd Tank Division*, and numerous smaller units in the Bambang area. General Yamashita, headquartered at Baguio, kept personal command of the units in the Baguio and Bontoc areas.

With his army spread out and with fewer forces available than had been originally planned General Krueger had to scrap his original plans and start over. His first plans called for a two-division attack against Baguio, an amphibious one-division attack somewhere in northern Luzon, and another one later at Aparri. These plans also came to nothing. General MacArthur's orders to redeploy units like the 6th Infantry, 43rd Infantry, and 158th Infantry RCT all combined to make General Krueger's second series of plans moot. There was then much intelligence-gathering and planning of individual sectors' operations, but by late February the Sixth Army had finalized the plans to carry it into northern Luzon.

These plans described a main effort on the Bambang Front with the 25th and 32nd Infantry Divisions. The 33rd Infantry Division would probe along the Baguio Front until the 37th Infantry Division became available, after which the two divisions would launch a major attack on Baguio. An organized group of Filipino guerillas, led mostly by American Army officers and known as U.S. Army Forces in the Philippines, Northern Luzon (USAFIP[NL]), would drive along Route 4 toward the junction of Routes 4 and 11 at Bontoc.

The 33rd Infantry Division had been organized from the National Guard of Illinois and served in Hawaii before conducting mopping-up operations in New Guinea and Morotai Island. It had landed on Luzon on February 10 and relieved the 43rd Infantry Division at Damortis. The division commander, Major General Percy W. Clarkson, had graduated from Texas A&M in 1915 and accepted a commission in the infantry, serving in World War I. After the usual inter-war assignments, including graduating from the Command and General Staff College, the Army War College, and teaching at the Military Academy at West Point, he rose to division command, taking command of the 33rd Infantry Division in 1943. He was now about to lead it into its first major combat assignment.

The division began its probing attacks by clearing the Japanese from the hills dominating Routes 3 and 11 above Rosario. The newcomers quickly learned that Route 11 was the most strongly defended and easily defended path to Baguio. One of the reasons for this was the sharp ravines over which an attacker would have to pass, not to mention crossing the Bued River at least five times. These each had a bridge across it along Route 11, but between Philippine guerillas and retreating Japanese of the *23rd Division*, few if any of these remained standing when approached by the Americans. One report lists at least 19 crossing sites on Route 11 before reaching Baguio.

The advance north became one of attacking the Japanese in dominating terrain, crawling up a ridge under fire, crossing the crest under fire, and then repeating the process on the far side of the same ridge. Terrain had to be cleared inch-by-inch, with the Japanese refusing to allow one uncontested step forward. Meanwhile, engineers of the 108th Engineer (Combat) Battalion, aided by I Corps engineers, struggled with providing bridges across each and every ravine and river crossing as the division moved north.

General Clarkson and his staff began looking for alternate routes. They found one possibility seven miles north of Rosario, at Pugo, where a fair road ran north over easy terrain. This trail, known as the Tuba Trail, wound a tortuous path to Tuba, only two and a half miles southwest of Baguio. From there another good road led back to Route 11 at the southern edge of Baguio itself. But here again, the terrain favored the defenders. A third route started at Caba and ran to an abandoned railroad line which in turn ran, with deviations, to Route 9 near Baguio. Finally, there was a fourth route, Route 9 itself, a good road from Bauang 20 miles north into Baguio. Although this route was physically the easiest, it also crossed easily defended terrain.

General Clarkson divided his division into three regimental combat teams and assigned each a sector. One covered the east coast inland as far as Route 11. A second was to reconnoiter along Route 11, while the third would clear the enemy off Hills 600–1500 that blocked the way north. Ironically, the Japanese had structured their defenses very similarly. A Japanese regiment defended against each regiment of the 33rd Infantry Division. The battle for Baguio began February 21 when the first patrols moved forward.

CHAPTER 13

The Villa Verde Trail

General MacArthur and General Krueger had served together in the Philippines before World War II.[1] As General MacArthur recorded in his memoirs, he wrote to the U.S. Army Chief of Staff, General George C. Marshall, on January 11, 1943, requesting that General Krueger, then commanding a training army in the United States, be sent to him to command his growing forces. "Experience indicates the necessity for a tactical organization of an American Army. In the absence of such an echelon the burden had been carried by General Headquarters. I recommend the U.S. Third Army under Lieutenant General Walter Krueger, which would provide an able commander and an efficient operating organization. I am especially anxious to have Krueger because of my long and intimate association with him."[2] Despite General Marshall's aversion to having "older" officers commanding combat forces—General Krueger would celebrate his 62 birthday on January 26—General MacArthur's request was granted. By February 23 of that year, General Krueger was in the South Pacific commanding the newly established Sixth U.S. Army.[3]

Although it is not unusual in General MacArthur's memoirs to barely mention subordinates, this is the only mention of General Krueger, who commanded General MacArthur's ground forces all through the New Guinea, Leyte, and Luzon campaigns—and who was selected to command the first invasion of Japan—other than two or three brief passing references. One factor may be that by late February 1945, General MacArthur was becoming dissatisfied with General Krueger's performance.

Simply put, General MacArthur began to regard General Krueger's operations as too slow. General MacArthur made it clear that he intended to liberate his "home" in Manila on his 65th birthday. He had made it equally clear that he wished to free as many Allied prisoners of war and civilian internees as possible early in the campaign. Neither of these happened in accordance with General MacArthur's wishes. Nor did he consider the fact that he himself had slowed the operations by pulling units from General Krueger for his other objectives, including the complete liberation of the Philippines. Other factors also contributed. General MacArthur was unhappy with his U.S. Navy supporting forces, considering them too reluctant to risk their ships in the Philippines' constricted waters to support his ongoing amphibious operations. He was also looking over his shoulder as he launched his Philippine liberation campaign, since he had never advised nor requested authorization from his superiors, the United States Combined Chiefs of Staff, to conduct such an operation. The first they learned of it was when the landings on lesser Philippine islands were publicized. Only the ongoing operations on Iwo Jima and later Okinawa diverted their attention. No one mentioned to General MacArthur, nor did he himself realize, that the assets he was expending—Lieutenant General Robert L. Eichelberger's Eighth U.S. Army—could have been put to better use on Luzon.

Nor was that all that was influencing General MacArthur. "His [MacArthur's] own household was in some disarray, since MacArthur and his abrasive chief of staff, Richard K. Sutherland, had argued heatedly over the status of Sutherland's mistress, an army secretary he had secretly brought to Leyte against orders. The lady in question rapidly departed, along with Sutherland's power. Unfortunately, Sutherland's not-unwelcome fall did not redound to the advantage of the long-suffering professional officers around MacArthur but only strengthened the power of his two top courtiers, General Charles Willoughby and General Courtney Whitney."[4] Indeed, it was intelligence chief Major Genera l Willoughby who, as befits a sycophant, consistently underestimated enemy strength to placate his commander's intentions. It was General Willoughby's wildly inaccurate estimate of Japanese forces on Luzon, less than one-third of the actual number, later revised to two-thirds, that first caused trouble for General Krueger. Colonel Horton V. White, General Krueger's own intelligence officer (G-2), reported far more accurate enemy numbers and urged caution. After explaining his plan of advance to General MacArthur at a pre-invasion meeting, General MacArthur demanded a swifter advance on Manila, believing that Japanese forces on Luzon were outnumbered by the Sixth Army, when in fact, the reverse was true. General Krueger wrote, "General MacArthur did not seem to be impressed by my arguments. He did not appear to take very seriously the danger that the enemy might well take advantage of any overextension of our forces to attack them in the flank as we moved south."[5] All to no avail, as it happened. When General Krueger's operations officer (G-3), Colonel Clyde D. Eddleman, briefed General MacArthur and his senior staff on Leyte before the Luzon invasion, his estimate of Japanese numbers on that island was greeted by shouts from General MacArthur saying, "Bunk! Bunk!"

At a conference on January 12, the discussion between the two men became heated. Having made his case that to order both of his assault corps on Manila would leave his beachhead vulnerable to a Japanese counterattack by the *Shobu Group*, General Krueger refused to change his original plans. General MacArthur was not satisfied, demanding, "Where are your casualties?" Why are you holding the I Corps back? It ought to be moving south." Unimpressed, General Krueger replied, "And abandon my base here? What other base do I have?" Colonel Eddleman, who was present, remembered, "The old man [Krueger] stuck to his guns, but he didn't feel too good going back across Lingayen Gulf to our flag ship."[6]

As was his nature, General MacArthur never put anything in the record about this crisis in command. However, two of his closest friends, Frazier Hunt, and Dr. D. Clayton James, reported that General MacArthur gave serious consideration to relieving General Krueger at about this time. This version goes on to state that General Sutherland was sent as an emissary to General Krueger's headquarters to urge him to action, indicating that if General MacArthur had to personally visit Sixth Army Headquarters, he might lose his temper and relieve his old comrade.[7] Instead, General Krueger was bombarded by repeated messages from General MacArthur urging rapid movement to Manila, Bataan, and Manila Bay. On an inspection tour of the veteran 37th Infantry Division, General MacArthur, who often bypassed Sixth Army when visiting the front, radioed General Krueger that "there was a noticeable lack of drive and aggressive initiative today."[8] During January 1945, General MacArthur also met with General Krueger several times, still trying to win his point about a rapid advance on Manila. At one such meeting General Krueger again refused to change his plans and after General Krueger left, General MacArthur turned to a staff member and remarked, "Walter's pretty stubborn. Maybe I'll have to try something else."[9]

"Something else" was General MacArthur moving his own headquarters ahead of General Krueger's Sixth Army headquarters. This attempt to embarrass General Krueger failed, as did his bringing the 11th Airborne Division, assigned to General Eichelberger's Eighth Army, ashore at Nasugbu Bay. By giving General Eichelberger permission to strike for Manila, an original Sixth Army objective, General MacArthur continued his earlier policy of playing his two ground force commanders off against each other. The two army commanders did not like each other, a fact well known to General MacArthur and which he exploited as it suited him.[10] But General Krueger, more interested in reaching Manila with safety, not only did not object, but encouraged the Nasugbu Bay plan. Meanwhile, he continued to have I Corps protect Sixth Army's rear while advancing as fast as possible with XIV Corps. As he explained, "Our advance toward the south was slower than desirable, but its pace depended upon reconstruction of the many destroyed bridges, some very large ones, rehabilitation of the roads and the Manila–Dagupan Railroad. Shortage of vital bridge material, lack of locomotive[s], and limited rolling stock complicated matters."[11]

All the impatience, arguing, and petty bickering came to nothing. In the event, once Manila had been "liberated," such as it was, Corregidor taken, and Manila Bay opened to Allied traffic, General MacArthur seems to have lost all interest in the rest of the Luzon campaign. From the end of February to the end of the war, he took minimal interest in Luzon and instead concentrated on liberating the rest of the Philippines, then preparing for the invasion of Japan. General Krueger kept his job and was in fact scheduled to lead his Sixth U.S. Army to Japan in the invasion scheduled for late 1945. The tempest in a teapot evaporated.

Not so the *Shobu Group*. It was still in northern Luzon and presenting a potential threat to Allied operations on that island. General Krueger was left to deal with them.

* * *

None of these maneuvers among the generals interested the men of the 33rd Infantry Division. After four years of training and garrison duties, they were about to enter their first major combat situation. Coming ashore on Luzon, they found themselves facing a towering, tree-covered mountain range which rose suddenly from the Central Plain and stretched to the north as far as the eye could see. The higher peaks were shrouded in mist and fog. Palls of smoke rolled off many of the slopes, the results of recent bombing attacks.

First to move up was Colonel Paul C. Serff's 123rd Infantry RCT. They relieved the 158th Infantry RCT ("Bushmasters") on high ground above the Damortis–Rosario road on February 13. Major Sanford I. Wolff's 3rd Battalion held the left flank, while Major James L. Cregg's 2nd Battalion held the center, and Lieutenant Colonel Charles F. Coates placed his 1st Battalion on the right flank. They were followed the next day by the 130th Infantry Regiment of Colonel Arthur S. Collins, Jr., who relieved the 43rd Infantry Division's 172nd Infantry Regiment. Last to arrive at the front was Colonel Ray E. Cavenee's 136th Infantry RCT, which relieved additional battalions of the 43rd Infantry Division. Behind these infantrymen, the 122nd, 124th, and 210th Field Artillery Battalions took their support positions. To the rear the heavy guns (155mm) of Lieutenant Colonel George McClure's 123rd Field Artillery Battalion took up positions. The newcomers expected trouble, especially after reading a captured document signed by a Japanese division commander which read in part, "if the battle situation develops unfavorably for us and we find ourselves under continuous enemy pressure, we must be able to hold a route of withdrawal to the mountainous terrain around Baguio. Therefore, in order to hang on doggedly in the Philippines and await the plans of later years, it is necessary to organize quickly and in such a manner as to be able to establish permanent installations which can hold out for months and years. The mountainous terrain in the vicinity of Baguio is suitable for this purpose."[12] And that is precisely where the division was headed.

The Illinois National Guard men's introduction to Luzon began at Bench Mark and Question Mark Hills. The latter hill rises 2,500 feet at the edge of the Central Plain. It is covered with dry cogon grass and many wooded gullies which sharply indent the steep slopes. Its position gave the Japanese a panoramic view of the Central Plain. To get to Question Mark Hill, the Americans had to first clear Bench Mark Hill. A 600-foot-wide draw separates the two hills, both of which provide clear observation to the rear of Sixth Army. These hills would occupy the 33rd Infantry Division for the next four days.[13]

Twenty-six-year-old Lieutenant Colonel Orville Minton's 3rd Battalion, 130th Infantry, was assigned Bench Mark Hill. After relieving the 169th Infantry of the 43rd Infantry Division, they discovered an unusual situation. The 169th Infantry held the reverse slope of Bench Mark Hill, but the Japanese still held the forward slope and both flanks of that hill. Only yards separated the opposing forces on the hill. Colonel Minton immediately assigned Captain Elbert J. Hicks and his Company K to the reverse slope. Captain Norman H. Litz and Company L took position in a perimeter on a small knob behind the Company K positions. Heavy machine-gun squads of Company M were distributed to each company. Company M's 81mm mortars were grouped together 1,000 yards from the hill. Captain Alan J. Kennedy and his Company I was retained in battalion reserve with the battalion headquarters in a grove of mango trees.

Patrols began at dawn on February 16. They sought enemy strength and defenses on the hill. The best—indeed, the only—way to accomplish this in such proximity was to contact the enemy and force him to reveal his positions and guns by opening fire on the patrol. From this dangerous plan estimates could be made of the enemy and his defensive preparations. Colonel Frank J. Sackton, the division intelligence officer (G-2), reported that the enemy facing the 130th Infantry was from the *58th Independent Mixed Brigade* and the *71st Infantry Regiment, 23rd Division*. How many enemy were present and how they were deployed remained unknown, hence the patrols.

Lieutenant Colonel Minton planned his attack for February 19. Companies K and L would attack up the reverse slope and seize the crest and forward slope of Bench Mark Hill. Captain Kennedy and Company I would move around the right flank of the hill, using a deep ravine for cover while they attacked the side of the hill. Artillery support from two artillery battalions, the 123rd (105mm) and 210th (155mm) Field Artillery Battalions, was carefully planned. Meanwhile, the patrols would continue with their probing. At night, the Japanese returned the favor, sending raiding parties into American lines, instigating grenade duels and sniping but causing no serious damage.

February 19 began hot and hazy. A thousand miles from Luzon the V Marine Amphibious Corps was landing on the beaches of Iwo Jima. At Bench Mark Hill the artillery barrage began with daybreak and lasted for 15 minutes. The last shell was a smoke round, signaling to the infantry that the barrage had ended. Companies K and L attacked alongside each other. Almost immediately difficulties appeared. Poor visibility strained contact between the two assault companies. As they moved up the hill, they drifted apart until only radios maintained communications. Within moments, each company was involved in its own separate fight.

Company L was struck by fire from an exposed knob on the north slope of the hill. The Japanese had chosen their positions poorly, as the knob had no cover and stood out from the rest of the hill. Company L veered toward the enemy and within moments were mopping up the enemy knob, suffering fewer than 10 casualties. Company L then moved forward, seeking to support Company K. But as they moved forward, enemy fire from Question Mark Hill cut down nearly one entire squad. Heavy machine guns supported Company L only to find themselves in a duel with Japanese machine guns from across the draw. One gunner was killed, and two crewmen seriously wounded. Captain Litz, realizing the need for superior firepower, crawled to the heavy machine gun, pulled the two casualties to safety, and took over as gunner on the heavy Browning machine gun.[14] He succeeded in silencing one Japanese machine gun, but another opened fire and killed Captain Litz. The company executive officer assumed command and tried to move the company to more tenable positions. However, every move was struck by Japanese mortar and machine-gun fire. Finally, the company was directed to dig in on the knob. Five men had died and 17 more were wounded in this brief battle.

Meanwhile, Company K experienced much the same kind of battle. After encountering minor resistance as they started forward, there was a brief hand-to-hand encounter on the hill's crest. After pausing to reorganize, Captain Hicks began his push down the forward slope of Bench Mark Hill. As they moved past the crest the lead scouts noted a drop, then a rise in front with two more knobs jutting out. Captain Hicks directed his two lead platoons on the knobs. Concealed in caves and bunkers, the Japanese waited until the company began to move down the first depression before opening fire. Lieutenant Robert R. Kimball's platoon was laced with machine-gun fire from hidden locations. Hand grenades shocked the trapped platoon. Now heavy machine guns and mortars began to strike among the platoon, firing from Question Mark Hill. Because the infantry was so close to the enemy positions, American artillery observers could not safely put down artillery on the enemy. Company K's light machine guns were constantly chased from one position to another by Japanese fire.

Seeing no option, Lieutenant Kimball ordered his men to attack the closest knob. His platoon rose, firing as they advanced. Urged on by Lieutenant Kimball, the platoon followed him up the knob. Moving ahead alone, the lieutenant was seriously wounded by shrapnel. Seeing two enemy machine guns which seemed to be halting his platoon, Lieutenant Kimball advanced upon the first, firing as he advanced. After killing the crew with his M-1 carbine,[15] he charged the second gun using the same tactics but was shot down before he reached the enemy gun position. His Distinguished Service Cross was posthumously awarded.[16]

Company K tried again, and again. In one attempt, Staff Sergeant William E. Pavlick, a squad leader, came close to breaching the enemy defenses. He knocked out an enemy machine gun alone with his rifle, then had his squad cover him as he repeated this feat again, knocking out a second gun. Twice wounded, he continued to point out targets to his men, exposing himself each time. He kept this up until he collapsed from loss of blood. His squad, now under heavy mortar fire, dragged him to safety. He lived to receive his Distinguished Service Cross.[17] By the time this fight ended, the Americans had given the two hills names. One was Hooker Hill, after the new platoon commander, Staff Sergeant Gerald W. Hooker, and the other Dead Man's Hill after a dead Japanese soldier prominently lying on the forward slope of the knob.

It was now apparent to Colonel Minton that no advance on Bench Mark Hill could be successful until the supporting fires from Question Mark Hill were stopped. He ordered Captain Kennedy and Company I to "Move your outfit along the southern slope of Bench Mark. Cut down into the draw and attack Question Mark. King Company can't do a thing until the pressure coming from Question Mark is knocked out. Leave as soon as you can."[18]

In war, sometimes the simplest things can make or break a battle. In the case of Company I, 130th Infantry, that simple thing was water. Although the men had a full load of ammunition and food, they were low on water. Most had less than half a canteen and they carried only one. Captain Kennedy was not disturbed, however. The map showed a stream running along the edge of the spacious draw separating Question Mark Hill from Bench Mark Hill. It seemed a simple matter to fill the men's canteens as they moved forward. But it wasn't. When the company arrived at the stream, it was an arid, rock-strewn dry bed. There would be no water for Company I this day.

Captain Kennedy counted on surprise to begin his attack. He declined the use of artillery and launched his attack in the late afternoon, when usually the Americans were preparing their night positions. His plan came close to succeeding. The men of Company I moved silently up Question Mark Hill, unseen by the enemy, whose attention was riveted on the Americans on Bench Mark Hill. Not until the leading scouts were within 75 yards of the Japanese did the enemy spot them. Then every Japanese opened fire on Company I. Using predetermined lines of fire, the Japanese struck the assault teams from front and flank. Despite this heavy fire, the Americans continued to advance, using fire and movement tactics.[19] Soon they were within grenade range of the Japanese defenses. But that was as far as they could get.

The attack stalled, and the Japanese had established fire superiority. The number of grenades the Japanese rolled down the hill surprised the Americans. By now hunger and thirst were taking a toll on the attackers, as well. Captain Kennedy asked for instructions from Colonel Minton. Ordered to dig in and hold his position, Captain Kennedy was promised protective artillery fires. But Captain Kennedy had other problems. His wounded men, including several who were seriously wounded, could not be evacuated because there was no safe route for evacuation. Japanese mortars and machine guns covered every possible avenue in or out of Company I's position. Undaunted, Captain Kennedy decided to establish two defensive perimeters. One was established just below the crest of Question Mark Hill into which most of his command moved. The second was some 400 yards to the rear into which the wounded were placed guarded by one squad of able-bodied men.

As soon as Company I began to dig in the Japanese saw their opportunity. Their firing increased against the company. To protect the troops, First Lieutenant James E. Finn, a platoon leader, took over the job of directing the protective artillery and mortar fire. Almost as soon as he did so, a group of Japanese left the protection of their bunkers and attacked the company which was preoccupied with digging in. Lieutenant Finn saw them coming, and radioed calls for artillery and mortar fire close to his own position. Standing erect in his partly finished foxhole, he coordinated the fires until the Japanese withdrew. But they soon returned, and once again Lieutenant Finn rose to direct the artillery. Again, the enemy was turned back, but not before one Japanese soldier recognized what Lieutenant Finn was doing and killed him with a rifle shot. His Distinguished Service Cross was posthumously awarded.[20] Captain Kennedy took over the task of directing the supporting artillery.

Captain Kennedy brought in the artillery so close that the artillery commanders protested, but Captain Kennedy insisted. Satisfied that no Japanese would dare to venture into the protective fires, he walked back to his command post. Along the way he saw his men suffering terribly from thirst. Lips were cracked; others sucked in gulps of air to ease the pain of aching throats. Others ate condensed food, hoping to stifle their thirst. None of this worked. Captain Kennedy contacted his battalion headquarters and explained that unless water could be brought forward soon, his company was finished as an effective fighting force. Colonel Minton promised to try to send carrying parties forward, and there would be air drops in the morning. As to the wounded, Company I would have to do the best they could for the moment.

The assistant division commander, Brigadier General Donald J. Myers, had been overseeing the operation on the hills.[21] He recognized that unless the situation was corrected, operational success was jeopardized. He immediately reported to General Clarkson on the situation. As a result, the 3rd Battalion, 130th Infantry, was reinforced during the night. Captain James W. Cavender's Company A, 136th Infantry, was ordered out of reserve and to report to Colonel Minton. Once at the 3rd Battalion headquarters, Captain Cavender was ordered to attack at dawn and relieve Company I, 130th Infantry.

Meanwhile, General Clarkson addressed the water problem. Realizing that the air drops held little prospect for success, he began searching for a carrying party to hand-carry water to the beleaguered rifle company. With all his infantry and artillery committed to the battle, he ordered Lieutenant Colonel Francis P. Kane, the division engineer, to form a 100-man carrying party and to personally report with it to him at his advance headquarters at Cauringan by dawn. The division supply officer was directed to produce 100 water cans and pack-boards by dawn for the carrying party. The cans would be filled at the advance command post and the engineers would carry them forward. Seeing that his combat engineers found their task distasteful, particularly in the hot, humid weather conditions, General Clarkson first gathered them together and reviewed the critical importance of their new assignment. This "pep talk" worked, and the engineers set off with a renewed spirit.

Up on the hill, Company I spent a relatively quiet night as division artillery kept the Japanese within their defenses. But the lack of enemy action only gave more attention to the growing thirst among the soldiers. Men's lips cracked, food could not be absorbed, sleep was impossible, and even speech became extremely difficult. As dawn broke, the heat rose, increasing the level of thirst suffered by the Americans. As they began to move about their position, Japanese machine guns opened fire from new locations, and reports began to arrive of enemy reinforcements joining the original defenders of the hill. One enemy platoon had even established itself between the two perimeters of Company I, cutting off communication between the two. Captain Kennedy identified four new machine guns established between the two halves of his company. Company I was now worse off than ever, with Japanese in front, within, and behind them. Any attempt at movement would be struck from the front, flank, and rear. With no choice, Captain Kennedy ordered his men to remain in their defensive positions until they could be relieved.

The first relief attempt arrived overhead in mid-morning when a C-47 transport aircraft appeared. Dozens of crates and containers were dropped on the hill. Desperate riflemen risked death or wounds to retrieve these crates, only to find that there was not a drop of water among the air-dropped supplies. Captain Kennedy immediately radioed his anger to Colonel Minton, who explained that a communications error had caused the mistake. Colonel Minton promised that the plane would be reloaded with water and would soon return. While waiting, Captain Kennedy and his officers decided on removing the threat of the Japanese platoon between his two perimeters. Artillery was out, as it was not accurate enough to drop its shells safely between the two American groups. Instead, Captain Kennedy called upon Captain Arthur L. Wallace, Company M commander, to use his heavy 81mm mortars to "walk" his explosives into the enemy position directed by Captain Kennedy. The difficult operation succeeded without friendly casualties, and the enemy platoon was placed under a constant harassing fire by the mortars.

Once again, the C-47 aircraft appeared and dropped five-gallon water cans at the end of parachutes. But adverse winds carried every drop of it to the enemy. Only the calm and steadiness of Captain Kennedy managed to avoid a panic. He repeatedly assured his men that Company A was about to break through to them with water and medical aid.

Although Captain Kennedy was unaware of the details, Company A was indeed moving to succor Company I. Captain Cavender had led his men to the draw between the two hills and then sent out a patrol to find the best and least opposed route to Company I. One of the patrols spotted Company I's smaller perimeter. With this information, Captain Cavender prepared to attack to reach Company I. Along with Colonel Minton, he agreed that artillery was not accurate enough given the close quarters of the opposing forces. Once again, the 60mm mortars of Company A and 81mm mortars of Company M were relied upon to provide covering fire for the attack. Smoke shells would provide cover under which Company A would advance.

Technical Sergeant Emil B. Weber's 2nd Platoon led the attack and advanced beyond the small perimeter of wounded before the Japanese spotted them and opened fire. Caught in a crossfire, Sergeant Weber was killed. Staff Sergeant Alphonsus L. Leary, the platoon guide, took command and led the platoon forward until they were within grenade range of the enemy. Casualties were heavy, and many of the leaders fell to enemy fire. Technical Sergeant Leary, a 37-year-old who had repeatedly refused offers to attend Officer Candidate School, was already fighting hand-to-hand when he identified an enemy machine gun holding up the advance and moved forward alone. Using his rifle and grenades, he destroyed the enemy position, but as he turned to direct his squad forward, a second enemy gun cut him down.[22]

The 2nd Platoon was left leaderless. Seeing the attack falter, First Lieutenant Samuel B. Harbison left his weapons platoon in command of his sergeant and took charge of the assault unit. Captain Cavender sent up a second platoon in support. With Lieutenant Harbison, an attorney in civilian life, in the lead, the Americans closed for another hand-to-hand encounter. But as they did so, Japanese machine guns and mortars from Question Mark Hill opened fire on the group. Seeing this, Captain Cavender realized that his attacks could not succeed unless artillery knocked out the distant enemy defenses that were supporting those on Bench Mark Hill. He ordered a withdrawal by Lieutenant Harbison and then carefully directed supporting artillery to hit the enemy positions.

A renewed attack met less enemy resistance. With all three platoons of Company A in line, the advance fought through the afternoon until it reached the Company I perimeter. Here they found men delirious after 36 hours without water. Others lay unconscious in their foxholes. The carrying party from the 108th Engineer (Combat) Battalion arrived and distributed water to all. As the men recovered, Company I was relieved by Company A. Captain Kennedy's men returned to the rear under cover of a smoke screen, picking up their wounded at the second perimeter as they left.

The first battles for Question Mark and Bench Mark Hills had gone to the Japanese, but General Myers had learned a lot about their defenses, strengths, and weaknesses. After Company B, 108th Engineer (Combat) Battalion scraped a trail from the base of Bench Mark Hill to the draw separating the two hills, four rifle companies assaulted Question Mark Hill on February 22 and seized it against heavy opposition. The cost to the *23rd Division* was 460 killed, while the Americans of the 33rd Infantry Division's two assault regiments lost 33 killed, 82 wounded, and two men missing in action.

Meanwhile, Major General William H. Gill's 32nd Infantry Division was also heading north along the Villa Verde Trail. Attacking north along what was referred to as the "Bambang Front," the division had been ordered by I Corps to capture the junction of Route 5 and the Villa Verde Trail as the beginning of an advance on Baguio. The advance began on February 19, with the 25th Infantry Division attacking alongside. General Swift hoped that the 32nd Infantry Division, supported by the 25th Infantry Division, would seize Santa Fe after driving up the Villa Verde Trail, then turn and strike the Japanese forces facing the 25th Infantry Division in the rear. Such an advance would create a decisive breakthrough of the enemy defenses facing I Corps.

The Villa Verde Trail fell to Colonel Frederick R. Stofft's 127th Infantry RCT. Supporting it by struggling up several river valleys on the division's left was Colonel Raymond G. Stanton's 126th Infantry Regiment. The 128th Infantry Regiment would protect the division's rear. It quickly became clear that the river valleys were lightly defended and that the rugged terrain within them made progress painfully slow and difficult. Further along, strong outposts of the *23rd Division* blocked progress against Baguio. Clearly the main advance was along the Villa Verde Trail.

Created originally as a foot and carabao path in the 1880s and named after a Spanish priest, Juan Villa Verde, the route ran from Lingayen Gulf over the Caraballo Mountains to the Cagayan Valley in northeast Luzon. From its beginning at Santa Maria, it ran for 27 miles (43 kilometers) to Santa Fe. The straight-line distance between Santa Maria and Santa Fe is but 11 miles. The trail twisted erratically up the eastern slopes of a ridge between the Cabalisiaan River on the east and the Ambayabang River on the west. The Villa Verde Trail began a meter wide at Santa Maria, then widened to three meter about five miles to the northeast. There were so many twists in the trail that the straight-line distance between Santa Maria and the Cabalisiaan River crossing site is five miles, but nine miles along the trail. Beginning at 400 feet above sea level, it rose within those nine miles to 3,500 feet above sea level. As it continued north, it rose and fell to between 3,500 feet and 4,500 feet above sea level. Beginning in wide open terrain with grass-covered ridges, the trail gradually became heavily wooded amid dense jungle forest. Only when within two miles of Santa Fe did it again run through open country. The gradually rising terrain gave the Japanese good observation over the American advance.

The 2nd Battalion, 127th Infantry, advanced directly up the trail. Initial efforts were stopped by strong Japanese resistance near Santa Maria. For two days, February 23 and 24, the battalion was pinned down by Japanese forces on commanding ground. Determined to overcome this resistance, the commander of Company K, 127th Infantry, requested and received permission to attack a key enemy position. In mid-morning on February 23, he sent his 3rd Platoon, only 19 men, to take the hill. It was a very steep hill with no cover or concealment. After a 90-minute struggle, the platoon reached the top of the hill, taking the enemy in the rear and catching them by surprise. There some 31 Japanese, armed with machine guns, grenades, mortars, and small arms defending from six-foot-deep holes, met the attack. For the next six hours, the men of Company K's 3rd Platoon and the Japanese fought for the hill. Hand-to-hand combat was the norm. The struggle ended only when all the defenders lay dead. That evening the Japanese launched a counterattack to regain the hill, but despite the small American force, they were driven off. The taking of that hill secured some 4,000 yards of the trail and allowed critical supplies and equipment to move forward.[23]

The Balete Pass–Santa Fe–Imugan area was the key to the defensive system protecting the Cagayan Valley and General Yamashita's mountain stronghold. From strongly held positions in that area he could send reinforcements to any threatened Japanese positions on the Villa Verde Trail or Route 5 to the east. General Gill's men moved along the trail, while General Mullins's 25th Infantry Division took the path up Route 5.

Colonel Stofft's regiment continued up the trail to Salacsac Pass Number 2, so named to distinguish it from another pass further east. Here the Japanese put up stiff resistance. At what was known to the men of the 32nd Infantry Division as "Yamashita Ridge," the battle became continuous. To get the vital supplies and equipment forward, the division engineers had to struggle along with the infantry. Lieutenant Colonel Charles B. Rynearson's 114th Engineer (Combat) Battalion had to move with the forward infantry elements. They were building a road to support the main assault under intense sniper and artillery fire. Armored bulldozers were used to break open a way forward and set up new firing positions for the supporting M4 Sherman tanks. But despite becoming a priority target of the enemy, the engineers managed under the most difficult conditions to build 18 miles of road usable by American vehicles.

General Krueger was aware of the difficulties. He commented, "The 32nd Division found it increasingly difficult to reduce the cleverly organized and stubbornly defended position of the enemy. Moreover, the necessity of making the extremely poor, winding Villa Verde Trail passible for heavy vehicles to meet logistic requirements and the difficulty of supplying troops in the rugged terrain off the trail by native cargadores [porters] restricted enveloping movements and compelled the division to assault one hill after another and slowed up the advance. Repeated visits to this front had made me fully cognizant of the tough conditions facing the 32nd Division, but I was confident that it would overcome all difficulties successfully."[24]

The veterans of the 32nd Infantry Division were not going to be stopped. The initial Japanese defenses, an outpost line of defense, was manned by the *10th Division's* *10th Reconnaissance Regiment*. This unit found itself not only attacked frontally but outflanked by another battalion and with a roadblock behind it by yet a third American battalion. The *10th Reconnaissance Regiment* melted into the thick jungle, and its survivors, estimated at no more than 250 men, prepared another position at the Cabalisiaan River crossing. Yet no sooner had they arrived than the 127th Infantry was upon them once again. Pushed aside again, the Japanese broke contact for the next two days, March 1–2, before stopping again to delay the American advance.

The Japanese area commander, Major General Haruo Konuma, became concerned with the *10th Reconnaissance Regiment's* failure to hold its forward positions. Just three miles from the Cabalisiaan River was the Salacsac Pass area, the best defensive terrain in the Japanese zone. If the retreat continued, he feared that General Gill's men could easily slip through the Salacsac Pass, denying that terrain to the Japanese and seizing Santa Fe. This would also cut off the *10th Division* defending Route 5 against the 25th Infantry Division. Seeking reinforcements for the *10th Reconnaissance Regiment*, General Konuma dispatched several small infantry and artillery units to the Villa Verde Trail. Even this effort brought the strength of the regiment to only about 550 men. On March 3, he ordered the *10th Division* to send four infantry companies to the Salacsac Pass. Yet there would still be only about 1,100 Japanese troops to defend the vital pass. Looking further, he ordered General Iwanaka, commanding the remnants *2nd Tank Division*, to take command of the Villa Verde Trail defense.

The *2nd Tank Division* now consisted of 4,350 men, but no tanks. The force was now four infantry battalions, each understrength, eight artillery pieces, and 1,000 service troops. Additional troops from the *10th Division* were coming to join General Iwanaka, and other reinforcements arrived in small driblets. Meanwhile, the 127th Infantry leapfrogged its battalions up the trail. As each American battalion encountered resistance, almost always on the high ground bordering the trail, it would turn to the attack while another battalion continued up the road. As a result, just as the 127th Infantry arrived at the Salacsac Pass, so did the *2nd Tank Division*.

The Japanese were acknowledged masters at the use of terrain for defense. This they proved once again at Salacsac Pass Number 2. The men of the *2nd Tank Division*, heavily armed with automatic weapons, covered every twist of the Villa Verde Trail and every fold of ground with a mutually supporting defensive system. Attacking such a defense became a series of monotonous strikes by the Americans. First, a frontal attack to discover the enemy defenses, followed by strong air and artillery attacks, followed by another frontal attack which might, or might not, succeed. Outflanking attacks followed, some successful, others not. Usually a final frontal attack would decide the issue. These days repeated themselves, seemingly endlessly in extreme heat and humidity, or under cloudbursts, fog, and mud. Because the Japanese employed mutually supporting positions, attacks would have to engage two or more such positions to succeed. Often the support was not revealed until a major attack was in motion. Caves, once seized, would need to be sealed to avoid re-occupation by the Japanese. Daily patrols were necessary to find ways to outflank the enemy defenses. The combination of mountain and jungle warfare wore down the attacking Americans at an alarming rate.

The intensity of these battles is epitomized by the fight on March 10, 1945. Company A, 127th Infantry, was holding a defensive position along the trail. At three o'clock in the morning, the Japanese counterattacked. Private First Class Thomas E. Atkins, from Campobello, South Carolina, was holding a post with two companions on a hill. Attacked by two companies of Japanese, armed with machine guns, grenades, TNT charges, and mines, Pfc Atkins was severely wounded and his two buddies killed. Despite heavy fire and intense pain from his wounds, Pfc Atkins held his ground and returned fire. The Japanese withdrew, but Pfc Atkins refused to report for medical attention and leave his position undefended. He remained in position, and a Japanese machine-gun team set up within 20 yards of his position, trying to drive him off. Despite four hours of nearly constant attacks, Pfc Atkins remained at his post, driving off each enemy thrust. By dawn, 13 enemy dead lay to his immediate front, and he had fired over 400 rounds of ammunition, all that he and his two companions had carried up the hill. Each of their three rifles was burned out. During a lull, Pfc Atkins withdrew for a rifle and more ammunition, and was persuaded to permit medical attention. As he waited, he saw a Japanese infiltrator within the perimeter and killed him. Later, while lying on a litter awaiting evacuation, he spotted an enemy group behind his platoon and, despite his severe wounds, opened fire and forced them to retreat. For his actions on March 10, 1945, Pfc Atkins received a Medal of Honor.[25]

Reinforced with the 2nd Battalion, 128th Infantry, the attack continued. Yet the fighting remained the same, one hill after another. The attempt of the 3rd Battalion, 127th Infantry, to outflank the pass defenses was stymied by more defended hills. In the end, the two regiments spent most of March 1945 attacking one hill after another, slowly but steadily moving north along the deadly Villa Verde Trail. Even when the Americans reached the crest of a hill, the Japanese would hold on to the reverse slope. American losses weakened their attacking battalions, and few reinforcements were available. On the other hand, the Japanese could freely reinforce their Salacsac Number 2 Pass defenses from the vast reserves hidden in the Cagayan Valley. It took two weeks for two battalions of the 127th Infantry to advance from Hill 502 to Hill 505, a distance of 1,000 yards. In March, the regiment lost 110 killed, 225 wounded, and 500 non-battle casualties, mostly from heat and illnesses. Most of its original leaders had been killed or wounded. Few officers who had been with the regiment when it landed on Luzon remained. Many of the platoons within the regiment were now led by privates, all higher-ranking men having become casualties. With a shortage of over 1,100 men, and with barely 1,500 men left, the regiment was clearly in need of relief.

Yet the fighting continued. Company F, 127th Infantry, attacked an enemy position on March 20. The leading squad was led by Staff Sergeant Ysmael R. Villegas, a soldier from Casa Blanca, California. Facing the enemy defending from caves and foxholes on high ground, Staff Sergeant Villegas went from man to man in his squad, directing their efforts and encouraging them as they attacked. Under heavy machine-gun and rifle fire, the squad moved forward, but the Japanese refused to yield. They continued throwing demolition charges and grenades at the advancing Americans. As the Americans reached the crest of the hill, the Japanese fired upon them from numerous foxholes. Refusing to be stopped, Staff Sergeant Villegas alone charged each enemy position, rushing to each foxhole under direct enemy fire, and using his rifle to knock out one enemy post after the other. He repeated his efforts five times, all the while under enemy fire from machine guns, rifles, and grenades. It was as he attacked the sixth enemy position that the enemy fire cut him down. Inspired by his gallantry, his men cleared the hill and drove the enemy off.[26] Yet the battle continued. Indeed, the 32nd Infantry Division felt that the Japanese will to resist increased with each yard they moved north.

In the Ambayang River Valley on the left of the Villa Verde Trail, the 126th Infantry faced similar opposition, backed by difficult terrain. The advance moved forward only with the combined use of air attacks, artillery, mortars, and machine guns. The infantry fought with rifles, bazookas, flamethrowers, explosive charges on long poles to insert into enemy caves, and personal courage. They were supported by tanks and armored bulldozers, when terrain permitted, and by combat engineers, quartermaster, ordnance, signal, and medical units, all of whom operated under the most difficult conditions. These support units often found themselves forced to defend their own positions when enemy patrols made fanatical attacks on the division's rear areas.

Once again, General Krueger expressed it best when he wrote, "The terrain in this area was much worse than any which the Division had so far encountered. Hills with nearly perpendicular slopes and deep, precipitous ravines made all movements exceedingly difficult. The enemy had, moreover, utilized the terrain to best advantage by constructing numerous, mutually supporting cave positions, which had to be reduced one by one, to permit the eastward advance of the Division to continue. This advance was, moreover, flanked 1,500–2,000 yards north of and parallel to the Villa Verde Trail by Mt. Imugan, on the forward slopes of which the enemy had established defensive positions and artillery observation posts. The Mt. Imugan positions dominated a stretch of over two miles of the Villa Verde Trail and his observation stations enabled the enemy to adjust his artillery fire on troops and vehicles moving along the trail, which ran along the crest of razor-back ridges and formed the only route of advance. Besides, the Mt. Imugan positions enabled the enemy to repulse any direct attack through the valley north of the trail and constituted an ever-present threat to the line of communications of the 32nd Division. Under the circumstances, with the enemy holding Mt. Imugan, the 32nd Division had no choice but to crack the enemy defenses on the dominating hills directly in its front some four miles west of Imugan village, since by-passing them was impossible."[27]

CHAPTER 14

San Jose, Digdig, and Baguio

The rugged Caraballo Mountains are split by a narrow terrain corridor over which National Highway (Route) 5 winds its way from San Jose to Balete Pass and then into Santa Fe at the southern entrance to the Cagayan Valley, General Yamashita's stronghold on Luzon. This was the route assigned to General Mullins's veteran 25th Infantry Division.

Originally it had been believed that the main Japanese defenses protecting Baguio and the Cagayan Valley would be found along Route 5. As a result, General Swift had assigned the 25th Infantry Division a narrower sector to assault than the adjacent 32nd Infantry Division. Both divisions were veterans of the early days in the South Pacific, and their experience and leadership were expected to be useful in dealing with the Japanese defenses they would face.

The 25th Infantry Division was assigned to clear Route 5 from San Jose north to Digdig, then open Route 100 from Rizal, 10 miles north of San Jose, to Carranglan. They were then to follow Route 100 from Carranglan west to Route 5 at Digdig. Route 5 was a good two-lane gravel road running northeast. The first four miles ran along open, flat terrain between San Jose and Barrio Rosaldo, which the division had taken on February 14. Here the highway swings north through the Talavera River Valley. The river's name changes when it reaches the village of Digdig, becoming the Digdig River. Thereafter, the road leaves the river and runs through a wooded area where it rises sharply some 1,000 feet to a generally open and grassy area. At Rizal, Route 100, a narrow dirt road, runs 10 miles over rough hills as high as 1,000 feet over open country to Carranglan. It continues from Carranglan west to Digdig.

Two other routes interested the 25th Infantry Division. One was Route 8, a narrow trail originating at Lupao and running east across rough heavily forested terrain over the Caraballo Mountains to Puncan, on Route 5, three miles south of Digdig. Another trail, unnamed, began near Rosaldo and ran north over the same mountains to near Route 5, where it merged with the Route 8 trail near Puncan.

General Mullins deployed his division according to their earlier relief of the 6th Infantry Division. His choices were to conduct a frontal attack up Route 5 or to use flanking moves on the other routes available. Realizing that a frontal attack was expected by the Japanese who no doubt had prepared for just such an eventuality, he decided to send his 35th RCT along Route 100 to Digdig, where it was to cut across to Route 5 at Puncan, cutting off the advance Japanese defenders. The 27th Infantry RCT would keep the Japanese busy along Route 5 by applying pressure to prevent their premature withdrawal. His last regiment, the 161st Infantry RCT, would strike over the smaller trails toward Puncan and hopefully continue to Digdig. The operation began February 23 with a relatively easy advance by the 35th Infantry to Carranglan, which it reached three days later. From there a rough trail, known as the Old Spanish Trail, of which there were several in the Philippines, ran north through the Sierra Madre to Route 5 at Aritao.

Attacking on the division's left, the 161st Infantry's 1st Battalion led the way, ordered to clear all the high ridges that dominated the highway from the left. In one such action, a large enemy cave was discovered hidden under a huge boulder. A flamethrower was called forward, and the operator opened fire on the cave. Twenty-six Japanese rushed out, some ablaze, only to be cut down by the waiting American infantrymen. One Japanese decided to use a small rear exit to the cave, only to run into the flamethrower operator who, unfortunately, was now out of fuel. Instead, the operator dispatched the enemy soldier using his weapon's nozzle as a club.

North of Rosaldo the 27th Infantry exerted pressure on the defending Japanese and prepared to launch a full-scale attack. The enemy intent was made clear by a captured document which read in part, "Positions will not be yielded to the enemy even though you die. Our only path is victory or death; therefore, defend to the last man. Those who retreat without orders will be decapitated."[1]

The 35th Infantry's initial objective was Pantabangan. The 1st Battalion moved up the Pampaanga River Valley, and the 2nd Battalion followed the high ground along the Rizal–Pantabangan road. The march was difficult, with no fewer than 19 river crossings required by the advance battalions. Often after crossing waist-deep water, they had to search for the trail which disappeared time after time in the underbrush. Pack horses had to be pushed, dragged, and half-carried along the difficult terrain. Despite these difficulties, Company B reached Pantabangan in the late afternoon of February 23 and blocked all access to the town. The 2nd Battalion arrived a few hours later. The following day the 1st Battalion entered the town, while the 2nd Battalion continued to Conversion, a small village further north. The 3rd Battalion motored up by truck and joined in the advance.

The 27th Infantry ("Wolfhounds") Regiment occupied the Japanese defending Route 5 by attacking to secure the high ground along the road at Lumboy. As expected, the Japanese resisted fiercely. As Company B, 27th Infantry, attacked one strong Japanese group of defenses, Staff Sergeant Raymond H. Cooley, a platoon guide in the company, distinguished himself. Staff Sergeant Cooley, from Richard City, Tennessee, saw that his platoon was pinned down by two enemy machine guns, rifles, and mortars. On his own initiative, he advanced to within 20 yards of one machine gun and attacked it with a hand grenade. Before the missile could explode, however, the Japanese hurled it back. Arming a second grenade, Staff Sergeant Cooley held this grenade for several seconds before again tossing it into the enemy position. This explosion destroyed the enemy gun and crew. Moving forward again, Staff Sergeant Cooley repeated his actions at the second machine-gun position. As he advanced, he tossed grenades into several enemy foxholes, knocking out the defending riflemen protecting the machine guns. In the act of tossing yet another armed grenade, he was attacked by six enemy soldiers. Knowing he could not dispose of the grenade safely without risking injury to his own men, Staff Sergeant Cooley dropped to the ground and covered the grenade with his own body. He was severely wounded as the grenade exploded, but none of his buddies were injured and the attack succeeded in knocking out the enemy defenses. Staff Sergeant Cooley survived to receive his Medal of Honor.[2]

The actions of the 27th Infantry RCT in attacking up Route 5 succeeded in diverting the Japanese attention, which is why the other regiments enjoyed relatively easy advances. The Japanese defending force, known as the *Puncan Sector Defense Unit*, had failed to defend the left and rear of their defenses, allowing the Americans to advance in those areas. Once the American attack began, these Japanese rushed their artillery and much of their infantry, to defend against the 161st Infantry, but too late to halt that regiment's drive to Puncan, which it reached on February 28. The rapid re-deployment left the Route 5 sector relatively undefended, resulting in a swifter advance of the 27th Infantry RCT. Both units joined on Route 5 on March 2. They were soon joined there by the 35th Infantry. The 161st Infantry then continued north along high ground west of Route 5. Enemy resistance steadily diminished, and the leading troops arrived above Digdig on March 5.

The advance of the 25th Infantry Division in those 13 days cost it 40 men killed and 165 wounded. Behind them they left 1,250 enemy killed, and the *Puncan Sector Defense Unit* annihilated. Japanese diaries explained the wide difference in casualty figures by blaming the heavy and widespread American artillery and mortar support for the losses. That, taken with the fact that many of the Japanese defenders were not trained infantrymen, and the fact that retreat had been cut off by the envelopment movement of the 35th Infantry Regiment, accounted for the heavy Japanese losses. The Japanese also made serious errors in their deployment. They had not adequately reconnoitered the area beyond their individual defensive positions. They also ignored the advance of the 35th Infantry up Route 100, expecting the Americans to continue up that road to where the *11th Independent Infantry Regiment* was digging defenses. When, instead, the 35th Infantry turned west for Puncan, the Japanese had no forces in position to halt its advance. General Konuma, in whose sector Puncan fell, was so optimistic about the defense of Puncan that he was planning a counterattack when he learned of the *Puncan Sector's* demise.

General Swift, commanding I Corps, was pleased with General Mullins's progress, and added six more miles to his division's zone of responsibility. On March 2, he ordered General Mullins to push north along Route 5 from Digdig to Putlan, a small village along the highway. Since mopping-up operations were nearly completed, the division began the move immediately. Using the same formation and plan as before, the division moved north. So poor were the Japanese defenses in this sector that the 35th Infantry, marching up the Bonga River Valley and then crossing over to the Putlan River, reached Putlan in just two days. The following day, March 9, the 27th Infantry joined them, having marched up Route 5 against light opposition. Determined Japanese holdouts required mopping-up operations until March 15.

Difficult terrain and more determined Japanese opposition slowed the advance of the 161st Infantry, which did not reach Putlan until March 10. The regiment had to fight its way over Hoshi and Honshi Ridges, strongly defended by the enemy. After counting 228 enemy dead, the regiment finally cleared its way to Putlan. Once again, General Swift was delighted with the division's progress, and as before rewarded it with additional objectives. Twice more he extended the division's zone of operations further northward. First, it was to continue along Route 5 for five miles to the village of Kapintalan. After that, considering the 32nd Infantry Division faced stiff opposition along the Villa Verde Trail, General Mullins was to seize and pass beyond the critical Balete Pass, two miles south of the junction of Route 5 and the Villa Verde Trail.

With the bulk of the reconstituted *2nd Tank Division* facing General Gill's 32nd Infantry Division, and considering the unexpected rapid collapse of the *Puncan Sector Defense Unit*, the 25th Infantry Division seemed now to be in a better position to seize the corps' main objectives. Unknown to the American commanders, however, was the fact that the Japanese intended to defend Balete Pass and had in place a unit as determined as the *2nd Tank Division* then facing the 32nd Infantry Division, the *10th Division*.

The *10th Division* was what the *Imperial Japanese Army* referred to as a "Type A Strengthened (Modified) Division." It had originally been activated in 1895 as a two-brigade four-infantry regiment division and had participated in the Russo–Japanese War of 1904–05. By 1944, the division had been reorganized into a triangular structure, with three infantry regiments (*10th*, *39th*, and *63rd*) of three battalions each. At full strength, it contained 14,840 officers and men and included an artillery regiment (the *10th*), an engineer regiment (the *10th*), a reconnaissance regiment (the *10th*), and the usual signal, transport, ordnance, and medical units. It had served in China and Manchuria between 1932 and 1934, after which it was returned to Japan. Commanded by Lieutenant General Yasuyuki Okamoto, it arrived in the Philippines in the fall of 1944 and joined the Luzon garrison.

General Mullins had to adjust his planning for the Balete Pass objective. Route 5 follows the deep, sharp valley of the Digdig River north, rising abruptly some

3,000 feet above sea level to the Balete Pass area. Once at the pass, the road drops to about 2,500 feet above sea level as it reaches Santa Fe. Innumerable large and small ridges border the road along its length. Some of these ridges are heavily wooded, some grassy slopes, and others bare. Balete Pass itself is a low point on an extended ridge complex forming the watershed of the streams running north into the Cagayan Valley. Balete Ridge, on which the pass stands, ran 11 miles across the Americans' path. Mount Imugan, which we heard about earlier in the 32nd Infantry Division's battle for the Villa Verde Trail, overlooks the area from a height of 5,580 feet a mile and a half north of the Salacsac Pass Number 1 on that Villa Verde Trail. The Americans would have to cross a series of ridges along their path under Japanese observation from Mt. Imugan, Mt. Minami (4,530 feet high) and Mt. Kabuto (4,600 feet high).

Patrols from the 25th Infantry Division soon discovered that the ravines between ridges were largely impassable due to heavy thick undergrowth and woods. They would have to move along the razor-backed crests of the ridges to advance. Room to maneuver was severely limited. Both sides would have plenty of cover and concealment. The Japanese, expecting the attack, had placed the understrength *11th Independent Infantry Regiment* along the Old Spanish Trail several miles east of Carranglan. A battalion of the *10th Infantry Regiment* held the eastern end of Balete Pass at Mts. Minami and Kabuto. Other units of this regiment also held Mt. Kanami, two miles northeast of Santa Fe. The *63rd Infantry Regiment*, reinforced with three provisional infantry battalions, defended Mt. Myoko, which was on Balete Ridge a mile west of Mt. Minami. These troops also defended Lone Tree Hill, halfway between Mt. Myoko and Balete Pass. Others held Kapintalan Ridge. Battalions from both the *10th* and *63rd Infantry Regiments* blocked Route 5 north of Minuli. Of the approximately 8,000 Japanese troops defending Balete Pass, 6,000 were west of Route 5 and the rest east of the road.

Some of this General Mullins knew from a captured fire plan of the *10th Field Artillery Regiment*. But considerable information about the exact positions of the Japanese infantry and mortars was lacking. Nevertheless, the attack began as planned. Initially, the 35th Infantry Regiment attacked up the Old Spanish Trail and advanced seven miles by March 11. But as they came up against a series of defended ridges, heavy resistance stopped the advance. Strong enemy artillery and mortar fire from undetected positions prevented further advance for the moment. Engineers of the 65th Engineer (Combat) Battalion reported that the Old Spanish Trail was unsuitable for military traffic unless significant rock fill, grading, and compacting was performed on it. Unwilling to delay his attack, General Mullins ordered the 35th Infantry to halt its attack.

To the Japanese, however, the attack of the 35th Infantry, which they estimated at battalion strength, was disturbing. General Konuma sent two battalions to the area, including some highly trained paratroopers, reinforcing the *11th Independent*

Infantry Regiment. These reinforcements arrived the same day that the 35th Infantry halted its attack. But, uncertain of the American intentions, General Konuma left the reinforcements where they were for the time being. Thus, the 35th Infantry, remaining in place, tied down about 3,000 of the enemy's best troops. They would remain there until late April, when General Konuma finally learned that the Americans did not have the strength to mount two full-force attacks against his defenses.

Between March 12 and 15, the 27th and 161st Infantry Regiments attacked along Route 5. Progress was made, but slowly. The 1st Battalion, 161st Infantry, went against what they soon called "Norton's Knob." This densely wooded knob lay 1,500 yards southwest of Kapintalan and was defended by a strong enemy defense based in the bottom of a saddle between hills from which machine-gun fire covered all approaches. On March 18, a flanking movement by the battalion surprised the enemy and critical ground was seized. The 3rd Battalion was immediately brought forward to hold the newly won ground and complete the seizure of Norton's Knob. Unwilling to concede the hill, the Japanese launched a series of strong night counterattacks, each of which was turned back with heavy Japanese losses. Indeed, so many attacks hit Companies C and L that the ridge was given a new name, "Banzai Ridge."

The effort to hold Norton's Knob continued for days. Air strikes, artillery, mortars, assault guns, and machine guns blasted the enemy-held area. More than 10,000 rounds of artillery and mortar fire was sent against Norton's Knob. Finally, on March 27, two M4 Sherman tanks armed with 105mm guns arrived and supported another attack. Led by a "tankdozer"—a tank equipped with a bulldozer blade—the battalion overran the Japanese defenses after an all-day and all-night battle. But the Japanese were not through just yet. A major counterattack hit the defenders the night of March 28, but it too was repulsed. Norton's Knob, also known as "Banzai Ridge," was safely in American hands.

The 27th Infantry Regiment had been pushing forward until they encountered Mt. Myoko. This was the first of three hills—Mt. Myoko, Myoko Ridge, and Lone Tree Hill—that they would have to secure to reach Balete Pass. Supported by the 35th Infantry, the attack began, while to the rear the 65th Engineer (Combat) Battalion struggled under enemy fire to build combat supply roads to the rear of the assault regiments.

Mount Myoko marked the Japanese main line of resistance. Alongside the 27th Infantry Regiment, the 35th Infantry bypassed the crests of Mt. Kabuto and Mt. Minami and reached the western side of Mt. Kanami. Using inaccurate maps, and moving in thick jungle, the leading companies had little idea of where they were, making supporting fires dangerous. It is believed that the leading companies reached the crest of Mt. Kanami before hitting enemy opposition. Moving away from that opposition, the leading companies of the 35th Infantry seemed to have reached the northern slope of Balete Ridge, two miles from the pass, on March 22. This movement concerned the Japanese, who began to move reinforcements from the Old Spanish Trail to Mt. Kanami and committed the remainder of the *10th Division* to the battle. The Japanese also launched a series of counterattacks against the supply line of the 35th Infantry Regiment. The combination of reinforcements and threats to the supply lines halted the advance of the 35th Infantry once again.

General Mullins faced a problem. He could not advance as his forces now stood. Each was blocked by the enemy and rough terrain. Intelligence estimates raised the original total of enemy defenders from 4,000 to over 10,000 enemy troops. Faced with this information and the conditions under which his troops were fighting, General Mullins did not have enough strength to continue his attack. To address his problem, General Mullins decided on March 29 to place his 35th Infantry Regiment along Route 5 between the 27th and 161st Infantry Regiments. Once in place, the 35th and 161st Infantry Regiments would attack along the highway, while the 27th Infantry attacked up Myoko Ridge, enveloping Balete Pass from the southeast. For the next two months, this was the form the fight for the pass would take.

Meanwhile, along the coast, on I Corps' extreme left flank, General Clarkson remained dissatisfied with his assignment. His 33rd Infantry Division had been enjoying success against the *58th Independent Mixed Brigade* and *23rd Division*. Aided by the Japanese belief that the main American effort would come up Route 11 to attack Baguio, patrols of the 33rd Infantry Division had been able to progress north along the weakly defended coast roads. A weak defense line along the Hills 600–1500 ridge line had fallen to the Illinois Guardsmen without a casualty. A sharp fight at the entrance to the Arodogat Valley had been won by the Americans, and the remaining Japanese stragglers easily cleared. Only along Route 11, where the *71st Infantry* of the *23rd Division* blocked rapid progress north, did the Japanese stand fast. These Japanese conducted a fighting withdrawal, slowing the American progress. Upon reaching another route, known as the Tuba Trail, patrols found that elements of the *64th Infantry Regiment, 23rd Division*, blocked that access road. Yet along the coast American patrols encountered few if any Japanese troops. These patrols soon discovered that there were no Japanese defending Route 3, which ran along the coast, as far north as the Aringay River.

General Clarkson saw an opportunity. With the Japanese withdrawing on his right, and few opponents on his left along the coast, he pushed General Swift at I Corps for permission to attack for a new line from Aringay through Pugo to Route 11 at Twin Peaks, near an objective known as Camp 2, a former Philippine Army military base. Included with General Swift's permission was authorization to reconnoiter further north if the opportunity arose. General Swift authorized this advance to begin March 7.

The 33rd Infantry Division moved swiftly. Patrols secured Aringay and Caba against no opposition. The Japanese defenders of the Tuba Trail were pushed back. Although any progress to the right, or east, on the division's front was strongly opposed, the coast roads continued to appear either weakly or completely undefended.

General Clarkson was encouraged to learn from Philippine guerilla informants that there were no Japanese troops at Bauang, seven miles north of Caba. Here Route 9 began, running off Route 3. Patrols also reported that these roads were in good condition and would require little engineering effort to bring them up to American military road standards.

General Clarkson prepared to act. He planned to send battalion combat teams up Route 11, the Galiano Road, and the Tuba Trail. Each would be directed on Baguio as a final objective. Two of his regiments would be concentrated along Route 9 for a rush to Baguio. He planned for his troops to be ready to move by April 1, and expected to have his leading elements in Baguio by April 15. His plan relied heavily on Philippine guerilla forces to hold the division's exposed northern flank. General Swift agreed fully with General Clarkson's plan, seeing an opportunity in taking advantage of Japanese weakness in the area. But just as this plan was to be implemented, Sixth Army Headquarters intervened. Pre-invasion plans called for opening a third front against the Japanese in northern Luzon, and the forces for this operation were to come from the USAFIP(NL) guerilla forces in the San Fernando area, the same guerilla forces General Clarkson planned to use to cover his flanks.

And although he supported General Clarkson's plan, General Swift was concerned about the 33rd Infantry Division becoming overextended and having to use scarce I Corps assets to rescue isolated 33rd Infantry Division units in trouble. As a compromise, General Swift allowed General Clarkson to put his plan into operation, but only in staged limited objective attacks. General Swift directed that an attack be made up Route 11 to Camp 4, six miles north of Twin Peaks. If this was successful, then the division was to halt all attacks along the Galiano Road and Tuba Trail, to avoid bringing Japanese attention, and possibly reinforcements, to those areas. Third, General Clarkson was directed to send a battalion into Bauang and then inland four miles along Route 9. The battalion was not to force a battle and was to withdraw if the Japanese opposed its advance. Although unsatisfactory to General Clarkson, he moved to implement the orders.

On the east flank, troops pushed slowly up Route 11, avoiding a pitched battle. It took them a week to reach Camp 3, where they discovered that the *23rd Division's* main line of resistance lay just north of Camp 3. The Japanese defended Route 11 and all trails on both sides of the highway. In accordance with orders not to bring on a pitched battle, the advance halted. Other patrols found no enemy defending the central trail, leading to Galiano. However, those probing the Tuba Trail found strong Japanese opposition.

Ever since entering the front lines on Luzon, the 33rd Infantry Division's intelligence and operations officers had been receiving unconfirmed reports of an abandoned trail that led from the 123rd Infantry's sector through the Caraballo Mountains to the outskirts of Baguio. This route supposedly began at Pugo, 10 miles north of Rosario, and ended at Tuba, just a few miles south of the Philippine summer capital, Baguio. This trail did not appear on any maps. But if it existed it would be a shorter and likely undefended route to the I Corps' objective. Interrogation of local residents seemed to support the existence of this trail. Many claimed to have used it, and others named it as the Old Spanish Trail. With this seemingly positive information, General Clarkson decided to send one arm of his reconnaissance-in-force to find and use this avenue.

In order not to alert the Japanese to their intention to use the Old Spanish Trail, American patrols were sent forward to find it and determine its usefulness. Company B, 123rd Infantry, under Captain James J. Itule, was assigned this task. Equipped for a five-day mission, the company set out on February 18 to pass through Pugo and find the trail. After five days, Captain Itule returned to report that despite his search, he could find no trace of the Old Spanish Trail. He added that there was no way for an American force to advance undetected in that direction since all supply and supporting arms would have to follow a narrow road through a clear valley which was open to enemy observation. He did report that enemy defenses in the area, however, consisted mainly of a string of observation posts strung out along the front of the 123rd Infantry.

With his advance stymied for the moment, General Clarkson again tried to convince General Swift that a run along the coast had a chance of success, especially since the Philippine guerilla forces he would depend upon to cover his flanks had not yet departed the San Fernando area for their next assignment. Instead, General Clarkson received orders to use his forces to relieve the guerillas at San Fernando to allow them to move north as directed by Sixth Army.

Colonel Russell W. Volckmann commanded the USAFIP(NL) forces in the San Fernando area. Another of several American Army officers who had refused to surrender in 1942 and instead gone into hiding while forming guerilla groups from Philippine soldiers and citizens, he now had a battalion of the 121st Infantry, USAFIP(NL) in the San Fernando area. Even before Sixth Army landed on Luzon in January, this force had begun gathering intelligence and harassing the Japanese forces in the area. A second battalion arrived in February and, supported by U.S. Marine Corps aircraft flying from primitive airstrips at Lingayen Gulf, made an attack on San Fernando at the end of February. Their opponents were the 3,000-member *Hayashi Detachment*, three infantry battalions, and some artillery that defended the area.[3]

To defend the San Fernando area, the *Hayashi Detachment* had withdrawn all the troops formerly defending the Route 3 and 9 junctions at Bauang. Exactly why they did this remains unclear, other than an attempt to concentrate their defenses around an area in which they had accumulated adequate supplies and where reinforcements might arrive by sea. The USAFIP(NL) attacks in January and February had only limited success, but in early March a third battalion, formerly attached to the 33rd Infantry Division, arrived. At this same time, the *Hayashi Detachment* lost one battalion, which the *58th Independent Mixed Brigade* recalled into reserve. Shortly after this battalion was withdrawn, the remaining units of the *Hayashi Detachment* left San Fernando, and on March 14 the guerillas marched into the town unopposed.

When advance elements of the 33rd Infantry Division had reached Bauang, the *58th Independent Mixed Brigade* decided to pull the entire *Hayashi Detachment* back to reinforce its main line of resistance at Sablan. Most of the detachment moved back over small backcountry trails with the guerillas in pursuit. One group, however, boldly withdrew up Route 3 to Bauang, not knowing that the Americans had already secured the area. This error cost them some 200 casualties. The withdrawal allowed the USAFIP(NL) forces to mop up the San Fernando area before moving to their next assignment. That came from Sixth Army, which directed them to move inland along Route 4, in effect creating a new front against the Japanese in northern Luzon. This move, however, deprived General Clarkson of his hoped-for flank protection.

To further disrupt General Clarkson's plans, with the 32nd Infantry Division struggling along the Villa Verde Trail, General Swift reduced its zone of responsibility to allow it to use more of its own troops in the main drive north. This, however, required the 33rd Infantry Division to stretch its own zone to cover the area left by General Gill's division. With his forces now thinly spread, General Clarkson had no choice but to return to the patrolling and holding actions he felt were unnecessary.

General Krueger at Sixth Army Headquarters had been monitoring, and often visiting, the I Corps front. Seeking to reinforce General Swift, he had begun to press General MacArthur's headquarters to release some troops then garrisoning Manila and its environs. Finally, in late March, General Headquarters, Southwest Pacific Area (GHQ, SWPA) released the 129th RCT of the 37th Infantry Division. General Krueger sent this regiment to take over the Route 9 advance, freeing up several battalions of the 33rd Infantry Division. Immediately, General Clarkson began making plans for a renewed advance on Baguio.

The forces under General Clarkson were redistributed. The attached 129th Infantry was assigned Route 9. The 123rd Infantry Regiment would patrol toward Baguio using the Galiano and Tuba Trails. The 136th Infantry was assigned an advance of five miles from Camp 2 to Camp 4 on Route 11, while the 130th Infantry covered the ground recently vacated by the 32nd Infantry Division. Facing them was the same *58th Independent Mixed Brigade* and *23rd Division*. But neither of these units was in the same condition as when the advance first began. Each had suffered considerable losses in March, and lack of food and adequate medical supplies had further diminished their ranks. By mid-March the supply situation had become critical. Allied air forces constantly slowed supply deliveries, those that they did not destroy. The difficult terrain which slowed American progress did the same for the Japanese supply convoys. Around the village of Aritao, the 66th Infantry, USAFIP(NL), had all but closed Route 11 north of Baguio, and the 11th Infantry, USAFIP(NL), had done the same in portions of the Cagayan Valley. Finally, the Japanese themselves overstretched their resources by trying to supply the

23rd Division, the *58th Independent Mixed Brigade*, the *19th Division*, and *Fourteenth Army Headquarters*, plus the large civilian population at Baguio while at the same time withdrawing supplies deeper into the mountains for the eventual withdrawal.

As expected, the burden of insufficient supplies was felt most by the combat troops. In mid-March, the combat troops at Baguio were getting less than half a pound of rice per day, when requirements were two and a half pounds per day. This level of food continued to decline as the battle wore on, and it was not long before signs of starvation and related diseases began to appear, filling the hospitals and weakening the front-line units. This, in turn, increased the use of already insufficient medical supplies, adding yet another crisis to the Japanese dilemma. General Yamashita, already pessimistic, directed that a new defense line be reconnoitered to the north, northeast, and east of Baguio, where he had his headquarters. Attempting to alleviate his food and medical situation, in mid-March General Yamashita also ordered all Japanese civilians and the puppet government of the Japanese-controlled Philippines to evacuate the city. Although it was clear that a withdrawal was necessary, General Yamashita decided to wait until the situation became hopeless before ordering a full-scale withdrawal.

At the front Major General Bunzo Sato, commanding the *58th Independent Mixed Brigade*, reinforced his main line of resistance. Expecting the main American attack along Route 9 in his sector, he was also aware that the Galiano Road was vulnerable. He ordered the *1st Battalion, 75th Infantry* of the *19th Division* to move from Baguio and defend the road at Asin. This, however, left only three provisional battalions, perhaps 750 soldiers, to defend Baguio itself.

The 33rd Infantry Division was still limited to patrolling and minor advances. But in the last days of March patrols along the Tuba Trail managed to secure another three miles, although they reported increasing Japanese resistance as they moved northeast. The situation was similar along the Galiano Road, where a battalion managed to reach a position only one mile east of Galiano by the end of March. But it was on the left of the division, where the attached 129th Infantry pushed forward to within a mile of Salat, that the Japanese main line of resistance was most threatened. Here, despite another battalion of the *58th Independent Mixed Brigade* being rushed in as reinforcements, the 129th Infantry broke through the outpost line of resistance and began to maneuver against the main enemy defenses. The Americans now began to feel that the Japanese defenses along Route 9, the Galiano Road, and the Tuba Trail were unexpectedly weak. Perhaps this was another opportunity which could be exploited with the application of a little more strength. Once again, General Krueger provided the necessary strength.

CHAPTER 15

Baguio Falls

General Krueger had continued with his efforts to provide more striking power for the I Corps in northern Luzon. By April 7 he had persuaded GHQ SWPA to release the remainder of the 37th Infantry Division, less its 145th Infantry RCT, from its garrison duties at Manila. With this news to General Swift came authorization for a two-division drive on Baguio as soon as the 37th Infantry Division took over a sector of the I Corps' front. As conceived, the plan called for the 37th Infantry Division to take over responsibility for Route 9, while the adjoining 33rd Infantry Division used all three routes to attack north, with emphasis along the Galiano Road in support of General Beightler's division. From the American viewpoint, the Galiano Road was also the least difficult terrain over which to advance.

General Clarkson assigned his 136th Infantry Regiment, reinforced with the 33rd Reconnaissance Troop and the 2nd Battalion, 66th Infantry, USAFIP(NL), to Route 11. The 123rd Infantry was to push northeast up the Tuba Trail, while the 130th Infantry RCT would continue up the Galiano Road. Inland, the 129th Infantry rejoined its parent 37th Infantry Division to attack along Route 9 while the 148th Infantry RCT remained in reserve.

The Japanese remained ignorant of these changes and still believed the main American attack would come up Route 11. They did not redeploy any units while the new American units moved into position. There was some indication that the Japanese had developed a fatalistic, or defeatist, attitude strengthened by the recent evacuation of civilians from Baguio. Even General Yamashita prepared to leave Baguio, departing on April 19. Behind him he left yet another independent command, under Major General Naokata Utsonomiya, one of his assistant Chiefs of Staff. This unnamed command covered the Baguio front and included the *19th Division*, north of Baguio, the *58th Independent Mixed Brigade*, and the *23rd Division*. Because of communication difficulties, contact with the *19th Division* was impossible, and this unit was in effect outside the Baguio front. Nevertheless, General Utsonomiya prepared to defend Baguio to the last, issuing the by now standard order to fight to the last man.

The two right-flank regiments of the 33rd Infantry Division were badly placed to strike for the Philippine summer capital. Rain, fog, particularly bad terrain, and determined Japanese resistance slowed them to a crawl. Nevertheless, the 123rd and 136th Infantry RCTs did tie down strong enemy forces defending Route 11 and the Tuba Trail. In doing so, they paid he usual high price.

Even the rear areas were deadly. Galiano was a small power-plant town. Supposedly a "rear" area, it had been under intermittent artillery fire from Japanese batteries further north. To secure the area, Company B, 130th Infantry, sent out patrols regularly. One such patrol consisted of the 2nd Platoon, which completed a routine security check along the battalion's left flank. As they began to move down a valley to their bivouac area, they were struck by a barrage of artillery. As they sought cover, a small party of Japanese infiltrators opened fire with a machine gun. One of the first wounded was Private First Class Doneivon L. Weeks, a scout.

Private First Class Weeks was wounded in the legs and fell to the ground. He immediately shouted warnings to his buddies behind him to seek cover. Then the scout took out a grenade, armed it, and began painfully crawling toward the enemy. Seeing this apparently helpless target, the Japanese concentrated their fire on Private First Class Weeks as he advanced on them. The gallant scout was instantly killed, but his diversion identified the enemy's position to the rest of the platoon who then surrounded and wiped out the party of infiltrators. For his gallantry, Private First Class Weeks received a posthumous Distinguished Service Cross.[1]

One of the obstacles facing the 123rd Infantry was what they termed "Hill X." This was a long knob running down a slope at Bilbil. The job fell to Lieutenant Colonel Charles F. Coates's 1st Battalion, which attacked the hill seven times only to be caught each time by heavy enemy fire as they became exposed on an open razor-back ridge leading to the hill. Exhausted, the battalion was replaced by Major Richard Askren's 2nd Battalion, 130th Infantry. Aware that the enemy troops, from the *58th Independent Mixed Brigade*, were determined to hold Hill X to the last man, Major Askren's men moved up and prepared to assault the hill. Patrols searched for a weak spot but found none. No matter how hard they looked, the only way up to Hill X was along that exposed razor-back ridge.

Determined to try, Major Askren asked Captain William F. Dellinger, commanding Company F, to attack the hill without preparatory fires, which alerted the Japanese to an incoming attack, basing his entire plan on surprise. It was hoped that Company F could at least secure a foothold on Hill X before they were discovered, giving the battalion an advantage for the next attack. The attack went in early on April 11.

Initially, the surprise attack went well. The enemy outposts were overrun, blasted by Company F's grenades and rifle fire. Caught completely by surprise, the Japanese died in place or withdrew to higher defenses on the hill. Fox Company immediately began to construct defenses for the inevitable counterattack. But before they finished, Japanese artillery and mortars came down followed by a wave of Japanese troops

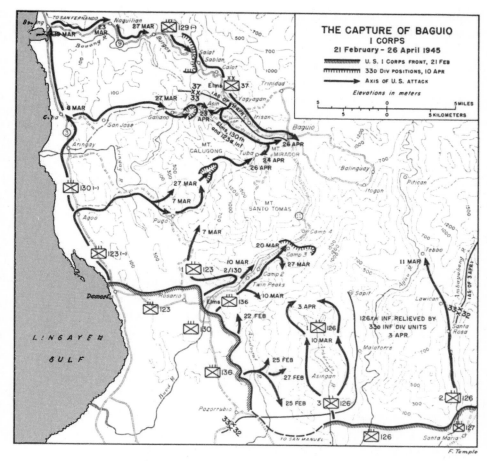

The Capture of Baguio, February–April 1945

Robert Ross Smith. *United States Army in World War II. The War in the Pacific. Triumph in the Philippines.* Washington, D.C.: Center of Military History, 1984. p. 473.

screaming obscenities in Japanese and English. Captain Dellinger and his men tried desperately to halt the attack with rifle and machine-gun fire, but the Japanese attack was overwhelming and had the advantage of height, from which supporting fire struck within Company F. Over the next several minutes the Japanese gained fire superiority, and then enemy artillery and mortars began a plunging fire directly into Company F's positions. Still Company F fought on, but soon the Japanese gained their flanks. Despite repeated failures to overrun "Fox" Company, the Japanese still attacked. Finally, carrying its dead and wounded, Captain Dellinger's company withdrew, leaving the Japanese still in possession of Hill X. It would take 12 hours of bombardment by the 124th Field Artillery Battalion and a costly two-day attack by Captain Patrick Kelly's Company C, 130th Infantry, before Hill X fell.

It was during Company C's attack on Hill X that Private First Class Dexter J. Kerstetter distinguished himself. The soldier from Centralia, Washington, was with the lead squad as it moved under heavy Japanese fire along the razor-back ridge. Enemy machine guns, rifles, mortars, and artillery fire opposed the advance. Sheltered by spider holes, tunnels, caves, and being well camouflaged, the Japanese had the upper hand. When the five men ahead of him were wounded, Private First Class Kerstetter moved to the front of the assault team, leading his squad forward. He continued to work his way up the steep ridge, under constant enemy fire. Using well-aimed rifle shots and rifle grenades, he forced the Japanese to seek cover, thus reducing the amount of fire that came against him and his squad. Spotting an enemy cave, he dropped from the trail along a cliff using precarious footholds and wiped out four enemy soldiers sheltering in the cave. Climbing back to the trail, he attacked a machine gun protected by riflemen and mortar fire. After knocking out the gun with his rifle and grenades, he used up all his remaining ammunition repelling an attack by 20 enemy soldiers, forcing them to scatter. He returned to his squad for more ammunition and first aid for his left hand, which had blistered from the heat of his rifle. With fresh ammunition, he guided a new platoon to a position from which a new attack could be launched, killing three enemy troops on the way forward. Due largely to his actions, Hill X was taken that day, and held for the next three days despite ferocious Japanese counterattacks. For his leadership on April 11, 1945, Private First Class Dexter J. Kerstetter received a Medal of Honor.[2]

Nor was it a one-man show on Hill X. Following Private First Class Kerstetter up the hill was Private First Class Joseph Papez, Jr., who attacked a pair of enemy machine guns despite the fact that they concentrated their fire on him, as did the supporting riflemen. Enemy grenades shrouded him in smoke and dust as he made his way up the hill and knocked out both guns with grenades and bullets. Indeed, Company C, which the division's own history claims was "one of the finest units in the division,"[3] stormed Hill X and blasted every enemy gun position and drove off any surviving enemy soldiers. Company C, those who survived, were left standing in a haze of smoke and acrid smells amid dozens of enemy dead, but they had seized the hill. It had also earned itself a rare award for so small a unit, the Distinguished Unit Citation.[4]

But the Japanese, whose orders directed them to hold to the last man, were not quite finished with Company C. Over the next three days, and nights, the Japanese counterattacked repeatedly. When the attacks finally ceased, Company C had less than half the men it had started with up Hill X four days ago. One of the casualties was Private First Class Kerstetter, who was wounded by a sniper's bullet in the leg. The Japanese concentration on Hill X, however, had allowed the regiment's 2nd Battalion to move through the valley below and take the town of Asin. A provisional force, consisting of the Regimental Intelligence and Reconnaissance Platoon and the Antitank Company, seized a position on a hill near Lomboy, preventing the Japanese from striking at the supply lines into Asin. By April 12, Major Askren had his command post established in Asin.

With the fall of Asin and patrol probes toward the mountains east of Asin, it became clear that the enemy's main line of resistance had been reached. Each patrol found that every avenue of approach to the enemy was covered by "an abundance of automatic weapons. He let you get in close, and just when you thought you had him, he opened up."[5] Colonel Collins and his 130th Infantry ("Blackhawks") Regiment also noted that the Japanese had stopped their regular harassing fire, raiding parties, and fanatical banzai attacks. The enemy, identified by a prisoner as a battalion of the *75th Infantry Regiment*, had his back to Baguio and was saving his resources for the defensive battle about to begin.

The 129th Infantry of the 37th Infantry Division had left Manila by truck and by train, along with Lieutenant Colonel Stewart L. Brown's 6th Field Artillery Battalion. Leaving Manila was hard for the men of the 37th Infantry Division. In the weeks that they had garrisoned the Philippine capital city, many had made friends with the civilian population. Many Filipinos came to say goodbye to the troops who were about to return to combat, others said prayers for them, and little girls placed necklaces of flowers around the necks of many. It was a parting not unlike that which had taken place more than two years before when the division left the United States. As the narrow-gauge 10mph diesel locomotive struggled north, every stop along the way saw more Filipinos, particularly children, come out to ask for cigarettes, or sell coconuts and bananas. Each of the small railroad cars was filled with 60 soldiers and their gear, resulting in an uncomfortable ride. Sleep, when possible, was difficult.

The regiment unloaded at San Fabian, where trucks carried the regiment and artillery forward to a point where they dismounted and began a march to relieve the 130th Infantry, 33rd Infantry Division. In the initial advances, only sporadic minor resistance was encountered. A few enemy machine guns, a few mortar rounds, were all that disputed the initial advance until April 3. Demolition charges placed along the roadway were easily spotted and removed by the Mine Platoon of the regimental Antitank Company. Tanks from Company D, 775th Tank Battalion, led the advance, encountering no opposition. In one instance 37th Infantry Division Military Police encountered three Japanese soldiers in civilian clothes hiding in a native hut whom they quickly dealt with. At night, minor infiltration attempts were easily brushed off.

Trouble began near the village of Salat when the lead truck was attacked by a Japanese soldier tossing a bag of grenades, damaging the vehicle but causing no casualties. The leading reconnaissance patrols now found themselves along a concrete road winding up into the mountains with granite cliffs on one side and a perpendicular chasm dropping off on the other side. This canalized the advance along the single road with no maneuver room. Allied air power was used to try to destroy any enemy defenses along the road and the nearby hills as the infantry advanced. Once again mines had been placed in bomb craters to stop the American armor, but these were usually poorly camouflaged and easily removed by Company B, 117th Engineer (Combat) Battalion.

Further along the road a large crater halted the tanks. As the tankers sought a way around the roadblock and the infantrymen stopped for a lunch of frankfurters and beans, the Japanese opened fire. Machine guns and heavy artillery fire stymied the advance patrol. Some ran for the shelter of the tanks, but two men were seriously wounded even as they sheltered behind a tank. Japanese 47mm antitank fire then joined in the barrage. The tanks began to search for the source of the enemy fire while more infantrymen fell dead and wounded. Finally, after locating and suppressing the enemy weapons, the wounded were evacuated and the dead carried to the rear. The patrol report clearly indicated that the Japanese, believed to be at company strength, were strongly dug in along the Nagulian–Baguio road near Salat.

The following day the advance resumed against snipers, antitank fire, and artillery which struck among the 6th Field Artillery Battalion, causing several casualties. A 52-man detachment of the attached 66th (Igorot) Battalion, USAIP(NL), moved forward during a cold, windy, and rainy night. Within an hour a loud barrage of gunfire was heard by the Americans waiting along the road. Moans and screams followed, but the Americans had no idea of what had happened nor who had won this obvious nocturnal battle. The following morning, after some sporadic machine-gun and rifle fire, the half of the native detachment who survived marched down the highway chanting "sixty-six, sixty-six" as both their password and victory song.[6]

But still the advance remained blocked. More and more patrols were sent out. These became truly a deadly trial to the men assigned to them. Nearly every patrol encountered the enemy, and those who sought out the enemy's flanks were particularly grueling. As one patrol leader expressed it, "Men, we have fought, at one time or another, in the jungles, in the valleys, in barrios and even in cities. Now men, something new had been added, MOUNTAINS!"[7] The climb up the nearly vertical slope to get to the rear of the enemy exhausted the men, as did the heat and humidity, so that when the Japanese opened fire they were so exhausted that opposition was feeble, and the patrols were easily turned back.

Still, the Ohioans pushed ahead. On April 8, a Japanese attack struck Company G, supported by artillery. The Americans turned back this attack with automatic weapons and rifle fire. Later, Staff Sergeant Joseph J. Podsiedly of Chicago led the counterattack against enemy soldiers who were overlooking his Company E's position, using a BAR. Rushing up the high ground firing his BAR, he dodged quickly from one cave to a foxhole and on to the next. He killed several of the enemy and then led his squad in a drive to secure the hill, leading them forward into heavy enemy fire. Nearly a platoon of the enemy was eliminated by Staff Sergeant Podsiedly, who was awarded the Distinguished Service Cross.[8]

It was the next day, April 9, that the Japanese targeted a forward observation post of the 6th Field Artillery Battalion. As he usually did, Colonel Brown had gone forward to this post to observe the enemy and to control counterbattery fire against the enemy's artillery. But the Japanese struck first, and a direct hit killed Lieutenant Colonel Brown, Captain Wayne A. Kepler, and Technician Fifth Class Thomas E. Tickle. Lieutenant Colonel Chester W. Wolfe was sent up to take command of the 6th Field Artillery Battalion.

The advance continued in this manner day after day. Each fortified hill had to be taken individually, with air and artillery pounding the Japanese and then infantry and tanks attacking against rifles, machine guns and mortars, usually supported by distant artillery. The enemy and the terrain controlled the speed of the advance. Roving enemy patrols ambushed supply convoys that were technically "behind" the front lines. The infantrymen were constantly exhausted and had to be rested frequently to keep them in shape to fight again. One unidentified infantryman from Company D, 129th Infantry, is reported to have muttered that he couldn't go any faster "even if the opposition were nude women and not scrappy yellow men."[9]

On April 14, after a breakfast of powdered eggs and simulated toast, the 148th Infantry RCT came up to relieve the 129th Infantry. The scenario remained the same. Coming to a hairpin turn in the road, one of many, the leading squad came under fire from a Japanese-held cave. A tank from the 775th Tank Battalion came up and fired directly into the cave, then repeated the action. The attack moved on.

More often, it was not as simple. As the leading force moved up the road some 300 yards from the last encounter, enemy mines and landslides halted the advance. As the tanks and infantry stood aside for the combat engineers and bulldozers to work, the leading platoon moved beyond the obstacle to see what lay ahead. As First Lieutenant Gerald E. Van Pelt led his men forward, they came under intense machine-gun and rifle fire from commanding ground along the road. Lieutenant Van Pelt fell, mortally wounded. Two of his men were seriously wounded as they ran for cover. One of them dragged himself into a nearby cave and became the focus of much of the enemy's fire. Private First Class Fred Ogrodnick ignored the flying bullets and dashed into the cave to give medical aid to his wounded friend. Fifty yards further back, Private First Class Melvin Kidd jumped on a tank and, despite withering fire directed at him, rode the tank forward to a position near the cave. He then jumped down and assisted Private First Class Ogrodnick in providing first aid. Suddenly, the cave collapsed due to the intense impact of the hundreds of bullets thundering into it. All three men were buried alive. Five other men of the platoon, firing their rifles as they ran, raced to the cave and began to dig the buried men out. Using their bayonets, pick mattocks, and bare hands, they managed to save the three men.

A call went out for support, and a platoon of self-propelled guns rolled forward. They saturated the hostile hills with direct fire, allowing the trapped platoon to withdraw. That night, in a pitch-black darkness, the Japanese tried to sneak into the Americans' perimeter, but the 148th Infantry were old hands at this game, having played it on New Georgia, Bougainville, and earlier on Luzon. Not a rifle was fired, so the Japanese could not locate the Americans' positions. Instead, led by Sergeant Harniack of Company I, the battle raged with hand grenades only. The Japanese inflicted no casualties, but apparently dragged off several of their own wounded.

And so it went. From Hairpin Turn to Hairpin Ridge to Monglo Hill to Banana Ridge, the battles followed each other with a dangerously similar pattern. Progress remained slow but steady. The occasional night attack, such as the one by Captain Buster Ferris and his Company B, sometimes gained a success with minimal casualties, but even then, the inevitable Japanese counterattack continued the flow of American casualties.

These battles signaled the beginning of a two-division attack General Swift planned to reach Baguio. Both the 33rd and 37th Infantry Divisions were to make this attack beginning April 12, but in fact both divisions simply continued with attacks already in progress by that date. Ironically, although the American commanders viewed these attacks as slow and costly, the Japanese grew increasingly concerned about them. The 148th Infantry, for example, captured several large stocks of ammunition that the *19th Division* had left behind when it moved north. Other critical supplies also fell into American hands during this drive. Yet another concern for the Japanese was that the combined air and artillery attacks on the supporting Japanese artillery had nearly destroyed all the *58th Independent Mixed Brigade*'s artillery support in the area. The Japanese tried to rush reinforcements forward, but the Americans were moving so rapidly, or so it seemed to the Japanese, that the reinforcements could not reach their designated posts before they were overrun by the enemy.

One such place was the village of Yagyagan. Here a trail led down steep slopes to Asin on the Galiano Road where the 130th Infantry, 33rd Infantry Division, had been stalled by determined Japanese resistance. If the 37th Infantry Division could seize this small barrio, then the 130th Infantry Regiment could bypass that resistance and hit it from the rear. But to get to Yagyagan the attackers would first have to pass through the Irisan gorge, holding the Irisan River, the last natural defensive position along Route 9. It would take them six days.

Determined to halt the advance of General Beightler's division, General Utsunomiya rushed reinforcements to the Irisan area. They were ordered to make a last stand and halt the American drive. Baguio was stripped of able-bodied soldiers to form this new reinforcement group. Others were taken from outposts in the Ambayabang, Agno, and Arboredo Valleys, stripping those defenses. Even Route 11, which the Japanese still believed was the Americans' main thrust, lost men to the Irisan front. All in all, at least 1,500 men were rushed to the area, although they arrived in separate groups and were rarely coordinated in their efforts.

There were a group of high ridges that overlooked the Irisan gorge area and dominated Route 9. These became known to the 148th Infantry as Hills A through F. Each held defensive positions manned by the enemy. On April 17, the 2nd Battalion, 148th Infantry, reinforced by medium tanks, 105mm self-propelled guns, and 76mm armed tank destroyers tried and failed to attack along the east-west section of Route 9. Two tanks were knocked out by Japanese antitank fire. Japanese machine guns and small-arms fire blocked the infantry's advance.

"Of all the natural defensive positions in the Baguio mountains, the ones covering the Irisan were the most ominous. The bridge itself was in a valley, surrounded by eight distinct ridges, and it resembles a drop of water in a teacup with the bridge being the drop and the high ground, the rim. The ridges were all defended, were mutually supporting, and yet any one could be held independent of the others. The terrain was heavily wooded and the minor trails leading to the Japanese position were few, narrow, steep and, of course, covered by automatic fire. A stretch of road about two hundred yards on each side of the bridge, could be swept by machine gun and rifle fire from any of the right ridges and the flat-trajectory artillery, concealed in caves and dragged out for special occasions could pound any remunerative targets within this 400-yard zone. The 90mm mortars were zeroed in on the bridge and surrounding areas, and American commanders agreed that any attempt to enter this no man's land without first conquering the ridges would be suicidal."[10]

That afternoon the 148th Infantry tried different tactics. Supported by Company B, 754th Tank Battalion, a platoon of Company F occupied Ridge A's defenders while the rest of Company F infiltrated to the rear of the Japanese positions and took the high point on Ridge A from behind. They held this position despite repeated Japanese counterattacks. The seizure of Ridge A opened the way to Ridges B, G, and F. Company G attacked along the road supported by tanks and self-propelled guns. Enemy fire halted this advance, and one tank, trying to get out of the line of fire, slipped off the narrow roadway and fell down the cliff, hitting bottom 50 yards below. A patrol from Company G was dispatched to rescue the crew, arriving just in time to fend off a Japanese patrol intent on finishing off that same crew. Four of the five-man tank crew survived.

The 2nd Battalion, 148th Infantry's commander, Lieutenant Colonel Herbert Radcliffe, came forward and, with regimental commander Colonel L. K. White, was deciding on what to do next. As they conversed, two Japanese tanks came racing down the roadway toward the Americans. Tank-mounted 47mm guns and machine guns blasted the road ahead of the onrushing Japanese armored vehicles. Behind each tank rode a dozen Japanese infantrymen on specially designed towed platforms, blazing away at the surprised Americans. The lead tank had antitank mines strapped to its front, intent on ramming an American tank and knocking it out, along with themselves. One succeeded in ramming an M4 Sherman Tank, ripping off its tread and disabling it. But after 10 minutes the enemy tanks were destroyed, and the enemy riflemen annihilated. But Colonel White was badly wounded in the leg and knocked over the cliff where he was caught by the regimental chaplain, Captain (Chaplain) Elmer Heindl. Chaplain Heindl received a Silver Star for saving the colonel's life while under heavy enemy fire. A medical officer, Captain James Watson, continued administering plasma despite receiving a hundred shrapnel wounds all over his body. His survival, despite a prognosis to the contrary, amazed everyone. More than a score of enlisted men and several officers were also wounded in this attack. Colonel A. R. Walk, formerly the division chief of staff, came forward to assume command of the 148th Infantry Regiment.

Meanwhile the 3rd Battalion was conducting a wide envelopment, crossing the Irisan River 500 yards downstream to attack Ridge C. Later they would strike for Ridges D and E. Moving down steep wooded ridges, terrain considered impassible by the Japanese, they remained undetected and were soon behind enemy lines. Supported by direct fire from a platoon of self-propelled guns of Company B, 637th Tank Destroyer Battalion, the attack completely surprised the Japanese on Ridge C, who offered no opposition. Some killed themselves and others were killed or raced away. By lunchtime, Ridge C was secured.

The 2nd Battalion, however, had no options such as surprise. Continuing their attack along the road, Company E ran into the usual intense automatic weapons, mortar, and artillery fire. Supported by their own artillery, the infantrymen took half of Ridge B by dark. That night a Japanese counterattack resulted in hand-to-hand fighting, but the Americans held their positions. April 19 saw heavy air and artillery preparation as Companies E and G renewed their assault. A bitter fight ensued. A machine-gun crew from Company E managed to get behind the Japanese and opened fire. Although two of this crew were subsequently killed, their fire allowed the rest of Company E to break through Japanese lines, securing Ridge B.

The 3rd Battalion, 148th Infantry, covered by its own machine guns, mortars, and rifle fire, successively struck at ridges D and E. So stunned and distracted were the Japanese on what the Americans were calling "Chocolate Drop Hill" that it was seized without a single casualty. There remained only Ridges F, G, and H. To give the assault battalions a rest, the 1st Battalion was brought forward to initiate the rest of the advance. By noon on April 20, Ridge G was in American hands. The 37th Infantry Division would spend another few days fighting off counterattacks and digging out determined holdouts among the ridges, but in effect the battle had been won at a cost of 40 killed and 160 wounded. At least 500 Japanese had been lost at the Irisan gorge.

While General Beightler's men fought at the gorge, General Clarkson's men were taking advantage of that distraction. A battalion of the 130th Infantry was withdrawn from the Asin–Galiano zone and sent to the rear. Here it enjoyed mobile showers, hot food, and canvas cots to sleep upon. The next morning, they were sent along the 129th Infantry's route to Irisan. In what they later called the "130th Infantry merry-go-round," they were followed by Major James B. Faulconer's 2nd Battalion, released from division reserve status. While the 3rd Battalion remained at Asin putting pressure on the enemy, the rest of the regiment moved up the road to new positions. With dawn came the realization that the day's attack would be downhill! For the first time on Luzon, the 130th Infantry Regiment was on top of the enemy and attacking downhill.

Supporting weapons were set up. The regimental Cannon Company placed its guns, as did guns from an antiaircraft battalion firing multiple-mounted .50-caliber and 40mm weapons. Heavy machine guns of both D and H Companies took up positions. As dawn rose on April 21, Captain James L. Brown's Company B launched the attack, followed by the rest of the 1st Battalion, 130th Infantry. The attack caught the Japanese completely by surprise. Not expecting an attack from the north, behind them, the entire Japanese defense was rendered impotent. Covered by a rolling barrage of artillery, mortar, and machine-gun fire, the advance rolled downhill.

As the attack progressed, and as the Japanese had time to organize themselves for the new situation, resistance stiffened. Lieutenant Colonel Ernest D. Jessup, the battalion commander, was up front with the leading company. While directing fire on enemy defenses, he was struck by enemy machine-gun fire. As he lay in an exposed position, a Japanese machine gunner targeted him again. This time the battalion commander was hit in the arms and legs. Captain Patrick Kelly, mentioned earlier, crawled out to Colonel Jessup and dragged him to a concealed position. Undaunted, Colonel Jessup continued to observe direct cannon fire against an enemy position holding up his battalion. The self-propelled guns knocked out that position under his direction, destroying three machine guns and four mortars. For his gallantry and leadership, Colonel Jessup received a Distinguished Service Cross.[11] Major Charlie Y. Talbot, Sr., assumed command of the battalion.

That night came the usual strong counterattacks. Companies E and F were particularly hard hit but refused to yield, knowing that they would only have to attack this same ground again. After the usual artillery and mortar bombardment, the 2nd Battalion took up the attack again on the morning of April 23. With its heavy losses of the night before, the *1st Battalion, 75th Infantry*, had insufficient strength to put up a strong defense. Still contesting every yard of the advance, the Japanese were pressed back steadily. Captain Gerard Unrein's Company E pushed forward, breaking up the Japanese defenders into small groups that were pushed aside. Captain Marinos G. Maniatty's Company G destroyed those small groups as they followed in Company E's trace. To reach some hidden caves alongside the hills, some Americans had to use small saplings to support themselves while they leaned over and fired into those caves. As each company became low on ammunition, Major Faulconer replaced it with another of his companies. With this constant supply of fresh and equipped troops, the advance continued. By the end of the day the Asin area and its tunnels along the road had been secured. In exchange for knocking out 350 enemy troops, the 130th Infantry suffered 72 casualties, of which 13 were killed.

Along Route 9, General Beightler's division was experiencing little opposition after passing the Irisan gorge. But reports soon began to arrive from guerilla sources that the survivors of the gorge battle, and possibly the previously uncommitted *379th Independent Infantry Battalion*, were massing on the division's north (left) flank for a counterattack. With all his own troops committed, General Beightler called for reinforcements to guard his exposed flank. Unfortunately, General Swift had no reserves to offer. Instead, the division was ordered to halt in place and clear the ground along Route 9 between Sablan and Irisan and set up strong defenses in the area. The 33rd Infantry Division was likewise ordered to halt and ensure that there was no threat to the 37th Infantry Division's southern (right) flank. Once this had been accomplished, both divisions were to attack Mt. Mirador, on the outskirts of Baguio.

Mount Mirador had to be seized. It dominated the Galiano Road and Route 9 junction and could cover the entire town of Baguio with fire. But things were in rapid movement on the Japanese side of the front. General Utsunomiya had decided to place his main line of resistance closer to Baguio. But even as he did so, his new line evaporated. One anchor of the new line, the Irisan gorge, was gone. The 123rd Infantry was about to overrun another strategic point, Mt. Calugong. The Asin position had disappeared. It became clear to General Utsunomiya that he had no main line of resistance left, and his forces were significantly diminished.

Being a reasonable man, General Utsunomiya ordered a withdrawal north and east from Baguio. He would leave a rear guard in Baguio and another to delay the 37th Infantry Division along the Irisan–Trinidad trail. This latter force was to delay the Americans reaching Route 11 until all Japanese forces had successfully withdrawn. The Japanese, many of whom no doubt expected the order, moved swiftly. A patrol of the 129th Infantry, 37th Infantry Division, entered Baguio on April 24 and in two days had the city secured against negligible opposition. The remaining force on Mt. Mirador was destroyed by the 123rd and 130th Infantry Regiments of the 33rd Infantry Division between April 24 and 26. Tuba was reached by the 123rd Infantry on April 24 after an unopposed march. Major units of the 33rd Infantry Division entered Baguio on April 27. Baguio had fallen.

Although General Utsunomiya had managed to withdraw with about 10,000 Japanese troops from the Baguio area, largely due to the necessary halt by the Americans on April 22, the battle had been otherwise successful. Terrain problems and a lack of available intelligence, particularly once the 66th Infantry USAFIP(NL) were withdrawn, slowed the American advance unavoidably. Nor should Japanese resistance be discounted. On the other hand, both the *58th Independent Mixed Brigade* and the *23rd Division* were severely injured during the battles. American intelligence estimated that the *23rd Division* had no more than 7,000 troops left to it, while the *58th Independent Mixed Brigade* was at less than the strength of a battalion, perhaps 350 survivors. They had also lost much in the way of supplies, ammunition, and artillery. Indeed, the *58th Independent Mixed Brigade* had no artillery left and the *23rd Division* was down to three or four guns. Further, one of the three main anchors of General Yamashita's defensive triangle had been overrun. Those Japanese who had retreated had only gone deeper into a mountain fastness from which there could be no escape.

CHAPTER 16

Balete Pass

From the end of April to the end of May, the 37th Infantry Division cleared the area around Trinidad of enemy stragglers and holdouts. Isolated pockets of Japanese resistance in the high ground of Route 9 and Route 11 were eliminated by combat patrols. Only near Trinidad itself did the division encounter organized resistance.

Meanwhile, along the Tuba Trail the 33rd Infantry Division did much the same work. After clearing its area, General Clarkson's men garrisoned Baguio and its environs. The 130th Infantry marched to Balinguay, and eventually the division again was tasked with a holding mission, this time north of Baguio securing the Baguio–Bauang–San Fernando area. It also had to maintain contact between itself and the units still fighting in the Ambayabang and Agno Valleys.

Things cooled off for the Japanese in the area as well. With the 33rd Infantry Division being held to the Baguio area, they could supply themselves better than they had the past several weeks from several large supply dumps hidden north of the Philippine summer capital. They could also dig defensive positions at leisure since they were under no immediate pressure from the Americans. From all sources, it appears that both General Swift at I Corps and General Clarkson at 33rd Infantry Division were willing to push north, but Sixth Army Headquarters was concerned about security in the vast area guarded by the 33rd Infantry Division and felt it needed time to rest and rehabilitate itself before conducting another advance. There was also the concern that if the division pushed north and became involved in a fight, there were no reserves available on Luzon to support it. Finally, Sixth Army still had little in the way of concrete intelligence as to how and where the Japanese intended to make their next stand. That they would was not in doubt, only where and when.

General Krueger had, back in March, believed that the main Japanese resistance to his army's northern push would be along Route 5. It was with that in mind that he gave the 25th Infantry Division a narrower front and ordered it to attack north from San Jose to Digdig, then open Route 100 another 17 miles north from Rizal to Carranglan. The junction of the two roads at Digdig was also to be secured.

The 35th Infantry attacked on February 23 against negligible opposition. Upon reaching Carranglan three days later, patrols were sent forward to probe enemy defenses along Route 100. Their surprising reports indicated that the Japanese were nowhere to be found, and the leading elements of the 35th Infantry Regiment entered Digdig without opposition. It was later concluded that the nearby operations of the 27th and 161st Infantry Regiments south of Puncan had diverted Japanese attention, allowing the 35th Infantry an unopposed advance.

The *Puncan Sector Defense Force* was a conglomeration of seven infantry battalions drawn from as many larger units, including several recently organized provisional units. The Japanese had little time to prepare adequate defenses and had little in the way of artillery support. The rapid and unexpected advance of the 35th Infantry to their rear produced an unusual sense of demoralization among the *Puncan Sector Defense Force*. As a result, the command-and-control organization within the unit soon broke down. This is illustrated by the fact that, as earlier noted, as late as February 25 General Konuma, commanding the *Bambang Branch, 14th Army Area Army*, was planning a counterattack using the *Puncan Sector Defense Force*. It was only on March 2 that he learned of the situation and cancelled the proposed counterattack.

Pleasantly surprised by the rapid advance to Digdig, General Swift ordered General Mullins to continue his offensive another six miles to Putlan. General Mullins was prepared for this new corps order, and sent the 161st Infantry to clear the high ground west of Route 5, while the 27th Infantry cleared the ground east of the highway. The 35th Infantry was again sent on a wide envelopment of the expected Japanese positions. It was to march up the Bonga River and then swing toward the Putlan River and then into Putlan over a good trail from the north. Once again, the Japanese had left the door open, and the 35th Infantry walked right in to Putlan after two days' hard marching, meeting the 27th Infantry there only three days after the advance began. The "Wolfhound" Regiment had likewise met little opposition in their advance. The most difficult time was that of the 161st Infantry Regiment, which faced stiffer Japanese resistance. But it, too, made rapid progress and reached the vicinity of Putlan two days after its sister regiments.

General Swift was getting optimistic with the rapidity of General Mullins's advance. As mentioned in the previous chapter, he twice—on March 11 and March 13—extended the sector of the 25th Infantry Division. First, another five miles of Route 5 was to be cleared. Then, with the 32nd Infantry Division tied up fighting the *2nd Tank Division* along the Villa Verde Trail, General Swift ordered General Mullins to move forward and secure the critical Balete Pass area. This objective had originally been assigned to General Gill's 32nd Infantry Division, but the rapid advance of the 25th Infantry Division convinced General Swift that General Mullins had a better chance of securing the pass than did General Gill. Unknown to the Americans, however, the bulk of the *10th Division* was holding a main line of resistance at the pass.

Balete Pass is a low point on a large ridge complex which forms a watershed for many streams flowing into the Cagayan Valley and the Central Plain. The ridge, known as Balete Ridge, is over 11 miles in length. The high point is Mt. Imugan, 5,580 feet north of Salacsac Pass Number 1 on the Villa Verde Trail, where the 32nd Infantry Division was engaged in heavy fighting. As noted earlier, another prominent height is Mt. Minami, 4,530 feet high, where the ridge turns to the south and then ends at Mt. Kabuto, 4,600 feet of wooded heights. Like the 32nd Infantry Division on their flank, the men of the 25th Infantry Division would be attacking across ridges and valleys heavily jungled and with no paths. Here again, so thick was the vegetation that it soon became clear that the advance could only proceed along the generally razor-backed crests of the ridges. Outflanking was unlikely, since none of ridges had fingers connecting them to each other. There was plenty of cover and concealment, but that advantage was shared with the Japanese. Observation was limited.

The Japanese holding this area were from the *10th Division*. Lieutenant General Yasuyuki Okamoto's men had been deployed mostly east of Route 5. The weakened *11th Independent Infantry Regiment* was blocking the Old Spanish Trail north of Carranglan. Part of the 10th Infantry Regiment held the eastern end of Balete Ridge at Mt. Minami and Mt. Kabuto. There were also troops on Mt. Kanami, two miles northeast of Santa Fe. The *63rd Infantry Regiment*, heavily reinforced with provisional units, defended Mt. Myoko. The Japanese had troops dug in on Lone Tree Hill, Myoko Ridge, and Kapintalan Ridge. In all, there were an estimated 8,000 enemy troops dug in on or near the Balete Ridge–Balete Pass region.

The captured fire plan of the *10th Artillery Regiment* showed the positions of the Japanese artillery as well as attached heavy mortars and some infantry units. Several other Japanese plans had been captured by patrols or found in overrun enemy defenses, and these filled in many blanks concerning the dispositions of the enemy's infantry defenders. Although lacking information on light artillery, mortars, and some infantry units, General Mullins's "Tropic Lightning" division began its attack on Balete Pass with reasonably good intelligence on the enemy.

With the 35th Infantry Regiment stymied along the Old Spanish Trail, but nevertheless holding the attention of four battalions of General Konuma's best troops, the 27th and 161st Infantry Regiments continued their attacks along Route 5 with limited success. The battles for Digdig and Norton's Knob were but examples of the daily advances accomplished by the assault battalions. The first half of March was used up in these early advances. So thick was the jungled terrain that advance companies often could not say with any certainty where they were or what positions they had occupied. Nevertheless, by the end of March the division was well engaged with the main line of resistance of the *10th Division*. It was then, around March 28, that the Japanese command realized that the Americans did not have enough strength to conduct two main axis of attacks, and so rushed reinforcements to

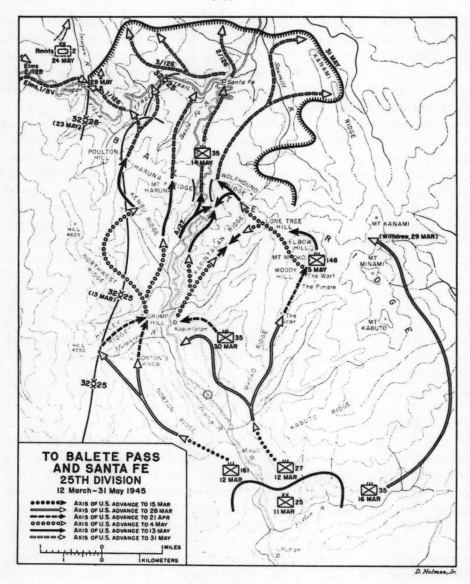

The Battle for Balete Pass, March–May 1945

Robert Ross Smith. *United States Army in World War II. The War in the Pacific. Triumph in the Philippines.* Washington, D.C.: Center of Military History, 1984. p. 521.

Mt. Myoko, where the 35th Infantry Regiment had tried an enveloping maneuver. These reinforcements came from the battalions defending the Old Spanish Trail as well as others from the *10th Division* reserve. These moves once again stymied the advance of the 35th Infantry. Renewed attacks against its supply lines and repeated counterattacks halted any advance for the moment. General Mullins called off the attack, remarking, "First, that the casualties incurred in continuing the advance would be prohibitive as the terrain permitted no room whatsoever for maneuver; second, the supply problem could get out of hand should the Japanese elect to attack in force using the Putlan River Valley as a route of approach; third, a desire to keep the division front as tight as was tactically possible."[1]

General Mullins's division was in a difficult situation. His three regiments were attacking along a six-mile front. Every inch of that front was rough, densely covered, and wooded terrain. It was impossible to bring the full strength of the division to bear against any one enemy point. Spread out as they were, the enemy resistance was made even more effective than usual. Unable to move his other two regiments, which were in close contact with the enemy, General Mullins decided to move the 35th Infantry.

Faced with revised, and subsequently proven accurate, estimates that the Japanese now numbered in excess of 10,000 troops opposing his understrength division, and understanding that their main line of resistance lay south of Balete Pass, General Mullins drew up a new plan of attack. Accepting that he did not have the resources to continue a broad-front attack, General Mullins turned to the military principles of mass and economy of force. He directed, on March 28, the 35th Infantry to move to Route 5 between the 27th and 161st Infantry Regiments. Once in position, the 35th and 161st Infantry would attack up Route 5, while the 27th Infantry struck at Myoko Ridge to get at Balete Pass from the southeast. The attack began at the end of March after yet another strong enemy counterattack attempting to regain Norton's Knob.

Using Norton's Knob as a base of fire, the 161st Infantry attacked along one of the few ridges that ran southwest to northeast and led to Kapintalan. Supported by heavy machine guns, 81mm mortars, 4.2-inch chemical mortars, 37mm antitank guns, and guns from the regimental Cannon Company as well as tanks and 105mm howitzers, the attack began March 28. It would take the regiment 12 days and 23,500 round of artillery ammunition to move to and secure "Crump Hill," named for the first American fatality there. But here General Mullins called a halt, for the regiment's right flank was dangerously exposed, the 35th Infantry not having kept pace with the Washington State National Guard regiment. The 161st Infantry spent the rest of April mopping up determined holdouts and stragglers in and around Crump Hill.

The reason for the delay by the 35th Infantry was its assignment to protect the division's rear areas, which were under near constant attack from Japanese infiltrators and bypassed stragglers. As a result, only one of its battalions could be made available for the attack. Leaving Company C behind to block the valley road, the rest of the regiment was moved to join the rest of the division. Soon after dark on March 30, the Japanese struck Company C in a vicious attack which lasted all night. With dawn came the realization that the company was cut off. The soldiers attempted to withdraw to the nearby supply road, only to discover that they were blocked by about three groups of Japanese numbering perhaps 150 soldiers in all. Company A was immediately dispatched to rescue Company C, only to learn that the Japanese had established three roadblocks between them and the trapped company. The Battalion Headquarters Company, Company F, and an attached company of Filipino guerillas were added to the rescue force, and by late on March 31, the junction between rescuer and rescued was complete.

Meanwhile the 3rd Battalion, 35th Infantry, had joined the 27th Infantry Regiment along Route 5 and pushed toward Kapintalan. The Japanese strongly defended this area from caves and pillboxes, all of which were mutually supporting and aligned in depth along the wooded ridge tops. Flank attacks proved impossible because the enemy flanks could not be located in the dense underbrush. The attack became one of identifying each enemy position and then blasting them out with artillery, bazookas, flamethrowers, explosives, and riflemen. Clearing one such ridge, known as "The Fishhook," took the battalion a week amid heavy rains and fierce opposition.

General Krueger was one of those American generals who genuinely cared for the men under his command. He had been noted for this trait by the well-known combat artist William ("Bill") Mauldin, who had served under him before moving to journalism. Evidence of his concern for his men's welfare began to appear in the rear areas of the combat divisions. A division rest area was developed near Puncan, opening on April 6. After 78 days of constant combat, one battalion of each regiment returned to the rest camp while the rest of the regiment continued the offensive. After a two-week rest the battalion would rotate with one of the front-line battalions. As the division history noted, "The two-week recuperation period was desperately needed."[2]

General Mullins also brought up some more power to strengthen his drive north. Two 90mm antiaircraft guns were manhandled forward and placed on Norton's Knob, where they fired in direct support of the 35th Infantry as it advanced. The results were reportedly very satisfactory, with pillboxes being destroyed at distances of up to 5,000 yards.

Pushing toward the high ground, the 35th Infantry continued with its attack, the 2nd Battalion relieving the 3rd Battalion on April 12. Caves and pillboxes again barred the way, and each had to be seized individually. Deserted positions even delayed the advance, as each had to be individually searched to ensure no enemy stragglers or snipers remained behind to harass the supply, medical, and engineer services, yet each search took up precious time. On April 17 the attack turned west toward Kapintalan and immediately faced heavy mortar, antitank, and machine-gun fire.

After three days of bitter fighting, Company E reached Kapintalan Bridge and destroyed a defending pillbox. Behind the 2nd Battalion, the 1st Battalion mopped up the many Japanese that had been bypassed in the deep draws between the ridges. By April 21, Route 5 was open as far as Kapintalan, but it took another week before all enemy resistance was eliminated in the area.

Meanwhile, the 161st Infantry held Crump Hill under observed Japanese artillery fire. Here, too, while the 2nd Battalion, 161st Infantry, held the hill, the regiment's 3rd Battalion mopped up around the hill until the approval came for a renewed advance. Nearby, the 27th Infantry had encountered a main line of resistance two miles up Myoko Ridge and was having a tough time continuing forward. A plan to envelop the enemy from two flanks while a third company attacked frontally included the addition of one M4 Sherman tank from Company C, 775th Tank Battalion. After moving forward over the supply road built by the 65th Engineer (Combat) Battalion, the tank attempted to get up to the forward infantrymen but found the terrain so poor for armored operations that it had continuous difficulty in gaining traction and was in constant danger of "bellying down"—hitting the ground with its hull's bottom—that it proved of little value. The battalion historian would later write of the northern Luzon campaign with regard to American armored vehicles, "In some of the most difficult fighting in the southwest Pacific, over terrain not suited for tank employment, [C] Company slowly pushed with elements of the 25th Division through Balete Pass."[3]

The "Tropic Lightning" division had originally believed that the enemy positions had been hastily prepared on Myoko Ridge, and the hope was for a rapid advance past that obstacle, bypassing any strongpoints to reach Balete Pass. In implementing this plan, a large Japanese pocket had been bypassed on a finger jutting out from Myoko Ridge. Known as "The Scar," this was the larger of two such strongpoints bypassed. Yet by April 12 the regiment had advanced no more than 1,000 yards beyond "The Scar." One problem was that Japanese within "The Scar" continually harassed the rear of the attacking infantrymen. As a result, the regiment was forced to deal with the bypassed enemy enclaves.

Company C drew the assignment of reducing "The Scar." After an aerial and artillery bombardment, the infantry, supported by 775th Tank Battalion tanks, attacked. They soon found themselves in a maze of interconnecting caves and pillboxes that took them a week to clear. Meanwhile, enemy infiltrators stepped up their activities behind the front lines. They concentrated on the supply road built by Company B, 65th Engineer (Combat) Battalion. Moving under the cover of darkness, these Japanese soldiers set up machine guns on the ridge past which the supply road ran, firing on any vehicles that came under their guns. Others placed mines on the road, hoping to disable American tanks and armored vehicles. Once again, a detachment, this time Company G, was necessary to clear the supply road and keep it open. But despite these battles, the attack continued.

That attack became a repetitive rotation of battalions, and tank companies, pushing forward against determined opposition. One ridge after another became the day's objective. There was the "Pimple," only 300 yards from the crest of Myoko Ridge. There was the "Wart," just 200 yards beyond the "Pimple." Then, a ravine with no name lay another 350 yards further along the way to Balete Pass.

Progress was accomplished routinely by the methods in which the ravine was cleared. On April 15 Company A, 27th Infantry, attacked and managed to get across the ravine. But once on the other side, they could not dig defensive positions due to the heavy and continuous enemy fire rained down on them. As darkness began, the company withdrew to the American side of the ravine. The following day, Company B made a frontal attack on the ravine while Company C moved to the west to try an enveloping maneuver. Tanks supported both companies with overhead fire, since the enemy positions could not be identified in the thick underbrush. Meanwhile, the regimental commander decided to use his 2nd Battalion to bypass the ravine and seize a hill further north. Company G, only recently returned from its efforts to clear the supply road, was given the lead.

Moving forward on April 18, Company G hit a wall of enemy fire and suffered heavy casualties after advancing some 400 yards. Then, three strong enemy counterattacks struck the company in quick succession. Company G repulsed the attacks, and, hoping that the attacks had weakened the enemy defenders, a platoon of Company F rushed through Company G to disrupt the enemy defenses. The platoon soon found themselves facing a perpendicular stone cliff covered on each side by strong enemy defenses. The platoon, joined by the rest of Company F, managed to advance 75 yards toward the cliff but was forced to withdraw as night fell.

On the other flank, the 1st Battalion, 27th Infantry, had managed to work with the 65th Combat Engineers in creating a "road" of sorts for the supporting M4 Sherman tanks of the 775th Tank Battalion. With armored support, the 1st Battalion managed to fight its way up the ravine's slopes, clearing it on April 21. Operations to clear out the remaining enemy resistance began immediately. There remained only one major obstacle between the "Tropic Lightning" division and Balete Pass, known as Lone Tree Hill.

Located at the junction of Kapintalan Ridge and Balete Ridge, some 2,000 yards northwest of the deepest American penetration onto Myoko Ridge, Lone Tree Hill was the commanding terrain between the ridge and the pass. Unless the Americans controlled Lone Tree Hill, they could not reach Balete Pass. Once again Company G drew the assignment of leading the advance. On April 21, it sent a platoon in a wide enveloping movement through a deep ravine to reach a grassy saddle at the base of Lone Tree Hill, a journey of about 2,500 yards into enemy territory. The platoon made the hazardous trip without being detected by the Japanese. The rest of Company G followed and arrived undetected despite passing within 100 yards of enemy positions. The entire 2nd Battalion, 27th Infantry, soon followed, completing the trip by April 24.

The next day, April 25, an artillery and mortar barrage, directed by the 2nd Battalion, pummeled the top of Lone Tree Hill. Supported by the direct fire of M7 motor carriages mounting 105mm howitzers, Company G led the attack on Lone tree Hill. The attack was a complete surprise to the Japanese who, despite having had more than two days to find them, had never detected the presence of the Americans at the foot of their mountain. So surprised were the Japanese that their resistance broke quickly, and the Americans found enemy guns unmanned and positions abandoned. The 2nd Battalion continued its attack down the mountain toward Balete Pass. After three days of clearing Lone Tree Hill, the battalion had advanced another 1,200 yards.

While the fight at Lone Tree Hill continued, the 3rd Battalion struck Elbow Hill. This was a connecting link between Mt. Myoko and Lone Tree Hill. The hill was necessary to provide a route of supply and evacuation for the regiment's continuing attack. Resistance was fierce and tanks were called forward. An American light tank armed with a flamethrower arrived to support Company K. Flamethrower tanks were new to the northern Luzon campaign and constituted another unpleasant surprise for the Japanese, who either fought and died in their positions or ran from the horror of the flame only to be cut down by the supporting infantrymen.

With the fall of Lone Tree and Elbow Hills, there remained three more obstacles for the 25th Infantry Division in its drive to secure Balete Pass. The first hill fell after an all-day battle and a fierce enemy counterattack that night. Repeated assaults with two tanks in support, one of which was knocked out by a 75mm gun, failed to clear the second hill. The 148th Infantry, 37th Infantry Division, was moved forward to relieve the exhausted 27th Infantry Regiment.

At the same time, the 2nd Battalion, 27th Infantry, was relieved on Balete Ridge and ordered to attack from Lone Tree Hill down Kapintalan Ridge to join with the 35th Infantry, attacking toward it along that ridge. The 3rd Battalion of the "Wolfhound Regiment" was ordered to stand by to strike for Balete Pass. As usual, the Japanese on Kapintalan Ridge "had burrowed into the ground like so many gophers,"[4] and the battle for Kapintalan Ridge took a few more days to be completed.

Meanwhile, the division's third regiment, the 161st Infantry, had been occupied with reconnaissance missions to the west of Route 5 until April 23 when it received orders to attack and envelop Balete Pass. They were to attack from the west. Before the attack, two more of the effective 90mm antiaircraft guns were winched to the top of Norton's (Banzai) Knob and placed into action. These had a field of fire that included Kembu Plateau and Kapintalan as well as Balete Pass itself.

Its reconnaissance had alerted the 161st Infantry to the fact that the Japanese had some of their highly effective 70mm guns defending the Kembu Plateau, and so the assault force, the 2nd Battalion, decided upon a night attack. Launched during the night of April 25–26, the advance moved swiftly and secured its objective, a launching position for the attack on Kembu Plateau, after a 24-hour advance. The attack jumped off on May 1, with four infantry companies attacking from the base of the plateau. The 1st and 2nd Battalions pushed forward on a 700-yard front northeast. The 1st Battalion made rapid progress, but the 2nd Battalion was slowed by terrain obstacles and Japanese opposition. But by the next day, May 2, both battalions had a block across the top of the plateau. Here fanatical resistance stopped the advance in its tracks.

The 161st Infantry spent the next three days trying to clear the plateau, but every attempt was repulsed by the Japanese. By the fourth day, the Japanese resources were exhausted, and the two battalions managed to clear the rest of the plateau. As they did, the regiment's 3rd Battalion attacked Mt. Haruna and Balete Ridge. Using small-unit maneuvers, Mt. Haruna fell despite strong resistance. By late afternoon, the military crest of the hill was in American hands. Over the next two days, May 5–7, the battalion mopped up along Balete Ridge and moved to within 300 yards of Balete Pass.

Heavy and desperate fighting continued behind them, however. The ongoing reduction of Kapintalan Ridge was miserable, bloody work. The Japanese continued to defend from deep caves, some so deep a ladder was needed to enter it, and pillboxes expertly sited and camouflaged. Only after prolonged bombardments from 81mm mortars, flamethrowers, M7 cannon fire, and artillery were the Japanese overcome. It took six more days to clear Lone Tree Hill. A similar time was spent clearing Kapintalan Ridge, where 954 enemy dead were counted. Hundreds more were sealed up in caves by the American advance. In one instance on the ridge, a soldier from Company K, 35th Infantry, was busy digging his foxhole when he opened the roof of a cave and almost fell into a group of Japanese hiding therein. The hole was quickly filled in and the soldier chose another spot, digging a little less deep than before.

The 161st Infantry spent several days clearing enemy resistance south of Balete Ridge and Mt. Haruna. Soldiers of the 148th Infantry cleared the Mt. Myoko positions. The 27th Infantry Regiment, after seizing Lone Tree Hill, turned onto a long, southeast-northwest ridge leading from Lone Tree Hill toward Balete Pass. Companies E and F led the advance against moderate resistance until they were relieved on May 4 by companies I and L. The advance continued, and on May 9 a platoon scout from Company I reached the ruins of the Rest House, which was in the center of Balete Pass. The goal of the last two months had been achieved after an advance of 33 miles of the most bitter, desperate, yard-by-yard and confused battles of the campaign.

Four days later, after the 35th Infantry cleared the last organized enemy defenders from a large draw where Route 5 joined Balete Pass, General Mullins declared Balete Pass secured and Route 5 opened from San Jose to the pass. Enemy casualties were counted as 6,427 dead and hundreds of others sealed in caves throughout the area. Some 79 Japanese had surrendered. Japanese losses in arms and supplies were significant. Most importantly, however, was that they had lost the gateway to the critical Cagayan Valley, leaving General Yamashita's remaining forces vulnerable to attack, starvation, and capture. The cost to the 25th Infantry Division was 2,195 battle casualties, including 545 killed in action. The attached 148th Infantry Regiment added another 20 killed and 95 wounded in its phase of the battle.

It seemed to many, particularly those in the "Tropic Lightning" division, that the capture of Balete Pass marked the end of their participation in the northern Luzon campaign. But that was not the case. One more place name was included on their list of objectives—that of the road junction at the town of Santa Fe. Putting the pass behind them, the exhausted infantry moved forward yet again.

CHAPTER 17

The Bambang Front

United States Marine Corps aviation had flourished during the South Pacific campaigns of 1942–43, but since then had been severely restricted because of various factors, not the least of which was that the United States Navy delayed their deployment on the Navy's aircraft carriers, reserving that role for its own naval aviation. While the naval aviators provided good support for the various amphibious landings performed by both the Army and Marine Corps, there remained the issue of close air support once the assault forces had established themselves ashore. Before the war the Army Air Corps had concentrated on long-range bombing, following the then-in-vogue theory that bombing alone could force a nation to sue for peace. It had little interest and no training in close air support. Similarly, the Navy devoted its air assets to the destruction of enemy shipping and the support of amphibious landings but had little interest in close air support of prolonged ground battles, for to engage in such activities placed the valuable carrier task forces in greater jeopardy by tying them to a restricted area in which their mobility—a major piece of their defensive assets—was lost.

But the Marine Corps had developed a system of close air support during the inter-war years in small-scale wars in Haiti, the Dominican Republic, and Nicaragua. They had exhibited this system during maneuvers with Army forces in Louisiana and North Carolina, while still developing their system. At the same time, in Europe, the German Air Force, the Luftwaffe, was displaying to the world the effectiveness of close air support. This was particularly true in the use of the German dive-bomber, known as the Stuka,[1] which bombed enemy positions close to the front lines. But objections to close air support of ground troops remained, principally that it was not effective, too dangerous, and too expensive. Infantry officers were leery of close air support's accuracy. "Friendly fire" incidents during close air support attempts were widely known and strengthened the belief that close air support was simply too dangerous to implement.

But gradually, through the South Pacific, the Gilbert Islands, and the Marshall Islands, the Navy and Marine Corps improved their records. An improved communication system and greater training of both air and ground officers resulted in the Marshall Islands campaign having the most successful air support program yet. The 7th Infantry Division, after participating in that campaign, reported that it preferred naval aviation close air support and termed it, "very effective and desirable as executed by Naval air."[2] The report went on to state that the Army Air Corps had no system of close air support and was unable to control its aircraft sufficiently to be effective.

While the Navy provided close air support in the Central Pacific during 1943–44, Marine aviation languished in the backwaters of the South Pacific. It wasn't until October 1944 that Marine Air Group (MAG)-24,[3] then on Bougainville, received orders to move to the Philippines and provide close air support to Army troops about to invade those islands. Training and gathering assets began immediately, and soon Marine aviation was supporting Army troops on Leyte. Because of the ground situation, a limited front, jungle cover, and enemy defenses, the team developed a system whereby the aircraft were controlled, or "talked on to," a target by a ground controller at the site of the battle. Usually riding in radio-equipped jeeps, these ground controllers—Marine pilots themselves detached to ground control duty—would literally talk to the pilots and direct them to a target using smoke shells, landmarks, and any other means to clearly identify the target for the pilot who would then make a dive-bombing or strafing run on that target.

The aircraft the Marines used were at the end of their life span but still suitable for the close air support mission.[4] After the initial landings at Lingayen Gulf were covered by naval aviators of the Seventh Fleet, the Marines came ashore and began to set up for business. But they found that the available airfields were already crowded with Army Air Corps aircraft and that they had not been assigned to any specific field. Searching for space with a suitable ground for his airfield, Colonel Clayton C. Jerome, USMC, traveled north until he located a suitable spot at a rice paddy near the town of Mangaldan.[5] With previous experience in the Philippines, Colonel Jerome knew that by collapsing the rice paddy walls and covering them over, a suitable airstrip would exist until the next rainy season, when all would be washed away. Estimating MAG-24's tour of duty to be about the next three months, in the dry season, the airfield was established over the rice paddy. From here MAG-24 and MAG-32 would operate in support of the Sixth U.S. Army until late in April. By the end of January, the Marines had seven squadrons, 174 SBDs, 472 officers, and 3,047 enlisted Marines on the base, which they soon shared with as many as 300 Army aircraft. Their first combat mission took place on January 27 against San Fernando and Clark Field. Before long they were covering the flanks of the 1st Cavalry Division as it made its dash for Manila. The success of this and other missions is best evaluated by the infantrymen themselves, who reported in their history, "Much of the success of the entire movement is credited to the superb air cover, flank protection, and reconnaissance provided by the Marine Air Groups 24 and 32. The 1st Cavalry's drive down through Central Luzon was the longest such operation ever made in the Southwest Pacific Area using only air cover for flank protection."[6]

That episode was the opening for the use of close air support. Colonel Jerome, commanding the base, visited the commanders of the Sixth Army's combat units promoting his Marines' abilities. He met with General Swift at I Corps and General Griswold at XXIV Corps, both of whom gave him permission to speak to their division commanders about close air support. Lieutenant Colonel John L. Smith, executive officer of MAG-32, then made the rounds of the division commanders, promoting Marine close air support. He offered the division operations and intelligence officers a ride in the rear seat of an SBD as it performed a dive-bombing mission. These promotion efforts paid off, and by the end of February there were seven jeep-mounted forward air control parties assigned to the various divisions. By March the activities of both Marine and Army aircraft, particularly around Balete Pass, had forced the Japanese to make all movement, especially truck movements, by night using torches to light the way. Enemy artillery, noted the Sixth Army, was often silenced by these aircraft and remained silent when they were in the skies over Japanese lines.

The Marines also supported the many guerilla units fighting the Japanese well in advance of the Sixth Army's front lines. Methods were different here since no American radio jeep would last long in the heavy jungles and mountains in which the guerillas operated. Instead, the request was radioed from guerilla headquarters to the air base. The pilots were briefed while on the ground and then flew to their targets. Sometimes it was possible for them to receive ground signals, such as panels or smoke signals from mortar shells, but many were performed successfully without ground aids. "Friendly fire" casualties were rare. Occasionally, Army Air Corps A-20 light bombers or P-51 fighters joined in with the Marines in these missions.[7]

So successful was the Marine contribution to the Leyte and Luzon campaigns that when General MacArthur began his Southern Philippines campaign, in which he cleared the rest of the major Philippine islands of the enemy, MAG-32 was dispatched to Zamboanga to support these southern island operations. Originally set for early March, requests by Sixth Army for a delay to allow the Marines to continue to provide close air support delayed the departure until the end of March, although some squadrons moved earlier.

While in general the move went well, there was one tragic moment. As Marine Scout Bomber Squadron-142[8] flew to Zamboanga, one pilot experienced engine trouble. A Marine transport plane accompanied the squadron, precisely to pick up any crews that were forced to land their aircraft along the way. Advised that a small airstrip at San Jose was in friendly hands, the bomber pilot and his gunner made a successful landing. The emergency strip was too small for the transport plane to land, however, so with a wave goodbye the transport resumed its journey. Although both pilot and gunner had been seen safely on the strip, they were later captured and executed by the Japanese.

MAG-24 remained on Luzon and continued to provide close air support to Sixth Army, concentrating mostly in and around Balete Pass in support of the 37th Infantry Division, until late April when they were moved to Mindanao to support that campaign.

The capture of Balete Pass and the departure of the Marine Corps air groups did not complete the destruction of the Japanese on the Bambang Front. There remained the enemy stronghold at Santa Fe, where the Villa Verde Trail and Route 5 joined. Until Santa Fe was captured, the *2nd Tank Division* could continue to prolong the Villa Verde Trail battle, and it was even possible that the *10th Division* might reorganize and renew operations there. The Japanese command could easily send reinforcements through Santa Fe to either front, making any American advance costlier.

Generals Swift and Mullins were aware of this danger, and plans had been prepared well before Balete Pass was secured. In accordance with those plans, the 27th Infantry was sent north to clear the Sawmill River Valley, an avenue the Japanese could use to bring forward reinforcements and supplies, or conversely, provide a route of withdrawal for the *10th Division* remnants. That job proved difficult, as fanatically resisting Japanese groups fought to the death amid the heavily forested and rough terrain. About the only thing the regiment could favorably remark upon was the fact that for the first time in the campaign, the regiment was attacking downhill.

The 27th Infantry's first objective was to seize the high ground 2,000 yards east of Santa Fe and block all approaches to the town from that direction. The 35th Infantry was to attack along Route 5 and seize the town proper. The 161st Infantry was to attack north to reach the Villa Verde Trail and then secure the high ground southwest of Santa Fe, blocking all approaches from the west. The attached 148th Infantry Regiment was to finish clearing Mt. Myoko, relieving the 27th Infantry, and mop up the 25th Infantry Division's rear areas on Kapintalan Ridge.

Before any movements could begin, however, the 161st Infantry had to clear one last major pocket of resistance west of Mt. Haruna. Here the Japanese resisted fiercely from reverse slope positions guarding the junction of Balete Pass and Santa Fe Ridge. Using the 1st and 3rd Battalions, the regiment attacked on May 11. Even when supported by mechanized 105mm guns, the attack made only limited progress. Daily attacks were made between May 11 and May 21, weakening the Japanese until a coordinated attack by both battalions wiped out the remaining defenders.

It was during these operations that another American flag officer met his death. Brigadier General James L. Dalton II (USMA, 1933) was the recently appointed assistant division commander of the 25th Infantry Division. He had gone forward to reconnoiter the battlefield area when a Japanese sniper cut him down. He had previously served as the 161st regimental commander and was highly regarded within the "Tropic Lightning" division.[9]

The battle continued. Patrols extensively covered the area to the north and northeast, trying to locate the enemy's new main line of resistance. The strongest enemy defenses were located to the front of the 27th Infantry in the Sawmill River Road sector. The Santa Fe Ridge itself was found to be lightly defended while Route 5 had the usual cave defenses. The enemy was on Bolong Ridge, across the Sawmill River, as well as in the Sawmill River Valley itself. The attack began on May 14, with the 1st Battalion, 27th Infantry, attacking Bolong Ridge and the 3rd Battalion attacking the high ground over the Sawmill River and trail.

Heavy Japanese resistance slowed and then stalled the attacks. An enemy strong-point on Bolong Ridge halted the 1st Battalion, and a similar position stopped the 3rd Battalion on high ground dominating the Sawmill Trail. It took two days of intense fighting for the 1st Battalion to clear its opposition, and the 3rd Battalion required nearly a week and the support of tanks and mechanized 105mm howitzers before they could overcome their zone. Companies K and L immediately formed a block along the Sawmill River and trail to prevent the Japanese from using it to either reinforce or withdraw troops.

In the 35th Infantry Regiment's sector along Route 5, resistance was sporadic and came mostly from Japanese sheltering in caves along the roadway. But on May 15 the Japanese launched a strong counterattack, taking advantage of a heavy fog and rain, which made visibility nearly zero, even for the infantry. Nevertheless, Companies E and F held their positions, and when the fog cleared that afternoon, forty enemy dead lay around their positions. The advance of the "Cacti" regiment had compressed the defending Japanese into small pockets. Each was subjected to concentrated artillery and mortar fire, after which combat patrols moved in to mop up and eliminate any remaining resistance. In one such instance, a patrol from Company A, 35th Infantry, fired a bazooka into a cave some 900 yards north of Balete Pass. The resulting explosion and collapse of the entire side of that hill clearly indicated that the Japanese had lost another ammunition supply post. In another instance, a Company B patrol on May 20 threw a grenade into a cave after seeing an enemy soldier dart into it. Another huge explosion resulted, causing a landslide of the hill directly over the patrol, which cost Company B a total of 23 casualties, along with two combat engineers who were killed.

The steady advance of the 25th Infantry Division toward Santa Fe, while the adjacent 32nd Infantry Division was held up along the Villa Verde Trail at Salacsac Pass Number 1, prompted a change of boundaries between the two divisions. The "Tropic Lightning" division, now reinforced by the 126th Infantry of the 32nd Infantry ("Red Arrow") Division, was tasked with the area around Imugan, north and west of Santa Fe. Indeed, the steady advance of General Mullins's men had sowed some confusion in the Japanese ranks. For several consecutive nights in early May large groups of Japanese troops marched down Route 5 from the north to reinforce the already eliminated defenders around the Balete Pass area. Blocks placed on rivers, trails, and roads took a heavy toll on these reinforcements, who never reached their destinations.

By the last week of May the division was mopping up west and south of Santa Fe. The attached 148th Infantry continued to clear the Mt. Myoko area while the 35th Infantry cleared Route 5. May 25 and again on the 26th saw patrols of the 35th Infantry advance to the outskirts of Santa Fe. Finally, on the morning of May 27, Companies B and C entered the town and cleared it of Japanese stragglers. By noon of that day, Route 5 was declared open for all traffic from San Jose to Santa Fe. The entrance to the Cagayan Valley was open to the Americans. More than a thousand Japanese troops had been counted killed in the advance.

The next two weeks, until the middle of June, were spent in mopping-up operations. Some enemy groups continued to hold out and had to be destroyed by air, artillery, mortars, and the inevitable infantry assault. Troops of the 2nd Battalion, 161st Infantry, were sent by sea to Baler Bay where they landed unopposed and began to conduct an extensive prisoner-gathering expedition, collecting 252 prisoners without a single casualty to themselves. Surrender leaflets were dropped along the coast, while offshore an LCM broadcast surrender messages to the trapped Japanese. Along Route 5, the 126th and 35th Infantry Regiments shared mopping-up duties. In addition to roadblocks along the route, patrols went into the mountains alongside the route and contacted stragglers and small groups of Japanese who either surrendered or were eliminated. The only effective remaining organized enemy resistance now lay along the Old Spanish Trail. Clearing of this last enemy opposition fell to General Mullins's men.

Like the situation of Balete Pass, the Old Spanish Trail lies along an east-west ridge which in effect extends Balete Ridge and separates the Cagayan Valley to the north from the Central Plain on the south. Objectives were the Suzuga Pass over which the trail ran, and another pass further east forming an exit from the Cauco Valley. American intelligence estimated that the enemy defenders in this area numbered between 600 and 800 men who were poorly equipped and supplied. General Mullins assigned his 27th and 35th Infantry Regiments the job of securing Suzuga Pass.

The 1st Battalion, 35th Infantry, drew the assignment of blocking the numerous enemy trails in the vicinity. This required no fewer than 14 trail blocks, preventing any escape by retreating Japanese. The 2nd Battalion, 35th Infantry, began a 6,000-yard drive to San Francisco, occupied on June 12. Little opposition was encountered. But as the battalion moved south of the town, a strong enemy position revealed itself. A strong mortar and artillery barrage weakened this defense so that by the end of the day the infantry had cleared it. The battalion, now followed by the 3rd Battalion, pushed on to within 4,000 yards of an interim objective, the Marang River. This advance cleared six enemy trail blocks, but the Americans were seeing that the Japanese in this area were more inclined to retreat than to fight to the death, as they had previously. On June 17, Company G was hit by heavy 150mm artillery, 90mm guns, and grenade launchers or "knee mortars,"[10] but when the infantry advanced upon the position, they found it abandoned. The two battalions continued to move forward and reached the Marang River, covering 17,000 yards, in nine days.

North of Carranglan, the 3rd Battalion, 27th Infantry, relieved a trail block manned by the 25th Division Reconnaissance Troop and began a drive up the Old Spanish Trail, reaching Suzuga Pass on June 22. Nearby, the 1st Battalion captured a series of Japanese field orders which revealed that the enemy commander was aware of his situation, understanding that he was under attack from the north, south, and west, and that his only chance of escape was to the northeast, to Cagayan Valley, which was blocked by American trail blocks. His only option was a withdrawal to the east. To remain in place invited extermination.

That withdrawal began on the evening of June 23. The Japanese took the trail passing north of the Suzuga Pass toward the Cauco Pass, along a river valley. The Americans, alerted by the captured documents, poured a steady artillery fire on their route, constantly harassing all escape attempts. Those Japanese that succeeded in escaping were thoroughly beaten and discouraged. Earlier, on June 20, the 35th and 27th Infantry Regiments advance elements made contact near the Marang River. For all practical purposes, the Caraballo Mountains had been seized.

As always on Luzon, mopping up took another 10 days along the Old Spanish Trail and in scattered bypassed pockets of resistance elsewhere. For the 25th Infantry Division, the junction marked the end of 165 days of continuous combat, always on the attack. In this last drive, they recorded 14,569 enemy counted dead and 614 prisoners of war. Uncounted thousands more had been sealed in caves and bunkers along the way. In exchange the division, between February 21 and May 31, 1945, had suffered 685 killed and 2,090 wounded, for a total of 2,775 casualties.[11] The division had played a decisive role in the converging I Corps drive to Santa Fe.

While the "Tropic Lightning" division had been clearing Balete Ridge and Santa Fe, General Gill's 32nd Infantry Division had continued its own fight along the Villa Verde Trail. Here the division was tying down the *2nd Tank Division* fully, making the advance of the adjacent 25th Infantry Division somewhat easier. Some of the severest fighting took place at Salacsac Pass Number 1.

General Iwanaka had decided to hold a north–south line from Mt. Imugan to Hill 508, some two and a half miles south of the Villa Verde Trail. In addition to his main line of resistance, he had stationed units of 500 men each on high ground southwest of Imugan, ready to be called forward in the event of an American breakthrough. General Gill learned of these reserves and set as an intermediate goal the ridges on which those reserves were posted. To do this General Gill had sent the 126th Infantry Regiment against Salacsac Pass Number 1 and the 127th Infantry to the east. Patrols would mount diversionary attacks and be reinforced by the efforts of the Buena Vista Regiment, another of Colonel Volckmann's guerilla units now attached to the division.

After relieving the 128th Infantry Regiment on April 17, the 127th Infantry began to clear the Japanese from Hill 507 but had some difficulty in doing this as rapidly as expected. It took until May 3 before the Villa Verde Trail was cleared between Hills 506B and 507D for division traffic. The ongoing battle descended into a series of costly frontal attacks interspersed with strong enemy counterattacks. To continue progress, enemy positions that were too well defended were bypassed and left to the mercies of air attacks, ground mounted antiaircraft artillery, and sustained artillery fire. Once it had been determined that these positions had been sufficiently weakened, they were surrounded, cut off from supplies, and eliminated when their capability to resist had sufficiently diminished.

General Gill remained concerned about his division's slow progress, despite the ample justification of a strong Japanese resistance in rugged terrain. After a battalion of the 127th Infantry was held up at one strongly defended hill south of the trail for 10 days and had to be withdrawn because it could not be supplied, he expressed his concerns to General Krueger during one of the Army commander's frequent visits to the front lines. Reassured by General Krueger that his progress was the best that could be expected while operating in "the incredibly difficult terrain conditions and the enemy resistance facing it,"[12] General Gill resumed his planning to expedite the advance.

He replaced the 127th Infantry with the now rested 128th Infantry Regiment along the Villa Verde Trail. The 127th went into reserve for a well-earned rest. On March 27, five days after the 128th Infantry took over the Villa Verde Trail advance, its commander, Colonel John A. Hettinger, was killed in action. A former enlisted man in the Kansas National Guard before the war, Colonel Hettinger was commissioned in the Regular Army in 1917. Colonel Merle H. Howe assumed command of the 128th Infantry Regiment.[13]

The intensity of the combat during this late March period is exemplified by the actions of Private First Class William R. Shockley of Company L, 128th Infantry. This 27-year-old soldier from Selma, California, had enlisted in 1940 and had participated in the Saidor, Aitape, and Leyte campaigns, suffering wounds at Saidor. He was serving as a machine gunner with Company L on March 31 when their hill position along the Villa Verde Trail came under a concentration of Japanese artillery fire, followed by a heavy counterattack. When the enemy pressure became too great, he directed his fellow soldiers to withdraw, saying that he would "remain to the end" to provide cover for their withdrawal. This he proceeded to do, despite being forced to clear two stoppages of his machine gun amid the enemy attack. When he observed enemy troops moving past his left flank, he re-positioned his machine gun and opened fire on them. Again, he ordered his remaining buddies to withdraw before they were completely cut off but remained in position himself. He covered the withdrawal of his squad with devastating fire against the onrushing enemy. With his buddies safely off the hill, he remained at his chosen position until overwhelmed by the enemy. For his self-sacrifice in saving his buddies, he was awarded a posthumous Medal of Honor.[14]

"For the 32nd Division April was just another month of hard fighting," states the division's history.[15] Japanese resistance remained firm, and the terrain continued to be formidable. Casualties were not being timely replaced, and the shortage of men and their weariness after months of constant combat took a toll on the division's ability to make progress. At one point the assault regiments were down to half of their authorized strength. With no reserves available to them, General Krueger and General Swift had little choice but to push forward as best as the situation permitted. Losses in experienced leaders, such as the death of Lieutenant Colonel Claudie A. Bailey, commanding the 1st Battalion, 126th Infantry, exacerbated the already difficult situation. Major Elee L. Tyler took command of the battalion.

With General MacArthur's Southern Philippines campaign in full swing, both reinforcements and supplies for Sixth Army became increasingly difficult to find. The 32nd Infantry Division soon found shortages in certain types of ammunition as well as a shortage of personnel. General Swift ordered the tired and depleted 126th Infantry Regiment replaced in the front lines by attaching the 130th Infantry of the 33rd Infantry Division to General Gill's "Red Arrow" division in early April.

The objective was now Salacsac Pass Number 2. The kind of struggle that ensued was typical of the ongoing campaign in northern Luzon. Lieutenant Colonel Robert B. Vance was commanding the 1st Battalion, 128th Infantry Regiment, which was attacking Hill 505 on the approach to Salacsac Pass Number 2. He remembered, "By the third night our positions were past their first line of defense and several positions were directly on top of their dugouts. The openings in the rear of our front line that could not be closed permanently, were guarded continuously. When any movement of any kind in the holes was heard, the guard would use hand grenades in it or try to seal it up better with sandbags. Some of the entrances to the firing parapets would go down fifteen to twenty feet with ladders leading up to the positions, which made them very difficult to close."[16] An estimated fifty enemy soldiers committed suicide in these holes, while as long as a week later several were found trying to dig their way out of a sealed dugout. A sister battalion, Lieutenant Colonel Maurice B. Holden's 2nd Battalion, 128th Infantry, later reported wiping out two enemy machine-gun companies and killing 223 enemy troops by actual count in 137 different caves. They captured 13 heavy machine guns, two BARs, a Thompson submachine gun, and an American flamethrower.

Battles such as these quickly depleted the attacking battalions. Once again, Colonel Howe's 128th Infantry was exhausted and dangerously short of infantrymen, so General Gill replaced it with Colonel Frederick R. Stofft's rested 127th Infantry Regiment. Colonel Howe's men moved to an assembly area near Asingan, where they would have a chance to recuperate over the next two weeks. Meanwhile, the 127th Infantry cleared more of Hill 508 and established trail blocks along the Villa

Verde Trail. Small-scale Japanese counterattacks came in nightly over the next few weeks, but none seriously threatened the American hold on Hill 508.

Behind the Japanese lines, the Buena Vista Regiment, stationed at a base in the small village of Valdez, operated against the Japanese rear areas around Imugan. To the front both the 126th and 127th Infantry Regiments pressured the Japanese main line of resistance, steadily pushing it back. During these attacks a rare, at this stage of the war, enemy air attack hit a building in which Captain Paul Keene, Jr.'s 732nd Ordnance Company had stored its supplies. The resulting blast wiped out the entire supplies of the company as well as inflicting numerous casualties.

On April 25, Lieutenant Colonel Powell A. Fraser's 1st Battalion, 127th Infantry, continued its attack. Company A, 127th Infantry, was advancing along the Villa Verde Trail when it was pinned down by enemy resistance. During the ensuing firefight a 500-pound bomb exploded in the company's midst. Five of the Americans were buried by the blast. Private First Class David M. Gonzales, who had only joined the division in December 1944 but already earned his Combat Infantryman's Badge, grabbed his entrenching tool and crawled 15 yards to their rescue despite the intense enemy fire covering the entire area. The soldier from Pacoima, California, began digging to rescue the trapped men, while his commanding officer assisted. As they began to make progress, the officer was killed by enemy fire, but Pfc Gonzales continued digging despite the obvious danger to himself, using his tool and his hands while Japanese snipers and machine gunners tried to cut him down. He pulled the first man out of the rocks and sand, and then to make better progress he stood up in clear view of the enemy to better use his shovel. He pulled a second man, then a third, from the rubble. Just as the third man escaped, Pfc Gonzales was hit and mortally wounded, but the trapped men had been saved. For his self-sacrifice in giving his life to save others, Pfc David M. Gonzales was awarded a posthumous Medal of Honor.[17]

General Iwanka realized by early May that his position was being overrun and that any chance he might have to set up a new line of defense depended upon slowing the American advance. He hoped to accomplish this by cutting the American supply lines. On May 10 Japanese forces cut the supply line between Hills 525 and 516, forcing the 128th Infantry and a battalion of the 127th Infantry to devote their efforts to clear this critical block. It took them a week, until May 19, before this Japanese pocket was eliminated. Ten days later the 1st Battalion, Buena Vista Regiment, captured Hill 528, marking the end of the division's drive on Santa Fe.

Despite the apparent slow advance of the division, which had concerned General Gill earlier, General Krueger and General Swift again visited the division on May 12 and General Krueger later recorded in his memoirs, "An inspection of elements of the 127th and 128th Infantry Regiments, some artillery units and evacuation hospitals impressed me as on previous occasions with the fine performance of the 32nd Division under extremely difficult conditions."

Throughout the month of May 1945, the division battled its way forward. On May 23, the division came up against what the Japanese referred to as the "Kongo Fortress," believed by them to be impregnable. It took the Americans five days to overcome resistance within that fortress. That same week General Iwanaka, with the 25th Infantry Division threatening his rear and the 32nd Infantry Division crushing his front, began withdrawing his troops north up the valley of the Imugan River. The American advance continued until, on May 28, the following entry was made in the division's Operations Report: "This morning elements of the 128th Infantry and the 32nd Cavalry Reconnaissance Squadron captured the important village of Imugan. This village, the center of enemy activity for deployment of troops to the east, south and west was secured at 10:00 when contact was made with elements of the 126th Infantry, now attached to the 25th Infantry Division, on Hill 530 (1,000 yards north of Imugan)."[18] The pincer movement had been completed and the Villa Verde Trail was open to American traffic from Santa Maria to Imugan.

During the four-month campaign the 1st and 3rd Battalions, 128th Infantry Regiment, had earned a Presidential Unit Citation, as did the 126th Field Artillery Battalion and the 114th Engineer (Combat) Battalion.[19] In turn, the division had suffered 51 officers and 865 enlisted men killed in action, with 11 officers and 2,162 enlisted men wounded. Nearly 5,000 men had been evacuated with non-battle casualties, mostly illness and exhaustion. The division had in turn received 238 officers and 6,661 enlisted men as replacements during the campaign. The "Red Arrow" division had begun the Luzon campaign directly from the Leyte campaign[20] and was understrength by over 2,000 men when it began the Luzon campaign. An additional infantry division, allowing the others to rotate rest periods, might have made a difference. But General MacArthur's Southern Philippines campaign made such a reserve impossible.

Japanese casualties were estimated at 5,750 killed.[21] The *2nd Tank Division* was finished as an effective fighting force. The *10th Division* had suffered considerably and had been pushed back into the Cagayan Valley, whose entrance lay open to American entry at their convenience. The two Japanese divisions had between them lost a total of 13,500 men killed in the two months of fighting. The *Bambang Branch, Fourteenth Area Army*, had perhaps 5,000 survivors to stop the Americans. Two of the three critical anchors of General Yamashita's line protecting the Cagayan Valley had fallen, and the third at Bonton was under attack by Colonel Volckmann's USAFIP(NL) forces and about to fall as well. Sixth U.S. Army was prepared to exploit its successes and move north into the critical Cagayan Valley.

CHAPTER 18

Aparri

General Krueger had ordered the USAFIP(NL) forces to attack inland from the west coast of Luzon to achieve possession of a critical road junction leading into the Cagayan Valley around Bontoc. If Colonel Volckmann's forces could secure the road junctions in that area it would in effect isolate General Yamashita's *Fourteenth Area Army* while blocking lesser routes for the Japanese to draw sustenance from Cagayan Valley, their only remaining source. The *Shobu Group* would be trapped in a limited area, unable to move troops or supplies, and in effect be surrounded. The capture of Route 4, which ran inland from the coast to Bontoc, would open for Sixth Army a back door into General Yamashita's stronghold.

The town of Bontoc is the capital of Mountain Province and is in the Caycayan River Valley some 2,750 feet up in the Cordillera Central Mountains, the backbone ridge of Luzon. It is at the junction of Route 4, to the coast, and Route 11, which leads to Baguio. The latter route was an unpaved road of one narrow lane that followed the Chico River Canyon into the Cagayan Valley and then on to Bontoc. It merges with Route 4 at Sabangan, 16 miles southwest of Bontoc, and the two then combine to go on to Bontoc. The area contains several critical military objectives, including the road junction at Sabangan, the road junction town of Cervantes, the Malaya Range, Mankayan, Bessang Pass, and the Amburayan River Valley. Mankayan was particularly important because it provided the *Shobu Group* with suitable assembly areas for the movement of troops to any threatened area on either Route 4 or Route 11. The Lepanto Copper Mine, near Route 4 at Cervantes, had been exploited by the Japanese who had shipped its ore to Japan. Native populations in this portion of northern Luzon were scarce. As in the Cagayan Mountains, the tangled, rough, and steep mountains presented problems for any military movements. Later, some I Corps officers would declare that the terrain along Route 4 was much worse than any they had encountered along the Villa Verde Trail.

Colonel Volckmann's guerilla forces had been active in the area well before the Sixth Army had landed on Luzon in January. Here Lieutenant Colonel Robert H. Arnold was in command of the 15th Infantry, USAFIP(NL). This force of about

2,900 officers and men was under strength, badly equipped, and poorly trained. Its three battalions were widely scattered to avoid making a worthwhile target for a major Japanese attack. Around San Fernando Colonel George M. Barnett led the 121st Infantry, USAFIP(NL). The 3rd Battalion, 66th Infantry, USAFIP(NL), last heard of with the 33rd Infantry Division, was harassing Japanese movements along Route 11 coming from Baguio.[1] In the Cagayan Valley itself the 14th Infantry, USAFIP(NL) operated.[2]

The original assignment for the USAFIP(NL) units in northern Luzon was to gather intelligence and harass the enemy with sabotage and demolitions. These were intended to cut Japanese lines of communication and supply. But with the landing and attack of the Sixth Army the guerillas became emboldened, and soon direct attacks, including the 11th Infantry's USAFIP(NL) siege of San Fernando, began occurring on a more regular basis. Similarly, the 15th Infantry, USAFIP(NL), began a campaign to clear northwestern Luzon.

The Japanese in northern Luzon had concentrated around the airfield towns of Vigan and Laoag, which they had captured early in the 1941–42 Philippine campaign. Here a regimental-sized force, Major General Shoji Araki's *Araki Force*, defended the area.[3] It had a few 70mm guns available to it, but food and ammunition were in short supply even before Sixth Army landed. In addition, the *357th Independent Infantry Battalion, 103rd Division*, guarded Route 4. Japanese command arrangements were poor, with General Araki reporting to the *103rd Division*, and the *357th Battalion* reporting directly to *Shobu Group* headquarters, then in Baguio. Supporting these two defense groups were some 4,500 antiaircraft, *Imperial Army Air Force*, and service and support troops. Small garrisons of from 20 to 200 men dotted the area. Many of these were made up of conscripted Formosans and Koreans whose motivations for battle were suspect.

Within days of the landings at Lingayan Gulf, the 15th Infantry, USAFIP(NL), began harassing the *Araki Force*. Using guerilla tactics of raids and ambushes, these attacks were designed to force the smaller Japanese garrisons out of position while capturing much needed supplies and weapons for use by the guerillas. By mid-February they had cleared Route 3 north of Vigan and captured Laoag. The Japanese garrison retreated to the Salomague Harbor area, but under continued pressure they again moved south to Vigan. Sustained stress from the guerillas prompted another withdrawal by the *Araki Force*, and by mid-April all Japanese forces had been pushed south of Vigan. While this was going on, the 121st Infantry, USAFIP(NL), cleared Route 3 south of Vigan and opened that road all the way up the west coast from Lingayan Gulf.

The *Araki Force* assembled its scattered elements along Route 6 and attempted to deny the guerillas access to the Abra River Valley, a rich farming area covering some 20 miles inland from Vigan. As noted, General Araki's men were in poor shape by this time, short on supplies and ammunition of all types. He had lost contact with the headquarters of the *103rd Division*, and finally in mid-March General Yamashita had subordinated the *Araki Force* to his own *Shobu Group* headquarters. Despite this attempt at control, General Araki was soon out of touch with any higher headquarters.

Supported by Fifth U.S. Army Air Force and Marine Corps aircraft, the 15th Infantry USAFIP(NL), attacked astride Route 6 with two battalions while a third attempted an enveloping maneuver using narrow native trails. This attempt at encirclement failed when General Araki saw the writing on the wall and again retreated. A general Japanese withdrawal began in mid-April and soon the *Araki Force* disappeared southward toward Gayaman, forced in that direction by a block placed by the 121st Infantry, USAFIP(NL), at the entrance to the Abra Valley. Blocked yet again, General Araki turned east over trackless, unexplored territory of the Cordillera Central Mountain Range, every step losing Japanese troops to starvation and disease. Nearly a month later, the survivors of the *Araki Force* began to straggle into Besao, a village seven miles west of Bontoc. Here fewer than 1,500 survivors settled down for a rest. Of the 8,000 Japanese defending northern Luzon in January, 4,000 had been killed, 2,000 had scattered into the mountain vastness that covered northern Luzon, and only 1,500 survived to arrive in Besao. Those that scattered were accounted for by guerilla patrols. The cost to the guerillas was recorded as 125 killed and 335 wounded. More importantly, at the end of the struggle the 15th Infantry, USAFIP(NL), was up to full strength, had equipped itself with captured weapons and supplies, received additional supplies from Sixth Army, and gained valuable experience in more conventional fighting against the *Imperial Japanese Army*. It was ready to join the 121st Infantry, USAFIP(NL), in the fighting along Route 4.

It was in early January that the 15th Infantry USAFIP(NL) began its operations to clear Route 3 north from Vigan. At that same time the 3rd Battalion, 121st Infantry, USAFIL(NL), had begun its own operations to seize the highway between Vigan and Libtong, at the junction of Routes 3 and 4. This task was completed by the end of that month, and Colonel Volckmann believed that to ensure his progress remained undisturbed, he should also clear Route 4 inland from Libtong to Cervantes to prevent the *357th Independent Infantry Battalion* from counterattacking. The 121st Infantry, USAFIL(NL), was instructed to attack Cervantes along Route 393 and Route 4. At the time, only the regiment's 3rd Battalion was available for this task.

The 3rd Battalion's attack began well, with the seizure of the small village of Bitalag and the destruction of the Japanese garrison there. In early February the battalion moved on to the town of Suyo, but there Colonel Volckmann called a halt to operations. He needed all the troops he could muster for the seizure of San Fernando, and so the 3rd Battalion, 121st Infantry USAFIL(NL), was recalled, less Company L which remained at Suyo.

Meanwhile, the *357th Independent Infantry Battalion* had not been idle. It had pulled in its outposts and moved to Bessang Pass, where it began to construct defensive positions. Company L, 121st Infantry, USAFIL(NL), which had been left at Suyo, avoided the pass, and captured Cervantes on February 24 after pushing the small Japanese garrison out of the town. Barely had they settled in, however, when elements of the *19th Division* appeared and pushed the guerillas out in turn. Determined to stand their ground, the guerillas recaptured the town on March 13, but now found themselves under constant Japanese artillery attacks.

Colonel Volckmann knew that Company L could not hold against continued Japanese attacks, so he formed a Provisional Battalion under Captain Serafin V. Elizondo of the 11th Infantry, USAFIL(NL). The battalion included Company A, 11th Infantry, Company L of the 121st Infantry, Company D of the 66th Infantry, some 81mm mortars, and two platoons of the replacement battalion. This group held Cervantes under increasingly severe Japanese attacks until April 3, when Japanese pressure forced a withdrawal into the hills north of the town.

While the Provisional Battalion fought for Cervantes the rest of the guerilla force had captured the San Fernando area. As soon as they did, new orders arrived from General Krueger. A third offensive in northern Luzon was to begin, with the guerillas driving along Route 4 to capture Bontoc. The intermediate objective was to permanently secure Cervantes. It would take the next three months for the guerillas to obtain the new goal.

Colonel Volckmann had only the Provisional Battalion on the scene, and the 121st Infantry, USAFIL(NL), available for this new mission. Two of his other regiments, the 11th and 14th Infantry Regiments, USAFIL(NL), were scattered throughout the Cagayan Valley and could not be brought out. His 66th Infantry, USAFIL(NL), was assigned to the 33rd Infantry Division while the 15th Infantry, USAFIL(NL), was busily engaged with the *Araki Force*. However, the 121st Infantry, USAFIL(NL), was his best equipped, best trained, and strongest regiment, with just under 3,000 men available to it. It had supporting artillery—captured Japanese weapons—that included 70mm guns and 47mm antitank guns. The Fifth U.S. Army Air Force was on call.

With the Provisional Battalion and a company of the Military Police Battalion, USAFIL(NL), attached to it, the regiment moved along Route 4 until it arrived near Bessang Pass on March 29. There the terrain was highly defensible, with ridges rising as high as 5,000 feet and at least one hill, Mt. Namogoian, rising to a height of 6,830 feet. The Japanese had, as usual, taken full advantage of the opportunities the terrain offered them for defense. A week of frustrating battles began, with the guerillas trying to outflank and outfight the Japanese, with limited success. The Provisional Battalion, ordered to hold Cervantes on Route 4 to prevent Japanese reinforcements arriving, was unable to accomplish its mission. As mentioned, it was soon pushed aside and out of the battle.

By the middle of April, the guerillas held strong footholds within the Japanese defenses, manned by elements of the *357th Independent Infantry Battalion* and the *73rd Infantry Regiment, 19th Division*. Slow and costly progress continued, and

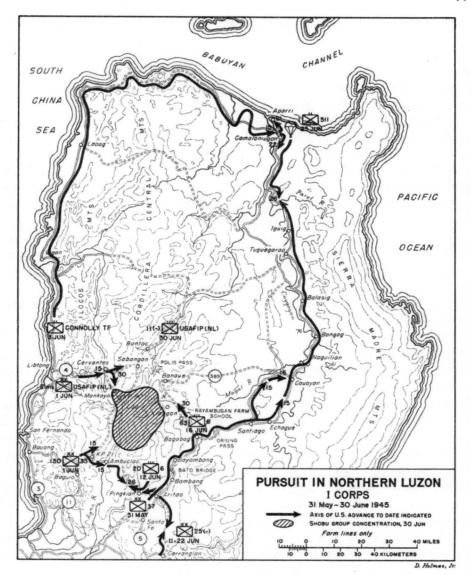

Pursuit in Northern Luzon, I Corps, May–June 1945

Robert Ross Smith. *United States Army in World War II. The War in the Pacific. Triumph in the Philippines.* Washington, D.C.: Center of Military History, 1984. p. 565.

at the end of the month a newly formed unit, the 1st Field Artillery Battalion, USAFIL(NL), arrived to join the fight. This unit was armed with captured 105mm howitzers, 75mm guns, and four American 75mm pack howitzers, especially useful in the mountainous terrain. Their arrival was timely, particularly since the

121st Infantry USAFIL(NL) had recently lost its two 70mm guns to a Japanese counterattack.

Yet despite these reinforcements the attack continued, only to inch forward. In addition to the difficult terrain, the *19th Division* began to feed reinforcements into the battle. These forced the guerillas to cover a wider area with the same resources, and as a result the guerilla front line was stretched perilously thin. The Japanese took notice, and on May 17 the *73rd Infantry Regiment*, supported by a strong artillery barrage, counterattacked. Their attack was successful, pushing the guerillas off most of the real estate they had captured at such cost. The 1st Battalion, 121st Infantry, USAFIL(NL), was so hard hit that it scattered and took days to reform. Although the 3rd Battalion, despite being surrounded, held most of its positions, the gains of the past month had largely been lost. At the same time a 600-man battalion of the *76th Infantry Regiment, 19th Division*, had bypassed the guerilla positions and had moved to the south, cutting Route 4 at the village of Butac, two miles behind the 121st Infantry's front lines. Although there were few troops at Butac to oppose them, the Japanese seemed confused and wasted several days before attacking the village itself.[4] Colonel Volckmann had used this time to rush a strong garrison to Butac. The 2nd Battalion, 15th Infantry, USAFIL(NL), had been rushed there and counterattacked the Japanese, who, having accomplished nothing, withdrew.

Clearly more power was needed to renew the drive on Bessang Pass. Colonel Volckmann ordered the 15th Infantry, USAFIL(NL), into the battle while allowing the 121st Infantry, USAFIL(NL), to rest and reorganize. During the remainder of May, the two regiments attacked the Japanese again, bypassing some resistance and flanking others. By the end of the month Colonel Volckmann was planning on a major attack to seize Bessang Pass. As he did so control of the USAFIL(NL) forces was transferred from the Sixth U.S. Army to General Swift's I Corps. General Swift, who was closer to operations and more familiar with the ground, was ordered to capture Cervantes, reinforcing Colonel Volckmann with the 66th Infantry, USAFIL(NL), from the 33rd Infantry Division. At the same time, the 33rd Infantry Division was to detach its 122nd Field Artillery Battalion (105mm howitzers) and the 1st Battalion, 123rd Infantry, as reinforcements for Colonel Volckmann.

General Swift ordered the guerilla command to mount a major attack toward Cervantes. Colonel Volckmann obliged, sending the 121st Infantry to clear Route 4 and the 15th Infantry to clear Lamagan Ridge, a major enemy position. The 66th Infantry was to deal with the Japanese battalion that had infiltrated Allied lines. The Provisional Battalion,[5] now commanded by Captain Herbert Swick,[6] was assigned to clear Magun Hill, another prominent Japanese defensive position. The 1st Battalion, 123rd Infantry, 33rd Infantry Division, was in reserve at Butac, protecting the guns of the 122nd Field Artillery Battalion.

The attack was scheduled to begin June 1, but the 121st Infantry had suffered heavy casualties and was still somewhat disorganized. To strengthen it, Colonel

Volckmann attached two companies of his 14th Infantry and three Military Police companies to the regiment for the June attack. The 1st Field Artillery Battalion USAFIL(NL) had lost all its captured Japanese guns during the enemy counterattack but had saved its American pack howitzers. The arrival of the 122nd Field Artillery Battalion would be of considerable assistance during the new offensive.

Intelligence sources reported that the Japanese holding Bessang Pass by June 1 were in poor shape. They were estimated to number 2,250, a combined total from both the *73rd Infantry Regiment* and the *76th Infantry Regiment*, both from the *19th Division*. Many service and supply troops were also present. But the entire force was suffering from malaria, beriberi, and other diseases. Ammunition was low, both for the infantry and the remaining artillery. No reinforcements were available, since the rest of the *19th Division* had been ordered to secure Mankayan, Lepanto Mine, and the road junctions at Sagangan and Bontoc. This situation became apparent when the guerillas resumed their attacks, with Lamagan Ridge and Cadsu Ridge falling to them with little trouble. Then, the 121st Infantry, USAFIL(NL), supported by the Provisional Battalion, struck directly for Bessang Pass from several directions. A week of bitter fighting saw them seize the critical pass. Meanwhile, the other regiments had cleared and secured their area as well. By June 14 Japanese survivors were streaming east along Route 4 toward Cervantes. The next day that town was secured by the 15th Infantry, USAFIL(NL).

The cost of securing Bessang Pass and Cervantes was calculated at 117 dead guerillas, with another 217 wounded. American losses, from the 1st Battalion, 123rd Infantry, and 122nd Field Artillery Battalion, were two killed and three wounded. Japanese losses were totaled at 2,600 killed, which seems excessive considering the total number of Japanese defenders, some of whom are known to have escaped. More importantly, the guerillas had tied down the entire *19th Division*, making it unavailable to be inserted in the fighting against Sixth U.S. Army. In addition, they had enabled General Krueger to use his limited forces to the best advantage by making it unnecessary to employ an American infantry division along the coast to contain Japanese forces there. The guerillas had also been responsible for the elimination of at least 10,000 enemy troops between January 9 and June 15 that could otherwise have been used against American forces in northern Luzon. The cost to the guerillas was estimated to be 3,375 total casualties, of which about 900 were killed.

By mid-June, the USAFIL(NL) forces, now a part of General Swift's I Corps, were ready to join the rest of the invasion forces in the pursuit of the rapidly retreating *Shobu Group* as it withdrew even deeper into the wilderness of northern Luzon.

The town of Aparri, which lies 175 miles north of Lingayen Gulf on Luzon's northern shore at the end of the Cagayan Valley, is the only other area on Luzon where there is ample maneuver room for mechanized military forces. In between Aparri and the Central Luzon Plain lie 50 miles of rugged, mountainous terrain, already experienced by the Sixth U.S. Army. In the original planning for the invasion of Luzon, an airfield was to be established in northern Luzon to support the main landings at Lingayen Gulf. Major General Stephen J. Chamberlin (USMA, 1912), General MacArthur's assistant chief of staff, had considered a subsidiary landing at Aparri prior to the main landings at Lingayen Gulf to develop an air base from which such support might be based. Another such site under consideration was at Legaspi, at the eastern end of the Bicol Peninsula. The air support from these fields was to protect American convoys to Luzon while later giving support to the ground troops.

The Legaspi proposal was soon dismissed due to logistical considerations. Likewise, the Aparri operation, for which a corps of two reinforced divisions was required, created concerns. In one of the several plans drawn up for the Luzon campaign, General MacArthur's staff had proposed that the First Australian Corps of two divisions make that assault at Aparri. The isolated corps would be 600 miles from the nearest friendly air bases but only 300 miles from the nearest Japanese air bases, on Formosa. There was also Japanese air power based on Luzon to consider. Knowing that the development of the air bases was the primary purpose of this Aparri landing, and that such bases usually took up to a month to develop, during which the isolated corps would be on its own, gave the planners pause. General MacArthur, however, liked the plan and kept it viable, even after the U.S. Navy's chief of operations, Fleet Admiral Ernest J. King, believed that such an operation was doomed unless Japanese air power could be neutralized beforehand. He objected to routing convoys around the island unless and until that air power was destroyed. Vice Admiral Thomas J. Kinkaid (USNA, 1908), General MacArthur's naval commander, agreed with Admiral King. Admiral Kinkaid added the concern that the many typhoons for which the area is noted would further endanger the operation. Instead, he recommended that the assault convoys use the previously discarded Visayan Passage route. Here were more protected waters, and Allied air power from Mindoro Island could provide air cover. After reconsideration, both General MacArthur and General Chamberlin agreed. Not the least consideration was the fact that General MacArthur did not want any but United States military forces to participate in the Luzon campaign, even though the Australian Army, Navy, and Air Forces were under his overall command as a part of the Southwest Pacific Theater of Operations. The Aparri operation, known as "Love II," was cancelled.[7]

As early as mid-February General Krueger understood that General Yamashita was aligning his forces for a protracted stand in the mountain vastness of northern Luzon. He was anxious not to allow the enemy much time to dig defensive positions. Meanwhile, General Yamashita needed time to reorganize and rehabilitate the units under his command, many of whom had been shattered by battling the Sixth U.S. Army. He also had the problem of re-positioning his supplies and gathering as much sustenance as he could from the Cagayan Valley and distributing it to his troops as soon as possible. As a result, both generals were closely watching the clock and the battle's progress.

As noted, the Cagayan Valley is about 40 miles wide and runs south some 200 miles from Aparri almost to Bambang along the Magat River. The largely unexplored Sierra Madre Mountains seal it off from the Pacific Ocean to the east. The equally harsh Cordillera Central Range joins with the Ilocos Mountains (Malaya Range) to seal the valley off from the South China Sea on the west. The southern boundary, the Caraballo Mountains, had already been breached by Sixth U.S. Army. All entrances to the valley, except for that from Aparri, were along poor roads, usually no more than trails, over mountain passes that were easily defensible. Even the much-fought-over Route 5 was barely two lanes wide and twists and turns through the mountains. Route 11 was little better, and in some places worse, becoming above Bontoc a mere horse trail. Simply put, the easiest entrance to the Cagayan Valley was from Aparri. Route 5, through Balete Pass, was next best, and Route 11 from Baguio was a poor third choice.

General Yamashita's original plan had been to establish a triangular defensive system using Baguio, Bontoc, and Bambang as the apexes of his triangle. This would allow him to strip the Cagayan Valley of all its produce for as long as possible. He expected the American attacks at Baguio and Bambang, and even feared an airborne attack directly into the Cagayan Valley. Equally aware of the American amphibious capability, he had stationed his *103rd Division* at Aparri to address just such an eventuality. As mentioned earlier, he also stationed the *Araki Force* in the area, protecting the airfields. Guerilla activity in late January around the Baguio and Bontoc areas raised concern about another amphibious landing there, and much of the *19th Division* was moved to Bontoc and Libtong to address those concerns. Elements of the *105th Division*, those that had escaped from the *Shimbu Group* east of Manila, held the Bontoc area reinforced with elements of the *10th Division*.

These movements to address General Yamashita's concerns about American attacks into his defensive area required much shifting of units, and the resulting unit shuffling reduced the time for building defenses as well as moving supplies. The result was a strengthened defense of the Baguio area and a consolidation of forces, allowing the Japanese better use of their limited resources.

General Krueger had four American divisions available for the push into northern Luzon—the 6th, 25th, 32nd, and 33rd Infantry Divisions—as well as the USAFIP(NL) forces making up in effect a fifth division. He also expected to receive, albeit piecemeal, the 37th Infantry Division, parts of which had already arrived. With these forces he would have to complete the conquest of Luzon.

By mid-June General Krueger had breached the Japanese defensive triangle. General Krueger now believed that the enemy would make his last stand within the Cagayan Valley. Because of those beliefs, he saw the need to seal off that valley as quickly as possible. He wanted General Beightler's 37th Infantry Division to make a push up the west coast to Aparri, sealing off the last entrance to the Cagayan Valley and cutting off any hope, however remote, of the *Shobu Group* receiving additional reinforcements or supplies from outside Luzon. Such an effort, however, risked endangering the division's long and tenuous lines of supply and communication. General Krueger hoped that a rapid advance would so disorganize the Japanese defenses that they would be unable to strike effectively at those lines of supply. In any event, with the limited forces available to him, the division would have to take its chances, guarding its own supply lines.

It was while these plans were under discussion that intelligence reported that the *Shobu Group* was withdrawing into the Cordillera Central Mountains between Route 4 and 11. This new information prompted General Krueger to order his 6th, 25th, and 33rd Infantry Divisions to finish clearing the Baguio and Bontoc areas, sealing off the *Shobu Group* to the south. He ordered USAFIL(NL) forces to attack east of Cervantes and seize the Route 4 and Route 11 junction at Sabangan, while the 63rd Infantry, 6th Infantry Division, would strike up Route 4 to Kiangan.

The advance of the 37th Infantry Division was slowed by a Japanese force, known as the *Yuguchi Force*, which was moving in the opposite direction along Route 5.[8] Beginning on May 28, the 129th Infantry, with Company C, 775th Tank Battalion, Company C, 85th Chemical Mortar Battalion, Company B, 637th Tank Destroyer Battalion, and the 37th Cavalry Reconnaissance Troop assembled at Santa Fe and two days later began marching up Route 5. Enemy resistance was encountered at several points along the way. The *Yuguchi Force* was determined and well equipped, with two infantry battalions, seven tanks,[9] eight antitank guns, four 75mm guns, and eight 105mm howitzers, along with engineers, medical, and signal units from the *103rd Division*. As the Ohio Division struggled north, they knocked out much of the enemy's equipment while counterbattery fire from the divisional artillery knocked out the enemy guns. The Americans, using superior firepower not previously available to them, including self-propelled howitzers and 240mm artillery guns as well as on-call ground support aircraft, soon struck so hard that the Japanese defenses became obviously disorganized.

With the three infantry battalions rotating turns leading up Route 5, the combat team advanced against resistance which ranged from light to severe. In one instance a leading light tank was knocked out by Japanese antitank fire, which in turn was destroyed by other American tanks. Three enemy tanks were also destroyed on the road. Many of the Ohio Division soldiers began to compare the campaign to that of the "rat race" to Manila four months earlier. By June 5 the division had secured the town of Aritao and advanced 4,000 yards beyond that objective, which they had been allotted 30 days to achieve. The 3rd Battalion, 129th Infantry, reached Bambang the following day. As General Krueger intended, the stretching supply lines were left largely untouched due to the Japanese disorganization.

On June 7 the Magat River was crossed, and bulldozers rushed forward to prepare crossing sites for vehicles. The town of Bayombong fell that day. Here the Americans found an abandoned Japanese military hospital where a lone Japanese doctor awaited them. As they tried to convince him to surrender, he pulled his sword and charged them, making less than 10 yards before being cut down. Inside the hospital were 183 dead Japanese patients who, unable to be moved, had been killed by their comrades, or ordered to kill themselves with grenades and knives. Only one man, who had crawled into the underbrush, survived to tell the tale. As Sergeant John Riggle, of Company M, 129th Infantry, inspected the buildings, he noticed three dead bodies covered by a blanket. As he passed, he noted one of the "dead" men move slightly. Moving past the group, Sergeant Riggle hurled a tin can at them, and when they rose prepared to open fire, he shot them down with his BAR.

As the forward elements reached the town of Solano, antitank fire knocked out the leading vehicles. The leading troops had moved so fast that their support elements were lagging. A brief rest was conducted while the mortars came forward and dealt with the enemy guns. Being late in the day, the advance halted for the night. Two observation aircraft landing strips were built, at Yangiren and Bayombong. With these the supporting artillery—Lieutenant Colonel Chet Wolfe's 6th Field Artillery Battalion—kept the advance within range. When the advance resumed the next morning, June 7, Private First Class Lee E. Sullinger remembered, "I trudged along, when in back of me, I heard shouts of 'Hi, Joe.' I looked back to see who this guy was. Coming toward me, in the front seat of the Division Commander's jeep, was the largest mouth ever seen in the Southwest Pacific. It was attached to the face of Joe E. Brown, the famous comedian. He put out his hand for me to shake, but I missed it by inches. We learned later that he rode into Bayombong on the lead tank. When the town was secured, we were able to pose with Joe for some pictures."[10]

Behind the front the battered 145th Infantry of Colonel Loren G. Windom received 1,000 replacements while moving from Manila to Digdig. They then advanced to Aritao where they assumed the responsibility for guarding the 129th Infantry's extended lines of supply and communication. Similarly, the 148th Infantry moved up to Putlan and soon was also guarding Route 5. Both regiments guarded the supply line and sent combat patrols deep into the hills bordering the road to prevent any enemy from infiltrating the route. Small ineffective groups of Japanese were found and pushed away from the main supply route. An airstrip capable of handling large transport aircraft, C-47s,[11] was built near Bagbag. Piles of enemy dead became a problem, and Filipino civilians were hired to help dispose of them. Meanwhile, at the front, the Japanese made a stand at the town of Lantap, where the 1st Battalion, 148th Infantry, used mortars, tanks, fighter-bombers, and artillery to eliminate this opposition. Eight enemy tanks and 103 enemy dead were counted when the town fell to Company C on June 11. Other groups found 10 light tanks, 10 trucks, and three 20mm antiaircraft/antitank guns abandoned by the fleeing enemy. On June 9 the 148th Infantry was relieved at Lantap by the 20th Infantry, 6th Infantry Division.

Although the advance was moving better than expected, there may have been another factor slowing it down. A new system of relieving men from combat duty had recently been instituted by the U.S. Army. "Old" soldiers like Private First Class Calm H. Wittebort, one of the few remaining original Ohio National Guard members of the division, were "sweating it out" until they acquired the required number of "points" to be able to go home. Although there was no sign of it, these men certainly moved a little more cautiously when sent into the Cagayan Valley.

When orders finally arrived, a group of "high-point" men jumped into two jeeps and started for the rear. As they went down Route 5 a Japanese tank, heretofore silent, opened fire on the road along with 90mm mortars hidden in the jungle. The men in the jeeps—veterans of Munda, Bougainville, Manila, Baguio, and Balete Pass—all had the same thought: "This would be a helluva time to get killed." They jumped out of the jeeps and headed for cover. Shortly thereafter, the enemy fire stopped. The veterans jumped back into their jeeps and hastily left the area and reported the enemy position to headquarters. As they did so, enemy artillery began to explode around the headquarters area. Once again threatened with death just as they were about to return to life, they began to think the enemy had it in for them personally. Finally, friendly mortars got the enemy's range and knocked out the guns. The seven staff sergeants again mounted the jeeps and headed south without further incident.[12]

Major Stephen Bailey's 3rd Battalion, 145th Infantry, took over the lead on June 8. Supported closely by the 775th Tank Battalion, the 85th Chemical Mortar Battalion, and the 209th Antiaircraft Automatic Weapons Battalion, the advance pushed into Solano. Enemy resistance was still sporadic but occasionally strong, as when at the town of Bascaran an enemy strongpoint knocked two American tanks out of action. Such actions continued as the American advance rolled along the west coast. By June 12 the advance battalion, Lieutenant Colonel Hareld Smith's 1st Battalion, 145th Infantry, was approaching Aparri. Counterattacks remained strong, with suicide attacks being made against the American armor. It took the 145th Infantry most of June 12 to eliminate this defense. That night the 1st Battalion, 129th Infantry, relieved the 145th Infantry near Aparri. Back down Route 5 the 6th Infantry Division took up positions to relieve the rest of the 37th Infantry Division protecting the main supply route. The *Yuguchi Force*, what was left of it, scattered into the wilderness of the Sierra Madre Mountains, separating the Cagayan Valley from Luzon's east coast.

Even as the Ohio Division struck north, General Swift had organized a force to assist the guerillas in denying the use of Aparri to the enemy. This task force, known as Connolly Task Force after its commander, Major Robert V. Connolly of the 123rd Infantry, 33rd Infantry Division, was a composite force consisting of Company G, 127th Infantry, 32nd Infantry Division; Company B, 6th Ranger Infantry Battalion; Battery C, 694th Field Artillery Battalion, and several supporting units. The task force was to work with a battalion of the 11th Infantry, USAFIL(NL), in moving up Route

3 around the northern tip of Luzon and occupy the Aparri region until relieved.[13] Once in the area they were to prepare minor port facilities and a liaison aircraft airfield. Combined with a reinforced battalion of the 11th Infantry, USAFIL(NL), Connelly Task Force moved out over Route 3 on June 6. Major Connelly, who had commanded another such task force at Dingalan Bay in May, moved quickly against no opposition. Moving through territory cleared earlier by the USAFIL(NL) forces, Major Connolly arrived at Aparri on June 11, and the combined forces attacked to clear the area of the remaining Japanese troops. As it turned out, they were the rear elements of the already departed *Yuguchi Force*.

Even before the 37th Infantry Division had begun its drive north, General Krueger had wanted to make some move to ensure the success of that drive to Aparri. He decided that an airborne operation was necessary to finally seal off the Cagayan Valley. Probably also under pressure to clear up northern Luzon before his Sixth U.S. Army was relieved by General Robert L. Eichelberger's Eighth U.S. Army on July 1, General Krueger also believed that the Japanese were disorganized and ineffective as an organized fighting force.[14] On June 21 he ordered General Swing's 11th Airborne Division to prepare a battalion combat team for an airborne attack on Aparri. That same day Connelly Task Force entered Aparri unopposed. The following day Colonel Volckmann's 11th Infantry, USAFIL(NL), secured Camalaniugan Airfield, 10 miles south along Route 5.

General Swing organized what came to be called Gypsy Task Force around the 1st Battalion, 511th Parachute Infantry Battalion. It was commanded by the executive officer of the 511th Parachute Infantry Regiment, Lieutenant Colonel Henry Burgess. He organized a force of 1,030 men of the 1st Battalion, 511th Parachute Infantry, reinforced with Company G and Company I of the same regiment. Included was Battery C, 457th Parachute Field Artillery, Company C, 127th Airborne Engineer Battalion, and a platoon of the 221st Airborne Medical Company. Small detachments of the 511th's Signal Company, a language detachment, intelligence, and parachute maintenance units finalized the task force order of battle.

After a personal inspection by General Krueger on June 22 at Lipa Airfield, the troopers boarded 54 C-47s and 13 C-46 aircraft[15] of Colonel John Lackey's 317th Troop Carrier Group. Two days earlier, airborne pathfinders from the division had dropped and contacted Colonel Volckmann's forces near the Cagayan River and then moved to prepare the Camalaniugan drop zone. On the morning of June 23, the pathfinders popped colored smoke to mark the drop zones and the aircraft dropped their paratroopers in the correct area. Two men were killed in the drop due to parachute malfunctions while another 70 were injured, an unusually high seven percent drop injury rate caused by the higher-than-normal wind of 20–25 miles per hour over the drop zone.

Colonel Burgess assembled his task force and contacted Major Connolly and Colonel Volckmann before setting out south along Route 5. Contact was made on

June 27 with the 37th Infantry Division 35 miles south of the airstrip at the Paret River. As Colonel Burgess later wrote, "The Aparri operation was one long, hot march, but militarily it was not difficult."[16] With both task forces under command, General Beightler's division now moved against the 10,000 Japanese service troops hidden in the Sierra Madre Mountains. The *Shobu Group* was now surrounded.

CHAPTER 19

Pursuit

General Yamashita had become concerned about his defenses well before the USAFIL(NL) forces had captured Bessang Pass or General Mullins's 25th Infantry Division had captured Balete Pass. The fall of the strongest anchor of his line of defense at Baguio prompted new plans for a withdrawal of the *Shobu Group* deeper into the Cordillera Central Mountain Range. By May 5, two weeks after Baguio's fall, the plan was distributed to all senior commanders within the *Shobu Group*.

General Yamashita's plans were based upon three basic beliefs. First, he understood that General Krueger's Sixth U.S. Army would continue driving north along Route 5 and attack Bontoc along Routes 4 and 11. Second, he knew that his *Shobu Group* had at most three months in which to complete stripping the Cagayan and Magat Valleys of all food and military supplies available there. These same three months would be necessary to move those supplies into the Cordillera Central Range using Routes 4 and 5 near Bagabag, some 25 miles north from Bambang on Route 5. Finally, he knew that the success of his planned withdrawal and future delaying actions required that the *Shobu Group* maintain control over the Routes 4 and 5 junctions if possible. He expected that his defenses south of Santa Fe would hold until mid-June, allowing him to construct new defenses on Route 5 between Santa Fe and Bambang to delay I Corps. He hoped to hold the junctions of Routes 4 and 5 until the end of July.

With the capture of Aparri, any illusions of succor General Yamashita might have harbored from outside Luzon were gone. Although he had managed to delay the Americans, he still had insufficient food and supplies for a prolonged stand. Meanwhile, the Americans were compressing his forces into a pocket which they called the Kiangan Pocket. The most dangerous threat to the Kiangan Pocket was the attack by the 6th Infantry Division up Route 4 from Bagabag. This route presented the most direct threat to the Japanese along the Asin River Valley. However, General Swift did not neglect other avenues of attack. He directed the USAFIP(NL) forces to strike from Cervantes toward Mankayan and Sabangan. The remnants of the *19th Division*, numbering perhaps 2,000 effective soldiers, withdrew from Bontoc and Sabangan to the area of the Lepanto Mine near Mankayan. To the south the 33rd Infantry Division had pushed aside the remnants of the *23rd Division* and contacted the 6th Infantry Division near Pingkian. The *2nd Tank Division* remnants had escaped north over mountain trails and river valleys 20 miles to Tubliao by early July. Along Route 4 the attack of the 63rd Infantry, 6th Infantry Division, had swiftly cracked the outpost line of resistance of the *105th Division* by June 17 and reached the enemy's main line of resistance two miles north of the Rayambugan Farm School on June 19. Here Japanese resistance stiffened. It took a reinforced 63rd Infantry until June 30 before they cracked this MLR and chased the *105th Division* west toward Kiangan.

At the end of June, with the war in Europe now over for nearly two months and Okinawa "secured," American and Filipino forces were attacking the *Shobu Group* on all fronts. As planned before the invasion, at this juncture General Krueger's Sixth U.S. Army and General Swift's I Corps were relieved of responsibility and pulled off the line to begin to plan for the invasion of Japan, in which they would participate. Strategically, the campaign was over with the seizure of Aparri and the surrounding of the *Shobu Group* in northern Luzon. Sixth U.S. Army estimated that only about 23,000 enemy troops remained in northern Luzon and that they were disorganized and incapable of effective resistance. About half were believed to be within the Cordillera Central Range between Routes 4 and 11, while the remainder were believed to be within the Sierra Madre Mountains east of the Cagayan Valley.

In fact, at least 65,000 enemy troops remained alive in northern Luzon, 13,000 in the Sierra Madre Mountains and the rest in the last stand—or Kiangan—area. While it was true that organization and morale were deteriorating, and supplies were growing extremely short, these men were still capable of effective resistance. Despite being poorly armed, ill with a variety of diseases, and with little hope of success, these Japanese soldiers had no intention of surrendering.

General Robert Lawrence Eichelberger was born in Urbana, Ohio, in 1886 and after attending Ohio State University graduated from the U.S. Military Academy at West Point, New York, in 1909 with classmate George S. Patton. He was commissioned into the infantry and served in Panama and along the Mexican border before serving in the American Expeditionary Force sent to Siberia in 1918. Service in the Philippines and China followed. He graduated from the prestigious Command and General Staff School in the same year as future General Dwight D. Eisenhower. Graduation from the Army War College followed. Service with the War Department under General Douglas MacArthur led to command of the 30th Infantry Regiment at San Francisco. Over the next few years, with the Army expanding to meet the new world crisis, he rose in rank and responsibility so that in 1940 he was promoted to brigadier general on the same list as his former classmate, George S. Patton. He served as the superintendent at West Point until 1942 when he was again promoted, to major general, and given command of the newly organized

77th Infantry Division. He then received command of the XI Corps, and then I Corps. He retained this latter command, leading it in action in the South Pacific Theater, until 1944 when he was given command of the newly created Eighth U.S. Army. Having been promoted to lieutenant general, he led the Eighth U.S. Army in the Southern Philippines campaign and, in June 1945, brought part of his army to Luzon.[1]

The Eighth U.S. Army had been created by using the Australian forces under General MacArthur's command to replace the several United States infantry divisions that had been holding the more than 100,000 bypassed Japanese troops in New Guinea and the Solomon Islands in place. The First Australian Army replaced United States Army units at Aitape, New Guinea, New Britain, Bougainville, and other bypassed battlefields. These American units were then forwarded to reinforce the Sixth U.S. Army and build the Eighth U.S. Army.[2]

The Eighth U.S. Army had been busy while the Sixth U.S. Army was occupied on Luzon. It had conquered most of the Southern Philippine islands and all but eliminated the Japanese presence there. It was still engaged on mopping-up operations in many of those places, including Leyte, and now it was about to do the same in northern Luzon.[3]

General Eichelberger brought one of his own corps headquarters to handle the troops in northern Luzon. This was the XIV Corps, whose war began as far back as Guadalcanal. It had fought its way west ever since. Under the command of the experienced Lieutenant General Oscar W. Griswold (USMA, 1904),[4] the XIV Corps would have available to it the 6th, 32nd, and 37th Infantry Divisions, all USAFIP(NL) forces, including the Buena Vista Regiment and the two American field artillery battalions assigned to the USAFIP(NL).

General Griswold adopted General Swift's I Corps plans for dealing with the *Shobu Group*. Those plans called for continued pressure on the Japanese wherever they might be found. To the east of the Cagayan River the 37th Infantry Division, reinforced with a regiment of the 6th Infantry Division, pushed the enemy ever deeper into the Sierra Madre Mountain Range. Here it was as difficult to get supplies forward in the constant torrential rains as it was to defeat the Japanese. To the north and west where opposition was stronger and better organized the USAFIP(NL) fought over the Sabangan junction of Routes 4 and 11 and captured Bontoc. The 11th Infantry, USAFIP(NL), captured the Lepanto Mines and Mankayan after the *19th Division* defenses collapsed. The 66th Infantry, USAFIP(NL), captured the road junction of Routes 11 and 393 near Sabangan, forcing the *19th Division* into another withdrawal which brought them into the Agno Valley in front of Toccucan, forming the western end of the last stand area. Here resistance stiffened, and the guerillas spent the next several weeks attacking against strong defenses.

Things on the Japanese side were barely recognizable from a mere three months earlier. The *2nd Tank Division*, for example, had barely 1,800 men left of its original complement, and had filled out its ranks with thousands of men from the *Hayakawa Naval Unit* and another 1,700 *Imperial Japanese Army* service and supply units. These 5,300 soldiers and sailors, without any armored vehicles left, had assembled at Tubliao. Of that total, barely 3,600 were armed, and these men had about 80 rounds of ammunition for each rifle, no artillery, and a few mortars and machine guns. They had no food stocks and were living off the land daily. Their attempt to reach the last stand area had been blocked by the 20th Infantry, 6th Infantry Division, when the Americans had cut their route on August 7. Heavy rains, muddy trails, flooded rice paddies, and rugged terrain had prevented the two forces from engaging in more than patrol actions.

Along Route 11 it had become vital to secure the road north from Baguio since the annual monsoon rains had made supplying the forward troops difficult. This job was assigned to the 66th Infantry, USAFIPL(NL), who joined with the 127th Infantry, 32nd Infantry Division, after defeating the *58th Independent Mixed Brigade* and elements of the *19th Division*. To the east the 6th Infantry Division joined with the 11th Infantry, USAFIP(NL), at Polis Pass, thereby finally encircling the last stand area itself on July 21. The last element of the attacks against the *Shobu Group* was a strike south along an old horse trail, upgraded with the name Route 390, on which the 1st Infantry Regiment, 6th Infantry Division, and the 11th Infantry, USAFIP(NL), attacked the northern tip of the last stand area. This soon halted due to a lack of troops and supply problems.

The main effort was the 6th Infantry Division's attack along Route 4, but by July 1 most movement had halted due to the torrential rains which destroyed the roads and trails. What wasn't destroyed by the rains had already been blown apart by the air support previously used in the campaign. Opposition here was from the remnants of the *105th Division*. During this period General Eichelberger made several visits to the front. During one such visit he and General Griswold visited General Hurdis at 6th Infantry Division headquarters and then went to the front of Colonel Everett Yon's 63rd Infantry Regiment. Despite General Eichelberger's previous service in the Philippines, "There I had my first glimpse of almost naked savages, armed only with spears, who were fighting side by side with our troops. These were Ifugaos. The tribesmen had come down from their villages and thrown in their lot with us. They were tall, broad-shouldered, splendidly muscled, and despite the cold climate wore only G-strings."[5]

General Eichelberger then went on to visit General Beightler at 37th Infantry Division headquarters. "The job of the 37th was to eliminate by-passed Japanese units, a discouraging job indeed. This meant going into sections altogether without roads. The enemy was incapable of offensive action, but the heavy rains aggravated the problem and made it sheer drudgery. The 37th could supply its own troops and evacuate the wounded only by the use of rivers which were often turbulent and unruly. Vehicles with tracks helped on the native trails. Jeeps in the eastern reaches could get nowhere."[6] During a subsequent visit to General Chase at the 38th Infantry Division headquarters, then clearing central Luzon, General Eichelberger recorded, "From a high hill Chase and General Bill Spence[7] pointed out to me the Ipo Dam area and other battlefields of the 38th; although the tempo of the fighting was now slowed, two hundred and fifty-nine Japanese were killed between dawn and dusk the day I visited there and twenty-nine were captured. The 38th and elements of the 43rd Division inflicted appalling losses on the enemy during a six-week period."

Because of these visits, General Eichelberger wrote to General MacArthur that he found morale "very high" and that his own morale was equally high. Later, however, he remarked, "I might not have been so optimistic if I had known that, considerably after the official Japanese capitulation, General Yamashita was to come out of the mountain wilderness northeast of Baguio and surrender forty thousand well-disciplined troops."[8]

While the view from headquarters was improving daily, that of the front-line troops was far deadlier. Yet there could be moments of macabre humor as well. At midnight on June 12 Corporal Thompson of Headquarters Company, 145th Infantry, was guarding an ammunition dump near Orioung when a Japanese soldier appeared and began to count the boxes. Corporal Thompson dispatched this intruder only to hear sounds behind him half an hour later. Investigating the disturbance, he found two more Japanese soldiers prying the lids off the ammunition boxes, apparently believing they held food. These were also dispatched quickly.

But usually any humor, however macabre, was lacking. The following day an armored column of the 37th Reconnaissance Troop, a platoon of medium tanks, a platoon of M18 tank destroyers,[9] multi-mount antiaircraft machine guns, a platoon of the Cannon Company and Company B, 145th Infantry, with a motorized Company C, 117th Engineer (Combat) Battalion, moved east toward Cordon. Along the way they smashed into an enemy infantry platoon on the road and eliminated it. Once in Cordon, Company B dismounted to secure the town while the trucks returned to bring forward Company A.

As the truck convoy returned along the road to Cordon, it was taken under enemy automatic weapons fire. The Japanese battalion had let the armored convoy—against which they had no effective weapons—pass without revealing their positions and then ambushed the unarmored trucks loaded with vulnerable infantrymen. Company A quickly deployed off the trucks and called for help. Tanks, Cannon Company guns, and multi-mount machine guns responded to the call, as well as Company C of the same battalion. The 3rd Battalion, 145th Infantry, moved off the road into the hills and flanked the enemy position. The combined attacks pushed the Japanese out of position, leaving behind 245 dead. The survivors scattered into the mountains. Ten were captured. American losses were two killed and 12 wounded.[10]

Near Tabio on June 6, 1945, a year after D-Day in Europe and two months after VE Day, Company I of the 130th Infantry, 33rd Infantry Division, was awaiting an attack to begin by Philippine guerillas attached to the regiment. When no attack began as scheduled, Staff Sergeant Howard E. Woodford, from Barberton, Ohio, volunteered to find out why. He moved to the leading guerilla company and discovered that it was the first time this unit had been under fire, and the reaction was to freeze in place under the intense mortar, machine-gun and rifle fire which had knocked out most of the company leaders. Knowing that continued failure to attack would endanger Company I and other nearby units, he immediately took command of the company, evacuated the wounded, reorganized the unit under enemy fire, and prepared it to attack. He repeatedly exposed himself to enemy fire to locate the source of that fire and then led a five-man assault force to determine their exact position. Although all five of his men became casualties during this movement, Staff Sergeant Woodford continued his patrol alone before returning to the company. He then guided his guerillas up a barren hill and captured the objective, knocking out two machine guns. He organized the defenses for the night and radioed his battalion for permission to remain with the guerillas during the night, when men new to combat experienced the most fear. With permission granted, he held the company within its defenses until dawn when the Japanese struck with a fierce suicide attack supported by mortars, grenades, and small-arms fire. Staff Sergeant Woodford remained at his self-assigned post despite being wounded and radioed for mortar support until his radio was destroyed. He seized a rifle and worked his way around the perimeter, encouraging the Filipinos and directing their defense. Finding a hole in the line where two guerillas had been killed, he filled that gap himself and fought off the enemy. When the fight was over, he was found dead in his foxhole with at least 37 enemy dead in the immediate vicinity. His Medal of Honor was posthumously awarded.[11]

Small-unit actions marked the remainder of the fighting in northern Luzon. The advance of the 20th Infantry, 6th Infantry Division, was marked by one such fight after the other. Moving up a road near Barat on June 12, the Japanese ambushed a company. Private First Class Charles S. Swimmer was outside the ambush zone when he spotted a camouflaged machine gun that was pinning down the lead company. He crawled through thickets and across broken ground to within 25 yards of the emplacement, then charged across a clearing, firing his automatic rifle from the hip. He destroyed the gun and killed the crew, then turned the gun to fire on adjacent enemy positions to cover the evacuation of American wounded. Despite being alone in an exposed position, he remained there because it provided the maximum protection to the wounded. Private First Class Swimmer was killed at his self-appointed post by an enemy sniper.[12]

Not far away Private First Class David J. Kirkland was a lead scout for his company when it was ambushed. Seeing an enemy position, he crawled forward along a ditch, took up a position only 20 yards from the enemy, and fired four rounds from his bazooka. The enemy gun and crew were destroyed.[13] When a roadblock stopped a convoy of self-propelled artillery, Technical Sergeant Roy P. Hanson crawled to the block under machine-gun fire, sawed the key log in half, then made two trips to attach chains to the support logs, after which the self-propelled guns collapsed the roadblock. Technical Sergeant Hanson then led patrols throughout the area to ensure the safety of the convoy.[14]

Meanwhile, the division's 63rd Infantry Regiment continued to push up Route 4. For the first few days there was no enemy contact. Then, on June 14 they encountered a company of Japanese infantry moving south on the same road. Company I raced to the nearest high ground and drove off the enemy counterattack that followed. Continuing north, Companies K and L, with the 6th Reconnaissance Troop, came upon a large undefended motor pool and supply area. Repeated ambushes marred the continuing advance, and an armored car and two trucks were lost to these. By now, however, the Americans had become accustomed to being ambushed, although they never got used to it. When the 6th Reconnaissance Troop was escorting a supply convoy to Payawan, it was ambushed. Technician Fifth Grade Albert H. Green, Jr., deliberately exposed himself to draw enemy fire and identify their positions. He fired his 37mm gun into those positions, then turned his gun to destroy American vehicles which had been disabled by Japanese fire to prevent them from falling into enemy hands. Captain Jean E. LaPlace, commanding the escort troop, so directed the defense that numerous enemy machine guns were knocked out, despite himself being under direct enemy fire. He received his second Silver Star award for this action. The convoy, damaged but basically intact, reached its destination.

June turned into July, and still the fighting continued. Nearly three months after VE Day in Europe, the XIV Corps was still fighting the *Shobu Group* in northern Luzon. There was no more maneuver room for the Japanese, and both sides understood that it was simply a matter of time before the end. Yet both sides continued the struggle, as the *Shobu Group* presented a technical threat to the security of Luzon, which was undergoing rapid development as a major base for the invasion of Japan. Having tens of thousands of enemy troops, regardless of their equipment status, in the rear of a major support base was illogical.

By July General Yamashita estimated that he could hold out until mid-September when all his food would be exhausted. When this happened, he hoped to stage a major breakout with all effective remaining troops and head for the extreme northern end of Luzon, where another mountain range might provide a food source and extend the life of his *Shobu Group*. In the interim, he would hold his positions as long as possible, pinning American forces to his front and thereby keeping them from the invasion of his homeland.

The fighting continued. The Americans and USAFIP(NL) forces struggled in some of the worst country and worst weather conditions to find and attack the Japanese. The Japanese, in turn, fought to hold their positions and keep the Allies away from their few remaining supplies. Once again, these were small-unit fights, such as the one on July 29, 1945, deep in the Cordillera Mountains.

Company D, 20th Infantry, 6th Infantry Division, was supporting a guerilla attack against a Japanese stronghold. Two of the Filipino companies were pinned down by Japanese fire. Corporal Melvin Mayfield saw the problem and rushed from shell hole to shell hole until he reached four enemy caves from which the fire was coming. From the top of the barren hill, he tossed grenades and fired his M-1 carbine, assaulting each cave in turn while constantly under enemy fire. As he finished off the last cave, an enemy machine gun shattered his carbine and wounded him in his left hand. Disregarding the wound, he secured more hand grenades and again charged into the teeth of the enemy fire. This time his target was an enemy observation post which was directing fire on the trapped guerillas. His gallant actions so inspired the guerilla companies that they followed him up the hill and overran the entire enemy defensive complex. For his leadership and personal gallantry on July 29, 1945, Corporal Melvin Mayfield received the Medal of Honor.[15] The Ohio native's award was the last ground combat chronological action for which this award was given in World War II.

Fighting such as this—small-unit fights against ambushes, dug-in Japanese defending high ground, and breaking trail blocks held by the enemy—characterized the remaining weeks of the Luzon campaign. More and more of the fighting was taken over by the USAFIP(NL) forces, but these could not operate successfully without the close support of the better-equipped and better-trained Americans. As a result, the divisions and support elements of XIV Corps continued to fight and suffer casualties until the Japanese surrender. One description from the Japanese side was given by Lieutenant General Akira Muto, General Yamashita's chief of staff: "Based on previous concepts of tactics, the terrain features of these areas provided impregnable fortifications. However, the Americans started attacking in the beginning of February and kept it up incessantly. The superior enemy bombardment and shelling gradually obliterated the jungle. Bulldozers accomplished the impossible. Tanks and artillery appeared in positions where we had thought they would never penetrate. Our front-line troops destroyed bulldozers, tanks and artillery by valiant hand-to-hand fighting. However, the enemy advanced inch-by-inch, capturing this mountain, taking that hill."[16]

When General Hurdis's 6th Infantry Division finally cleared the Kiangan area, fighting the remnants of the *2nd Tank Division* every step of the way, the Japanese pulled back into the Asin Valley. The 20th Infantry and 63rd Infantry RCTs fought over rain-swollen streams, flooded rice paddies, and impassable trails but never were able to pin the surviving members of the *2nd Tank Division* down. Once again, the Americans found themselves involved in mountain fighting, much as they had earlier in the campaign. As they battled closer and closer to the Asin Valley—now the last redoubt of the Japanese forces on Luzon—the enemy opposition, helped by constant rains and miserable terrain, stiffened. In the last six weeks of the campaign, before the Japanese surrender on August 15, 1945, the combined American–Filipino forces suffered an additional 440 killed and 1,210 wounded, totaling 1,650. Of these, 1,000 were members of the USAFIP(NL) forces.

As noted, General Yamashita had estimated that he could hold out in the rugged mountains of northern Luzon until mid-September, when his food supplies would be exhausted. When that occurred, he planned to use his remaining effective soldiers for a breakout operation from the Asin Valley to another group of mountains in the far north of Luzon where he hoped to find additional food supplies, thereby prolonging his defense. This was not to be a banzai attack, but a carefully planned change of base, attacking through enemy lines to reach a more sustainable area for defense. Those of his soldiers too weak or ill to make the move were to remain behind and cover the others' breakout. Expecting that his breakout attempt would destroy any remaining command and control over his forces, he planned for himself a ritual suicide, hara-kiri, at some point during the breakout attempt. Fortunately for the general, the surrender of Japan a month before his scheduled death saved his life, albeit temporarily.

The surrender of Imperial Japan on August 15 found American forces tied down in northern Luzon, precisely as General Yamashita had planned before the first Americans landed there. He understood from the outset, unlike General MacArthur in 1941, that his forces were incapable of holding the entire island, and that the best he could hope to accomplish was to tie down significant American forces, keeping them from additional attacks against the Japanese homeland. In this he succeeded, tying down an entire American army for six months, and then a three-division American corps plus significant USAFIP(NL) forces for another two months. Even then, he was prepared to continue his struggle at least for another month, perhaps longer, depending upon circumstances. Using his soldiers' vaunted determination to fight to the last and incorporating the excellent defensive terrain of the northern Luzon battlefield, he accomplished much more than expected when the campaign began.

General Yamashita was one of the few Japanese leaders who understood that the futile counterattacks usually made against invaders by Japanese forces were out of place in his plans. Surrounded by the enemy, who held complete mastery of the air and seas around the island, he correctly understood that only by a prolonged defense would he contribute anything to the ongoing Japanese struggle in the Pacific. He divided his forces into three main combat groups, keeping the main and strongest force, the *Shobu Group*, under his command and occupying the most defensible terrain. There he held out until the end of the war, fulfilling his self-imposed mission.

General Krueger, on the other hand, had been assigned the mission of containing and then destroying the Japanese defenders of Luzon. In this they had also succeeded. The *Shimbu* and *Kembu Groups* were eliminated or rendered impotent early in the campaign, and the main force, the *Shobu Group*, was in fact contained and pushed deep into the northern mountains of Luzon, where it did no harm to the budding Allied bases developed on Luzon for the coming invasion of Japan. In fact, by mid-March all strategic objectives—Manila, Manila Bay, and the airfields—had been secured by the Sixth U.S. Army. By June 30 the *Shobu Group* was clearly no longer capable of effective or even significant offensive efforts, although American intelligence reports consistently underestimated its strength, its condition and that the constant pressure exerted by the Sixth and later Eighth U.S. Armies kept it offensively harmless.

With the end of the war General Yamashita and his survivors came down out of the mountains and surrendered. There were approximately 50,500 of them, many sick and suffering from malnutrition, but nevertheless capable of sustaining a defense for another month or more. Most of these soldiers, perhaps 40,000 or so, had come out of the Asin Valley. In any estimate, like General Krueger, he had accomplished his mission.

There are, of course, questions about the Luzon campaign, as there are about most military operations. Some raise the valid question of how the campaign would have progressed had the forces originally assigned to the Sixth U.S. Army not been diverted to clear all the other Philippine islands. Was this diversion of strength—five American divisions[17] and the attendant air and naval support—necessary, and was it necessary at the time it was implemented or could it have awaited a greater advance on Luzon before being put into effect? There is no doubt that General Eichelberger's Eighth U.S. Army performed magnificently, making 52 landings in all, including 14 major and 24 minor landings in one four-day period. But that very success highlights the question, given the Japanese strength, or rather lack of it, at the time, was it necessary to clear every island, or to do that before Luzon had been significantly cleared? There was no strategic reason for the Southern Philippines campaign. The Joint Chiefs of Staff had not been consulted about it and had therefore not approved it. The Japanese had little or no air and naval strength in the area, and other than the constant submarine and kamikaze danger, presented little in the way of an organized threat to the Allied forces. Or would it have been better if General MacArthur had used General Eichelberger's fresher Eighth U.S. Army on Luzon rather than the tired Sixth U.S. Army, particularly considering General MacArthur's reservations concerning General Krueger? Further, once Manila was captured, General MacArthur seems to have lost any interest in the continuing Luzon campaign, concentrating rather on the recapture of the other islands and future operations, none of which were imminent. The removal of two and a half veteran combat divisions certainly restricted Sixth U.S. Army's advance into northern Luzon and quite probably increased casualties, since tired soldiers, no matter how experienced, make deadly mistakes.[18] And would the overall cost of the campaign have diminished because of fresh troops and equipment being supplied to it?

Whatever the responses to such questions, General Yamashita was still obeying his orders. On the afternoon of August 26, a Japanese Army captain, carrying a flag of truce, entered American lines and presented General Yamashita's reply to a letter that General Gill of the 32nd Infantry Division had air-dropped into Japanese lines a few days earlier. Using the most courteous and correct language, General Yamashita advised General Gill that he had received his letter but was awaiting authorization from Imperial Headquarters to enter direct negotiations with United States forces in the Philippines. In the interim, General Yamashita had ordered a cessation of hostilities until Tokyo responded to his query. He promised that "upon receipt of this order, negotiations can be immediately entered into."[19] A series of letters back and forth resulted, during which one of the senior messengers, Colonel Merle H. Howe, a veteran regimental commander of the 32nd Infantry Division who had begun his war back in New Guinea in 1942, was killed in a plane crash. Finally, a group of American radiomen were escorted by the Japanese directly to General Yamashita's headquarters, and communications improved considerably. On the morning of September 2, 1945, General Yamashita and Vice Admiral Okochi, accompanied by a small escort, entered American lines at Kiangan. From there the party was escorted to Baguio where the formal surrender document was signed, covering all Japanese Army and Navy forces in the Philippines. The Luzon campaign was over.

CHAPTER 20

The Luzon Campaign

When Imperial Japan surrendered to the Allies in mid-September 1945, there were still 115,000 Japanese—including noncombatant civilians—at large on Luzon and the Southern Philippine islands. General Yamashita's *Shobu Group* was still tying down an American corps of nearly four infantry divisions plus more than 20,000 Filipino guerillas in the inhospitable terrain of northern Luzon. Another American division was similarly tied down reducing Japanese positions in the Southern Philippines. An additional 22,000 guerillas were engaged in patrolling and mopping-up activities on Luzon. Nearly 75,000 guerillas were mopping up on smaller Philippine islands throughout the archipelago. This army-sized force was still engaged in the Luzon campaign when Japan surrendered.

While tactically the Luzon campaign was unfinished when Japan surrendered, the *Fourteenth Area Army* had been decisively defeated and was incapable of any offensive activity. It was no longer a threat to the American advance toward Japan. In turn, the American military had established themselves on Luzon and were rapidly developing it as a base for future operations. Both the Sixth and Eighth U.S. Armies were assembled within the Philippines and preparing for Operation *Olympic*, the first invasion of the Japanese home islands on Kyushu. General Krueger's Sixth U.S. Army, with nine Army and three Marine Corps divisions, would attack the southern end of this home island near the end of 1945. Included in the invasion force was I Corps and XI Corps, veterans of Luzon, along with the 1st Cavalry, 25th, 33rd, and 43rd Infantry, and 11th Airborne Divisions, also Luzon veterans. General Eichelberger's Eighth U.S. Army would participate in the second home islands invasion on Honshu in early 1946, bringing with it veterans of Luzon such as the 6th, 32nd, 37th, and 38th Infantry Divisions and the 13th Armored Group.

Strategically, the objectives of the Luzon campaign had been achieved. The airfields on the Central Plain and the harbor at Manila Bay had been secured and were already in use by Allied forces. From these, Allied forces emerged to cut Japanese lines of communication to the Indies. In addition, support from these same bases aided the efforts of the Australian First Corps in its invasion of Dutch Borneo at

Tarakan Island (26th Australian Brigade, May 1, 1945), Brunei (9th Australian Division, June 10, 1945), and Balikpapan (7th Australian Division, July 1, 1945).

By the end of April all the necessary sites for supporting bases to carry on the war effort had been secured. By August, the first American troops redeployed from the European Theater of Operations had arrived in the Philippines, prepared to participate in the invasion of Japan. Civilian government had been restored to nearly all the Philippines. Over 380,000 enemy troops had been contained or eliminated from the defense of the Japanese mainland. Another 70,000 had been lost on Leyte. Nine enemy divisions had been destroyed on Luzon, and another six had been decimated within the Philippines. Several independent regiments and brigades had also been eliminated.

On Luzon alone, more than 275,000 Japanese had been accounted for during the campaign. Of these 205,000 had died from all causes, including combat, disease, and starvation. An additional 61,100 surrendered at the end of the war, while another 9,000 had become prisoners of war during the campaign. Combined with the 105,000 Japanese lost in the Central and Southern Philippines, nearly 400,000 troops had been lost to Japan.

The cost to the Americans had not been light. The ground combat losses for the Sixth and Eighth U.S. Armies on Luzon and in the Southern Philippines came to nearly 47,000 battle casualties. These included 10,380 killed in action and another 36,550 wounded in action.[1] Sixth Army on Luzon suffered 93,400 non-battle casualties, mostly from disease and heat exhaustion. Of the latter, 260 died. As expected, the infantry accounted for about 90 percent of Sixth Army casualties on Luzon. The battle casualty rate was higher than any other World War II campaign, including the European Theater of Operations and the Okinawa campaign. As noted earlier, the reasons for the high casualty rate include disease, heat exhaustion, torrential rains, the mountainous terrain, and the fact that all but one of the divisions which fought on Luzon had already been exhausted from earlier battles in the Pacific. Many of these men had been overseas three years or more, and had fought in at least one, usually two, campaigns. This resulted in a debilitation that only increased when these units were retained in the front lines for months on end.

The greatest number of American casualties occurred battling the *Shobu Group*, as might be expected. In this eight-month-long battle some 16,190 American losses were incurred, including 4,035 killed. The *Shimbu Group*'s demise cost the American Army 4,635 casualties, of which 1,020 were fatal. Overall, the battle for Manila cost Sixth Army the second highest casualty rate, with losses of 6,575, including 1,010 killed in action. Total American casualties incurred during the Luzon campaign were 37,870, of which 8,310 were killed.

Unlike many previous campaigns in the Pacific, the Luzon campaign was marked by an intelligent and tactically flexible enemy defense. General Yamashita understood that the mechanized power of the American Army of 1945 was beyond his capabilities to resist or defeat. Instead, he chose a defense in depth, designed to tie down large enemy forces to delay, perhaps postpone, the invasion of his homeland. He did not try to defend at the beaches, despite the fact that he selected the correct invasion beaches. The tactic of "defend at the water's edge" had failed numerous Japanese commanders, as well as General MacArthur, in previous battles. He maneuvered his forces by adapting to the terrain, supply situations, road networks, and enemy thrusts. Nor did he corral his forces in a dead-end location like Bataan, as did General MacArthur in 1941. Instead, he withdrew to a region which could support his forces with supplies for an extended period, and which would require a great effort by his enemy to eventually surround and destroy him. Even after eight months, his forces still had some maneuver room, and while hungry, were not universally starving or unable to engage in battle.

The Americans on Luzon engaged in the first large land mass battle of the Southwest Pacific Area of Operations. This presented problems for them. The terrain of northern Luzon prohibited the use of massive firepower upon which the average infantryman had depended previously. Artillery could not advance in force behind the infantry in many instances, stopped by mountains and jungles too thick for them to concentrate in. Tanks were largely road bound, easy targets for hidden antitank guns, land mines, and suicide attackers. Trucks, tracked vehicles, and even the ubiquitous jeep often failed to advance in such terrain. All these factors reduced the long-depended-upon mass and maneuver methods practiced by American armies, including those in the Pacific. To counteract this problem, innovations were made. Antiaircraft artillery, multiple machine guns, and automatic antiaircraft weapons were—in the absence of enemy air opposition—redirected against ground targets. Some even served as infantry. The small artillery liaison planes used for the spotting of enemy positions continued in that role, but also adopted the role of intelligence gatherer, casualty evacuation, and supply drops. Amphibious vehicles, including LVTs and amphibious trucks (DUKWs) were pressed into service to navigate the difficult roads and trails. Designed to land from sea to shore, they in most cases managed to complete their supply missions. When jeeps failed to navigate some trails, the wheels were "flanged" along the railroad beds until enough locomotives could be landed to restart the rail system on Luzon. The native carabaos were used as transport for supplies as well.

Close air support during the Luzon campaign mirrored previous campaigns. Army ground forces were supported by a variety of Army Air Force and United States Marine Corps aircraft during the campaign. While longer-range bombing missions were reasonably well conducted, close air support of ground troops engaged with the enemy resulted in a decided preference for Marine Corps aircraft in this supporting role. Although the Army air forces did improve their performance during the campaign, the issue remained unresolved at the end of the operation. Yet there can be no denying that air support of the 1st Cavalry Division's exposed flank during the "Race for Manila" was a major factor in that unit's success. Again, during the Corregidor operation air support was the only such support available for much of that battle.

Artillery support received mixed reviews. Although most infantrymen were in favor of close artillery support, it wasn't always possible during the campaign. Japanese prisoners were divided by the effectiveness of the artillery versus air support. Air support also could inhibit Japanese movements much further afield than could artillery. Yet the appearance of an artillery liaison aircraft in the sky over an exposed Japanese unit prompted every Japanese soldier to seek immediate cover. Artillery showed itself to great benefit in the battle for Manila. Once freed from General MacArthur's restrictions on firing into the city, it proved of immeasurable assistance to the infantry. The situation repeated itself during the 43rd Infantry Division's attack on the Ipo Dam.

Luzon provided no serious logistic problems. There were no shortages, other than artillery ammunition during the campaign, and the major obstacle, as mentioned earlier, was the impossible roads and trails that hindered forward movement of supplies to the troops. These were overcome by methods mentioned above and the quick attention to the repair of bridges and roads vital to supply lines. The use of Filipino volunteers as carriers of supplies, which began the moment the Americans landed at Lingayen Gulf, has already been described. The artillery ammunition shortage never appeared to influence the campaign, and while some units might have felt shorted during a particular phase of the battle, at no time did the artillery ammunition shortage decisively influence it.

Unique to the Luzon campaign was the presence and activities of the organized Philippine guerilla forces. The loyal population was eager to make its contribution to the defeat of Japan and, both prior to and during the entire Luzon campaign, played a significant role in liberating their home country from the invaders. Some issues developed, as American commanders were unsure how to put these forces to use. Many were poorly armed, few were well trained, and none were experienced in open warfare. Originally depended upon for intelligence gathering and service support, they soon became invaluable to the Americans. Many took on combat missions of their own. Others soon earned the respect of their allies and were considered dependable in most combat situations. Of course, there were ongoing issues. Local politics sometimes interfered with the duties assigned a guerilla force. In rare instances a guerilla leader refused to cooperate because that leader felt threatened in his personal domain. But regardless of the few issues, there is no doubt that the Filipino guerilla force saved thousands of American lives. They also served in service capacities, greatly relieving the Americans of providing those services to their own troops. To a large extent, the activities of the Filipino people reduced the problems of the American Army in clearing the Philippines of the common enemy.

The Luzon campaign also incurred one of the most heinous war crimes of World War II. Despite the stated intention of both opposing military commanders, the city of Manila, the "Pearl of the Orient," was wantonly destroyed and its population massacred. In what was to be the only major urban battle of the Pacific War between the Americans and the Japanese, an estimated 100,000 Philippine civilians were killed by a combination of deliberate murder by out-of-control Japanese military and accidental "collateral damage" of the firepower of the American military. Manila suffered second only to Warsaw as the most ravaged urban area of the entire war, yet today that fact is little remembered.

There was another aspect to the Luzon campaign. The fierce and prolonged defense by General Yamashita and his troops enhanced the fears of the Americans about the coming invasion of the Japanese home islands. If the Japanese had fought so fiercely, so determinedly for Luzon, how much fiercer would be their defense of their homeland? The estimates of American casualties for conquering Japan itself were made accordingly, and thus the need for use of a weapon to avoid such losses became more pronounced and immediate.

The use for which Luzon had been conquered never came to pass, although many of the occupation units destined for surrendered Japan came from the Philippines, including Luzon. The sudden end of the war negated all the plans for the invasion of Japan, and Luzon, as did the entire Philippines, returned to peacetime days capped off by the granting of their independence in 1946, another American promise kept.

Major U.S. Units in the Luzon Campaign

GENERAL HEADQUARTERS, SOUTHWEST PACIFIC AREA
General Douglas MacArthur, Commanding

SIXTH U.S. ARMY
Lieutenant General Walter Krueger, Commanding

EIGHTH U.S. ARMY
Lieutenant General Robert Lawrence Eichelberger, Commanding

ARMY SERVICE COMMAND
Major General Hugh J. Casey

I CORPS
Major General Innis P. Swift, Commanding

X CORPS
Major General Franklin C. Sibert, Commanding

XI CORPS
Major General Charles P. Hall, Commanding

XIV CORPS
Lieutenant General Oscar W. Griswold, Commanding

1st Cavalry Division (Special)
Major General Verne D. Mudge, Commanding (WIA February 27, 1945)
Brigadier General Hugh F. T. Hoffman, Commanding (to August 1945)
Major General William C. Chase, Commanding (from August 1945)

   <u>1st Cavalry Brigade</u>
   5th Cavalry Regiment
   12th Cavalry Regiment

2nd Cavalry Brigade
7th Cavalry Regiment
8th Cavalry Regiment

6th INFANTRY DIVISION
Major General Edwin D. Patrick, Commanding (KIA March 1945)
Major General Charles E. Hurdis, Commanding (from March 1945)
    1st Infantry Regiment
    20th Infantry Regiment
    63rd Infantry Regiment

11th AIRBORNE DIVISION
Major General Joseph M. Swing, Commanding
    187th Glider Infantry Regiment
    188th Glider Infantry Regiment
    511th Parachute Infantry Regiment

24th INFANTRY DIVISION
Major General Roscoe B. Woodruff, Commanding
    19th Infantry Regiment
    21st Infantry Regiment
    34th Infantry Regiment

25th INFANTRY DIVISION
Major General Charles L. Mullins, Jr., Commanding
    27th Infantry Regiment
    35th Infantry Regiment
    161st Infantry Regiment

32nd INFANTRY DIVISION
Major General William H. Gill, Commanding
    126th Infantry Regiment
    127th Infantry Regiment
    128th Infantry Regiment

33rd INFANTRY DIVISION
Major General Percy W. Clarkson, Commanding
    123rd Infantry Regiment
    130th Infantry Regiment
    136th Infantry Regiment

37th INFANTRY DIVISION
Major General Robert S. Beightler, Commanding
    129th Infantry Regiment

145th Infantry Regiment
148th Infantry Regiment

38th INFANTRY DIVISION
Major General Henry L. C. Jones, Commanding (to February 1945)
Major General William C. Chase, Commanding (from February 1945)
Major General Frederick A. Irving, Commanding (from August 1945)
149th Infantry Regiment
151st Infantry Regiment
152nd Infantry Regiment

40th INFANTRY DIVISION
Major General Rapp Brush, Commanding (to July 1945)
Brigadier General Donald J. Myers, Commanding (from July 1945)
108th Infantry Regiment
160th Infantry Regiment
185th Infantry Regiment

41st INFANTRY DIVISION
Major General Jens A. Doe, Commanding
162nd Infantry Regiment
163rd Infantry Regiment
186th Infantry Regiment

43rd INFANTRY DIVISION
Major General Leonard F. Wing, Commanding
103rd Infantry Regiment
169th Infantry Regiment
172nd Infantry Regiment

112th CAVALRY REGIMENT (Special)

158th REGIMENTAL COMBAT TEAM (Separate)

503rd PARACHUTE INFANTRY REGIMENT (Separate)

13th ARMORED GROUP

6th RANGER INFANTRY BATTALION

168th FIELD ARTILLERY GROUP (Motorized)

191st FIELD ARTILLERY GROUP (Motorized)

4th ENGINEER SPECIAL BRIGADE

ALLIED AIR FORCES, SOUTHWEST PACIFIC AREA
Lieutenant General George C. Kenney, Commanding

FAR EAST AIR FORCES
Lieutenant General George C. Kenney, Commanding

FIFTH U.S. ARMY AIR FORCE
Major General Ennis C. Whitehead, Commanding

THIRTEENTH U.S. ARMY AIR FORCE
Major General St. Clair Streett, Commanding

MARINE AIR GROUP 12
Colonel William A. Willis, USMC, Commanding

ALLIED NAVAL FORCES, SOUTHWEST PACIFIC AREA
Vice Admiral Thomas C. Kinkaid, USN, Commanding

LUZON ATTACK FORCE (Task Force 77)
Vice Admiral Thomas C. Kinkaid, USN, Commanding

SAN FABIAN ATTACK FORCE (Task Force 78)
Vice Admiral Daniel E. Barbey, Commanding

BOMBARDMENT AND FIRE SUPPORT GROUP (Task Group 77.2)
Vice Admiral Jesse B. Oldendorf, Commanding

CLOSE COVERING GROUP (Task Group 77.3)
Rear Admiral Russell S. Berkey, Commanding

REINFORCEMENT GROUP (Task Group 77.9)
Rear Admiral Richard L. Connolly, Commanding

SERVICE GROUP (Task Group 77.10)
Rear Admiral R. O. Glover, Commanding

LINGAYEN ATTACK FORCE (Task Force 79)
Vice Admiral Thomas S. Wilkinson, Commanding

Japanese Order of Battle, Luzon, 1945

IMPERIAL GENERAL HEADQUARTERS
(Tokyo)

SOUTHERN ARMY
Field Marshal Count Hisaichi Terauchi, Commanding
(Saigon)

FOURTEENTH AREA ARMY
General Tomoyuki Yamashita, Commanding
(Luzon)

SHIMBU GROUP
Lieutenant General Shizuo Yokoyama, Commanding

8th (INFANTRY) DIVISION (less elements on Leyte)
Lieutenant General Shizuo Yokoyama, Commanding

105th (INFANTRY) DIVISION
Lieutenant General Yoshitake Tsuda, Commanding

1st SURFACE RAIDING BASE FORCE
Lieutenant Colonel Nobotuka Kogure, Commanding

KOBAYASHI FORCE
Major General Takashi Kobayashi, Commanding

3rd SURFACE RAIDING FORCE
Lieutenant Colonel Masanori Kawagoshi, Commanding

FUJI FORCE (INCLUDES 2nd SURFACE RAIDING FORCE)
Colonel Masatoshi Fujishige, Commanding

31st NAVAL SPECIAL BASE FORCE (includes MANILA NAVAL DEFENSE FORCE)
Rear Admiral Sanji Iwabuchi, Commanding

KEMBU GROUP
Major General Rikichi Tsukada, Commanding

EGUCHI DETACHMENT (10th AIR SECTOR UNIT)
Lieutenant Colonel Seizuke Eguchi, Commanding

TAKAYA DETACHMENT (2nd Glider Infantry/1st Raiding Group)
Major Saburo Takaya, Commanding

TAKAYAMA DETACHMENT (2nd Mobile Infantry [-])
Lieutenant Colonel Koshin Takayama

YANAGIMOTO DETACHMENT (elements, 2nd Mobile Infantry)
Captain Yanagimoto, Commanding

NAVAL FORCES KIMBU GROUP (26th AIR FLOTILLA)
Rear Admiral Ushie Sugimoto, Commanding

NAGAYOSHI DETACHMENT (39th Infantry, 10th DIVISION [Bataan])
Colonel Sanenobu Nagayoshi, Commanding

SHOBU GROUP
General Yamashita, Commanding

2nd TANK DIVISION
Lieutenant General Yoshiharu Iwanaka, Commanding

23rd (INFANTRY) DIVISION
Lieutenant General Fukutaro Nishiyama, Commanding

103rd (INFANTRY) DIVISION
Lieutenant General Yutaka Muraoka, Commanding

19th (INFANTRY) DIVISION
Lieutenant General Yoshihara Ozaki, Commanding

10th (INFANTRY) DIVISION (-)
Lieutenant General Yasuyuki Okamoto, Commanding

TSUDA DETACHMENT (11th INDEPENDENT MIXED REGIMENT)
Colonel Tsukada Tsuda, Commanding

58th INDEPENDENT MIXED BRIGADE
Major General Bunzo Sato, Commanding

TOTAL JAPANESE GROUND FORCES, LUZON, JANUARY 1945 = 275,685

SUPPORT FORCES SUBORDINATE TO FOURTEENTH AREA ARMY

SOUTHWEST AREA FLEET
Vice Admiral Denshichi Okochi, Commanding
(Luzon)

3rd SOUTHERN EXPEDITIONARY FLEET
Vice Admiral Denshichi Okochi, Commanding
(Luzon)

4th AIR ARMY
Lieutenant General Kyoji Tominaga, Commanding
(Echague, Luzon)

2nd AIR DIVISION
Lieutenant General Seiichi Terada, Commanding
(Negros Island)

4th AIR DIVISION
Lieutenant General Kizo Mikami, Commanding
(Echague, Luzon)

30th FIGHTER GROUP
Major General Takezo Aoki, Commanding

Luzon Campaign Medals of Honor

Listed alphabetically, including place of enlistment. Italics denote those killed in action.

Private First Class Thomas E. Atkins, 127th Infantry, 32nd Infantry Division Campobello, South Carolina

First Lieutenant Willibald C. Bianchi, 45th Infantry, Philippine Scouts (1942) New Ulm, Minnesota

Sergeant Jose Calugas, Battery B, 88th Field Artillery, Philippine Scout (1942) Fort Stotsenburg, Philippine Islands

Private First Class Joseph J. Cicchetti, Company A, 148th Infantry, 37th Infantry Division Waynesburg, Ohio

Staff Sergeant Raymond H. Cooley, Company B, 27th Infantry, 25th Infantry Division Richard City, Tennessee

Commander George Fleming Davis, USN, Commanding Officer, USS *Walke* Philippine Islands

Private First Class David M. Gonzales, Company A, 127th Infantry, 32nd Infantry Division Pacoima, California

Private First Class William J. Grabiarz, Troop E, 5th Cavalry, 1st Cavalry Division Buffalo, New York

Private First Class Dexter J. Kerstetter, Company C, 130th Infantry, 33rd Infantry Division Centralia, Washington

Private First Class Anthony L. Krotiak, Company I, 148th Infantry, 37th Infantry Division Chicago, Illinois

Staff Sergeant Robert E. Laws, Company G, 169th Infantry, 43rd Infantry Division Altoona, Pennsylvania

General Douglas MacArthur, Commanding U.S. Army Forces in the Far East (1942) Ashland, Wisconsin

Corporal Melvin Mayfield, Company D, 20th Infantry, 6th Infantry Division Nashport, Ohio

Private Lloyd G. McCarter, 503rd Parachute Infantry Regiment Tacoma, Washington

Master Sergeant Charles L. McGaha, Company G, 35th Infantry, 25th Infantry Division Crosby, Tennessee

Major Thomas B. McGuire, 13th Army Air Force Sebring, Florida

Private John R. McKinney, Company A, 123rd Infantry, 33rd Infantry Division Woodcliff, Georgia

Second Lieutenant Alexander R. Nininger, Jr., 57th Infantry, Philippine Scouts (1942) Fort Lauderdale, Florida

Technician Fifth Grade Laverne Parrish, 161st Infantry, 25th Infantry Division Ronan, Montana

Private First Class Manuel Perez, Jr., Company A, 511th Parachute Infantry, 11th Airborne Division Chicago, Illinois

Private First Class John N. Reese, Jr., Company B, 148th Infantry, 37th Infantry Division Pryor, Oklahoma

Technical Sergeant Cleto Rodriguez, Company B, 148th Infantry, 37th Infantry Division San Antonio, Texas

Second Lieutenant Donald E. Rudolph, Company E, 20th Infantry, 6th Infantry Division Minneapolis, Minnesota

Private First Class William R. Shockley, Company L, 128th Infantry, 32nd Infantry Division Selma, California

Major William A. Shomo, 82nd Tactical Reconnaissance Squadron, Fifth Air Force Jeanette, Pennsylvania

Private First Class William H. Thomas, 149th Infantry, 38th Infantry Division Ypsilanti, Michigan

Second Lieutenant Robert M. Viale, Company K, 148th Infantry, 37th Infantry Division Ukiah, California

Staff Sergeant Ysmael, R. Villegas, Company F, 127th Infantry, 32nd Infantry Division Casa Blanca, California

Staff Sergeant Howard E. Woodford, Company I, 130th Infantry, 33rd Infantry Division Barberton, Ohio

Casualty Comparison

Battle Casualties of U.S. Army Ground Combat Forces, Luzon and the Southern Philippines, 1945[1]

Area	Killed	Wounded	Total
Shobu Area, Luzon	4,035	12,255	16,190
Shimbu Area, Luzon	1,020	3,615	4,635
Kembu Area, Luzon	835	3,380	4,215
Manila Area[2]	1,010	5,565	6,575
Corregidor	240	675	915
Bataan[3]	315	1,285	1,600
Southern Luzon[4]	255	880	1,135
Bicol Peninsula	95	475	570
Miscellaneous[5]	505	1,530	2,035
Luzon Campaign Totals:	8,310	29,560	37,870
Leyte Island	3,593	11,991	15,584
Mindoro and the Visayan Passages	125	255	380
Palawan and offshore islets	15	60	75
Zamboanga Peninsula	220	665	885
Sulu Archipelago	35	130	165
Panay and offshore islets	20	50	70
Northern Negros	370	1,025	1,395
Cebu and Mactan	420	1,730	2,150
Bohol Island	10	15	25
Southern Negros	35	180	215
Eastern Mindanao	820	2,880	3,700
Southern Philippines Totals:	2,070	6,990	9,060
Philippines Campaign Totals:	13,973	48,541	62,514[6]

Endnotes

Chapter 1

1 Samuel Eliot Morison. *Strategy and Compromise. A Reappraisal of the Crucial Decisions Confronting the Allies in the Hazardous Years, 1940–1945*. Boston: Little, Brown and Company, 1958. Part II, Chapter 5.

2 See Nathan N. Prefer, *Leyte 1944. The Soldier's Battle*. Philadelphia & Oxford: Casemate, 2012.

3 Postwar assessments concluded that an invasion of Formosa would have been strongly resisted by the Japanese garrison on that island, which was stronger than the Americans realized at this point in the war.

4 Hayashi, Saburo. *Kōgun. The Japanese Army in the Pacific War*. Tokyo: Marine Corps Association, 1959, p. 240.

5 Prefer, op. cit.

6 Edward J. Drea. *Japan's Imperial Army. Its Rise and Fall, 1853–1945*. Lawrence, KS: University Press of Kansas, 2009, p. 245.

7 For the composition of these groups, see Appendix B.

8 Quoted in Robert Ross Smith, *Triumph in the Philippines. U.S. Army in World War II. The War in the Pacific*. Washington, D.C.: Center of Military History, 1984, p. 92.

9 General Streett received a direct commission without attending college. General Kenney attended MIT for three years before enlisting in the Air Corps.

10 The true best sites for airfields were on the northwest section of the island, but constant rain in those areas made for poor flying weather.

11 Some sources list only one Japanese cruiser with this force.

12 Today's Vietnam.

13 The Japanese command in Saigon had also ordered General Yamashita to organize a counter-landing on Mindoro, but he refused and convinced them of the futility of the scheme. The Japanese naval forces were commanded by Rear Admiral Masanori Kimura, who had earlier fought in the Battle of Surigao Strait. The Japanese lost the destroyer IJN *Kiyoshimo*. There are some discrepancies over who first sighted the force, submarines or air searches.

14 The Lockheed P-38 "Lightning" fighter plane was produced by Lockheed and had the unusual characteristic of having its empennage carried by two booms supporting the main units of the aircraft. It was a single-seat long-range fighter and fighter-bomber powered by two 1,600-horsepower Allison V-1710 12-cylinder engines. It had a maximum speed of 414 miles per hour, a service ceiling of 44,000 feet, and a range of 2,600 miles. It was armed with one 20mm forward-firing cannon and four .50-caliber machine guns. It could also carry externally a bomb or rocket load of 4,000 pounds.

15 War Department General Order Number 24, March 7, 1946.

16 Probably the most widely known aircraft of World War II in the American inventory, the North American P-51 "Mustang" single-seat fighter and fighter-bomber aircraft was powered by a single 1,695-horsepower Packard V-1650 12-cylinder engine. It had a maximum speed of 437 miles per hour, a service ceiling of 41,900 feet, and a range of 2,301 miles. It was armed with six forward-firing .50-caliber machine guns and could carry an external bomb or rocket load of up to 2,000 pounds. The P-6D was a model specifically altered for photo-reconnaissance duties.

17 War Department General Order Number 25, April 7, 1945.

18 Another large relatively flat area is the Cagayan Valley in the northern portion of Luzon, of which more will be heard later.

19 The 13th Armored Group consisted of two tank battalions, a tank destroyer battalion, and a combat engineer battalion.

Chapter 2

1 General Walter Krueger, *From Down Under to Nippon. The Story of Sixth Army in World War II.* Nashville, TN: Battery Press, 1989, p. 3.

2 Walter Krueger was born January 26, 1881, in West Prussia and came with his family to the United States in 1889. He enlisted in the U.S. Army in 1898 and earned a commission from the enlisted ranks in 1901. He graduated from the Staff College in 1907, served in the Mexican Punitive Expedition 1916–17, and in France with the Tank Corps during World War I. He graduated from the Army War College (1921), the Naval War College (1926), before serving on the War Department General Staff. He was promoted to lieutenant general in May 1941 and given command of the Third U.S. Army the same month. He died August 20, 1967.

3 For an excellent detailed discussion of the U.S.–Australian relationships in the Southwest Pacific Theater of Operations, see Peter J. Dean, *MacArthur's Coalition. US and Australian Operations in the Southwest Pacific Area, 1942–1945.* Lawrence, KS: University Press of Kansas, 2018.

4 At this point in the war the Japanese still had available the super battleship *Yamato*, five other battleships, four aircraft carriers, four heavy cruisers, 35 destroyers, and 43 submarines. Samuel Eliot Morison. *History of United States Naval Operations in World War II. Volume Thirteen. The Liberation of the Philippines, Luzon, Mindanao, the Visayas, 1944–1945.* Edison, NJ: Castle Books, 1959, p. 14.

5 Ibid., p. 98fn.

6 The sloop HMAS *Warrego* and frigate HMAS *Gascoyne*.

7 Between December 13, 1944, and January 10, 1945, when the Americans landed on Luzon, Japanese aircraft sank 24 Allied ships and damaged 67 others.

8 Rear Admiral Chandler received a posthumous Navy Cross.

9 Morison, op cit., p. 114.

10 General Beightler was a rarity in that he was one of a handful of National Guard officers to command a division throughout the war.

11 Quoted in Gerald Astor, *Crisis in the Pacific. The Battles for the Philippine Islands by the Men Who Fought Them.* New York: Donald I. Fine Books, 1996, p. 355.

12 General Wing, a lawyer, was another of the very few National Guard officers to command a division throughout the war. He had no formal military training, having entered the service by enlisting in the Vermont National Guard and receiving a direct commission.

13 LVTs could carry 30 soldiers, a jeep, or supplies from ship to shore. The LVT-4 was the latest in a series of improvements which placed the engine at the front and a ramp at the rear. The 98th Chemical Mortar Battalion was equipped with 4.2-inch chemical mortars which were originally intended to fire gas shells at the enemy should that be necessary. Instead, throughout the war,

they were used as "light artillery," firing high-explosive shells or smoke shells out to a range of 3,200 yards.

14 War Department General Order Number 77, September 10, 1945.

15 Unlike other theaters, the Southwest Pacific Theater employed several independent infantry regimental combat teams, infantry regiments, and artillery battalions with other support troops. In addition to the 158th Infantry Regimental Combat Team, the Sixth Army had available the 112th Cavalry Regimental Combat Team and the 503rd Parachute Regimental Combat Team, all of which had seen previous combat.

16 See Appendix B for the order of battle.

17 Properly, Japanese divisions did not include the title of "infantry," but to conform to American Army usage, they will be so called herein.

18 The *23rd Division* was a Type A "Strengthened" (Modified) Division organized in 1939 and with service in Manchuria. It fought against the Russians at Nomonhan before being sent to the Philippines in November 1944.

19 Lieutenant General Yoshiharu Iwanaka's *2nd Tank Division* was activated in March 1942 in Manchuria. When it was sent to the Philippines in August 1944, it consisted of two tank brigades with a total of three tank regiments, a mobile infantry regiment, and the usual supporting arms.

20 The 147th Field Artillery Battalion.

21 Private First Class Smith received a Silver Star for this action. See Division Public Relations Section. *The 6th Infantry Division in World War II, 1939–1945*. Nashville, TN: Battery Press, 1983, p. 73.

22 Ibid. Staff Sergeant Kaufman received a posthumous Silver Star.

23 Staff Sergeant Mogab received the Distinguished Service Cross for this action, which he survived. See General Order Number 61, 1945, U.S. Forces Pacific, General Headquarters.

24 There are some indications that this was not a part of the planned counterattack, but an accidental meeting of the withdrawing *2nd Battalion, 64th Infantry*, from Hill 200.

Chapter 3

1 Quoted in Astor, op. cit., p. 363.

2 Named for its British inventor, Donald Coleman Bailey, the Bailey Bridge was widely used by Allied forces in World War II. Using flat panels which connected by pins and transoms to support decking, these bridges could span obstacles 30–220 feet wide. The bridges could support weights up to 100 tons and were comparatively easy to construct.

3 Kevin C. Holzimmer. *General Walter Krueger. Unsung Hero of the Pacific War*. Lawrence, KS: University Press of Kansas, 2007, p. 216.

4 Ibid.

5 It should be noted that the two commanders were making their judgments based upon two very different intelligence reports regarding Japanese strength on Luzon. General MacArthur's intelligence officer, Major General Charles A. Willoughby, reported that there was a total of 152,500 enemy troops on Luzon, a figure that barely covered the *Shobu Group* alone. General Krueger's intelligence officer, Colonel Horton V. White, on the other hand, reported the very nearly accurate figure of 234,500 Japanese troops on Luzon.

6 Holzimmer, op. cit., p. 217.

7 Major General Hugh J. Casey. *Engineers in Theater Operations: Engineers of the Southwest Pacific, 1941–1945*. Office of the Chief Engineer, General Headquarters Army Forces. n.p., n.d., p. 238.

8 The *19th Division* was another Type A "Strengthened" (Modified) Division. It had been activated during World War I and had been stationed in Korea before being sent to Luzon in January 1945.

This type of division contained three infantry regiments, an artillery regiment, a reconnaissance regiment, an engineer regiment, a transport regiment, and the usual supporting units.

9   The *105th Division* was a Type C "Special" or "Brigaded" Division with different variations in its composition. In this case, it included two infantry brigades of four infantry battalions each, along with supporting units including artillery, signals, engineers, medical, and transportation units. The *105th Division* had been organized at Hiroshima Depot, Japan, and sent to Luzon in the summer of 1944.

10 The *10th Division* was another Type A "Strengthened" (Modified) Division. It had been activated in 1895 and had participated in the Russo–Japanese War of 1904–05. After serving in Manchuria, it had returned to Japan, before returning to China in 1937. It was sent to the Philippines in the fall of 1944.

11 The composition of this force was not identified, but it probably came from either the *2nd Tank Division* or the *105th Infantry Division*, both of whom were withdrawing north.

12 For an order of battle of the *Kembu Group*, see Appendix B.

13 Stanley A. Frankel. *The 37th Infantry Division in World War II*. Washington, D.C.: Infantry Journal Press, 1948, p. 233.

14 Built around the *2nd Glider Infantry Regiment* and *1st Raiding Group*, under the command of Major Saburo Takaya.

15 The M-7 self-propelled howitzer was based on the M3 Medium Tank and intended to provide mobile fire support for infantry and tank units. It was an open-topped armored vehicle with a crew of seven armed with a 105mm howitzer and a .50-caliber machine gun. The latter was mounted in a circular side mount which led to the vehicle becoming known as the "Priest." It had a maximum road speed of 26 miles per hour and a range of 125 miles.

16 There is some discrepancy about the reasons the American tanks withdrew before the attack. The 129th Infantry's journal claims they withdrew to avoid Japanese artillery fire.

17 Frankel, op. cit., p. 237.

Chapter 4

1   General Krueger's Sixth Army numbered, including reserves, 175,000. General Yamashita's *Fourteenth Area Army* on Luzon numbered 250,000.

2   There are at least three different hills which the Americans in different units called Question Mark Hill.

3   General Shigemi's tanks could not negotiate the Villa Verde Trail to the east. The roads south were blocked by the 6th Infantry Division as was the way west. There were no roads leading north.

4   War Department General Order Number 55, July 13, 1945.

5   Captain Phelps received an Oak Leaf Cluster to his earlier Silver Star. Technical Sergeant Kitchens received a posthumous Silver Star.

6   Both Pfc Smith and Staff Sergeant Baker received Silver Stars for this action.

7   Lieutenant Canas, Pfc Van Winkle, and Pfc Guest all received Silver Stars, Pfc Guest posthumously.

8   Apparently, later in the campaign, General Patrick changed his mind. With General Krueger's support, Colonel Ives was given command of a regiment in the 33rd Infantry Division, which he retained throughout the war.

9   Hampton Sides. *Ghost Soldiers. The Forgotten Epic Story of World War II's Most Dramatic Mission*. New York: Doubleday, 2001, p. 324.

10 The Alamo Scouts were a small select group of specially trained scouts who went behind enemy lines to acquire intelligence on enemy troops, dispositions, defenses, and intention. They had been

created by General Krueger for use by his Sixth Army ("Alamo Force") during the New Guinea campaign.

11 Robert W. Black. *Rangers in World War II*. New York: Ivy Books, 1992.

Chapter 5

1 Prefer, op. cit.

2 For a detailed breakdown of these forces and how they were distributed, see B. David Mann, *Avenging Bataan. The Battle of Zigzag Pass*. Raleigh, NC: Pentland Press, 2001, Appendix A. See also Nathan N. Prefer, "Back to Bataan." *World War II History Magazine* (June 2018), p. 28.

3 Future President of the Republic of the Philippines.

4 Quoted in Gerald Astor, op. cit., p. 378.

5 See Mann, op. cit.

6 The 151st Infantry Regiment was in corps reserve, and the 149th Infantry Regiment was off making contact with XIV Corps.

7 Lieutenant General Robert L. Eichelberger, *Our Jungle Road to Tokyo*. Nashville, TN: Battery Press, 1989. p. 182.

8 Committee on Veterans' Affairs, United States Senate. *Medal of Honor Recipients, 1863–1978*. Washington, D.C.: Government Printing Office, 1979.

9 Quoted in Clay Blair, Jr., *Silent Victory. The U.S. Submarine War Against Japan*. Philadelphia and New York: J. B. Lippincott Company, 1975, p. 834.

10 Ibid.

11 Theodore Roscoe, *United States Submarine Operations in World War II*. Annapolis, MD: Naval Institute Press, 1949, pp. 450–51.

12 Astor, op. cit., p. 379.

13 Quoted in Smith, op. cit., p. 203.

14 *The 40th Infantry Division in World War II*. Nashville, TN: Battery Press, 1995, p. 114.

15 Astor, op. cit., p. 380.

16 Pfc Thomas was awarded a posthumous Medal of Honor. War Department General Order Number 81, September 24, 1945.

17 Astor, op. cit., p. 381.

Chapter 6

1 These bridges—there were two—had been destroyed by General MacArthur's forces in 1942, rebuilt by the Japanese, and again destroyed by them late in 1944 or early 1945.

2 During World War I, both men had served in France in the 42nd Infantry ("Rainbow") Division.

3 Smith, op. cit., p. 212, quoting from a radio message General Krueger sent to General Griswold, reports that General MacArthur complained to General Krueger after his January 30 front-line inspection that the 37th Infantry Division was demonstrating "a noticeable lack of drive and aggressive initiative …"

4 The Browning Automatic Rifle Light Machine Gun (BAR) was another of the developments of the noted firearms designer John Moses Browning. Developed because of a lack of light machine guns within the U.S. Arsenal in World War I, it became the standard squad automatic weapon of World War II and Korea. It had a firing rate of 350–550 rounds per minute, weighed 20.1 pounds, and used a 20-round ammunition magazine. It had an operational range of 875 yards.

5 Awarded under General Order Number 43, 1945 U.S. Forces, Pacific (GHQ).

6   See Frankel, op. cit., p. 240.

7   Ibid.

8   Unique to the World War II American Army, the 1st Cavalry Division did not contain three infantry regiments of three battalions each. Instead, it consisted of two cavalry brigades of two cavalry regiments each. Each cavalry regiment had only two instead of the infantry's three battalions (called "squadrons" in the cavalry). Each regiment was authorized 1,750 men versus the 3,000 men in an infantry regiment, but as noted, the division was understrength after the Leyte campaign.

9   Major B. C. Wright. *The 1st Cavalry Division in World War II.* Toppan Printing Company, Ltd. Tokyo: 1947, p. 126.

10 Colonel Ross received a posthumous Silver Star.

11 Lieutenant (j.g.) Sutton received a Distinguished Service Cross for this and other actions on February 8. See General Order Number 70, 1945, U.S. Army Forces, Pacific (GHQ).

12 Vice Admiral George Carroll Dyer, *The Amphibians Came to Conquer. The Story of Admiral Richmond Kelly Turner.* Vol. II. Washington, D.C.: Government Printing Office, 1969, pp. 974–75.

13 It should be noted that later in the war the 188th Glider Infantry Regiment was converted to a parachute infantry regiment, giving the division two parachute regiments and one glider infantry regiment.

14 Lieutenant General E. M. Flanagan, Jr. USA (Ret.). *The Angels. A History of the 11th Airborne Division.* Novato, CA: Presidio Press. 1989, p. 222.

15 Major Isaac Hoppenstein, Staff Officer, 187th Glider Infantry Regiment, quoted in Flanagan, op. cit., p. 236.

16 There is some confusion about this casualty. Some sources believe they are one and the same man, a seriously wounded trooper who later died of his wounds but was counted twice, once in each category.

Chapter 7

1   Vice Admiral Denshichi (Okauchi) Okochi was headquartered at Manila and under the direct command of GHQ, Tokyo. His fleet was disbanded in October 1944, but he was retained as commander of naval forces in the Philippines. He withdrew into the mountains with the *Fourteenth Area Army Headquarters* after ordering his naval forces to defend Manila to the last man, despite General Yamashita's orders to the contrary. He would later give testimony against General Yamashita at the latter's war crimes trial.

2   Not to be confused with the *Imperial Japanese Army's Manila Defense Force*, which was evacuating the city.

3   Rear Admial Sanji (Iwabachi) Iwabuchi was the commander of the 31st Naval Special Base Force under Southwest Area Fleet. It is believed he was killed or committed suicide at the end of the Battle of Manila. He had earlier in the war commanded the battleship IJN *Kirishima* when it was sunk during the battles for Guadalcanal. See Evan Mawdsley, *The War for the Seas. A Maritime History of World War II.* New Haven, CT: Yale University Press, 2019, p. 460.

4   Captain Manuel Colayco, formerly of the Philippine Army, who was killed during the brief ensuing battle, led this two-man force. See Richard Connaughton, John Pimlott and Duncan Anderson. *The Battle for Manila.* Novato, CA: Presidio Press, 2002, p. 91.

5   Ironically, Colonel Hayashi insisted on being escorted to the street leading to the Malacañan Palace. Once released they moved up the street only to come under fire from the American troops holding that palace. Colonel Hayashi and most of his men were killed in the ensuing firefight. Connaughton, et al., op. cit., p. 95.

6   Connaughton, Pimlott, Anderson, op. cit., pp. 92–95.

7   Frankel, op. cit., p. 254.

8   Astor, op. cit., p. 396.

9   War Department General Order Number 92, October 25, 1945.

10   Captain Knipp received the Distinguished Service Cross. General Order Number 171, 1945, U.S. Forces, Pacific (GHQ).

11   Smith, op. cit., p. 260fn.

12   Frankel, op. cit., p. 259.

13   Ibid., p. 260.

14   Captain West was awarded the Distinguished Service Cross, his second award of this decoration. See General Order Number 57, 1945, U.S. Forces, Pacific (GHQ).

15   Pfc John R. Reese, Jr., of Oklahoma, was awarded a posthumous Medal of Honor. See War Department General Order Number 89, October 19, 1945. Pfc Cleto Rodriguez, of Texas, was awarded a Medal of Honor and promoted to sergeant. See War Department General Order Number 97, November 1, 1945.

16   Pfc Joseph J. Cicchetti, of Ohio, was awarded a posthumous Medal of Honor. See War Department General Order Number 115, December 8, 1945.

Chapter 8

1   Also spelled Maraquina.

2   Wright, *The 1st Cavalry Division in World War II*, op. cit., p. 134.

3   Ibid., p. 135. Technical Sergeant Bridgewater received a Silver Star.

4   Ibid., p. 139. Pfc Ruede was awarded a Distinguished Service Cross (General Order Number 54, 1945, U.S. Forces, Pacific (GHQ)) and Pfc Wrights was awarded a Silver Star.

5   The howitzer motor carriage M8 was a close support weapon assigned to tank battalions. The light tank chassis M5 was equipped with a 75mm (2.96in) pack howitzer in an open-topped fully traversable turret. It carried a crew of four, had a maximum speed of 37 miles per hour, and a range of 99 miles.

6   Technical Sergeant Robert C. Steele was awarded a posthumous Distinguished Service Cross via General Order Number 41, 1945, U.S. Army Forces, Pacific (GHQ). His award was posthumous as he was killed during the following battle for Manila.

7   Flanagan, op. cit., p. 253.

8   Ibid.

9   Ibid., p. 253.

10   Ibid., p. 266.

11   Ibid., p. 268.

12   General Order Number 105, 1945, U.S. Forces, Pacific (GHQ).

13   Flanagan, op. cit., p. 271.

14   Ibid.

15   Frankel, op. cit., p. 277.

16   Although American artillery had been largely unrestricted after the first few days of the Battle of Manila, American air strikes continued to be limited to identifiable Japanese targets. No more than a dozen such strikes had been approved during the three-week battle thus far.

17   Teletype Message G-2 Sixth Army to G-2 XIV Corps, Mission Report, February 10, 1945. Quoted in Smith, op. cit., p. 294fn.

18   Artillery units conducting this bombardment included the following: 136th Field Artillery Battalion (155mm Howitzers), 6th Field Artillery Battalion (105mm Howitzers), 140th Field Artillery Battalion (105mm Howitzers), 756th Field Artillery Battalion (155mm Howitzers),

135th Field Artillery Battalion (105mm Howitzers), 82nd Field Artillery Battalion (105mm Howitzers), 465th Field Artillery Battalion (8-inch Howitzers), 544th Field Artillery Battalion (240mm Howitzers). In addition, elements of the 637th Tank Destroyer Battalion (76mm guns) participated.

19 Frankel, op. cit., p. 289.
20 Ibid., p. 291.
21 War Department General Order Number 115, December 8, 1945.
22 By unit, total casualties were as follows: 37th Infantry Division = 3,000; 11th Airborne Division = 1,075; 1st Cavalry Division = 1,500; XIV Corps Troops = 1,000.

Chapter 9

1 In 1942, the Japanese amphibious assault force lost half the troops in the leading wave to American defenders.
2 The 2nd Battalion, 503rd Parachute Infantry Regiment, was shipped to the Mediterranean Theater of Operations and subsequently renumbered the 509th Parachute Infantry Battalion. It took part in the North African, Italian, and Southern France campaigns. The 503rd Parachute Infantry Regiment organized a new second battalion.
3 During the landing on Noemfoor Island, Colonel Jones was severely injured by landing on the concrete runway and suffered a concussion.
4 The Consolidated four-engine B-24 "Liberator" heavy bomber was built in the largest numbers of any World War II long-range bomber by the U.S. It had a top speed of 303mph, a ceiling of 20,000 feet, and a range of 2,850 miles. It could carry a bomb load of up to 8,600 pounds. The North American B-25 "Mitchell" medium bomber had a top speed of 284mph, a ceiling of 21,200 feet, a range of 1,525 miles, and a bomb load of up to 3,200 pounds. The Douglas A-20 light attack bomber had a maximum speed of 339mph, a ceiling of 23,700 feet, a range of 2,100 miles, and a bomb load of 4,000 pounds.
5 Morison, op. cit., p. 199.
6 The A-20 light bomber was armed with six .50-caliber forward-firing machine guns, two .50-caliber trainable machine guns in a dorsal turret, and one .50-caliber machine gun in the ventral position.
7 Coincidentally, Colonel Postlethwait became a paratrooper after the war and commanded the 503rd Parachute Infantry in the postwar period.
8 Smith, op. cit., p. 343.
9 Pfc Prettyman received a posthumous Silver Star. Bennett M. Guthrie, *Three Winds of Death. The Saga of the 503rd Parachute Regimental Comat Team in the South Pacific*. Chicago: Adams Press, 1985.
10 Ibid., p. 152.
11 Pfc McCarter suffered severe pain from his wounds for the remainder of his short life. He committed suicide in 1956 after the death of his wife.
12 The 503rd Parachute Infantry suffered 780 casualties, including 165 killed. The 3rd battalion, 34th Infantry, lost 203, including 38 killed, and the subsequent garrison force, the 2nd Battalion, 151st Infantry, lost 22, including seven killed, for a total of 1,005 casualties.
13 Because the Japanese held many of the islands in the Philippines between New Guinea and Leyte and Luzon, Allied shipping was forced to take a roundabout route, which lengthened the journey and exposed the ships to enemy attack. By clearing the Southern Philippines, shipping could sail quicker and relatively safely using the San Bernardino Strait, the Sibuyan Sea and the Verde Island Passage directly to Manila Bay. It saved some 500 nautical miles and

was less hazardous for smaller vessels who suffered considerably in the storm-tossed waters of the Philippines.

14 In the end, General MacArthur cleared the entire Philippines, regardless of the threat or lack thereof to Allied shipping. He did this without advising the Chiefs of Staff and without their permission.

15 These included the 19th Infantry Regimental Combat Team and supporting units.

16 Another way of looking at the reduction is that General Krueger had the equivalent of 12 divisions (three of the separate RCTs equaled another division) plus the tank strength of an armored division. He had after the change nine divisions and tank strength less than an armored division.

17 See Wright, op. cit., p. 140.

18 Ibid.

19 Ibid., p. 141.

20 Colonel Charles E. Brady assumed command of the 8th Cavalry Regiment.

21 General Yokoyama had earlier divided his forces into a number of operational groups, as was common Japanese Army practice. Rather than list them all and describe their composition, a general overview is provided in Appendix B.

22 This was a deliberate withdrawal by General Patrick to concentrate his division for the mid-March attacks.

Chapter 10

1 Pfc Edwin N. Johnson received the Distinguished Service Cross. See General Order Number 14, 1945, U.S. Forces, Pacific (GHQ).

2 Staff Sergeant Charles H. Lanham received a Distinguished Service Cross. See General Order Number 163, 1945, U.S. Forces, Pacific (GHQ).

3 This figure is that of actual enemy killed reported by the assault regiments. However, there were hundreds, probably thousands, not included in this total who were killed "long distance," by artillery and air strikes. In addition, unlike the Americans, thousands of Japanese died of hunger, illness, and at the hands of Philippine guerillas.

4 Both American corps were forced to keep significant portions of their infantry strength off the assault lines. The 63rd Infantry, for example, had to be used to cover an exposed flank, while only two regiments of the 43rd Infantry Division were available during the assault phase. The 1st Cavalry Division was weak organizationally and suffering severe losses prior to this phase of the campaign.

5 Smith, op. cit., p. 394.

6 Marking was Colonel Augustin's nom de guerre. This unit was also known as the 1st Yay Regiment, Marking's Guerillas.

7 Alexander Newton Stark, Jr., was commissioned directly into the infantry in 1917 and fought in France during World War I. He graduated from the Command and General Staff School in 1928 and then served with the California National Guard before joining the New England National Guard's 43rd Infantry Division.

8 One 155mm general purpose gun used in these preparations had been captured by the Japanese in 1942, recaptured by the 43rd Infantry Division, and turned against the Japanese manned by a Filipino crew trained by the 43rd Infantry Division's artillerymen.

9 Colonel Joseph E. Zimmer (Ret.). *The History of the 43rd Infantry Division, 1941–1945*. Bennington, VT: Merriam Press, 2008, p. 154.

10 Quoted in Smith, op. cit., p. 414.

Chapter 11

1   Ōoka Shōhei. *Taken Captive. A Japanese POW's Story*. New York: John Wiley & Sons, Inc., 1952.
2   Japanese infantry weapons included the Arisaka Model 99 repeating rifle, the light machine gun model 99, caliber 0.3-inch, range 875 yards; the heavy machine gun Model 92, 0.3-inch with a range of 1,094 yards; and the 1.9-inch (50mm) Model 89 mortar, with a range of 700 yards. The latter was often mistaken for a "knee mortar" but was in fact designed to be fired from the ground.
3   The USS *Piranha* was a new submarine built at the Portsmouth Navy Yard and launched in 1944. It had 10 torpedo tubes and was manned by a crew of 80.
4   The Model 38 (1905) 6.5mm infantry rifle was a manually operated, clip-loaded, magazine-fed rifle. Commonly called the Arisaka, after its designer, it somewhat resembled the American 1903 Springfield rifle. It was light (9.4lb) and had an effective range of 400 yards. Issued in three different lengths, Japanese practice was to carry it with a fixed 20-inch, one-edged, Model 30 (1897) bayonet.
5   Ōoka Shōhei, op. cit., p. 319.
6   It is believed that these missing men made their way to the north through the mountains and were killed or starved to death, with their remains never being found.
7   Quoted in Gene Eric Salecker. *Blossoming Silk Against the Rising Sun. U.S. and Japanese Paratroopers at War in the Pacific in World War II*. Mechanicsburg, PA: Stackpole Books, 2010, p. 285.
8   Flanagan, op. cit., p. 299.
9   Ibid., pp. 297–305.
10 Ibid., p. 305.
11 A. Anthony, *Bushmasters: America's Jungle Warriors of World War II*. New York: St. Martin's Press, 1987, pp. 192–93.

Chapter 12

1   These tanks included the Type 97 "Te-Ke" light tank. They weighed 5.2 tons, had a crew of two, and were armed with a 1.5-inch type 94 cannon and/or a .30-caliber machine gun. The maximum speed was 26 miles per hour, and they had a range of 155 miles. There were also Type 95 "Ha-Go" light tanks of 8.1 tons, crew of three, and 1.5-inch cannon, with one or two machine guns. It had a maximum speed of 28mph and range of 155 miles. Some reports indicate that Type 97 "Chi-Ha" tanks were present. These weighed 16.5 tons, had a crew of four, and mounted a 4.7mm main gun and one machine gun. Its maximum speed was 24mph and maximum range of 130 miles.
2   The American M4A1 "Sherman" tank carried a crew of five, weighed 66,502 pounds, and had a maximum speed of 23mph. It was armed with a 75mm main gun and as many as three machine guns. It had a range of 99 miles and its armor ranged in thickness from one inch to over two inches. During the war, many variations of the tank, including flame-throwers, mine clearance, bulldozers, and others were produced.
3   6th Division Public Relations Section, op. cit., p. 90.
4   Ibid.
5   Private First Class Halverson, 20th Infantry Regiment, received a posthumous Distinguished Service Cross. See General Order Number 42, 1945, U.S. Forces, Pacific (GHQ).
6   Both Sergeants Johnson and Millious received Silver Stars for their performance this day.
7   First Lieutenant James L. Giangrosso, Company F, 20th Infantry, received the Distinguished Service Cross. See General Order Number 182, 1945, U.S. Army Forces, Pacific (GHQ).

8 The 1st Battalion, 63rd Infantry, was held in corps reserve.

9 Colonel Ives was later given command of a regiment of the 38th Infantry Division after Major General Charles E. Hurdis, who succeeded General Patrick in command of the 6th Infantry Division, revealed that General Patrick had changed his mind about Colonel Ives, and believed that the strong Japanese defense of Muñoz was to blame for the delay in securing that town.

10 War Department General Order Number 77, September 10, 1945.

11 For its performance at Muñoz, the 3rd Battalion, 20th Infantry Regiment, 6th Infantry Division, was awarded a Presidential Unit Citation (Army) Streamer embroidered Muñoz. See War Department General Order Number 90, 1945. The 6th Infantry Division history, op. cit., claims that the 80th Field Artillery Battalion received a similar award, but I have been unable to confirm this award.

12 Master Sergeant Charles L. McGaha, of Company G, 35th Infantry Regiment, from Tennessee, received a Medal of Honor. See War Department General Order Number 30, April 2, 1946.

13 Although sources disagree somewhat, it is believed by Japanese survivors that I Corps, between January 9 and February 7, destroyed 193 tanks of the 2nd Tank Division. Another five or six were destroyed by XIV Corps, leaving about 20 tanks within the 2nd Tank Division's inventory after February 7, 1945. It should be remembered, however, that independent smaller tank units were on Luzon and fought throughout the campaign.

14 The original planning for I Corps' advances north gave it five-plus divisions, but in February 1945, it had only three.

Chapter 13

1 General Krueger was unique in many ways with respect to the U.S. Army flag officers of World War II. He was foreign born (Germany), never graduated high school, had never attended college and had begun his U.S. Army career as an enlisted man, achieving commissioned status by competitive examination in 1901.

2 General of the Army Douglas MacArthur. *Reminiscences.* New York: McGraw-Hill, 1964, p. 170.

3 Although General Marshall approved General Krueger's transfer to the South Pacific, he denied the transfer of the entire Third U.S. Army Headquarters, which was destined for the Northwest European campaigns. As a result, a new army headquarters was organized.

4 Williamson Murray and Allan R. Millett. *A War to Be Won. Fighting the Second World War.* Cambridge: Belknap Press of Harvard University Press, 2000, p. 495.

5 Clay Blair. *MacArthur.* Garden City, NY: Nelson Doubleday, Inc., 1977, p. 202.

6 Kevin C. Holzimmer. *General Walter Krueger. Unsung Hero of the Pacific War.* Lawrence, KS: University Press of Kansas, 2007, p. 216.

7 Blair, op. cit.

8 Holzimmer, op. cit., p. 216. See also Smith, op. cit.

9 Roger Olaf Egeberg. *The General: MacArthur and the Man He called "Doc."* New York: Hippocrene Books, 1983, p. 115.

10 General MacArthur was not the only commander who employed this technique. It was used by Napoleon and even at this time was in use by Russian Premier Joseph Stalin.

11 Quoted in Holzimmer, op. cit., p. 217.

12 Quoted in 33rd Infantry Division Historical Committee. *A History of the 33rd Infantry Division in World War II.* Nashville, TN: Battery Press, 2000, p. 93.

13 Question Mark Hill, an unusual name, was awarded by air liaison pilots of the 43rd Infantry Division artillery. From the air, the hill seemed to resemble a question mark, hence the name.

Bench Mark Hill received its name from Philippine maps which depicted a surveyor's bench mark atop the hill.

14   The Browning heavy machine gun M2 was a .50-caliber weapon with a firing rate of 500 rounds per minute, weighing 84 pounds without tripod and a range of 2,187 yards. Each ammunition belt carried 110 rounds. It required a crew of four to move and operate. It was the heaviest automatic weapon in the infantry's arsenal.

15   The M-1 semi-automatic carbine was carried by officers and enlisted men whose jobs did not require a heavier rifle. The M-1 carbine fired .30-caliber bullets to an operational range of 273 yards from a 15-round box magazine. It weighed 5.2 pounds and could fire at a rate of 45 rounds per minute.

16   See General Order Number 110, 1945, U.S. Army Forces, Far East.

17   General Order Number 299, 1945, U.S. Forces, Pacific (GHQ).

18   Quoted in 33rd Infantry Division History, op. cit., p. 102.

19   Fire and movement tactics involved one unit firing while a second advanced. Then roles were reversed. This continued—in theory—until the objective was taken.

20   General Order Number 110, 1945, U.S. Army Forces, Far East.

21   Brigadier General Donald Johnson Myers (1893–1958) was born in Red Cloud, Nebraska, and received his Bachelor of Arts from the University of Colorado in 1917. Accepting a commission in the infantry that same year, he later graduated from the Command and General Staff School (1934) and the Army War College (1935). He would, in July 1945, receive command of the 40th Infantry Division.

22   Technical Sergeant Alphonsus L. Leary was awarded a posthumous Distinguished Service Cross. See General Order Number 55, 1945, U.S. Army Forces, Pacific (GHQ).

23   Major General H. W. Blakeley. *The 32nd Infantry Division in World War II*. Madison, WI: Bureau of Purchases, n. d., pp. 215–16. The platoon reportedly was cited in War Department General Orders, but the author has been unable to confirm this.

24   Ibid., p. 220.

25   War Department General Order Number 95, October 30, 1945.

26   Staff Sergeant Ismael R. Villegas was awarded a posthumous Medal of Honor. See War Department General Order Number 89, October 19, 1945.

27   Quoted in Lauer, 32nd Infantry Division History, op. cit., pp. 223–24.

Chapter 14

1   Quoted in Captain Robert F. Karolevitz (ed.). *The 25th Division and World War 2*. Nashville, TN: Battery Press, 1995, p. 116.

2   War Department General Order Number 77, September 10, 1945.

3   The *Hayashi Detachment* included the *544th Independent Infantry Battalion* (*58th Independent Mixed Brigade*), the *1st Battalion, 75th Infantry Regiment, 19th Division*, and artillery from the *58th Independent Mixed Brigade*. There were also provisional battalions made up of Japanese Army port and shipping units.

Chapter 15

1   General Order Number 68, U.S. Army Forces, Pacific (GHQ).

2   War Department General Order Number 97, November 1, 1945.

3 33rd Infantry Division History, op. cit., p. 185. Pfc Papez received the Distinguished Service Cross. See General Order Number 56, 1945, U.S. Army Forces, Pacific (GHQ).

4 See General Orders Number 159, Headquarters, 33rd Infantry Division, July 5, 1945, as approved by the Commander in Chief, United States Army Forces, Pacific.

5 33rd Infantry Division History, op. cit., p. 188.

6 Frankel, op. cit., p. 308.

7 Ibid.

8 General Order Number 51, 1945, U.S. Army Forces, Pacific (GHQ).

9 Frankel, op. cit., p. 309.

10 Ibid., p. 312.

11 General Order Number 48, U.S. Army Forces, Pacific (GHQ).

Chapter 16

1 25th Division Report Luzon Operations, P. 25. Quoted in Smith, op. cit., p. 524.

2 Karolevitz, op. cit., p. 134.

3 Salecker, op. cit., p. 314.

4 Karolevitz, op. cit., p. 139.

Chapter 17

1 The Stuka (short for *Sturzkampfflugzeug*) first flew in 1935 and was used during the Spanish Civil War and throughout World War II by Germany. Officially the JU-87 dive-bomber, it was powered by a 12-cylinder engine with 1,100 horsepower, had a speed of 242 miles per hour, a range of 373 miles, and a service ceiling of 26,250 feet. Its armament included two forward-firing and one rear-firing 7.92mm machine guns. It carried a crew of two and four 110-pound bombs.

2 Quoted in Robert Sherrod. *History of Marine Corps Aviation in World War II*. Baltimore: Nautical & Aviation Publishing Co. of America, Inc., 1952, p. 293.

3 Colonel Lyle H. Meyer, commanding.

4 Primarily, this was the Douglas SBD dive-bomber. Powered by a Wright R-1820-52 Cyclone 1,000 horsepower nine-cylinder radial engine, it could reach 245 miles per hour at a ceiling of 24,330 feet. It had a range of 1,100 miles and was armed with two forward-firing .50-caliber machine guns and two rear-firing .30-caliber machine guns. It could carry 1,200 pounds of bombs and was crewed by a pilot and radioman/gunner. Nicknamed "slow but deadly," it continued in service until the war's end, despite being declared obsolete.

5 Mangaldan lies halfway between San Fabian and Dagupan.

6 Wright, op. cit., p. 127.

7 The Douglas A-20 light bomber was a three-seater light-attack bomber powered by two Wright 1,700 horsepower R-2600-23 14-cylinder engines. It had a maximum speed of 339mph and a ceiling of 23,700 feet. With a range of 2,100 miles, it could carry 4,000 pounds of bombs. It was armed with six .50-caliber forward-firing guns, two .50-caliber dorsal-mounted guns, and one .50-caliber rear-firing gun. The widely known North American P-51 ("Mustang") fighter aircraft was a single-seater fighter-bomber armed with six .50-caliber forward-firing machine guns. Powered by a Packard V-1650-3 12-cylinder engine, it had a top speed of 440mph and a ceiling of 42,000 feet. It had a range of 2,200 miles and could carry a bomb load up to 2,000 pounds.

8 V=Navy, M=Marine, S=Scout, B=Bombing Squadron.

9   James Leo Dalton, II (1910–45) was born in New Britain, Connecticut, and commissioned into the cavalry from West Point in 1933. He served as a company commander, battalion commander, and regimental commander of the 35th Infantry Regiment in Hawaii and the Pacific. He commanded the 161st Infantry Regiment from 1943 to 1944 before being promoted to assistant division commander of the 25th Infantry Division in March 1945. He was promoted to brigadier general in March 1945. His decorations included two Distinguished Service Crosses, two Silver Stars, two Bronze Stars, and a Purple Heart. Balete Pass was later renamed Dalton Pass by the Philippine government.

10 As mentioned earlier, these were not mortars, but grenade launchers, and if fired from the knee resulted in broken legs.

11 These figures include 35 killed and 170 wounded of the attached 148th and 126th Infantry Regiments.

12 Blakely, 32nd Division History, op. cit., p. 230.

13 Colonel Howe's assumption of command of the 128th Infantry Regiment now made him commander at one time or another of all three of the division's infantry regiments. He commanded the 127th Infantry, 1943–44, and more recently the 126th Infantry in early 1945.

14 War Department General Order Number 89, October 19, 1945.

15 Blakely, op. cit., p. 233.

16 Ibid., p. 236.

17 War Department General Order Number 115, December 8, 1945. All five men survived and later returned to duty.

18 Blakely, op. cit., p. 240. This entry ignores the fact that it was the Buena Vista Regiment that made the initial entry into Imugan on May 28.

19 See War Department General Orders Number 74, 1946, and War Department General Orders Number 121, 1946, for the 128th Infantry awards. I have been unable to verify the Engineer Battalion award, but it is mentioned in the division history. The 126th Field Artillery Battalion award is verified in James A. Sawicki (ed.). *Field Artillery Battalions of the US Army*, Vol. 1. Dumfries, VA: Centaur Publications, 1977, p. 208.

20 See Nathan N. Prefer. *Leyte 1944: The Soldier's Battle*. Philadelphia & Oxford: Casemate Publishers, 2012.

21 This is the Japanese estimate. American sources claimed 8,750 enemy killed in action.

Chapter 18

1   The remaining two battalions of the 66th Infantry, USAFIP(NL), were assigned to the 33rd and 43rd Infantry Divisions along the Baguio Front.

2   Detailed descriptions of the operations of the guerillas in north Luzon may be found in the following sources: Maj. Billy Mossman, AUS, manuscripts at the Office of the Chief of Military History, "Volckmann's Provisional Battalion" and "Volckmann's Guerillas." See also Col. Russell W. Volckmann. *We Remained: Three Years Behind the Enemy Lines in the Philippines*. New York: W. W. Norton & Co., 1954.

3   The *Araki Force* consisted of two detached battalions of the 79th Infantry Brigade, 103rd Division. It included a machine-gun battalion and service troops.

4   When the Japanese arrived on May 7 there was only one Military Police company and some quartermaster units there to oppose them.

5   The Provisional Battalion now consisted of three companies of the 11th Infantry and one each from the 66th and 121st Infantry Regiments, USAFIL(NL).

6   Captain Swick had an interesting story. A civilian gold-mining engineer at the war's outbreak, he had gone into hiding and joined the guerillas in October 1942. He had been captured and interned as a civilian but escaped and rejoined the guerillas in April 1943.

7   For details, see Peter J Dean. *MacArthur's Coalition. US and Australian Operations in the Southwest Pacific Area, 1942–1945*. Lawrence, KS: University Press of Kansas, 2018, pp. 349–51.

8   The *Yuguchi Force* consisted of an understrength regiment of the *103rd Division* which was moving from Aparri to the last stand positions.

9   Some sources say two tank companies with 30 tanks. See Frankel, op. cit., p. 382.

10   Ibid., p. 334.

11   The Douglas C-47 Skytrain/Dakota was an unarmed transport aircraft powered by two Pratt and Whitney R-1830-92 14-cylinder radial engines. It had a maximum speed of 230 miles per hour and a service ceiling of 24,000 feet. It could carry troops, patients, or supplies of nearly any kind. It was also known in some services as the R4D.

12   Frankel, op. cit., pp. 337–38.

13   Supporting units included 81mm Mortar Platoon, Company H, 127th Infantry, 32nd Infantry Division; Company C, 339th Engineer Construction Battalion; detachments from the 543rd Engineer Boat and Shore Regiment, 3rd Engineer Special Brigade; 510th Engineer Light Pontoon Company; 276th Port Company, as well as from the 601st Quartermaster Graves Registration Company; 58th Signal Battalion; 24th Portable Surgical Hospital and 637th Medical Clearing Company.

14   This was a pre-planned relief to enable General Krueger and his staff to plan for the upcoming Sixth U.S. Army's invasion of Japan proper.

15   The Curtiss C-46 Commando transport aircraft was powered by two 1,600hp Wright R-2600 Cyclone engines and first flew in 1940. It was an unarmed transport aircraft that could carry general cargo or 40 fully equipped troops. It had a top speed of 270mph and a range of 3,150 miles. It earned its fame by flying the "Hump Route" to China throughout the war.

16   Flanagan, op. cit., p. 356.

Chapter 19

1   See Eichelberger, op. cit. General Eichelberger died September 26, 1961.

2   Dean, op. cit.

3   See Prefer, op. cit.

4   Oscar Woolverton Griswold (1886–1959) graduated from West Point in 1910. He had served in China before graduating from both the Command and General Staff School and the Army War College. During World War II he commanded the 4th Mechanized Division, the IV Corps, and the XIV Corps, which he led until war's end.

5   Eichelberger, op. cit., pp. 253–54.

6   Ibid., p. 254.

7   General William Spence (1893–1984) was the artillery commander of the 38th Infantry Division.

8   Eichelberger, op. cit., p. 255. The correct number of *Shobu Group* survivors was 50,500, 40,000 of which were in the last stand area at the time of the surrender.

9   The M18 tank destroyer "Hellcat" was developed in 1943 in response to a need for a fast-moving armored vehicle capable of dealing with enemy tanks. It weighed 18 tons, had a crew of five, a top road speed of 50mph, and a range of 105 road miles. It was armed with a 3-inch M1A1 cannon and had a .50-caliber antiaircraft gun mounted on the turret.

10   Frankel, op. cit., p. 341.

11   War Department General Order Number 14, February 4, 1946.

12 Pfc Charles S. Swimmer was awarded a posthumous Distinguished Service Cross. See General Order Number 147, 1945, U.S. Forces, Pacific (GHQ).

13 Private First Class David J. Kirkland received the Silver Star. See 6th Infantry Division History, p. 126.

14 Technical Sergeant Roy P. Hanson was awarded the Silver Star. See ibid.

15 War Department General Order Number 49, May 31, 1946.

16 MacArthur, op. cit., p. 253.

17 The Americal Division, 24th Infantry, 31st Infantry, 40th Infantry, and 41st Infantry Divisions.

18 General MacArthur removed the veteran 40th, 41st, and about half of the 24th Infantry Divisions beginning in February.

19 Eichelberger, op. cit., p. 256.

Chapter 20

1 It is estimated that of these casualties, some 2,070 were killed and 6,990 wounded in action during the Southern Philippines campaigns.

Appendix D

1 Smith, op. cit., Appendix H, p. 692.

2 Covers the period February 3–March 4, 1945 only.

3 Includes XI operations from the Zambales landing beaches to the northwestern base of Bataan Peninsula and operations on Grande Island.

4 Includes jump casualties of the 511th Parachute Infantry Regiment and all other 11th Airborne Division casualties through February 4.

5 Includes Army casualties from kamikaze raids at Lingayen Gulf, Army Service Command (ASCOM) units to February 13, the casualties of corps and army troops that cannot be placed on the ground (for example, the XIV Corps had simultaneous operations at Manila and against the Kembu and Shimbu Groups at the same time), and the casualties of attached service units after February 13.

6 Total does not include casualties of the USAFIP(NL) forces which ran into several thousand additional losses. For example, in the last six weeks of fighting within the Asin Valley/Final Redoubt area, the USAFIP(NL) forces lost 285 killed, 715 wounded, for a total of 1,000 casualties.

Bibliography

Alexander, Larry. *Shadows in the Jungle. The Alamo Scouts Behind Japanese Lines in World War II.* New York: NAL Caliber, 2009.

Anonymous. *History of the Second Engineer Special Brigade, United States Army, World War II.* Harrisburg: The Telegraph Press, 1946.

Arthur, Anthony. *Bushmasters: America's Jungle Warriors of World War II.* New York: St. Martin's Press, 1987.

Astor, Gerald. *Crisis in the Pacific. The Battles for the Philippine Islands by the Men Who Fought Them.* New York: Donald I. Fine Books, 1996.

Barbey, Daniel. *MacArthur's Amphibious Navy: Seventh Amphibious Force Operations, 1943–1945.* Annapolis, MD: United States Naval Institute, 1969.

Barker, Harold R. *History of the 43rd Division Artillery, World War II, 1941–1945.* Providence, RI: John F. Greene, 1961.

Beevor, Anthony. *The Second World War.* New York: Little, Brown and Company, 2012.

Belote, James H. and William M. *Corregidor: The Saga of a Fortress.* New York: Harper and Row, 1967.

Blair, Clay, Jr. *Silent Victory. The U.S. Submarine War Against Japan.* New York: J. B. Lippincott Company, 1975.

_____. *MacArthur.* Garden City, NY: Nelson Doubleday, Inc., 1977.

Boatner, Mark M., III. *The Biographical Dictionary of World War II.* Novato, CA: Presidio Press, 1996.

Boggs, Maj. Charles W., Jr. USMC. *Marine Aviation in the Philippines.* Washington, D.C.: Historical Division, HQMD, 1951.

Breuer, William B. *The Great Raid on Cabanatuan.* New York: John Wiley & Sons, 1994.

_____. *MacArthur's Undercover War. Spies, Saboteurs, Guerillas, and Secret Missions.* New York: John Wiley & Sons, 1995.

Buell, Thomas B. *Master of Sea Power: A Biography of Fleet Admiral Ernest J. King.* Boston: Little, Brown and Company 1980.

Cannon, M. Hamlin. *U.S. Army in World War II. Leyte: The Return to the Philippines.* Washington, D.C.: Center of Military History, Government Printing Office, 1987.

Chase, Maj. Gen. William C. *Front Line General.* Houston: Pacesetter Press, 1975.

Chwialkowski, Paul. *In Caesar's Shadow: The Life of General Robert Eichelberger.* Westport, CT: Greenwood Press, 1993.

Connaughton, Richard, John Pimlott and Duncan Anderson. *The Battle for Manila.* Novato, CA: Presidio Press, 1995.

Cook, Haruko Taya and Theodore Cook. *Japan at War: An Oral History.* New York: New Press, 1992.

Craven, Wesley Frank and James Lea Cate (eds.). *The Army Air Forces in World War II. The Pacific: MATTERHORN to Nagasaki, June 1944 to August 1945.* Volume V. Chicago: University of Chicago Press, 1953.

Dean, Peter J. *MacArthur's Coalition. US and Australian Operations in the Southwest Pacific Area, 1942–1945.* Lawrence, KS: University Press of Kansas, 2018.

Devlin, Gerard M. *Paratrooper! The Saga of U.S. Army and Marine Parachute and Glider Combat Troops During World War II*. New York: St. Martin's Press, 1979.

Division Public Relations Section. *The 6th Infantry Division in World War II*. Washington, D.C.: Infantry Journal Press, 1947.

Drea, Edward J. *Japan's Imperial Army. Its Rise and Fall, 1853–1945*. Lawrence, KS: University Press of Kansas, 2009.

_____. *MacArthur's Ultra: Codebreaking and the War Against Japan, 1942–1945*. Lawrence, KS: University Press of Kansas, 1992.

Dull, Paul S. *A Battle History of the Imperial Japanese Navy (1941–1945)*. Annapolis, MD: Naval Institute Press, 1978.

Eichelberger, Robert L., with Milton MacKaye. *Our Jungle Road to Tokyo*. Nashville, TN: Battery Press, 1989.

Ellis, John. *The Sharp End: The Fighting Man in World War II*. New York, 1980.

Flanagan, Lt. General E. M., Jr. *Corregidor: The Rock Force Assault*. New York: Jove Books, 1989.

_____. *The Angels: A History of the 11th Airborne Division*. Novato, CA: Presidio Press, 1989.

_____. *The Rakkasans. The Combat History of the 187th Airborne Infantry*. Novato, CA: Presidio Press, 1997.

Forty, George. *Japanese Army Handbook, 1939–1945*. Gloucestershire, UK: Sutton Publishing Limited, 1999.

_____. *U.S. Army Handbook, 1939–1945*. Gloucestershire, UK: Sutton Publishing Limited, 1995.

Frank, Richard. *Downfall*. New York: Random House, 1999.

Frank, Richard B. *MacArthur: A Biography*. Great Generals Series. New York: Palgrave Macmillan, 2007.

Frankel, Stanley A. *The 37th Infantry Division in World War II*. Washington, D.C.: Infantry Journal Press, 1948.

Fuller, Richard. *Shōkan, Hirohito's Samurai. Leaders of the Japanese Armed Forces, 1926–1945*. London: Arms and Armour Press, 1992.

Greenfield, Kent Roberts, Robert R. Palmer, and Bell I. Wiley. *The Organization of the Army Ground Forces, US Army in World War II*. Washington, D.C.: US Army of Military History, 1987.

Griffith, Thomas E., Jr. *MacArthur's Airman: General George C. Kenney and the War in the Southwest Pacific*. Lawrence, KS: University Press of Kansas, 1998.

Guthrie, Bennett M. *Three Winds of Death. The Saga of the 503rd Parachute Regimental Combat Team in the South Pacific*. Chicago: Adams Press, 1985.

Harkins, Philip. *Blackburn's Headhunters*. New York: W. W. Norton & Co., 1955.

Harries, Meirion and Susie Harries. *Soldiers of the Sun. The Rise and Fall of the Imperial Japanese Army*. New York: Random House, 1991.

Hashimoto, Mochitsura, with E. H. M. Colegrave (trans.). *Sunk: The Story of the Japanese Submarine Fleet, 1942–1945*. London: Cassell, 1954.

Hastings, Max. *Retribution. The Battle for Japan, 1944–1945*. New York: Alfred A. Knopf, 2008.

Hayashi, Saburo. *Kogun: The Japanese Army in the Pacific War*. Westport, CT: Greenwood Press, 1978.

Heavey, Brig. Gen. William F. *Down Ramp! The Story of the Army Amphibian Engineers*. Washington, D.C.: Infantry Journal Press, 1947.

Hodges, Peyton, et. al. *Avengers of Bataan*. Atlanta, GA: Albert Love Enterprises, 1947.

Hunt, Frazier. *The Untold Story of Douglas MacArthur*. New York: Devin-Adair Co., 1954.

Huston, James A. *Out of the Blue: U.S. Army Airborne Operations in World War II*. West Lafayette, IN: Purdue University Press, 1998.

Ienaga, Saburo. *The Pacific War*. New York: Pantheon, 1978.

Inoguchi, Rikihei, Tadashi Nakajima and Robert Pineau. *The Divine Wind*. New York: Ballantine, 1958.

James, D. Clayton. *The Years of MacArthur*, 3 vols. Boston: 1970–75.

Karolevitz, Capt. Robert F. (ed.). *The 25th Division and World War 2*. Nashville, TN: Battery Press, 1946.

Kenney, George C. *General Kenney Reports: A Personal History of the Pacific War*. New York: Duell, Sloan & Pearce, 1949.

King, Ernest J. and Walter Muir Whitehill. *Fleet Admiral King: A Naval Record*. London: Eyre and Spottiswoode, 1953.

Kotani, Ken. *Japanese Intelligence in World War II*. Oxford: Osprey Publishing, 2009.

Krueger, General Walter. *From Down Under to Nippon. The Story of Sixth Army in World War II*. Washington, D.C.: Combat Forces Press, 1953.

Lancaster, Roy. *The Story of the Bushmasters*. Detroit, MI: Lancaster Publications, n. d.

Larrabee, Eric. *Commander-in-Chief: Franklin Delano Roosevelt, His Lieutenants and Their War*. New York: Harper & Row, 1987.

Lauer, Edward T. (ed.). *32nd Infantry Division in World War II*. Madison, WI: Bureau of Purchases, n. d.

Leary, William M. (ed.). *We Shall Return! MacArthur's Commanders and the Defeat of Japan, 1942–1945*. Lexington, KY: University Press of Kentucky, 1988.

Lee, Clark and Richard Henschel. *Douglas MacArthur*. New York: Henry Holt and Co., 1952.

Leighton, Richard M. and Robert W. Coakley. *Global Logistics and Strategy, 1940–1943. U.S. Army in World War II*. Washington, D.C.: Government Printing Office, 1968.

Lewin, Ronald. *The American Magic: Codes, Ciphers and the Defeat of Japan*. New York: 1982.

Linderman, G. F. *The World Within War: America's Combat Experience in World War II*. New York: Free Press, 1997.

Long, Gavin. *MacArthur as Military Commander*. Conshohocken, PA: Combined Publishing, 1969.

————. *The Final Campaigns, Vol. 7 Australia in the War of 1939–1945*. Canberra: Australian War Memorial, 1963.

Luvaas, Jay (ed.). *Dear Miss Em: General Eichelberger's War in the Pacific, 1942–1945*. Westport, CT: Greenwood Press, 1972.

MacArthur, Douglas. *Reminiscences*. New York: McGraw-Hill, 1964.

————. *Reports of General MacArthur: The Campaigns of MacArthur in the Pacific, Vol. I*. Washington, D.C.: Center of Military History, Government Printing Office, 1994.

————. (V. E. Whan, ed.). *A Soldier Speaks*. New York: Praeger, 1965.

Manchester, William. *American Caesar*. Boston: Little, Brown and Company, 1978.

Mann, B. David. *Avenging Bataan. The Battle of Zigzag Pass*. Raleigh, NC: Pentland Press, Inc., 2001.

Miller, Edward S. *War Plan Orange. The U.S. Strategy to Defeat Japan, 1897–1945*. Annapolis, MD: U.S. Naval Institute Press, 1991.

Millett, Allan R. and Williamson Murray (eds.). *Military Effectiveness. Volume 3. The Second World War*. New York: Cambridge University Press, 2010.

————. *A War to Be Won: Fighting the Second World War, 1937–1945*. Cambridge, MA: Harvard University Press, 2000.

Morison, Samuel Eliot. *History of United States Naval Operations in World War II. Vol. XIII. The Liberation of the Philippines. Luzon, Mindanao, the Visayas, 1944–1945*. Boston: Little, Brown and Company, 1989.

Morton, Louis. *United States Army in World War II. The Fall of the Philippines*. Washington, D.C.: Government. Printing Office, 1953.

Palmer, Robert R., Bell I. Wiley and William R. Keast. *The Army Ground Forces: The Procurement and Training of Ground Combat Troops. The U.S. Army in World War II*. Washington, D.C.: Government Printing Office, 1948.

Perret, Geoffrey. *Old Soldiers Never Die: The Life of Douglas MacArthur*. New York: Random House, 1996.

Prefer, Nathan N. *Leyte 1944. The Soldier's Battle*. Philadelphia & Oxford: Casemate, 2012.

_____. *MacArthur's New Guinea Campaign, March–August 1944*. Conshohocken, PA.: Combined Books, 1995.

Potter, E. B. *Nimitz*. Annapolis, MD: Naval Institute Press, 1976.

Reel, A. Frank. *The Case of General Yamashita*. Chicago: University of Chicago Press, 1949.

Roscoe, Theodore. *United States Submarine Operations in World War II*. Annapolis, MD: Naval Institute Press, 1949.

Rush, Robert S. *GI: The US Infantryman in World War II*. Oxford: Osprey Publishing, 2003.

Salecker, Gene Eric. *Rolling Thunder Against the Rising Sun. The Combat History of U.S. Army Tank Battalions in the Pacific in World War II*. Mechanicsburg, PA: Stackpole Books, 2008.

_____. *Blossoming Silk Against the Rising Sun. U.S. and Japanese Paratroopers at War in the Pacific in WWII*. Mechanicsburg, PA: Stackpole Books, 2010.

Sawicki, James A. *Infantry Regiments of the U.S. Army*. Dumfries, VA: Wyvern Publications, 1981.

_____. *Tank Battalions of the U.S. Army*. Dumfries, VA: Wyvern Publications, 1983.

_____. *Cavalry Regiments of the U.S. Army*. Dumfries, VA: Wyvern Publications, 1985.

_____. *Field Artillery Battalions of the U.S. Army* (2 vols.). Dumfries, VA: Wyvern Publications, 1977.

Schaller, Michael. *Douglas MacArthur: The Far Eastern General*. New York: Oxford University Press, 1989.

Sears, David. *At War with the Wind. The Epic Struggle with Japan's World War II Suicide Bombers*. New York: Citadel Press, 2008.

Sides, Hampton. *Ghost Soldiers. The Forgotten Epic Story of World War II's Most Dramatic Mission*. New York: Doubleday, 2001.

Smith, Robert Ross. *U.S. Army in World War II. The Pacific. Triumph in The Philippines*. Washington, D.C.: Center of Military History, U.S. Army, 1963.

_____. *U.S. Army in World War II. The Approach to the Philippines*. Washington, D.C.: Center of Military History, Government Printing Office, 1984.

_____. "Luzon versus Formosa" in Kent Roberts Greenfield (ed.), *Command Decisions*. Washington, D.C.: Office of the Chief of Military History, United States Army, 1960: 461–66.

Spector, Ronald. *Eagle Against the Sun: The American War with Japan*. New York: Free Press, 1985.

Stanton, Shelby L. *Order of Battle, U.S. Army, World War II*. Novato, CA: Presidio Press, 1984.

Stern, Robert C. *Fire from the Sky: Surviving the Kamikaze Threat*. Annapolis, MD: Naval Institute Press, 2010.

Taaffe, Stephen R. *MacArthur's Jungle War: The 1944 New Guinea Campaign*. Lawrence, KS: University Press of Kansas, 1998.

_____. *Marshall and His Generals: US Army Commanders in World War II*. Lawrence, KS: University Press of Kansas, 2011.

Thorne, Christopher. *Allies of a Kind: The United States, Britain, and the War Against Japan, 1941–1945*. Oxford: Oxford University Press, 1978.

Toland, John. *The Rising Sun*. New York: Random House, 1970.

U.S. War Department. *Handbook on Japanese Military Forces*. Novato, CA: Presidio Press, 1991.

Volckmann, Col. Russell W. *We Remained: Three Years Behind the Enemy Lines in the Philippines*. New York: W. W. Norton & Co., 1954.

Wheeler, Gerald E. *Kinkaid of the Seventh Fleet. A Biography of Admiral Thomas C. Kinkaid, U.S. Navy*. Annapolis, MD: Naval Institute Press, 1996.

Whitney, Maj. Gen. Courtney. *MacArthur: His Rendezvous with History*. New York: Knopf, 1956.

Williams, Mary H. (comp.). *Chronology, 1941–1945. United States Army in World War II. Special Studies*. Washington, D.C.: Chief of Military History, 1960.

Willoughby, Maj. Gen. Charles A. and John Chamberlain. *MacArthur, 1941–1951*. New York: McGraw-Hill, 1956.

Wright, Major B. C. (comp.). *The 1st Cavalry Division in World War II*. Tokyo: Toppan Printing Company Ltd., 1947.

Yeide, Harry. *The Infantry's Armor. The U.S. Army's Separate Tank Battalions in World War II*. Mechanicsburg, PA: Stackpole Books, 2010.

_____. *The Tank Killers. A History of America's World War II Tank Destroyer Force*. Havertown, PA: Casemate, 2004.

_____. *Steeds of Steel. A History of American Mechanized Cavalry in World War II*. Minneapolis, MN: Zenith Press, 2008.

Zedric, Lance Q. *Silent Warriors of World War II. The Alamo Scouts Behind Japanese Lines*. Ventura, CA: Pathfinder Publishing, 1995.

Zimmer, Joseph E. *The History of the 43rd Infantry Division, 1941–1945*. Nashville, TN: Battery Press, 1945.

33rd Infantry Division Historical Committee. *The Golden Cross. A History of the 33rd Infantry Division in World War II*. Washington, D.C.: Infantry Journal Press, 1948.

40th Infantry Division. Nashville, TN: Battery Press, 1946.

Index